D1499626

ARMED WITH CAMERAS

ARMED WITH CAMERAS

THE AMERICAN MILITARY
PHOTOGRAPHERS OF WORLD WAR II

PETER MASLOWSKI

THE FREE PRESS
A Division of Macmillan, Inc.
NEW YORK

Maxwell Macmillan Canada
TORONTO

Maxwell Macmillan International
NEW YORK   OXFORD   SINGAPORE   SYDNEY

The Free Press
A Division of Macmillan, Inc.
866 Third Avenue, New York, N.Y. 10022

Maxwell Macmillan Canada, Inc.
1200 Eglinton Avenue East
Suite 200
Don Mills, Ontario M3C 3N1

Macmillan, Inc. is part of the Maxwell Communication
Group of Companies.

Printed in the United States of America

printing number

1 2 3 4 5 6 7 8 9 10

Library of Congress Cataloging-in-Publication Data

Maslowski, Peter
  Armed with cameras: the American military photographers of World
  War II/Peter Maslowski.
     p. cm.
  Includes bibliographical references and index.
  ISBN 0-02-920265-5
  1. World War, 1939–1945—Photography. 2. War photographers—
  United States. 3. United States. Army—Photographers. I. Title.
D810.P4M37 1993   93–7957
940.54—dc20   CIP

TO
PERN

CONTENTS

A Personal Note

Graying hair and a slight paunch were sure signs that the man was no longer in the prime of youth. Yet, although burdened with heavy motion picture camera equipment, he had just walked more than a mile with surprising speed across the tundra in the far northern reaches of Canada, just south of the Arctic Circle. Behind him, the tundra's spongy, uneven surface exacted a toll on the two increasingly breathless younger men trying to match the pace of Karl H. Maslowski. Suddenly the objects of their haste emerged from a fold of dead ground in front of them, closer than they had anticipated. The female grizzly bear reared on her hind legs, seemed to leer at the trio, and then she and her cub began to advance.

The bears' forward movement was not straight; they ambled to the left, then to the right, and then back again. Their speed varied from a slight jog to a mere walk, and occasionally they paused to stare at the intruders. Inexorably, however, the gap that separated them from the three men narrowed.

A grizzly bear is an awesome creature, and a female grizzly with a cub in tow is awesomely dangerous. Fortunately, one of the young men, a red-haired bush pilot, had brought along a high-powered rifle; unfortunately, he had not loaded it. The other young man began readying a Hasselblad still camera. I was that other young man, but I was having a hard time concentrating. My mind was elsewhere: The bear can easily outrun us ... no tree more than a few feet high grew within a thousand square miles ... if attacked by a grizzly bear curl into a fetal ball to protect your head and innards and then play dead ... the bear would maul you, but might not kill you—or at least so they said. Alas, the nearest hospital was ... well, I did not even want to think about the hundreds of miles between me and the nearest medical aid.

But most of all I was distracted watching my father. I marveled at his composure as he set up the bulky Akeley gyro tripod, leveled the tripod head and fastened the 16mm Arriflex camera to it, and attached a cord running from the camera to the heavy nickel-cadmium battery he carried on a shoulder strap. Pulling out his reading glasses, he stepped in front of the camera, held up a light meter toward the bears, and then turned his back on them so he could set the proper exposure on the camera's three lenses, which were mounted in a spider turret. Returning the glasses to his shirt pocket, he squinted through the eye-piece and began filming, periodically rotating the turret from lens to lens as the bears came closer.

Suddenly in my mind's eye the year was no longer 1969 and my father was no longer a professional wildlife photographer working on a documentary for the National Audubon Society's lecture circuit, no longer in his fifties, no longer in Canada, and no longer filming grizzly bears. It was 1944 and he was a member of the 12th Combat Camera Unit of the Army Air Forces, dark-haired and handsome, in his thirties, in Europe, filming the war against the Nazis near the front lines as German 88-millimeter artillery shells roared overhead with the terribly magnified hiss of a blacksmith dipping a hot horseshoe into a barrel of cool water.

A guide to the audiovisual records preserved in the National Archives warns that the "proper examination and use of motion-picture sources requires at least a rudimentary acquaintance with the film-making process itself."[1] Making a movie is like mastering a foreign language: without diligent study over an extended period, it cannot be done effectively. The same could be said about still pictures, though to a lesser extent. Understanding professional-quality still photography is like a white Anglo-Saxon American learning Spanish, but producing a motion picture is akin to the same person learning Chinese. Indeed, screenwriters and movie directors sometimes refer to a film's "grammar."

Thanks to the training I received from a master film linguist, my father, I have more than a passing knowledge of both still and motion picture photography. Long before World War II Karl H. Maslowski was already making his livelihood as a professional photographer, specializing in wildlife stills and movies. After the war he resumed his career, and even as I write this introduction he continues to dabble in the profession even though he "retired" years ago. His skills as a photographer and educator earned him an international reputation and many awards, including an honorary doctorate from Miami University—not bad for a gentleman whose formal education did not progress much beyond high school.

Under his tutelage I took still pictures that have appeared in various publications and also helped produce motion pictures ranging from a twenty-minute production on fishing in the Florida Keys to a seventy-minute travelogue/wildlife documentary on Canada's arctic regions. While working with my father I also earned a Ph.D. degree from The Ohio State University, specializing in military history. Since January 1974 I have taught military history at The University of Nebraska–Lincoln, save for one year when I had the honor of teaching at the Combat Studies Institute of the United States Army Command and General Staff College at Fort Leavenworth, Kansas. Whether this combined education in photography and military history makes me uniquely qualified to deal with wartime photography may be questionable, but it does give me insights into both film and war.

Without the assistance of dozens of former military combat cameramen this book could not have been written, as the notes and bibliography will amply attest. To say that I received the wholehearted cooperation of those World War II photographers whom I contacted would be an understatement:[2]

"If this material helps you record, for history's sake, how one World War II 'Cameraman Anonymous' did his best to cover the war, photographically, I'll be more than happy to have taken this effort to help you."

"Don't ever apologize, or feel guilty, about bombing me with requests. I'm very happy to cooperate in any way I'm able on your combat cameraman project."

"I realize I have made a short story long. I hope I have helped in some way. If I can help clarify anything let me know. I have enjoyed looking back."

"It is all over now—but the memories linger on. And suddenly we old bucks discover a young buck (probably not yet born, then) who wants to write about US. How can we RESIST?"

"SEE what you have done to me? You're making me recall long lost memories. But, SON, I bless you for it. It is a good feeling."

Joe Boyle, a proud soldier-photographer in the 163rd Signal Photographic Company, called me "son." No, Joe, I bless *you* and all the other cameramen-fathers who have treated me like a son as we (they and I) have worked on this project.

And how I regret that the ancient army adage popularized by Douglas MacArthur is not true. Old soldiers do not just fade away. They die.

———————

Apparently more curious than hostile, the grizzly bear and her cub approached to within twenty-five feet and stopped. The female sniffed the wind, evidently filling her nostrils with our strange scent; then, with amazing agility for such a huge beast, she turned and led her cub up and over a ridge.

None of my still pictures of this encounter was worthy of publication. My father's movie sequence was magnificent.

ABBREVIATIONS USED IN THE TEXT

AAF Army Air Forces

APS Army Pictorial Service

BuAer Bureau of Aeronautics (Navy)

CAT Combat Assignment Team

CCU Combat Camera Unit (AAF)

CINCPAC Commander in Chief, Pacific Fleet

CPS Combat Photography Section (Navy)

CPU Combat Photography Unit (Navy)

FMPU First Motion Picture Unit (AAF)

GSAP Gun Sight Aiming Point camera

OIC Officer in Charge

PSL Photographic Science Laboratory (Navy)

SCPC Signal Corps Photographic Center (Army)

SOP   Standing (or Standard) Operating Procedure

SPC   Signal Photographic Company (Army)

SSB   Signal Service Battalion (Army)

SWPA   Southwest Pacific Area

TCC   Troop Carrier Command

T/O&E   Table of Organization and Equipment

USMC   United States Marine Corps

In other words, there were situations I couldn't walk away from because all the elements for great photography were there, and to just walk away from it just to save my neck would've been stupid.

—William Teas, 166th Signal Photographic Company

Prologue

His first day at the front depressed Donald J. Morrow.

He and another combat cameraman were in a jeep heading north toward Cassino along Route 6, one of Italy's main highways. They passed a British military cemetery already sprouting more than a hundred white crosses, and noted that "a group of men were digging more graves for more men whose lives were stopped short of their time." And they encountered villages so thoroughly bombed and shelled that every building and dwelling had been hit many times. After arriving at their destination, a high peak across the valley from Cassino, an artillery duel began, which really dismayed them because it showed how difficult photographing the war was going to be. Numerous grayish-white puffs of smoke marked flashpoints of death and injury, but the plumes were so distant that the actual explosions, the wounded crying for help, and the body parts sprinkling the ground were beyond the range of both the human eye and a camera lens. "That was modern war," Morrow recorded in his diary, "*but* how could it be photographed?" As he learned during a year of combat photography in Italy, not easily.[1]

On the evening of February 5, 1945 Morrow was huddled in the

1

most northerly Allied observation post (known as an O.P.) in Italy, a mere two hundred yards from enemy lines atop Mount Castellaro. A recent order from his commanding officer to photograph artillery both at night and during the day had brought him to this forlorn and dangerous place, a "well-battered house" with no roof and a dirt floor under direct German observation and within reach not only of enemy artillery but even of enemy rifles and machine guns. He had lugged his equipment to the observation post the day before over a steep two-mile-long trail, sinking up to a foot deep in mud with every step and urging along three mules burdened with cameras, a tripod, and film. Situated in a tiny sandbagged room, Morrow could photograph through a small hole in the wall facing "Jerry-ward." Artillery officers had agreed to fire at Mount Castellaro when Morrow wanted them to so that he would not have to remain exposed at the hole any longer than necessary.

That night American forces attacked Mount Castellaro and the Germans responded ferociously. Around eight o'clock Morrow heard the first enemy artillery shell coming his way. "It landed just outside our window and the earth shook," he wrote. "From then on it was hell. For the next three hours they came in fast and close." Only after the enemy shelling abated did Morrow feel reasonably safe in setting up his camera. At his request an artillery officer ordered a concentrated barrage on the German position, and several seconds after Morrow began filming "the whole face of Mt. Castellaro was momentarily lit up with shell bursts. I called for one more concentration and the process was repeated."

With two action sequences on film, Morrow began retreating about one hundred yards to an old house where he would spend the night. But the Germans' ire had been aroused anew and they now unleashed a mortar barrage. At the first sound of incoming rounds Morrow flopped into the snow and mud, weathered the nearby concussions, then dashed for the house. When he reached it the shells whistling overhead sounded like a hurricane, while American and German rifles and machine guns beat a cacophonous undertone. Morrow slept only in snatches because the Nazis "shelled steadily all night—and they were damn close." Their impact shook the house.

Two days later Morrow was back at the O.P. to get daylight shots. As he photographed shells landing on Mount Castellaro, the Germans on Mount Castellaro fired back. Several of their "shells struck two yards in front of the O.P. throwing dirt and snow in the O.P. opening." Morrow used two cameras, one with a 20-inch lens "showing close ups of single barrages and low air bursts," and the other with a 4-inch lens "showing the whole mountain top with all bursts at once. It looked as though the whole mountain was erupting." He also discovered that the "house I slept in the other night has been evacuated because of heavy shelling." So he departed that night, trying to negotiate the precipitous trail in pitch blackness. "I became stuck in the mud several times," he recorded in his diary. "The mules would sink into the mud and wallow around like pigs. My equipment is caked with mud—and so am I." But a shower, a shave, and some hot food revived him and he almost immediately sought another front line assignment, even volunteering "to go behind the German lines on a special photographic mission of which I had conceived."

"I have a confession to make," Donald Morrow wrote in late October 1945 as he began his eleventh notebook. "This more than likely will be the last book of this diary and because it is, I dread starting it. No doubt this would seem strange to all that know what a fine home, and what wonderful parents I have to go back to. I know not how to explain myself other than calling attention to these rich experiences which are fast becoming part of the past."

Those "rich experiences" included Mount Castallaro and dozens of other assignments that could have cost Morrow his life. But like most military combat cameramen he loved his photographic duties despite (or perhaps because of) the danger. Donald Morrow was not alone in being a trifle saddened by the war's end.

I

For thousands of years most of the human race had never seen a battlefield, had been spared the eyewitness knowledge of the ugly indignities that war inflicted on those who engaged in combat. Non-combatants "saw" war only through the less-than-accurate tales of surviving soldiers and sailors, epic poetry, a few historical accounts, and stylized artwork. Before the mid-nineteenth century, as a *New York Times* reporter noted in late September 1862, "The dead of the battlefield come up to us very rarely, even in dreams.... We recognize the battle-field as a reality, but it stands as a remote one. It is like a funeral next door. It attracts your attention, but it does not enlist your sympathy." But now the situation had dramatically changed. The reporter had just visited Mathew Brady's exhibition on "The Dead of Antietam," consisting of photographs taken shortly after the battle by two of his assistants. "Mr. Brady has done something to bring to us the terrible reality and earnestness of the war," the correspondent mused. "If he has not brought bodies and laid them in our door-yards and along [our] streets, he has done something very like it."[2]

For people living miles away from the sound of the guns, and for those living long after the war ended, a battlefield's appearance was no longer confined almost exclusively to the imagination. Photography forever altered the human vision of warfare by preserving, with a vivid immediacy, its images. Memories dim and ultimately die, but photographs remain clear and crisp. Pictures are time machines, transporting an observer back "to the original moment when light fell upon these surfaces, these bodies and guns and fields; we all but feel the same rays of light in our own eyes."[3]

Less than a decade after Louis Daguerre perfected the daguerreotype photographic process in France in 1839, military photography made its debut during the Mexican War of 1846–1847. Although only a few dozen daguerreotypes survive, they represent the first link between the camera and warfare. The photographs include officers' portraits, static shots of troops in Mexico and of towns where Americans saw action, and a view of the burial site of Lieutenant Colonel Henry C. Clay, Jr., who died at the Battle of Buena Vista. But because of technological limitations, especially the bulky cameras and extremely slow film speeds, photographers could not record actual combat, so none of the Mexican War daguerreotypes depicted *action*.[4]

By the time the Civil War began in April 1861, photography had become so popular that it helped convert the war into a media event with modern overtones. The Union Army of the Potomac alone issued field passes to approximately three hundred civilian cameramen; Captain Andrew J. Russell became the country's first official military photographer; intrepid balloonists made a few aerial photographs; and some combatants recognized that a few good photographs could "impart more real useful knowledge than many pages of written description."[5] Although technology still barred the camera from direct battlefield participation, photographs of some of the post-battle scenes had such an intense impact that they impelled people, like the *New*

York Times reporter who "saw" the bodies littering the ground near Antietam, to near-poetic and philosophical musings.

During the Spanish–American War (1898) and the Philippine–American War (1899–1902) photographic improvements made warfare even more directly accessible to nonparticipants. The halftone reproduction process, first used in the United States in 1880, allowed photographs to replace engravings in newspapers and magazines. Roll film, daylight loading, faster shutter speeds, and less bulky equipment now permitted photographers with still cameras to record a handful of battlefield scenes. Even more dramatically, in 1896 Thomas Armat and Thomas Edison had projected the first motion pictures to a paying American audience, and a number of motion picture producers covered the Spanish–American War, with one of them actually recording Teddy Roosevelt's Rough Riders assaulting Kettle Hill.[6]

By World War I camera technology had further improved, so much so that photography had become an official military function. In the late nineteenth century the Army opened a photographic laboratory, published a photography manual, and offered regular instruction in the craft. In 1909 the Signal Corps used a motion picture camera to record a test flight by the Wright brothers, and seven years later the Army produced its first training film, *Close Order Drill*. Three months after the United States declared war in April 1917, the Signal Corps became responsible for all Army photographic coverage. It created a Photographic Section (soon upgraded to a Division) that contained only twenty-five men in August 1917, but by the war's end late in 1918 had almost six hundred, including both cameramen and laboratory personnel. The Signal Corps also established a school for land photography at Columbia University in New York City and another for aerial photography at the Eastman Kodak Company in Rochester, New York, and produced two long training film series, one for soldiers and the other for the Army's fledgling aviation units. Military cameramen shot tens of thousands of still pictures and almost 600,000 feet of motion picture film. However, cumbersome equipment, as well as the reluctance of officers to let photographers near the front for fear of drawing enemy fire, meant they shot little of this film on the battlefield. Still, seven army cameramen were wounded and one was killed.[7]

The Navy also integrated photography into its World War I operations. The "Father of Naval Photography" was W. L. Richardson, a ship's cook and camera hobbyist who had assumed the collateral duty of "official photographer" at the Pensacola Aeronautic Station late in 1914. In early 1917 the Navy added a second official photographer, and after the United States entered the war developments accelerated with the formation of a Navy Department Photographic Section and a Navy School of Aerial Photography, and with the deployment of the first U.S. Fleet Camera Ship, the U.S.S. *Lebanon*.[8]

Despite the overseas photographic effort, wartime censors permitted the public to see only the most mundane still and motion pictures. "In the First World War we were lucky to get views of our troops marching off to war, of our convoys sailing, of generals meeting far behind the front, of Y.M.C.A. doings and Red Cross parties," recalled one author. "Once in a while we saw a picture of some shell-shattered buildings, but never did we get a picture of actual combat." The pictorial coverage the public received was sketchy, superficial, and sanitized. More than 50,000 Americans died in action and almost 200,000 more suffered wounds, yet not one photograph of a dead doughboy was published and only a handful showed wounded men. Even in those, the wounded were always receiving medical aid and had "clean" injuries involving no gross disfigurement. As with noncombatants in ancient Greece, imperial Rome, or medieval Europe, the battlefield materialized only in the imagination and in dreams or nightmares. Authorities feared that showing even glimpses of the real war might lower home-front morale. Only military authorities and high-ranking civilian officials, such as congressmen and senators who had special projection facilities built for themselves, saw uncensored celluloid.[9]

In the postwar demobilization the armed forces' photographic programs virtually disappeared. For the next twenty years military photography nearly expired, kept barely alive by a handful of interested officers. When war clouds gathered and then burst on Asia and Europe during the late 1930s, the Army and Navy began rebuilding their photographic capabilities. But nothing in photography's first century foretold the varied and vital role film would play in the American war effort during World War II.

II

Combat photographers "are making this the most photographed War of all times," an Army document noted with a matter-of-fact tone in mid-1945. Indeed, photography and World War II were inseparable, as many wartime commentators recognized. "Total war is fought with cameras as well as cannons," said *Movies at War*, the annual publication of the Motion Picture Industry's War Activities Committee. The camera, wrote the author of a wartime photography guide, "has become a practical weapon of war, though it fires neither shot nor shell." And a *National Geographic* essay proclaimed that "Cameras and film have become as essential in this war as guns and bullets, on some occasions more so."[10]

Film was indispensable both on the home front and on the fighting fronts. Still pictures and motion-picture footage from the combat zones, which dominated home-front newspapers, magazines, newsreels, and documentaries, informed the civilian population about the war's progress and sustained domestic morale. Commentators have argued that television caused America's defeat in Vietnam by feeding the public a nightly diet of gore. But in 1943 President Franklin D. Roosevelt's administration made an explicit decision to show civilians more "blood and guts" as a way to stiffen their resolve. The armed services orchestrated special "industrial-incentive" film programs to inspire workers to greater productivity, and important endeavors such as selling war bonds and conducting Red Cross blood drives featured combat footage and photographs prominently in their publicity.

As on the home front, photography served multiple purposes within the armed forces. Many training films contained combat footage, which made them realistic enough to engage the attention of easily bored soldiers, sailors, and airmen. Experts estimated that good training films—films that troops did not sleep through—reduced training time by more than 30 percent, an important consideration when mobilizing millions of men and women as quickly as possible. Since World War II-style operations were complex bureaucratic tasks, many staff officers were essentially desk-bound managers rather than combatants. However, being effective administrators required that they understand the battlefield, and film was a vital educational tool in this regard. The Army, for example, produced a weekly *Staff Film Report* giving officers far from the fighting a "firsthand" glimpse of front-line conditions. Matters of tactical, technical, and intelligence value that might take dozens of pages to describe, and even then might not be clearly understood, could be readily grasped when pictorially presented. Thus, for instance, the Army produced *Film Bulletins*, *Technical Film Bulletins*, and *Project Technical Film Bulletins*, while the Army Air Forces produced *Combat Film Reports* and published *Impact*, a classified monthly magazine, to disseminate air intelligence information via still pictures. And film saved lives in an immediate sense: military surgeons in rear-area hospitals studying motion pictures and photographs of wounds and the treatment of casualties, devised better medical procedures and improved the training of doctors, nurses, and hospital corpsmen.

Film was so vital to the war effort that photographic coverage was an important aspect of campaign planning, and combat film was always marked "Top Priority" when being shipped from the battlefield to the processing lab. A few examples illustrate this point. In the spring of 1944 the Allies established a Planning Board, directly controlled by the Supreme Headquarters, Allied Expeditionary Force, to ensure complete coverage of D-Day by coordinating the cameramen from all the British, Canadian, and American armed forces as well as the Norwegian, French, Polish, Belgian, Czech, Dutch, and Greek photographic sections and the civilian photographic correspondents. The planners also made arrangements so that all film could be delivered from the cameramen to the labs with maximum speed.[11]

In the Pacific, several weeks before the Marines went ashore on Iwo Jima the chief photographic officer received access to the invasion plan so that he could orchestrate coverage accordingly. One result was a stunning documentary, *To the Shores of Iwo Jima*, which "was accomplished under fire according to a carefully worked out battle-plan script."[12] Equally detailed planning preceded the Tenth Army's invasion of Okinawa. And had it been necessary to carry out Operation Olympic, the ground assault on Kyushu, Japan, planned for November 1945, it would have been the war's most thoroughly photographed campaign. For the Army alone, pre-invasion charts detailed how the 167th Signal Photographic Company and the 4026th Signal Service Battalion would accompany the Operation Olympic invasion forces and how the film would be collected and processed in the shortest possible time.[13]

As people sat in darkened movie theaters during World War II gazing "enraptured upon the scenes of furious battle as released by the War Department," they rarely thought about the men who "got into this curious but highly important business of fighting the war with cameras and caption sheets as well as machine guns."[14] Yet military cameramen were ubiquitous along the fighting fronts, learning that combat photography entailed unique joys and special travails and that Hollywood's version of war and real war bore scant resemblance to each other.

The photographers discussed in this book were *military* combat cameramen rather than accredited civilian photographers or photographic aerial reconnaissance personnel. Their explicit mission was to photograph actual combat. Most of them served in the Army's Signal Photographic Companies (SPCs) and Signal Service Battalions (SSBs), the Army Air Forces Combat Camera Units (AAF CCUs), the Navy's Combat Photography Units (CPUs), or the Photo Sections of the individual Marine Corps divisions. Cameramen in these units sometimes worked with small special teams headed by famous Hollywood directors serving in uniform, such as John Huston for the Army and William Wyler for the AAF.[15]

World War II remains astonishingly vivid in the collective American memory. Almost nightly some small portion of the war's film record still appears on television, and someone going to the National Audiovisual Center in Washington, D.C., in the mid-1980s to "see" United States military history in the twentieth century could view six films or videotapes on Korea, three on Vietnam, and ninety-eight on World War II. The 1992 catalog from International Historic Films in Chicago has more than thirty pages devoted to World War II, but less than a page to Korea and about four pages to Vietnam.[16] Korea and Vietnam were big, long conflicts but it sometimes seems as if World War II was the country's most recent war, as if the 38th and 17th parallels never mattered, as if Chosin and Tet never occurred. Does the extraordinary World War II pictorial record have something to do with this? By preserving so much of that war for posterity, have combat cameramen had an undue influence on post-World War II perceptions of warfare? Definitive answers to these questions can probably never be given. But understanding the cameramen and what they did is an important first step toward probing their legacy.

1

"Those Guys Went Out Hunting Trouble"

The Ubiquitous but Anonymous Combat Cameramen

Gordon Frye was finally getting a well-deserved rest.

Frye was a long way from his home in Rhode Island and his bed would be a cement floor rather than a feather mattress, but a late-afternoon nap under any conditions was a luxury these days. His room was on the third floor of a former school building in Caiazzo, Italy, a structure that Frye's unit, the 163rd Signal Photographic Company (SPC), had commandeered for its headquarters. Frye and his colleague, Samuel Tischler, had arrived from the front lines the day before looking like typical dirty, unshaven, haggard Bill Mauldin GI Joe cartoon characters. While Frye rested, Tischler was getting one of those infamous GI haircuts on the ground floor. For the first time in months both were basking in the security of a rear-area billet.[1]

Within split seconds of each other Frye and Tischler, their senses honed by too many harrowing frontline experiences, recognized the droning of aircraft followed by the all too familiar sound of planes diving, with a musical accompaniment of machine-gun fire and bomb blasts. Military training decreed that during a bombing raid soldiers should get out of a building in case it collapsed, so in mid-haircut Tischler bolted out the doorway. After a hurried glance out of his win-

11

dow, where he could see red-hot tracers flashing by, Frye raced for safety down three flights of stairs. But neither man completely escaped the bomb concussions. They knocked Tischler flat; however, other than having "the runs for about a week" after this near-death experience he was unharmed.[2] Frye was not so lucky. Just as he started out of a hallway into the street a bomb exploded, spraying him with wood splinters, smashing him against a wall, and crushing him to the ground. "This is IT!" he thought. But he struggled to his feet. And, seeing devastation and human tragedy in all directions, he did what his mission as a "soldier-cameraman" required: he went back up to the third floor to get his camera to photograph the carnage. Re-emerging from the building into the rubble with motion-picture camera in hand, Frye observed that "the building across the street was GONE." Then his mind went black.

Frye awoke staring directly at the unexciting ceiling of a field hospital. A medic leaned into his field of vision and announced that he "looked like the wrath of God." Indeed he did. The skin of his face looked sandblasted, both eyelids were lacerated, his windpipe had been damaged, his left side was paralyzed, and he could not speak, not even to give his Army serial number. And, as he later realized, he had a world-class case of shattered nerves, known as "shell shock" in World War I but as "battle fatigue" in World War II. Adding to the bad news was the rumor Frye heard that *American* planes had done the bombing. That was no rumor. The 163rd's commander, Captain Ned R. Morehouse, had no doubt that the planes were American, a sentiment seconded by one of his successors, Robert Lewis, who recalled "that it was most difficult to explain to the Caiazzo natives why some of their ancient buildings were flattened by U.S. aircraft." Nor could he explain the seventeen dead civilians the planes left in their wake. Harold Culbertson, the dispatcher in the company motor pool who watched as the aircraft "bombed the tar out of that motor pool," suggested that they had mistaken Caiazzo for Cassino, one of the anchors in the German's Winter Line and the scene of brutal combat in the Italian campaign during the winter of 1943–44.[3]

The news was not all bad. Although seven other members of the 163rd had been hurt in the incident, none had been injured as seriously as Frye.[4] Moreover, three months earlier he had written his wife, Oleta, that getting a Purple Heart was fine "as long as you can *wear* it home and tell about it, but a lot of the boys never live to tell about it." Although his injuries bothered him for the rest of the war—in fact, fifty years later he was still receiving treatment for eye trouble caused by the bomb blast—Gordon Frye would eventually wear his Purple Heart and a Bronze Star home. Meanwhile, restored to adequate health by mid-March 1944, Frye was soon out once again "shooting 'em with my camera."

———————

Like Frye, the 166th SPC's Harry Downard had a nasty encounter with "friendly fire" under unusual circumstances, but unlike Frye he emerged unscathed. It seems Downard's entire wartime career consisted of getting into potentially mortal situations and then defying death, always without spilling any blood. An artillery shell went off so close to him that it knocked him flat and covered him with dirt but not a single jagged fragment found flesh or bone; a sniper's bullet swished by mere inches away; about a month after D-Day a Luftwaffe plane took dead aim on him with a strafing run and missed; in the gnarled hedgerow country of Normandy machine-gun fire had him pinned down until a tank (a modern-day knight in scruffy armor) rescued him; and while he was flying in a Piper Cub above the front lines an artillery shell hit the plane and forced it to make an emergency landing; Downard walked away, shaken and unsmiling but unhurt.[5]

Downard's most magnificent death-defying act came at Saint-Malo, a French port on the English Channel that the Germans had converted into a fortress city. When elements of General George Patton's Third Army laid siege to it in August 1944, Downard was there. The night before one of the assaults against the city he and a fellow photographer "sneaked in and got into a building inside German lines," climbing to the second floor, where they found a window from which, the next morning, they could photograph the Americans coming right at them. They would be behind the defenders, who were much in evidence in the streets below all night. As often happened during the war, in their single-minded pursuit of superb pictures the cameramen had not made an altogether reasonable calculation of risk versus value. What fascinated them was that "it would be a different [photographic] angle" of an assault. So intrigued was Downard by this prospect that he simply forgot that "the Americans always laid down a barrage before the attack." So they sweated out the "friendly" artillery fire that "just blew that town literally to hell." Some of the shells hit alarmingly close and showered them with dust and plaster, but when the barrage lifted and the attack commenced they inched their lenses out the window.

Alas, "the pictures weren't that great," though certainly not for lack of imagination and effort on the part of the two cameramen. On a more positive note, Harry Downard lived to tell the story.

Sunday, April 1, 1945, had the triple distinction of being April Fool's Day, Easter, and the day the American Tenth Army invaded Okinawa, initiating what became the war's last great battle. But for the 166th SPC's Joe Zinni, writing to his wife that evening from "somewhere in Germany," April Fool's/Easter was "just another day of war & photography." Zinni had come ashore on Omaha Beach in Normandy on D + 10 (ten days after D-Day), leading the six men—three photographers, two drivers, and a clerk—who comprised Detachment #2 of the 166th. From then until V-E Day, he and his men were attached to three different divisions, moving with the fighting front through France, Luxembourg, Belgium, and Germany, with a quick excursion into Czechoslovakia.[6]

In summarizing those eleven months Zinni was not boasting, but simply stating the facts without the beautifying retouching that characterizes so many reminiscences, when he recalled that "We covered quite a bit of action. We went right along with the infantrymen, with the tank men, with the engineers, with the Signal Corps, with the anti-aircraft people, and I think we did quite a job of covering their activities."

A random sampling of his letters to his wife demonstrates how continuously his detachment was close to the front. On July 31 he was writing the word "whenever" and had gotten to the the "v" when the ink darts down at a strange angle and then juts back up. A shell had "just burst a few yards away," startling him. On August 9 the Germans "surrounded and pinned down" Zinni and his men but "thanks to the bravery & courage" of two of his photographers, Jim Ryan and Bob Curry, "who risked their lives by going through machine-gun & rifle fire to deliver an oral message requesting support from our artillery we managed to get back alive." On September 1 artillery fire rattled an improvised table as he wrote that he was "up at *the* 'front' & have been for the past three days." November 18: the detachment was "in the *middle of an artillery duel* & every moment or so the building trembles and shakes" while the men prayed that enemy shells would either be duds or miss by a mile. "The Luftwaffe is up again," he noted on the first night of the new year, and "artillery duels, of great proportions, are in progress—the 'chattering' of machine-guns, that are not very distant, is heard at frequent intervals—mortar–fire is occasionally heard & there is an exchange of rifle fire that is periodical—about every ten minutes or so—aside from this, dear, things are rather quiet." On February 8th they "covered some very 'hot' action" that caused them some "slight nervousness & fear on several occasions," and the next day it seemed that "every enemy shell is bursting close" to their position. The detachment "procured some excellent combat pictures" on April 15 but the cameramen escaped unharmed only "thanks to Almighty God."

Through all of this Zinni was a nearly ideal frontline photo officer. As a 1937 graduate of a two–year course at the American School of Photography who had opened his own studio and also worked as a newspaper photographer, he understood the mechanics and demands of good camera work. Once in combat he learned its hard lessons quickly and well, thereby keeping his men from taking "unnecessary & foolish risks." He retained a sense of humor—"all the boys & myself are in the best of health, in excellent spirits (especially the hard cider & Calvados plus a little Bordeaux wine every now & then) & getting along quite well." And he admired and liked his men. But most of all Zinni had that rare and wonderful human quality called *empathy*— empathy for the cameramen and drivers with whom he worked, for the French people squeezed in war's violent vise-like grip, and particularly for American frontline soldiers. "It does hurt me," he admitted, "to see our boys die & become wounded & at times I'd like to see our air force level all of Germany, right to the ground!!"

Perhaps because of his close, personal perspective on combat Zinni resented what he perceived as a lack of home-front appreciation for what the infantrymen were doing. Speaking for almost all cameramen, he complained to his wife that too many civilians "don't give a damn about what so many American doughboys are going through. Yes, it really gripes me & I could almost scream at times." A civilian, he wrote on another occasion,

> could never fully understand or imagine what the "doughboy" really goes through, nor can we, despite the fact that we have been with them on several occasions for a few days at a time—only the "doughboy" & Almighty God knows about it; the former can't find words enough to fully describe his experiences & the "latter" isn't talking but it'll suffice to say that neither pictures nor words can describe the fears, discomforts, loneliness & hardships that the poor Infantryman has to go through.

Zinni had described one of warfare's universal themes: the innate tension between the fighting front and the home front. Starkly put, soldiers endured what civilians could not even conceptualize. By mid-1943 one of combat photography's foremost goals was to reduce this gulf of non-understanding "by attempting ever so much to get as many shots of the frontline soldiers as possible" for the home front's edification, a task that Zinni and other cameramen zealously embraced.

I

During World War II the U.S. armed forces mobilized many men like Gordon Frye, Harry Downard, and Joe Zinni, who felt compelled to try to complete their photographic mission despite acute danger. These men were ubiquitous along the fighting fronts not only because their specified mission was to photograph combat, but also because many had been civilian photographers for whom dramatic photo opportunities, which military operations offered aplenty, had a magnetic allure. Half a century after the conflict has ended, tens of millions of people continue almost routinely to look at, admire, and learn about that war from the still pictures and motion-picture footage shot by photographers who served in the armed forces; yet the cameramen themselves remain trapped in a black hole of historical anonymity. Two other photographic groups that ventured into the war zones—those engaged in aerial photographic reconnaissance and accredited civilian cameramen—avoided this fate. Since combat cameramen and aerial-recon photographers had distinctly different missions, they were not direct rivals. However, despite official efforts to dampen photographic competition, military cameramen and accredited civilians often engaged in a "friendly" rivalry. The former also competed against each other because high-ranking Army, Navy, Marine Corps, and AAF officials pressured them to provide pictorial publicity primarily for their respective services.

Cameramen were omnipresent near, at, and frequently *beyond* the front. "*Combat Cameramen!*" exclaimed a former glider pilot, itself an extremely dangerous military specialty. "Now, there's a profession that leaves me thinking I was lucky to be a glider pilot! Those guys went out *hunting* trouble."[7] Wherever and whenever soldiers, commandos, paratroopers, sailors, submariners, Marines, and airmen of all types entered harm's vortex, cameramen accompanied them. Sometimes, like Downard at Saint-Malo, they even preceded the fighting forces. "At present," Zinni wrote his wife, *"we are miles in front of the front & in German territory...."* In good husbandly fashion he assured her they were safe and that she should not worry, but only a wife yearning for widowhood could rest easily after receiving a letter like that.[8] Army photographer W. F. Lovell was reportedly the first American to enter Tunis and "had the fleeing Germans in range of his camera before the combat elements had them in range of their rifles."[9] In northern Italy the 3225 Signal Photo Production Unit's Donald Morrow, whose jeep had entered Pisa ahead of the engineers who were sweeping the roads for mines, volunteered "to go behind the German lines on a special photographic mission of which I have conceived." Morrow's plan went all the way to Lieutenant General Lucian K. Truscott but he rejected it as too dangerous.[10] The 163rd SPC's weekly newssheet, *Foto-Facto*, proclaimed in mid-December that the "163rd ENTERS GERMANY— SO DOES SEVENTH ARMY." Although this was a tongue-in-cheek headline, it did not exaggerate, since the unit's cameramen were with the first Seventh Army patrols piercing the Reich.[11]

Because these photographers seemingly courted trouble on purpose, people thought they "were nuts taking a picture with the enemy shooting at you."[12] Many sources confirm this view. In late November 1944 the 84th Infantry Division launched an attack against German defenses in Europe. As machine-gun squad leader Frank Gonzales moved forward he could not see any Germans but he did see a stranger who "was behind a tree with a big camera and was in uniform but he wasn't wearing a helmet. I asked him what in the hell he thought he was doing, and he told me he was taking pictures. I was really astonished to see him—I thought the guy was crazy." At approximately the same time, but half a world away on the war-stricken island called Peleliu, Marine private E. B. Sledge had a similar experience. When intense enemy fire ignited an amphibious assault vehicle (called an amtrac) loaded with ammunition right in front of Sledge, a man crawled over him and stood upright. "I looked up at him in surprise. Every Marine in the area was hugging the deck for the inevitable explosion from the amtrac. He carried a portable movie camera with which he began avidly filming the billow of smoke boiling up from the amtrac. Rifle cartridges began popping in the amtrac as the heat got to them." Sledge yelled out that the man should take cover. The photographer "turned and looked down at me with a contemptuous stare of utter disdain and disgust. He didn't demean himself to speak to me as I cringed in the ditch, but turned back to his camera eyepiece and continued filming."[13]

Yet these soldier-photographers were not crazy—at least not most of them, not most of the time, and not in the clinical sense. Nor were they necessarily displaying either inordinate foolhardiness or excessive bravery. Instead, two rational factors motivated them. One was professional pride. They had that obsession that characterizes great photographers—to take pictures that are technically perfect and that make a significant statement about the human condition. No one could *order* a photographer to take a superb picture, since he could readily do many things—soft focus, poor exposure, lopsided composition—to ruin it.[14] Only an inner drive bordering on missionary zeal could elicit excellent work. Engaging in photography under dangerous circumstances induced an adrenaline-like rush of excitement so overpowering that even amidst the battlefield's angry lead and jagged steel a cameraman could be oblivious to danger.

"Actually," recalled John Cooper of the 161st SPC, "some of our people would get so wrapped up in combat taking pictures that they seemed to forget they were in combat." Ed Newell of the 163rd SPC wrote that he always "wanted to stay close to the moving action—didn't want, or almost feared, getting left out or feared missing something big happening." Perhaps the 166th SPC's Charlie "Slick" Sumners phrased this craving most simply: "The most important thing was being where the action was."[15] Thus, when Jack Kill of the AAF's 4th CCU took a bullet in the shoulder, he "wouldn't miss out on the fighting" and refused to let the medics evacuate him to a hospital. With the slug still in his shoulder he simply "transferred into an an easier-riding tank and continued the advance." After volunteering "for a secret mission entailing unusual danger," Daniel Novak and William Safran of the 164th SPC participated in the glider attack on Myitkyina in northern Burma, performing their duties so assiduously that it endangered their lives "beyond the manner normally to be expected under combat conditions." In May 1944 Benedetto James Mancuso of the Navy's 3rd CPU went ashore with the third wave during the Wadke Island invasion. Amid heavy machine-gun, mortar, and sniper fire he "performed his tasks in a highly aggressive and skillful manner." Several times "when enemy fire was concentrated on his particular point of shelter, he refused to remain safely under cover. Instead, he unhesitatingly and with complete disregard for his personal safety moved forward to positions more advantageous to successful achievement of his mission, thereby obtaining photographs of great value."[16]

Reinforcing the professional ethos, and perhaps substituting for it in the case of photographers who had not been prewar professionals, was the mission of combat cameramen. Almost every military organization has an explicit mission and photo units were no exception. The emphasis was consistently on *combat operations*. The mission of the Army Pictorial Service (APS), which administered all the Signal Corps's photographic activities, was "to provide official photographs, both still and motion, of military activities, including combat," which had the highest priority. War Department Pamphlet 11-2, the *Standing Operating Procedure For Signal Photographic Units In Theaters Of Operations*, stated this emphatically: the primary function of these units "was to make and/or process still and motion pictures" that would "Convey to the War Department information on combat and field operations. When opportunities occur, combat photography is the first duty of all units." In a proposed lecture for the U.S. Army Command and General Staff College on photographic opportunities, Colonel William D. Hamlin, Chief of the Signal Corps's Military Training Branch, summarized the wartime mission when he emphasized that cameramen were *combat* personnel; he criticized an officer on Okinawa who restricted their battlefield access because he did not want to risk a man's life just to get pictures.[17] Throughout the war pertinent army documents reinforced the primacy of photographing combat, including the preparation of personnel and equipment, the departure of troops for the battle, all aspects of the fighting, seized or wrecked enemy equipment, and the return of personnel and equipment from the front.[18]

The AAF's commanding general, Henry "Hap" Arnold, took a personal interest in the CCUs and stated that their mission was to "Cover thoroughly with both still and motion pictures the activities of the Army Air Forces to which they are attached; particularly, whenever possible, combat operations both on the ground and in the air." AAF Memorandum 95-1, the Bible for the employment of CCUs, reinforced Arnold's view: CCUs were "to furnish motion pictures of AAF combat and other operational activities." This emphasis on combat appeared repeatedly in instructions that CCU officers and men received.[19]

Men who served in photographic units estimated they spent between two thirds and four fifths of their time striving to bring "a true combat picture of the war to all the world."[20] So assiduously did they perform their frontline duties that they occasionally needed a reminder to stay alive. The 10th CCU adopted a slogan: "Get it on film and get back with it." A high-ranking APS officer stressed that "the picture is no good if you can't bring it back" and a 166th SPC officer preached to his men, "What's the use of attempting to get something spectacular if you can't return to base alive & with it?" Lieutenant Commander Carleton Mitchell, Jr., who directed all the CPUs as head of the Combat Photography Section (CPS) of the Navy's Photographic Division, complained about one CPU that had run "an unnecessary risk" by going in with the first assault waves at Tarawa. He did "not think it fair to expect a man carrying only a camera to establish a beachhead on his own."[21]

As with other combatants who endured prolonged exposure to battle conditions, some cameramen required alcohol to "get a little mellow prior to going on a dangerous mission."[22] Others, such as Gordon Frye, suffered from battle fatigue, a phenomenon that was no reflection on a man's courage. Even the bravest could experience this syndrome; maybe some of them became afflicted *because* they were the bravest. The officer in charge (OIC) of CPU #7 became "jumpy as a jaybird," but with good reason. He had been through five major engagements including Tarawa, where he "saw enough dead men, or pieces thereof, to last me for half a dozen lifetimes."[23] Wounded cameramen became "a little jittery" or genuinely frightened and reluctant to go back into combat. Personality transformations occurred—invariably joyful, witty individuals became quiet and withdrawn, never vice versa. In other instances a cameraman simply "flipped out" under the stress of "little sleep, cold, and constant heavy guns both artillery and dive bombers." Often a short respite from combat duty restored a man's fighting spirit.[24] Meanwhile his colleagues continued peering through their viewfinders and deepening their foxholes.

II

Ned R. Morehouse had commanded the 163rd SPC from its inception until the spring of 1944, when he departed the Caiazzo headquarters building suddenly, unexpectedly, and in the dark of night. Most men in the 163rd were glad to be rid of Captain Morehouse, whom they despised. For more than thirty-five years after the war he neither saw nor spoke to anyone from his old company. But in 1980, learning that the 163rd was holding a reunion in nearby Anaheim, California, he chanced a telephone call to Robert Lewis to learn the details. The call both surprised and pleased Lewis, who had eventually become the company commander. Lewis suggested to Warren Kieft, who had been Morehouse's second-in-command and who was on the committee organizing the reunion, that Morehouse, once so bitterly loathed, should be "the chief recipient of praise at this reunion." After all, he had taken "green recruits and made soldiers of them, selected future leaders and organized what became an efficient team."[25]

Decades of reflection had convinced most of the 163rd's members that Lewis was right, that their hatred had been misplaced, that they, not their captain, had been wrong. During the war the cameramen had not understood the problems Morehouse confronted and had not appreciated all that he had done for the unit. Now the company belatedly made amends. With but one exception "each and every one of the individuals who were at the reunion came up to Morehouse and congratulated him on the good job he had done in training our company." At the final banquet one of Morehouse's most vocal wartime critics manfully "stood up and made a verbal commendation of Morehouse as to what a great job he had done."[26]

Few of Morehouse's men entering combat for the first time felt like Jerry Kahn of the 162nd SPC, who initially saw action during the fighting at the Falaise–Argentan gap in the summer of 1944. He and his colleagues had parked their vehicle and were moving forward on foot "and we passed what we thought were GIs advancing and we walked naively along and said, 'Where's the front line?' And they said 'Buddy, you're on it.'" Kahn recalled that he "really didn't know what I was doing up there and I shouldn't have been there in the first place because we weren't trained for any of this."[27] Thanks to Morehouse, those in the 163rd were reasonably well prepared for combat. Why, then, was he so disliked?

One fundamental reason was that combat cameramen were three things at once—soldiers, skilled technicians, and artists—and reconciling these different "personalities" created enormous tension. Photographers usually viewed themselves as technicians and artists first and soldiers second, but the Army often emphasized their soldierly duties, and properly so. Unless cameramen understood military procedures, the order of battle, and tactics they could not protect themselves in a combat environment or produce pictures that had continuity and were of the greatest military value.[28] Consequently, before 1943 commissioned officers in photo units were usually army officers with only a modest amount of photographic experience. They often had college degrees in physics or engineering, were trained for strictly administrative positions in the SPCs, and did not have a well-honed understanding of photographic practices and nomenclature. An officer in the 161st SPC, for example, peered though the ground glass at the back of a Speed Graphic and chided the photographer for having a defective lens because the image was upside down. As even novice cameramen knew, the image in a Speed Graphic was *always* upside down when viewed through the ground glass instead of the view-finder.[29]

Many high-ranking Signal Corps officers frowned on the idea of training professional photographers as officers. Most photographers had been too busy pursuing careers to get a college degree, and in a misplaced display of intellectual elitism army officers with university diplomas questioned whether such undereducated men were potential officer material. Army officers were also suspicious of "the so-called 'Hollywood touch' in its worst sense—an urge for questionable show-manship and publicity which are out of place in making serious combat or training films."[30]

A military-minded commanding officer might be good for instilling discipline but not for understanding photographic requirements and possibilities.[31] Overseas experience demonstrated that photo companies could not afford the luxury of having purely administrative officers; they needed officers who were also working photographers.

Belatedly realizing its mistake, in 1943 the Army transformed its definition of who would make good photo officers, stopped training officer-photographers, and began producing photographer-officers. Instead of budding physicists and engineers who would become photo company administrators, it sought experienced photographers who could be trained to become at least minimally acceptable military officers. The armed forces even dipped into the enlisted ranks to find suitable candidates; and seeing one of their own assume command often infused a unit's enlisted men with exceptionally high morale.[32]

Ned Morehouse was typical of the initial group of officer-photographers. A 1935 graduate of the University of Nevada with an engineering degree, he had been commissioned an infantry second lieutenant through ROTC. In college he had also done photography for the student newspaper, for his senior-class yearbook, and during ROTC summer training camps. Graduating in the midst of the Depression when no engineering positions were available, he found work in a photography studio for $10.00 per week. But in 1938 he went to work for General Electric, putting his engineering skills to use before being ordered to active duty in March 1941 with the First Signal Company, Photographic, which became the 161st SPC. While with the 161st Morehouse covered Patton's 2nd Armored Division and received a flattering commendation from the general for his fine efforts. On another occasion the Third Army's Public Relations Officer cited Morehouse as "ingenious, energetic, loyal and cheerful in his work."[33]

When the War Department formed the 163rd SPC in April 1942, First Lieutenant Morehouse (soon promoted to captain) and twenty enlisted men from the 161st provided the cadre. "With this," he wrote, "my career as a cameraman came to an end, and my responsibilities became those of command, responsible for preparing the unit in all ways to perform its combat mission." With this, he might have written, his ordeal began.

Assuming that the men already knew photography, Morehouse instituted a training program at Fort Sam Houston emphasizing basic infantry subjects. His philosophy was that "Emulsion may be mightier than the sword but it's also good to have a Tommy Gun handy." For three months the men did calisthenics, practiced the fundamentals of squad and platoon drill, and took classes in such subjects as marksmanship, defense against gas and air attacks, map reading, first aid, military courtesy, and army organization. Although Morehouse purposely stressed basic training, he really had no other option. Cameras were so scarce that photographic work was necessarily limited.[34]

Had the 163rd endured basic training only once, the enlisted men and most of the officers might not have become alienated. But the continuing equipment shortage and the constant arrival of untrained men dictated that Morehouse repeat the cycle several times.[35] No sooner had the twenty-man cadre from the 161st arrived at Fort Sam Houston to activate the 163rd than men began leaving. "We started off with high hopes and the determination to be the best photographic outfit in the USA," wrote Morehouse, "but then the termites started chipping away at the foundation." More than a third of the cadre soon departed to attend Officer Candidate School, and ultimately the 163rd supplied more than one hundred men to OCS. As replacements arrived they needed basic training, and since the photo equipment shortage had not abated the whole unit went through it again. Some of its men took basic training three or four times.

As the commanding officer Morehouse was the focal point for the 163rd's discontent. Men became bored with the training regimen and their morale fluctuated "from very low down to not very high." The unhappiness caused by the lack of photographic training, wrote Warren Kieft, showed "in the officers' and men's dissatisfaction and readiness to cause trouble."[36] All soldiers have an inalienable right to complain and the lower morale sank the more vigorously they exercised that privilege. "There was once a soldier who never complained about the way the Army was run," wrote one wag. "At last reports he was still satisfied with conditions in the psychopathic ward." Moreover, cameramen are often extreme individualists, ill suited for a collective enterprise and with little patience for regulations. As a 1944 Guide for Military and News Photography put it, "photographers are a peculiar clan of individualists, each sincere in his belief that he is creating something of great importance."[37] Since the essentially mechanical nature of basic training grated against a cameraman's creative instincts, talented photographers often had a hard time acquiring soldierly skills.

Despite the hatred directed against him, Morehouse had achieved his goal of teaching the men military skills and values by the time the 163rd SPC finally began deploying overseas. They were physically tough, disciplined, and well organized. As Lieutenant Brooks C. Noah's lab unit boarded ship in January 1943 bound for North Africa, Kieft noted that port officials "commended the company on having the unit so well prepared which in my mind [was] particularly due to the tireless but not very often appreciated efforts of Capt. Ned R. Morehouse."[38]

During the war Morehouse never reaped the praise he deserved. When the 163rd arrived in Italy he "lost direct control of the unit" because Colonel Melvin E. Gillette, a high ranking Signal Corps photographic officer in the Mediterranean Theater, ordered him "to remain at company headquarters, which essentially became simply an administrative headquarters, outfitting photographers, furnishing supplies of film, maintaining a place where men could come to when not needed or when awaiting further assignments." In short, Morehouse became a rear-area commander, and, as students of military history know, front-line soldiers often consider their own rear-area officers worse enemies than the other side's fighting forces. At the front, where fighting and surviving were the foremost concerns, formal military discipline and distinctions based on rank all but disappeared. But when a man returned to headquarters, where a garrison mentality often prevailed, he had to look and act military: wearing a clean uniform, snapping off finger-perfect salutes, and saying "Yes, sir!" became priority items. Such pettiness irritated individualistic-minded cameramen. As Sam Tischler bluntly put it regarding Morehouse's position, "Back there he's the enemy." Cameramen in other units had a similar attitude. Joe Zinni "hated to return to Headquarters for there is too much 'spit & shine' plus a great deal of discipline that has to be followed. . . . " And for years after the war Bill Teas had nightmares that centered not on gruesome combat scenes but on the agony of Army regulations.[39]

If few in his own company appreciated what a good trainer and administrator Morehouse was, his superiors did. The 3131st Signal Service Company had been formed as a provisional unit in Algiers to absorb a large number of small photographic units that had arrived in the Mediterranean theater and were simply "floating around." Originally the unit was not organized for combat coverage but when the 163rd left the Fifth Army in Italy to cover the invasion of Southern France, authorities decided to revamp the 3131st to replace the 163rd. To whip the 3131st into fighting trim the Army called upon the experienced Captain Ned Morehouse. So successful was he in completing this task that he received a Fifth Army commendation praising his initiative, resourcefulness, and foresight, all of which "materially contributed to the superior photographic coverage" of the Army's activities.

As usual, Morehouse's performance, so pleasing to the Army's high command, did not find favor among his photographers. Like the men in the 163rd, those in the 3131st severely criticized Morehouse. Donald J. Morrow confided to his diary that Morehouse "never passes up a chance to play soldier, and he does that in the same stupid way he administrates this company from the photographic viewpoint." The captain, for example, never would have approved of Morrow's decision, which violated all Army regulations, to shed his American uniform while at the front during the harsh northern Italian winter of 1944–45, and don a British uniform, which was much warmer.[40]

Since the problem of reconciling military discipline and subordination with artistic creativity was insoluble, the 163rd SPC's leadership problems were not unique. For example, when the 166th SPC assembled at Camp Crowder, a split developed almost immediately between its Hollywood-trained members (known as the "Kodachromes") and the officers who had graduated from OCS or been trained at the Signal Corps Photographic Center (SCPC). Like the 166th's commander, Captain Robert F. Downs, most of these officers had been in the army substantially longer than the men from Tinseltown and strongly believed in the virtues of basic training. The Kodachromes knew little about the army, drill, and tactics and did not care to learn much more about these matters since they had enlisted to serve as cameramen, not infantrymen. But while they wanted to concentrate almost exclusively on photographic training, Downs, like Morehouse, stressed the military aspects of combat photography. As a result the Kodachromes loathed him.[41]

Perhaps Downs was both a martinet and an unpleasant individual, or perhaps the Kodachromes collectively were not as introspective and as ultimately understanding as the men in the 163rd. But for whatever reason the Hollywood contingent never forgave Downs. Decades after the war Bill Teas still considered him "a son of a bitch" and Ted Sizer called him an arrogant, awful, terrible man; others echoed these sentiments.[42]

Warren Kieft was probably making a wish rather than a prediction when he confided to his diary in early 1943 that eventually the 163rd SPC would realize the importance of the "things beside photography" that Morehouse had taught the men. The 163rd had its share of casualties, but considering the extensive close-quarters violence it encountered during its lengthy overseas duty they were not unbearably high. "Now maybe it was a lot of luck," said Robert Goebel as he reflected on the unit's surprisingly low casualty rate, "but I'd like to think of it as the training...."[43] Like so many others he belatedly recognized that the 163rd's first commanding officer had made his men good soldiers as well as good photographers.

III

"I'd been wondering if anybody ever heard of combat cameramen," said Fred Bonnard of the 163rd SPC many decades after the war. And an AAF cameraman noted that "all during the war people would go to the theaters and see the newsreels and say, boy, look at that. No one ever said, hey, how much blood is on that film? Who is the guy that made this?"[44] War always has more unsung than publicized heroes, but certainly among World War II's most unsung heroes were the combat cameramen.

As a result of their ubiquity, professionalism, mission, and devotion to duty, cameramen compiled a fabulous pictorial record that has "kept history alive."[45] Paradoxically, in a figurative sense the cameramen themselves have always been "dead," suffering from an acute anonymity during the war and remaining invisible ever since. In part the wartime anonymity resulted from the ancient tradition that the closer to the fighting a man was, the less anyone knew about him. However unfairly, those in the higher ranks of the rear echelons reaped publicity and fame while the front-line personnel only bled and died. But the War and Navy Departments also purposefully imposed this anonymity as a security measure until late in the war. For example, only after it had worked for two years in the China-Burma-India Theater was the presence of the 10th CCU announced, a welcome bit of recognition for the unit members.[46] Individuals rarely received public credit for their work, as the services released almost all of their still photographs and motion picture footage under such innocuous bylines as "Official U.S. Navy Photograph" or "Photo by Signal Corps."

Only in the most unusual circumstances did photographers not crave credit for their work. Still photographer Martin Lederhandler of the 165th SPC had one of these exceptional experiences. He had gone ashore on D-Day and entrusted his negatives to a carrier pigeon, which, unfortunately, followed an eccentric flight pattern. Instead of flapping correctly toward London, it flew off over enemy lines. Shortly thereafter a German army newspaper ran the pictures, giving due credit: "Photos by 1st Lieut. Martin Lederhandler, U.S. Army Signal Corps."[47]

Under almost all other conditions many photographers resented the absence of bylines. Prewar professionals had been used to receiving personal credit and recognition, and those amateurs aspiring to professional status realized the importance of "making a name" through individual recognition. They especially disliked not getting bylines, since wartime picture magazines and newsreels were so immensely popular—primarily because of the dramatic photography provided by soldier-cameramen. Seemingly ignored and unappreciated, cameramen sometimes wondered why they tried so hard.[48]

"We feel," wrote the editor of the *Weekly Kodachrome*, the 166th SPC's newssheet, "that it would certainly be an added incentive to these men who are taking the pictures if they could expect credit lines."[49] Acting on its own suggestion, the *Weekly Kodachrome* gave photographers credit, as did the 163rd's *Foto-Facto*, *Stars and Stripes*, and *Yank*. As the war entered its last year even civilian journals and magazines occasionally gave military photographers a byline,[50] and the immediate postwar era witnessed a flurry of by-name recognition. The Navy, for example, issued special citations to 149 Navy, Marine Corps, and Coast Guard photographers; the Army publicly commended fifty Signal Corps photographers; and Marine Corps Captain Raymond Henri's book on Iwo Jima contained nearly a hundred pictures, most with by-name credit.[51]

Still, the wartime anonymity prevails. In 1981 Larry Sowinski published a book using many Navy photographs; in the acknowledgments he simply wrote "All photographs are official US Navy." John Pimlott's *World War II in Photographs* contains only a brief paragraph listing twenty-four agencies that supplied photos.[52] These two examples could be amplified many times over. More than forty years after the Japanese surrendered, Joseph Longo, who served in the AAF CCUs, felt so frustrated at seeing the work of combat cameramen used without attribution that he became a driving force behind the formation of the International Combat Cameramen's Association; one of its goals is to achieve greater recognition for World War II photographers.[53]

IV

Their specialized mission and anonymity differentiated combat cameramen from two other groups of wartime photographers—those in the Navy and AAF who specialized in aerial photographic reconnaissance and the "official" civilian photographers. The former had a different mission and the latter received effusive personal recognition. While combat cameramen concentrated on operations, photo recon's primary task was to provide pre- and post-operational coverage. Photo recon's vital role in World War II is indisputable, especially in supplying strategic intelligence such as identifying the location and disposition of the enemy's economic targets. But it was less adept at providing tactical intelligence of immediate use to a commander engaged in combat, because neither the appropriate equipment nor techniques for rapid printing and duplication had been developed. Only later, in the Korean War, did Navy and Air Force tactical recon become truly important.[54]

Aerial-recon missions could be dauntingly hazardous but as a general rule they were like detective work, involving a great deal of routine and only a little excitement.[55] As one Navy recon pilot, who was among the first to photograph Tokyo, wrote, "the cameras do all the work and we just fly and push buttons." He was fighting in "the gentleman's way (even though that sounds incongruous) because you are in solid comfort all the while." Guilt nipped at his conscience, for "the men in the other branches of service are taking all the weight. If we should fly constantly day and night under attack we wouldn't experience in twenty years what a Marine private has to go through in one day."[56] Down there with the Marine private was the combat cameraman.

Like their military counterparts, civilian still photographers and newsreel cameramen who received armed forces accreditation were "official" photographers and could take pictures in the war zones. An accredited civilian dressed in a uniform like an officer's and enjoyed many officers' privileges, but was unarmed. Around one arm an accredited civilian wore a green brassard with a white "P" on it, which identified the individual as a photographer. Unlike their military colleagues, civilians were not in for the duration; instead they were ordinarily on assignment for only a few weeks or months before returning home.[57]

The armed services tried to avoid competition among official civilian photographers and between civilians and combat cameramen by establishing a "pool" system. As an essay in *Popular Photography* proclaimed, "The day of the picture 'scoops' is over" since all still pictures and motion picture footage shot by civilians went into "pools." Accredited photographers from the Associated Press, International News Photos, Acme News Pictures, and *Life* Magazine comprised the Still Picture Pool, while Fox Movietone News, News of the Day, Paramount, Pathé, and Universal composed the Newsreel Pool. Stills and motion pictures shot by military cameramen also went into these pools.[58] Special Army, Navy, and AAF boards censored all the film coming into the pools and released for public use anything that did not endanger security. Thus, all official photography, civilian or military, once censored was equally available to all; of course, the armed services also had access to the material that the censors had deemed inappropriate for public release.[59] Although the War and Navy Departments occasionally used stills and motion pictures shot by civilians (and gave by-line credit when they did),[60] newspapers, magazines, and the newsreels were heavily dependent upon anonymous military personnel.

Controlling the photographers' competitive drive to get the best picture and have it published first was not as simple as establishing the pool system. Consequently, the relationship between civilian and military cameramen was often tense, with grave civilian fears being countered by intense military resentment. Civilians suspected that military photographers might replace them altogether and wondered if the military's accreditation system was actually a method of excluding them from covering the war. Even when it became evident that this fear was groundless, civilians dreaded excessive censorship. Pathé News cameraman David Oliver complained that only half his footage from Europe became public. And the *Motion Picture Herald* railed against newspapers and newsreels being subjected to military capriciousness. Military authorities assured pool representatives that they only wanted to supplement, not supplant, civilian coverage. Although this was true, military photographers so outnumbered civilian cameramen in the war zones that for all intents and purposes they did supplant them. Military officials also asserted that censorship was judicious and necessary. For example, the War Department insisted that 99 percent of Oliver's footage had been released and that the 1 percent withheld might aid the enemy.[61]

Combat cameramen often resented pool photographers who, they felt, were pampered and "treated like kings." Civilians frequently seemed to avoid the combat zone, staying snug and secure in the rear areas while combat cameramen tended the front lines.[62] Even when civilians ventured to the front, the combat cameramen still knew that they enjoyed the luxury of being able to depart whenever they wanted, even in broad daylight on a sunny, pleasant day. And in any event "they were not there for the whole period and did not slop in the mud day after day for two years." Warren Kieft of the 163rd SPC remembered his first day under fire. He was in a foxhole in Italy adjacent to one occupied by Margaret Bourke-White, one of *Life* owner Henry Luce's "lens-luggers." "I have a filter," he wrote, "which she left in her hurry to leave and would have returned it if I had seen her again." That is, while Bourke-White departed, Keift stayed.[63]

The poor opinions that many combat cameramen held regarding the photojournalists' bravery and dedication were not altogether accurate. No doubt a few civilians were unscrupulous laggards, even outright cowards; the same could be said about a few combat cameramen. But overall, as one Marine observed, "there weren't even a handful who weren't real professionals.... They shared the same hardships that we did. They could get killed or shot at just as easily as our people." And they did. *Life* sent twenty-one photojournalists to the war; five received wounds and a dozen contracted malaria. Newsreel cameramen, too, paid in blood the steep price of admission to frontline seats.[64] And officials in the still and newsreel pools were certainly gracious in thanking the combat cameramen for their assistance, praising their work, and commending their bravery.[65]

Combat cameramen perceived two other inequities. They knew that the civilians were "getting good money for the same stuff we shoot" for a soldier's pay, which was to say virtually for free.[66] And civilians received another type of "pay" that military photographers craved even more than money: bylines. *Life*, especially, trumpeted the exploits of its photojournalists. "Stuttgart Raid: LIFE Photographer Rides Through Flak and Fighters on Tough Fortress Mission to Southwest Germany" was the blaring headline for a story in the October 11, 1943 issue. "To *Life* Photoreporter Frank Scherschel," the essay began, "befell the rare and dangerous task of photographing the American bombing raid on Stuttgart, Germany, September 6."[67] The AAF CCUs also regularly flew on such hazardous missions, and *Life* repeatedly published their pictures, but in their case without by-name recognition. By April 1945 the 10th CCU had flown 257 combat missions totalling 2,500 hours of combat flying time, and between January 1944 and August 1945 the 5th CCU had more than 500 missions and well over 2,000 hours. Many CCU photographers had been on dozens of combat missions—Clifford M. Lefferts of the 16th CCU flew fifty-three in just six months and his colleague Harold E. Geer flew eighty-six missions by January 1945.[68]

For the military cameramen, even worse than not receiving credit was when they saw their pictures appearing over some other byline. Nothing galled them worse than when the Associated Press, International News Photos, or Acme News Pictures grabbed photos taken by military personnel out of the still-picture pool and then credited themselves with the work.[69]

V

Army Air Force Major General James P. Hodges was horrified. "The Navy has just released through 20th Century Fox the most spectacular picture of combat action I have ever seen," he wrote to the Commanding General of the Tenth Air Force. Hodges was referring to *The Fighting Lady*, a movie depicting life aboard an aircraft carrier in the Pacific, produced "in the most technically perfect color photography imaginable." "Needless to say," Hodges continued, "it has set us all back on our heels and every possible step is being taken to produce a comparable picture in the shortest possible time."[70] In the great battle fought among the services for public support, Congressional favor, and budgetary appropriations the Navy had inflicted a stunning defeat upon its budding archrival, the AAF, which now felt desperately compelled to counterattack.

Competition, not interservice cooperation or coordination, was the hallmark of the armed forces' photographic activities. High-ranking civil and military officials in each service recognized the utility of a shrewdly orchestrated public relations campaign built around its own photographic images. Secretary of the Navy Frank Knox was "vitally interested in presenting to the American public the Navy's part in the Pacific war," and the importance of pictures in this endeavor could not be overemphasized. In addition to looking at stills in newspapers and periodicals, millions of Americans attended movie theaters every week. Knox particularly desired naval-combat film reports "to show Congressional and other groups;" such films "would add immeasurably to the telling of the Navy's story of the war." Occasionally Secretary Knox and Admiral Ernest J. King, who performed the formidable dual roles of Commander in Chief of the United States Fleet and Chief of Naval Operations, took time from their busy schedules to view a rough cut (akin to the first draft of an essay) of film recently arrived from the front.[71] In their quest for recognition and taxpayers' dollars, Marine and Army officials also emphasized producing their own films for public distribution.[72] The Army and the Navy, to cite just one example of this competitiveness, each established a separate film division to get only its films shown at war plants as a way to spur worker productivity.[73]

No collective group of service authorities exceeded the AAF's in pursuing photographic publicity. Leading the AAF celluloid charge was General "Hap" Arnold, who "wanted to get publicity for the air force because he wanted to get money" from Congress. Beyond that, he strove to convince the public and the government that air power was so potent that the AAF should be an independent service, coequal with the Army and the Navy. When CCU film glorifying the AAF appeared in the newsreels, Arnold dashed off a commendatory telegram to the CCU that shot the footage. He screened AAF documentaries, made suggestions for revisions, and personally showed them to Congressional committees and at the White House.[74] His office also prepared a list of films that AAF generals might show when civilian organizations invited them to attend; the AAF had made them all, and all stressed the vital role of the AAF in defeating the Axis powers.[75]

Following General Arnold's fervent belief in film's public relations value, William Keighley, Chief of the AAF Motion Picture Branch, aggressively sought to get AAF films before the public on all occasions. As soon as its documentaries were ready the AAF moved into its "exploitation phase." *Target Tokyo* and *Fight for the Sky* were both finished in the spring of 1945, the former depicting the first B-29 raid on Tokyo and the latter detailing the role of American fighter planes in driving the Luftwaffe from the skies of Europe. A sergeant was placed on detached service in New York City to prepare newspaper stories, news clippings, advertisements, and press showings for each film. General Ira Eaker, the Deputy Commander of the AAF, and three other AAF generals attended a private screening of these two films with the members of the House Military Affairs Committee. And the AAF made special efforts to have the films shown to such influential civilian groups as the National Geographic Society. The AAF Director of Information urged all public-relations officers to cooperate with local movie representatives in showing another AAF documentary, *The Last Bomb*. In the words of General Curtis LeMay, who had directed the B-29 strategic bombing campaign against Japan, this film showed "how Japan's ability to wage modern war was destroyed by strategic air assaults, while her ground armies of 5 million men stood undefeated." That is, it showed why the United States no longer needed an army![76]

In their frontline niches combat cameramen felt pressure from above to compete not only against civilian cameramen but also against the other services. "You see," wrote Joe Zinni, "we have civilian photographers to compete with & I can't afford to have them 'scoop' us—i.e., to get their 'stuff' in before us for if they do I have to answer to my superiors."[77] Requests went out for the Navy's CPUs to concentrate only on naval operations, and AAF CCUs received pleas to make every effort "to provide interesting footage in order that the story of the AAF may be properly and constantly presented to the American public."[78] Driven by their own professional ethic and these demands from higher authority, photographers from each service went to great lengths to get their film back to the United States first so that it could be pooled, cleared by censors, and publicly displayed. For the invasion of Biak the OIC of CPU #3, Herbert S. Newcomb, carefully planned how he would get his photos to the States in the most expeditious manner, hoping that "this time we even beat the Signal Corps and civilian photographers."[79] Much to its bitter frustration, the Navy often lost these races. Because Army photographers had more frequent access to wirephoto machines, which could reproduce photos at great distances by means of electric impulses transmitted by wires, Signal Corps still photos often beat the Navy's by several days.[80]

Joe Boyle, known for good reason as "Shorty," was thinking only about his unit, but he really spoke for all World War II combat photographic units, when he wrote that the 163rd SPC was an outfit for which historians "should be eternally grateful, because without us then you fellows would have a much more difficult time writing history today and in the year 2000."[81] And beyond.

2

"Survival of the Cleverest"

The Joy and Travail
of Combat Photography

Before the war, John D. Craig was an internationally renowned produc-
er-director of travel and adventure pictures who had led expeditions
through forty-three countries and was a featured lecturer on Bell &
Howell's National Lecture Bureau roster. Without being unduly
immodest, he authored a book entitled *Danger Is My Business*. But no
peacetime adventures, no matter how thrilling, matched the concentrated danger of his wartime role. As the 9th CCU's commander he
flew thirty-five missions and logged 348 combat hours. Upon returning
to the States Craig assumed administrative control over all the CCUs.
Late in the war he left that cushy Washington, D.C. office job and
headed to the European Theater to eyeball combat through the camera's prisms again. "I wouldn't have it missed it for the world," Craig
said as he summarized his World War II experience, "but I wouldn't
like to go through it again. God, it was awful." Thus did he express
the ambivalence felt by many cameramen about combat photography,
with its alternating mixture of the wonderful and the woeful, of joy
and travail.[1]

I

Rare was the cameraman who did not consider himself fortunate. Photographers enjoyed their military specialty. As John S. Wever of the 196th SPC phrased it, "I'd rather be a private doing photography than a colonel doing some other sort of work." Most photographers felt privileged to utilize their civilian specialty in a wartime assignment. "It meant," wrote the 163rd SPC's L. Bennett "Elby" Fenberg, "that I was doing a job that I felt qualified to do and enjoyed doing. It was one of the few cases in the army where the bolt fitted into a proper hole instead of a square one."[2]

Cameramen also had extraordinary freedom and mobility. Considering that photographers rarely had an exalted rank—only a few were lieutenants, most were noncommissioned officers and privates— their independence may have been unprecedented. They referred to themselves as "gypsies" and "vagabonds" and moved around so much that they developed a keen sense of "how circus & carnival people live." It became big news when "we didn't move today—for a change!" Long after the war, when a slowed gait and potbellies belied their youthful vim, they still marveled that they had had more freedom than any other group of soldiers, sailors, or airmen. No one controlled them; they came and went as they pleased and lived and ate wherever they wanted. They "could just go out and pursue our instincts," though they always had to remember the important condition of their freedom: they had to produce quality combat photographic coverage.[3]

Sometimes Army photographers traveled so far so fast that "we overran our maps" and had no idea where they were, not even "what country we were in." Each month the 163rd SPC's several dozen cameramen traveled a distance equal to more than once around the globe. Harold Culbertson, the unit's motor pool dispatcher who had watched the mistaken bombing at Caiazzo, outfitted small photographic teams with a jeep and off they went. "They might go out and stay one day; they might go out and stay a week; they might go out and stay a month," he said. A few even stayed out more than a month. The prizewinner was probably Bob Goebel, who never once returned to company headquarters in eleven and a half months! These men had the time of their lives—romping or sailing all over the war zones, meeting fascinating local people, thriving on the action, and staring in wonder at amazing sights that the average foxhole dweller or boiler-room denizen never saw.[4]

Wartime photographic vagabondage, however, had three drawbacks. Two of them were minor irritations but one of them was a potentially serious problem. The first irritant was that jeeps suffered from "flat-tire-itis," a weakness in the otherwise astonishingly rugged vehicles that required the disgusted cameramen to change or repair as many as three or four flat tires a day.[5] The other minor difficulty was that each move required new quarters. When a photographer could not readily take up quarters in a building, it meant "once again digging slit-trenches, & fox holes & camouflaging our vehicles." Or it entailed striking a tent and pitching it elsewhere. Three members of the 6th CCU had "with loving care" just finished converting their tent into something akin to a penthouse apartment when the war required them to relocate. As the unit history relates, had the movement order also said the three men would be shot at dawn, their expressions "would not have needed any alteration." Although they re-erected a new penthouse elsewhere with all the original lavish appointments, the new domicile was "not quite the same in heart and spirit. Rancor lingers there."[6]

The potentially serious difficulty with such unrestricted movement was that low-ranking, unrestrained, free-spirited individuals irked higher authorities, who might try to constrain them and thereby prevent them from doing their job. "These guys have been roaming around unguided—have become so damned independent," complained a naval officer about one of the CPUs, "that you can never put your hands on them when you need them."[7] Fortunately for the cameramen, they had powerful protection against infringements on their wayfaring. Aside from wearing special patches and pins that identified them as photographers, they had "open orders" or special passes insulating them from interference by all but the highest-ranking officers. Shoulder patches identifying an individual as a photographer were an authorized part of the uniform but the pins were unofficial; hence, different units wore distinctive pins, some of them designed by the Walt Disney Studios.[8]

More important than the patches and pins were the "open orders." David Douglas Duncan, who took his first picture with a 39-cent Bakelite camera when he was a teenager, became such a skilled photographer that he worked for *Life* and *National Geographic*, then entered the Marine Corps in early 1943. Initially assigned to a photo laboratory in San Francisco, he requested more active duty and was soon in the Pacific Theater taking combat photographs. In early April 1945

Duncan received "dream orders" to photograph Marine aviation. Officers to whom he reported had to provide him transportation; he could photograph all phases of Marine aviation; and he could report to the various aircraft wings "in any sequence deemed expedient." These orders meant that even though Duncan was a mere lieutenant "he must be given air or surface transportation when he requests it; he can take photographs anywhere he desires; he must have top priority when changing stations—in short, he must be given the consideration a combat general or admiral receives. Some dream!"[9]

Although Duncan's extraordinary authority was individual in nature, sometimes open orders were all-encompassing, covering an entire photographic unit, all the cameramen serving an army or fleet, or even all of them in a particular service. James R. Palmer, the OIC of the 2nd CCU, was thankful for "the blanket movement order General LeMay had signed which enabled me to dispense with red tape in the movement of my men," who were scattered throughout the China-Burma-India Theater. The Seventh Army's Commanding General issued orders to all his corps and division commanders explaining that cameramen often went on missions with only verbal orders, and that as long as they had official passes they should receive complete assistance and be permitted to photograph anything they wanted no matter how secret or sensitive. "No person or organization in the military service," the orders intoned, "will prohibit or interfere with the activities of official photographers when engaged in official photographic duties." The Vice Chief of Naval Operations reminded all commandants and commanders that photographers often had to act on their own initiative and that the Secretary of the Navy "desired that the Navy photographers be given the whole-hearted support of all officers."[10]

Just as important as open orders were the special passes that identified the bearer as an "Official War Photographer" and, for all intents and purposes, liberated a cameraman from the tyranny of rank. A commonly-used Army photographer's pass in the European Theater was the "blue pass," known as such because of a blue stripe on it. Signed "By Command of General Eisenhower," it directed all unit commanders "to extend all necessary cooperation to this cameraman to enable him to complete his photographic mission." The "blue pass" was, one man remembered decades after the war, "a very powerful type pass (better than American Express)." Armed with this prophylaxis against arbitrary authority, "Elby" Fenberg, a mere enlisted man, did not hesitate to refuse a direct order from an officer on General Mark Clark's staff.[11] Much to their dismay, Navy CPUs never had a special identification pass, leading to several complicated situations. An "ID card for official Navy photographers, covering all situations, would be of inestimable value," wrote a CPU officer.[12]

Photographers rarely had to utilize their passes in forward areas, since troops engaged in combat were too busy trying to survive to question some oddball about his authority to be shooting a camera instead of a gun. But the passes were frequently useful for dealing with "rear-area martinets."[13]

Cameramen had yet another form of "currency" that gave them rare and special privileges in the rear areas. Photo units quickly learned that they could offer both civilians and other military personnel something that no other outfits could—pictures. Taking photographs "was just like printing your own money over there," said one cameraman, while another asserted that it allowed them "to get away with murder"—in a figurative sense, naturally.[14] Trading pictures for goods and influence was as old as the camera itself, but in World War II the cameramen honed the practice to a fine art. A few farsighted CCU cameramen who came from Hollywood had wisely brought to the war zones a few negatives of nude females; prints from these negatives were always a hot commodity. Moreover, every rear-area quartermaster, cook, and mechanic wanted to fancy himself up in a backpack and bayonet and have a picture snapped to send home for the family album or for his girlfriend. Some photographers even carried special cameras just for this purpose. In exchange photo units received jeeps and tires, pistols and shoulder holsters, steaks and booze, lumber and electrical appliances, a little folding money on the side, and even "one month's prayers free from the Chaplain."[15] Of course, "incurring of favors through direct or indirect use of pictorial coverage" was against regulations and "will not be tolerated." But wartime, said the 163rd SPC's Joe Boyle, "is survival of the cleverest" and the cameramen were clever.[16]

Another precious advantage cameramen had was vital information about forthcoming operations, a luxury enjoyed by few enlisted personnel with other specialties. The old adage that a soldier knew no more than what he saw from his foxhole did not apply to cameramen. The "poor GIs had no idea where the fuck they were," but the photographers could not perform their mission unless they knew in advance when and where combat operations would occur.[17] As a 10th CCU unit history stated, the "problem of having cameramen, cameras, and film at the right place at the right time requires careful planning, quick decisions, flexibility, and what might be called opportunism." Without prior knowledge, photographers lost opportunities to record dramatic and important events. "We have missed probably two dozen good picture-stories," lamented J. P. Drennan, the OIC of CPU #2, "because we learned about them too late."[18]

To avoid lost opportunities cameramen ingratiated themselves with intelligence and operations officers (known as G-2 and G-3 respectively), and as photography's importance became increasingly obvious G-2s and G-3s received instructions to keep photographers well informed. An APS "Handbook for Motion Picture Photographers" emphasized that photo officers had to maintain contact with G-2, G-3, and public relations personnel. "Officers and men rapidly learned their way around various headquarters," wrote a photo officer, "and got good information about impending action and were able to get good coverage."[19] One reason cooperation became so routine was high-level support for photo missions. The 14th AAF's Chief of Staff sent a message to the commanding officers of all 14th AAF tactical units and bases stressing the responsibility of operations and intelligence officers to "coordinate with camera team commanders sufficiently in advance of important missions to insure proper assignment briefing and coverage by combat camera teams...."[20]

Even in the war's latter stages cameramen occasionally encountered reticent staff officers who "just won't divulge anything,"[21] but in most instances they readily acquired information about future operations. They attended daily headquarters briefings and routinely visited Command Posts and War Rooms, looking at maps and consulting with G-2s and G-3s about the tactical situation and local terrain.[22] "I wish I could give you all the details," Joe Zinni of the 166th SPC wrote to his wife, "but since the operation is of a fairly secret nature & I'm entrusted with all the details, it's impossible for me to do so."[23] Like most of the soldiers embarking on this operation, she had to remain in the dark. But the glow of knowledge enlightened Zinni.

II

Keeping abreast of the tactical situation and always moving with or ahead of the action yielded two benefits that brought cameramen great pleasure. Arriving in an area first and with a jeep or other vehicle at their disposal, they had an excellent opportunity to engage in looting, although they commonly used euphemisms to describe what they did. They were not stealing; they were collecting junk or souvenirs, or "finding" things that had no owner, or "liberating" selected items. Moving into a town or village that was still hotly contested, cameramen commented that "it was really a field day for us—both for pictures & souvenirs." Others were more honest about what they did. "I think we spent most of our time looting," recalled a member of the 162nd SPC, "and that was the main preoccupation of most of the American army...."[24]

They "picked up" (note again their disguising euphemism) glassware and brass, jewelry and perfume, pistols and machine guns, and (as might be expected) cameras and film. One naval photographer needed "an LST to carry his souvenirs" and another sent Carleton Mitchell (the head of the Navy's Combat Photography Section and thus of all the CPUs) his newly acquired "arsenal" for safekeeping, prompting the latter to observe that the "German Supply Corps certainly took a beating when you arrived on the scene."[25] A particularly astute Signal Corps cameraman concentrated on getting film, since GIs often stole cameras but rarely took enough film. So the photographer worked a scam: he traded his stolen film to GIs for cigarettes and then sold the latter on the black market for a profit; he accumulated a bankroll of about $10,000, which he used to open a postwar photographic studio.[26]

Photographers also enjoyed the euphoria of being hailed as liberators, and since they repeatedly plunged to the foremost forward edge of the battle zone many experienced this exhilarating sensation more than once. One of the 161st SPC's lieutenants, Donald E. Mittelstaedt, was with the initial American forces entering Manila. As he and his men rode down Avenida Rizal people flocked to the sidewalks, windows, and rooftops, shouting, applauding, crying "Victory," pelting them with flowers and (from "some of the more aggressive maidens") kisses, lavishing liquor and cigars upon them. "It was more than a conqueror's or liberator's reception; it was a hero's welcome."[27] European Theater cameramen met the same exhilarating reception. According to members of the 166th SPC, "Whatever the fighting, wherever the village, town or city, the exuberant, sincere demonstrative gratitude of the French people toward their liberators was universal."[28]

Being greeted as liberators had been such a rapturous experience that cameramen needed no signposts to know when they had passed through Italy, France, Belgium, and Luxembourg and entered

Germany. Gordon Frye and Joe Zinni both wrote their wives about their "sudden change from the great Liberator, as in Italy and France, to that of the serious conqueror." On enemy soil they got "no smiles, no flowers, no wine, no V-for-Victory signs, with upraised hands, no cheering, no tears of joy or happiness, no banners with huge signs: 'Welcome To Our Liberators,'—no, none of these—but instead— sneers, scowls, hatred, fear, malice." Only a few attempted "to offer superficial smiles & gestures of 'friendship.'" Cameramen reciprocated these attitudes. "We had a reputation for great generosity in Italy and France," wrote Frye, "but we have no intention of playing Santa Claus to Hitler's children."[29]

III

The war "was a mighty grim affair, all in all," wrote Frye in August 1945 from Darmstadt, Germany, where he was participating in the postwar occupation. But as he admitted, he had mostly been an onlooker, "a kibitzer with a camera," and not a participant. Paradoxically, cameramen were intimately involved in combat and yet aloof from it, watching and filming but ordinarily not participating in the fighting. They were not quite like "rear-echelon personnel and their lack of knowledge, or imagination, as to the world of combat," but they were not like those who manned the front lines either.[30] With their mobility and independence cameramen could withdraw from the front at night, seeking warmth and shelter in the rear, avoiding the grinding ordeal of twenty-four-hour days in the open and in danger, in the cold and the rain, day after dreary, deadly day. And photographers had a rich choice of experiences because they could do something different tomorrow if they wanted—take stills instead of motion pictures (or vice versa), visit a new frontline sector, photograph engineers rather than artillery, or medics instead of chemical-warfare specialists.

Moreover, the traditional division among land, sea, and air did not prevail; cameramen in one service frequently accompanied combatants from another service. Army photographers took pictures from airplanes and ships; Navy CPUs "caught their share of hell in foxholes and on the beaches" and flew on bombing missions; and AAF CCUs went behind enemy lines with the Yugoslavian partisans and participated in parachute and glider operations. As a result cameramen gained a broad perspective about the war that eluded most participants.[31] "It was marvelous," exulted Ted Sizer of the 166th SPC. "It was front seat in the most dramatic kind of theater you could ever imagine." And Joe Boyle appreciated that "no one outfit had the grandstand seats as much as a photo company."[32]

Cameramen who were on the battle line during the day had compelling reasons to avoid the front at night. Taking pictures in darkness was next to impossible, and the Command Posts and War Rooms they needed to frequent for information were at rear-area headquarters. They also required shelter for their fragile and sensitive cameras and lenses, and space and lighting to make minor equipment repairs and write captions for exposed film. Thus, cameramen experienced "the contrast of working in the frontline area and then having it quite easy in the evening"; they conducted their own self-ordered mini-retreats and consolidated their position in some local homestead, chateau, or schoolhouse where they could have hot food, at least a tepid bath or shower, and a warm bed. The 163rd SPC's Ed Newell, for instance, was overseas for several years and spent all but a handful of nights in private residences in various towns. Sometimes the nightly rear-area billets were not very luxurious, but even an old barn with all the windows blown out and half the roof shot away could be made fairly comfortable with a modicum of effort.[33]

Most photographers did not "get in out of the weather & off the ground" every night, but they did so often enough to make them profoundly appreciative of what they frequently avoided and of what front-line troops regularly endured.[34] Being a good son, James LaFrano of the 162nd SPC wrote his parents often, and his letters were replete with references that would have made all infantrymen envious. His photo team often stayed in houses and chateaus, "living like kings" as they feasted on "plenty of steak and fresh eggs." At times he and his fellow photographers were "just like civilians again." But he knew how lucky they were. "We can go up to the front and then come back," he wrote. "But the other boys stay till it's all over."[35]

IV

"Caught flat-footed by our gunners and a combat cameraman," read the headline of an Eastman Kodak Company advertisement that showed an enemy submarine being "shelled to its doom," and that extolled the photographer as both a well-trained fighting man and a superb technician. "As a cameraman," the ad continued, "he has to be so expert that he is virtually a picture-taking machine, functioning at high efficiency under incredibly difficult conditions."[36] Whether most soldier-cameramen were good soldiers is questionable, even doubtful; but that they often performed their mission well under adverse circumstances is unquestionably true. Photographing the war was more than exhilaration, delight, benefit, and comparative comfort amidst misery. It also entailed terrible travail and intractable problems that arose from the tactical situation, the equipment that the cameramen needed, and the way in which photo units were administered.

The foremost tactical difficulty was danger. Although cameramen were technically combat support units rather than actual combatants, in certain ways their mission entailed *extraordinary* danger. "I don't believe," wrote an individual who saw Marine Corps photographers in action at Tarawa, "there ever was another group of men who had been so close to death so often in such a short time."[37] Did this observer engage in literary license? Perhaps, but not excessively so. Cameramen in all the services "tread the narrow thread between life and death" so regularly that few escaped feeling "the chill breath of the guy with the sickle."[38]

Although cameramen could retire from the front lines at night while combatants stayed out there twenty-four hours a day, a combat unit eventually withdrew from the line completely to refit and regroup and a new unit would take its place at the battle's forward edge. But photographers continued going to the front daily, focusing their lenses on new units as they rotated in and out of the fighting zone. In other cases they flitted from one dangerous assignment to another. In Burma the 164th SPC's policy was "to find out what military operation is to take place and to cover it by sending in a team by plane just to cover it and then to return to the base. In that way men do not stay in one place during a lull in the proceedings, and can be used more economically in other places."[39]   More so than cameramen, combatants enjoyed an occasional "lull in the proceedings."

Compared to combatants who were armed and trained to fight, cameramen were also defenseless. As Joe Zinni knew, "a cameraman has to expose himself a great deal while 'shooting' combat action & he can't very well operate a gun & a camera at the same time." Rifles and carbines were too heavy and cumbersome for cameramen laden with photographic gear to carry, so they normally opted for nothing more lethal than a .45 pistol and a knife. Some even found a pistol burdensome and did not pack even that much firepower, which was not much protection against rifle, machine-gun, mortar, and artillery fire anyway. When a cameraman pressed his eye to the viewfinder he was squinting down a tunnel, for he had lost his peripheral vision and could no longer see what was going on all around him. In this sense a still photographer had an advantage over a motion-picture cameraman, for the former could pop up from the ground, put his eye to the camera only momentarily, and then duck for cover, while the latter had to remain exposed for a longer period of time, his eye glued to the viewfinder.[40] On numerous occasions motion-picture men stepped into the middle of a firefight or had grenades land at their feet and did not know it.[41]

Movie men had three further disadvantages. First, a motion-picture photographer had to discard his helmet to handle his camera properly because the helmet's edge kept banging and jamming against the camera whenever he tried to look through the eyepiece. In battle, therefore, nothing protected his brain but tufts of hair, a few membranes, and the skull, all of which afforded little security against lead and steel traveling at high speed. Second, cameramen were always heavily burdened because they could never lighten their loads. "When the Infantry has it tough they drop their packs," wrote a Signal Corps photographer. "As you know in order to keep the film from being lost it is necessay to keep it on your person and trust *no one*." And third, their movie cameras were so noisy (they sounded like mini-machine guns) that they invariably attracted enemy attention.[42] When a United Press correspondent reported that "The men who shoot this war with a camera for the Signal Corps are poor insurance risks," he was providing good actuarial advice.[43]

Occasionally cameramen found themselves in such a tight situation that they dropped their cameras, picked up guns, and fought back. Donald E. Pringle of the 164th SPC in China had such an experience in November 1944. As his colleague, Louis W. Raczkowski, wrote, "Pringle got himself another Jap. He had to shoot the rifle instead of the camera or there would not have been any Pringle." A few months later Pringle was at it again, putting aside his camera to win a Bronze Star by killing a Japanese machine gunner with a grenade.[44] Sometimes cameramen were not forced to fight back but "just got mad and did it." Dewey Wrigley, OIC of CPU #10, was among the first Americans to enter Rome; he encountered sniper fire. Photo opportunities were nil, so he decided to fight rather than photograph.

Moments after he killed a sniper he went to the aid of a wounded Army lieutenant, and as he dragged him to safety he took a slug in the thigh that just missed his hipbone.[45]

Most cameramen never set aside their cameras to become actual combatants either through circumstances or anger, and some who did forget their photographic mission, no matter how temporarily, felt remorse long afterwards. During the fighting in Brittany, Ralph Butterfield of the 166th SPC helped string communications wire when one member of a two-man crew was wounded, and then he aided the stricken man to the rear. "The result was that I, under the opportunities of the moment and a sense of priorities, did not fulfill my own duties in taking pictures." Of course, fighting back never guaranteed safety anyhow. "In our unit we lost some fine comrades," Joe Boyle wrote, "who chose to keep taking pictures to the end—and LOST—and others who dropped the camera and became infantrymen—and still LOST."[46]

Even worse than simple danger was danger under miserable conditions, and in each theater the terrain and climate saddled cameramen with special problems. At times the elements superseded enemy soldiers as the photographers' worst foes.[47] In the North African and Mediterranean Theaters heat and wind-driven dust and sand plagued all combatants all the time, but the problems were especially acute during the periodic siroccos, the oppressively hot winds that blew non-stop for days from the Libyan desert across the Mediterranean and into southern Europe. After one sirocco that howled out of Libya for six consecutive days, it took the 12th CCU two days to dig itself out and overhaul its equipment. No matter how securely photographers wrapped their lenses and cameras in protective covering, the wind-borne desert grit always won, worming its way into every delicate mechanism.[48]

In arctic climes bitter cold was a brutal foe. Cameramen had to expose their fingers to change lenses and film, set the f-stop, tear film tabs off of film packs, and perform other operations requiring a high degree of manual dexterity difficult and painful to achieve when the temperature was in double digits below zero. Along with the men's numbed fingers, all the free moving parts of a camera would bind up, camera motors and batteries became weak, and film became so brittle it broke. Photographers had to remove all lubricating oil from their cameras (the contraction of metal camera parts made the fittings loose enough to operate temporarily without oil), tote extra batteries, and take extreme precautions when storing and handling film.[49]

Northern Europe had its share of heat as well as cold. During the Normandy campaign the 166th SPC's John Blankenhorn recalled that "GIs, radio sets, medics arm bands and dead cows were all exactly the same color from the dust." The living things that best thrived in the heat were the mosquitoes that nightly flew thousands of sorties and the bees that took over from the "skeeters" when daylight arrived, thereby subjecting vulnerable human skin to a round-the-clock strategic bombing campaign.[50] Cold weather brought relief from the insects but inflicted its own torments. The winter of 1944–45 was unusually severe, forcing men to seek improvised shelter during blizzards. Some of the 167th SPC's cameramen avoided a foot of snow by taking refuge in a basement. "With the exception of icy drafts, mice as big as small dogs, dripping water and choking waves of smoke from an open face stove," they reported, "all was lovely." Freezing winds, Zinni wrote, knifed "right through my overcoat, fur-lined jacket, field jacket, knitted sweater & undershirt!" Cameramen would have gladly endured these problems if they could fulfill their mission in an exemplary fashion. But this required sunlight, which was in short supply. Rain, fog, and dense forests made photography less than ideal, especially when compounded by the ground haze from shell explosions and ammunition dump fires and the artificial smoke that units often generated to conceal their movement. A team from the 163rd SPC reported that sometimes "the only thing there is a lot of is bad light."[51]

Conditions in the Pacific and China-Burma-India Theaters were no better. Heat and humidity caused film to deteriorate rapidly, gummed up film gates and camera shutters, oxidized chemicals used in processing, corroded or rusted metal parts, peeled off leather trim, loosened all types of glue, and nurtured fungus growth on lenses and filters. The Eastman Kodak Company eventually developed a method of "tropical packing" film that gave it a longer shelf life, but nothing alleviated the other problems. The climate remained so tough on cameras that they needed cleaning and oiling after almost every use, and the fungus buildup on lenses was so prolific that the cameramen frequently had to take them apart and wipe them clean.[52] Torrential downpours were also a problem. Men from the 164th SPC tried to photograph an engineer unit repairing a bridge near Ledo, India, but it rained so much that it took them "5 days to make 6 negatives, which were finally made in the rain anyhow. The engineers, of course, worked in spite of the weather, but a lot of rain can't damage a shovel very much." Another 164th detachment based in Calcutta photographed a construction project during such a severe monsoon that the photographers operated "from the backs of elephants in order to overcome the water hazards of the swamps."[53] When the rain ceased the sun blazed, creating lighting and exposure difficulties: anything in the sun was intensely bright, everything in the jungles was nearly black, and "you can't satisfactorily compromise between the two."[54]

Just as different regions of the world confronted cameramen with novel problems, so did photographers in each service endure peculiar difficulties. Marine cameramen shooting the amphibious assaults of the island-hopping Pacific campaign had to protect their equipment from the befouling effects of salt spray, as did the Navy cameramen who sometimes accompanied them and the Army photographers who made similar assaults. Worse than fending off the spray was having to wade through shoulder-deep salt water, for the landing craft often stopped far out from the beach.[55]

For the Navy's CPUs, ships had little spare space where they could set up their cameras; the trick was to find "a battle station with maximum camera coverage and minimum exposure to shrapnel or strafing attacks" and with a nearby nook to store extra photo gear. Few such havens existed even on a ship as big as an aircraft carrier. When the guns began firing the cameramen could not escape the deafening crescendo. The camera danced so vigorously that a photographer sometimes sported a black eye from looking through the viewfinder. A motion-picture man using a tripod could place its feet on life jackets to absorb some of the movement, but the vibrations could never be entirely eliminated. When Talbert N. "Bud" Reiman, OIC of CPU #7, went on a "business cruise" in the fall of 1943 he "had never been around when really big guns were fired, so when the first nine gun salvo sounded off, I was amazed. I swear that the cotton I put in my right ear was blown out my left ear!" Another cameraman reported that "the concussions seem to hit you in the chin with such rapidity that you feel as though you were a punching bag being pummeled by an expert."[56]

The AAF's CCUs probably confronted more difficulties than cameramen in other services. Airplanes were even more cramped for space than ships, and some of them, especially the B-29s, had "every convenience for each member of the crew but no allowance had been made for an extra man—the photographer." Even in planes with sufficient space, cameramen could not escape high-altitude temperatures that ranged from ~30° to ~50° F. The 13th CCU's Jack Stirling flew fifty-one combat missions and on each of them he shot only one roll of film because it "was too cold up there to reload film."[57] Those who tried reloading often ended up with frozen hands. But Stirling was comparatively lucky; many cameramen never got through an entire roll before their spring-wound cameras froze up or "the film broke in the extreme cold and the product of a hazardous mission was lost." The cold was tough not just on equipment but also on the men, who often lacked appropriate heavy winter flying clothes, gloves, and shoes, and who did not have adequate parachutes, oxygen masks, throat microphones, or earphones. Well into 1944 the conversion from spring-wound cameras to 24-volt electric-drive cameras that could be operated from an aircraft's electrical system was still incomplete, and suitable flying clothes and equipment remained in short supply. And not all men were born to fly: airsickness rendered some photographers incapable of fulfilling their mission even when other conditions were ideal.[58]

V

"If the rest of the Army had gone forth to war as poorly equipped as the early CCUs, it would have been a very short war and our side wouldn't have won," editorialized the 7th CCU's April 1944 "Newsletter." Every piece of equipment they needed "was practically nonexistent (and still is) and the difficulty in obtaining it was as plentiful as cameras were scarce." The editorial writer could think of "no known bitterness like that of a cameraman without a camera. He has as much right to be sore as an infantryman sent into combat without a rifle."[59] Every combat cameraman overseas would have vigorously nodded his head in agreement with these sentiments, for along with the tactical-level travails imposed by the enemy and the elements, cameramen also had severe equipment problems.

Combat camera organizations required enormous amounts of specialized equipment. With about a dozen photographers the 7th CCU had an authorized allotment of forty-eight cameras, and a CPU with four photographers had five authorized cameras.[60] During fiscal year 1944 the Navy alone added 33,000 cameras of all types, including those for photo reconnaissance, to its inventory to meet its burgeoning needs.[61] Without film, cameras were useless. Nine CPUs were in operation in early 1943. To supply them for six months, Carleton Mitchell estimated, they needed 394 400-foot rolls of motion-picture film, 76 200-foot rolls, 864 100-foot rolls, and 450 Kodachrome 100-foot magazines, plus a corresponding amount of still film. Cameras and film were only the basics; other necessities included lenses, exposure meters, tripods, batteries, film-changing bags, extra film spools, packing and shipping materials, repair kits, developing tanks and chemicals—the list went on and on. By the time the war ended the Signal Corps stocked 570 different photographic items.[62]

Almost all pieces of equipment were regular commercial items that the services bought directly from photo-supply houses; from private camera owners, who were urged to sell their equipment to the armed forces; even from pawnshops. The Signal Corps regularly had photography journals run stories about its need for photo equipment, and a Marine cameraman scoured "the second-hand stores, camera stores, and hockshops in New York City to try to buy" motion-picture equipment.[63] The "Army's photographic equipment was largely obtained not by the invention or development of new devices, as was the case with most communication and all radar equipment," admitted an unpublished "History of Signal Corps Research," "but rather by studying the products available from commercial manufacturers and selecting those most suitable to Army needs and capable of procurement in the necessary quantities."[64]

Procuring "the necessary quantities" was the hitch. The "problem of supplying the combat photographer with the still and motion-picture equipment best suited to his mission, acute in December 1941, had not been completely solved on V-J day," according to "Combat Photography," a study completed in late 1945 by the Historical Section of the Office of the Chief Signal Officer.[65]

The primary requirements for the timely acquisition of equipment were, first, determining what the best possible equipment was and, second, having it mass produced and getting it into the photographers' hands. Although the first of these tasks was done expeditiously, the latter, though it improved, remained a major problem. A foremost camera manufacturer, Bell & Howell, "inaugurated a tremendous expansion program to take care of Army and Navy needs but completely bogged down on production." The machinery necessary for plant expansion often took more than a year to build and install; moreover, it consumed large quantities of critical metals needed for manufacturing other tools of war. The armed forces also needed space in photographic factories to manufacture nonphotographic items such as telescopic gunsights.[66]

Supplies were sometimes so scarce overseas, frequently because of distribution delays, that some detachments had to curtail their activities. Lieutenant Commander Carleton Mitchell wrote to one CPU that all "shipments to your area, regardless of the addressee, seem to go astray" and the 7th CCU found that requisitioned items took at least three or four months to arrive. The 7th CCU may have been unusually fortunate; the 12th CCU considered the arrival of new equipment in July 1944 a matter of historical interest "because we had requisitioned this equipment nearly a year ago." One of the new cameras had no lenses but most of the other equipment was in excellent shape and the missing lenses could be re-requisitioned, leading to eager anticipation of their arrival a year later. Actually, the 12th was, like the 7th, lucky in a comparative sense. The 5th CCU lost most of its supplies during the landing on Leyte when the Japanese sank the ship carrying its equipment. The men worked with salvaged and borrowed equipment as best they could until twenty new cameras arrived—*finally* arrived since the equipment had been misaddressed, misrouted, and stored in the wrong depot for many weeks. Their joy was short-lived, however, for all twenty lacked lenses.[67]

One especially acute shortage was film, which "was even scarcer than cigarettes." Not only were the required quantities enormous and the plant manufacturing capacities limited, but the cotton linters, nitric and sulfuric acids, and certain solvents used in making film were also necessary to produce guncotton. The manufacture of film and explosives were in direct competition. Although the requirement for more and more film brought a surge in production of raw stock— 276,358,000 *square feet* of film in the first half of 1944, more than 300,000,000 in the first half of 1945—shortages never disappeared.[68] References to critical scarcities abound, as do pleas for cameramen to conserve film by not overshooting and injunctions against photographing mundane events such as parades and visiting dignitaries. "Got orders from the War Department," noted Don Morrow, "to conserve film for combat only."[69]

Even when film was available in the United States, distribution overseas was so slow that some cameramen claimed they never "received any film that was *in* date." One frustrated member of a Navy CPU wrote that film appeared "to be wasting the dependable part of its life in transit or in storage, only becoming available for use on the fighting front when its quality and reliability are growing questionable."[70] Emmett Bergholz, commander of the AAF's 3rd CCU, had an experience even worse than receiving outdated film. His unit actually received some film it had previously exposed, which had never been developed and was sent back as fresh stock, supposedly ready for use![71]

Regular commercial cameras were suitable for stateside, peacetime purposes when, in the ordinary course of events, the people being photographed were not trying to kill the cameraman. But they had grave limitations in combat. The standard still camera was the Speed Graphic, the long-time standby for press photographers. Speed Graphics used 4 × 5-inch negatives in either a cut-film holder that contained two shots or a film pack that held a dozen exposures; both the cut film and the film packs were awkward to use. The camera came with many shiny parts that sparkled in sunlight, making a convenient aiming point for the enemy, and it had a standard lens that was essentially a wide-angle lens, meaning that "you just had to climb on top of somebody to get a closeup."[72] Another problem was that it had a bellows and other leather parts, which were susceptible to fungus growth. But the worst defect was its bulk and its weight, which was almost seven pounds. Photographers commonly described it as "an ungainly & clumsy piece of equipment," "cumbersome," and "too heavy for front line work."[73] "Those cameras were awful bulky when you were crawling on your belly, attempting to avoid a sniper," said one Marine, and another complained that "when we went on a 3-day patrol through enemy territory my speed graphic was too big to pull out and take pictures here and there, and it would have been impossible to take any action pictures if the opportunity had presented itself."[74]

The motion-picture equivalent of the Speed Graphic was the Bell & Howell Eyemo 35mm camera, which came in several different models, some spring driven and others battery powered, some with only a single lens and others with a spider turret holding three lenses. The Signal Corps estimated that Eyemos accounted for about 90 percent of its combat motion-picture footage, and the percentage was approximately the same for the other services.[75] Here again the major problem was the camera's weight and bulk—and the film's. A 100-foot roll of 35mm film weighed about four pounds, and cameramen carried up to ten rolls. Bud Reiman of the Navy's CPU #7 "found that a man can carry an Eyemo and a tripod, or an Eyemo and a supply of film, but unless he is built along the lines of a dray horse he can't possibly carry all three."

One of his men who tried was soon "ready to drop from sheer exhaustion." As General Douglas MacArthur noted, the amount of gear motion-picture men "must carry sometimes precludes the possibility of getting that photographer to the scene of action since the only means of travel is on foot with native carriers to transport his equipment" and the situation did not always permit assigning native carriers.[76]

Eyemos had other problems beyond being cumbersome. Since setting up a tripod under combat conditions was rarely possible, most cameramen had to hand-hold their cameras. However, the Eyemo lacked special grips for steady hand-holding. Consequently much World War II footage bounces, jiggles, and wavers. Although an Eyemo could be modified to hold a 400-foot magazine, that made the camera impossibly bulky for front-line duty. But a 100-foot roll zipped through the camera in just a little more than a minute and then the cameraman had to reload, a tricky process even under ideal conditions, requiring him to thread the film carefully through the camera's inner rollers, gears, and gates. With a motor-driven model a photographer could shoot 100 feet without any interruptions, although then he had to tote along a battery that further burdened his already overburdened body. The spring-driven models eliminated the battery but in combat's fast-paced world they had their own special liability, "the reload–rewind headache." Only 45 feet of film could be used before the spring wound down. It took fifteen seconds to rewind, so a photographer shot 45 feet, then rewound, shot another 45 feet, and then either rewound again to shoot the last 10 feet on the roll, or reloaded immediately, wasting 10 feet of precious film and up to one full minute of irretrievable time. Eyemo cameramen swore that the best action always occurred during reloading and rewinding. Pity poor Robert B. Spafford, Jr., the OIC of CPU #13, who was aboard a carrier when the Japanese launched an aerial attack on the fleet. As an enemy plane dove at a nearby ship, Spafford "followed the Jap all the way down, just to deck level. Then I ran out of spring!" He was so angry that he almost pitched the unwound Eyemo overboard and swore so vigorously that a nearby officer thought someone had been killed.[77]

The "Handbook for Motion Picture Photographers" alerted cameramen to the obvious when it warned that "A motion-picture camera is a precise and intricate piece of equipment" that cost the government a lot of money "and therefore, should be treated with respect." The same could be said for still cameras. These precise and intricate instruments were susceptible to frequent malfunctions and, since combat was not always conducive to treating them with respect, to accidents as well. As the OIC of CPU #2, John P. Drennan, put it, "Cameras have a beautiful ability to go on the fritz...." One of the Eyemos in CPU #4 "invariably goes out of working order at the crucial moment. Although after each overhaul it appears to be working perfectly. Each time it goes haywire there seems to be a new defect." In some Eyemos graphite in the spring filtered down into the governor, causing the camera to either slow down or stop; in others the small gear train driving the take-up spindle stripped a few teeth, making the camera unusable. The spider turrets warped and bent too easily "when subjected to the inevitable bumps in forward areas."[78]

Accidents will (and did) happen. A member of CPU #8 wallowed in despair, practically weeping, when he "turned in some bad film on some good shows." The ship he was on had been hit by heavy shells and the concussions knocked the shutter loose from its pin, which then tore a running slit in the film. While covering the Okinawa campaign Robert Albright of the 3231st Photo Detachment badly damaged one camera "when there wasn't enough room for me and the camera to get into the foxhole at the same time," had a second one destroyed by either a shell fragment or a bullet, and had a third that "sort of died of old age near the end." A member of the 6th CCU flying in a crippled B-25 lost both his cameras when the pilot ordered all extra equipment thrown out in preparation for ditching at sea. Two other men from the 6th consigned their cameras to a premature burial at sea when they were aboard LST #738 participating in the invasion of Mindoro Island in the Philippines. A Japanese kamikaze hit the craft, forcing all hands to abandon ship and swim for their lives just "ahead of the blast which atomised #738."[79]

Were more compact still and motion-picture cameras with potentially fewer difficulties available? Yes, and yet no. In regard to the former, the Medalist produced a 2 1/4 × 3 1/4 negative, the Rolleiflex had a 2 1/4 × 2 1/4 negative, and both the Leica and Contax were 35mm cameras. The Signal Corps also designed a special lightweight "combat camera" with no leather parts, special protection for the lenses against rain and dust, and a 2 1/4 × 3 1/4 film-pack holder.[80] But none of these came close to replacing the Speed Graphic. Medalists were "too complicated and delicate," Rolleiflexes were "unsatisfactory for field and rough usage, especially where dust or rains are prevalent," and the "combat camera" became available only late in the war—the first one reached the 166th SPC in April 1945.[81] The best 35mm cameras were German made, and compared to the Speed Graphic's 4 × 5 negative a 35mm negative was difficult to handle and file. Standard prints were either 4 × 5 or 8 × 10 inches, so a 4 × 5 negative required either no enlargement or at most only a 2× enlargement, thereby providing less "grainy" prints than those enlarged from 35mm negatives. Less grainy prints provided the sharper detail that was often crucial for tactical intelligence.[82] Although many photographers carried 35mm cameras they used them primarily for personal photographs, employing them in combat "only where larger size cameras cannot be used."[83]

A number of other 35mm motion-picture cameras were available, such as the DeVry, Akeley, Cineflex (an imperfect copy of the superb German-made Arriflex), Wall, and Mitchell, with the latter two being single-system sound cameras totally unsuitable for combat because they required two or three men to operate. None of these had advantages over the Eyemo. One that did was the Cunningham Combat Camera, developed in 1942 and named after its designer, Hollywood's Harry Cunningham. The Cunningham had special grips for steady hand-holding, a simplified 200-foot magazine-loading system (it took only six seconds to change magazines), an electric motor powered by small batteries that could run several thousand feet of film before they went dead, a sturdy four lens turret, and lenses that were dust-, moisture-, and fungus-proof. The Cunningham was also lighter than the Eyemo since except for "a few small, highly stressed moving parts, necessarily built of steel, the entire camera is made of magnesium."[84] Cameramen in the field who knew of the Cunningham begged for one. "I could cut my throat," wrote Spafford, whose spring-wound Eyemo unwound at the critical moment, "for not stealing one before I left the States." But, like the combat still camera, the Cunningham did not get into large-scale production until late in the war. More than three years after Pearl Harbor Carleton Mitchell still could not get one for poor Spafford, or for anybody else.[85]

VI

World War II was primarily a black-and-white affair with only an occasional colorful hue brightening film's drab gray world. Looking at old newsreels and documentaries and thumbing through aged copies of

Life and *Look* are mildly boring experiences. Their pervasive monotone dullness sedates the modern eye, which is so accustomed to seeing a rainbow or a peacock with every glance.

When World War II began, color photography was just becoming popular for commercial purposes and the armed forces had been exploring its potential for only about a decade. In 1930 the Navy encouraged Melville Bell Grosvenor of the National Geographic Society to make the first aerial color shots. A decade later "Hap" Arnold, the World War II AAF Commanding General, published an essay in *The National Geographic Magazine* on aerial color photography that reported on joint experiments by the Eastman Kodak Company and the Army Air Corps (the AAF's predecessor). While stressing that color photography was still in its infancy, he predicted widespread future use as experts mastered the remaining technical difficulties associated with it.[86]

Arnold's prediction was essentially correct. Although color photography did not replace black and white during World War II, it increasingly supplemented it as the demand for color stills and movies grew. A year after Pearl Harbor magazines and newspapers were "clamoring for usable color" and the longer the war continued the louder the clamor became.[87] But the supply of high-quality color photographs never matched the demand because color, despite its obvious advantages, also had severe disadvantages.

Whether in stills or motion-pictures, color's most readily visible advantage was its realism, its ability to portray a subject accurately not only in regard to color but also in its form, texture, and illusion of depth. As *Life* editorialized in August 1944, "ordinary black and white photographs have not done full descriptive justice to the war in Italy. They have omitted the soft browns and grays of the ruined Italian towns, the bright, shocking redness of freshly spilled blood, the incongruously gay colors of spring in the midst of battle."[88] A training film shot in color on nighttime airplane landings could demonstrate how red lights indicated approach and takeoff zones, green lights marked the runway's end, clear lights its edges, and yellow lights a caution zone. Some types of ammunition were identified by color, camouflage could be more readily detected in color, and portraying even subtle shades of color was essential in medical films on the treatment of wounded and ill soldiers. Observers also believed color enhanced audience interest. A dull subject portrayed in black and white was doubly dull but in color it still might engage the viewers' attention.[89]

Motion-picture cameramen shot almost all their color with 16mm Kodachrome rather than in 35mm Technicolor. The latter was expensive and required three separate strips of film to run simultaneously through a camera that was much larger than an Eyemo, which was already too big for battlefield conditions.[90] Consequently, shooting color motion-pictures meant that cameramen carried lighter, less bulky equipment. Colonel Franklyn Adreon, the OIC of the Marine Corps Headquarters Photo Section, estimated that compared to 35mm movie equipment, 16mm cameras and their accoutrements weighed about one-fourth as much and occupied only about one-fourth as much shipping space (an important consideration when every soldier and weapon had to be transported overseas).[91] Another vital advantage was that cameramen could carry two and a half times more 16mm than 35mm film because one foot of 16mm was equivalent to two and a half feet of 35mm.[92] That was because 16mm film ran through a camera at the rate of 36 feet per minute so three minutes of 16mm film equalled 108 feet of exposed film, while 35mm film ran through a camera at the rate of 90 feet per minute so three minutes of 35mm film equalled 270 feet of exposed film. Therefore, a photographer armed with a 100-foot roll in a 16mm camera could shoot for almost three minutes before reloading, whereas a 35mm cameraman would have to reload twice to expose the same almost three minutes of film, potentially missing much action in the process.

Finally, 16mm Kodachrome was the only format that yielded four different types of copies: duplicate 16mm color prints, black-and-white 16mm prints, 35mm color enlargements, and 35mm black-and-white enlargements. Sixteen-mm black and white was not suitable for enlargement to 35mm because all black-and-white film contained grains of silver. When magnified the silver flecks gave a 35mm enlargement an annoyingly "grainy" appearance. Although Kodachrome, like black-and-white film, contained light-sensitive silver halide crystals, it was also a dye product. A "bleach" step during processing removed all the silver from Kodachrome, leaving an image composed only of extremely small clusters of dye deposits. Consequently it could be enlarged without producing a grainy effect.[93]

A fundamental problem with 16mm color was that in the early 1940s the weight of tradition and authority were against it. The standard format was 35mm black-and-white. An "Army Handbook for Motion Picture Photographers" said that "In combat the War Department has designated all motion-picture photography to be standard 35mm black and white.... the 16mm camera is an emergency camera." Signal Corps cameramen were to use 16mm Kodachrome "only when absolutely necessary, or if no other film is available." In a memo to all CPU OICs their commander, Carleton Mitchell, insisted that they use "16mm KODACHROME ONLY TO SUPPLEMENT" normal 35mm black and white, and as late as June 1944 both the Navy's Director of Public Relations and Director of Photography wanted "no more 16mm than absolutely necessary." Although CCUs received few definite directions governing the use of 35mm or 16mm, the AAF's emphasis was obvious since a CCU was authorized to receive four times more 35mm than 16mm cameras.[94]

The standard might have changed more rapidly had color not had other problems. Black-and-white film could be handled almost casually but color required an extremely precise exposure and carefully controlled processing, or the hues would not be natural looking. Black-and-white film could also be processed more quickly than color and in many labs around the world, while comparatively few specially equipped labs processed color. Kodachrome performed very poorly on overcast days and yielded really good results only when shot with flat light (that is, with the sun at the photographer's back). But combat neither waited upon the sun nor gave cameramen much maneuverability. So the cameramen frequently filmed under dreadful light conditions or in either side or back light (that is, with the sun to the side or directly in front, which would be in back of the subject a photographer was filming). With changing light conditions common during a battle owing to the time of day, cloud cover, smoke, or dust, matching up color sequences was more difficult than matching-up black-and-white ones. And color was costly. A 16mm color print cost about five times as much as a 16mm reduction print made from 35mm black and white.[95]

No doubt one important reason why some of the war's most dramatic footage came from the Pacific island-hopping campaigns was that the Marine Corps, unlike the other services, relied primarily on 16mm color. Marine photographers had cameras and film that were easier to handle in combat, did not have to be reloaded so often, and produced motion-pictures in startling living and dead color. The Army's Darryl Zanuck had used 16mm cameras in North Africa, finding them "light and simple to reload in a hurry. For combat action there is nothing to compare with them." But his disappointing results helped convince the War Department that 16mm color was unsatisfactory and that the Signal Corps should stick with 35mm and black-and-white.[96] No one seemed to care that too few cameramen had been on duty in North Africa, or that Zanuck's crews lost some of their best footage when the Nazis sank the ship on which they had stored it. For the Army, the AAF, and the Navy the war remained primarily 35mm and black-and-white. Between June 1943 and August 1945, the 3908th SSB (GHQ Pictorial) shot more than 20,000,000 feet of 35mm black-and-white, fewer than 5,000,000 feet of 16mm black-and-white, and only 70,000 feet of 16mm Kodachrome. During 1943 the AAF CCUs returned 557,000 feet of 35mm to the United States for processing, but only 40,000 feet of 16mm.[97]

Nonetheless, late in the war the standard began to change, both in response to demand and in response to experimentation and proven results with color photography. In late 1943 the Chief of APS sent four specially trained photographers overseas, two to England and two to Italy, to shoot color stills. They sent their exposed films directly to the War Department. From there they went to the Eastman Kodak lab for processing and then back to the Pentagon for screening and distribution. The results were impressive, demonstrating that color worked well at the front in the hands of competent craftsmen.[98] Soon color stills were no longer experimental and began appearing regularly in newspapers and magazines. Indicative of their increasing importance was the first color radiophotograph, which the Army transmitted from Germany more than three years after sending the first black-and-white radiophoto from Algiers. This novel color shot showed President Harry S. Truman, Prime Minister Clement R. Attlee, and Marshal Joseph Stalin at the Potsdam Conference in late summer 1945.[99]

Filmed in 16mm Kodachrome, blown up to 35mm, and produced in 1944, the Navy's movie *The Fighting Lady* not only horrified AAF General Hodge with its colorful brilliance, but also stunned General "Hap" Arnold. When John Craig (of *Danger Is My Business* fame), the former commander of the 9th CCU, was in Washington he saw the movie and considered it magnificent. Even though one flight of AAF bombers "carried more bombs than a whole carrier task force," he instantly realized that the Navy had scored a public-relations coup and insisted that Arnold see the film so that the AAF could plan a response. When the commanding general saw *The Fighting Lady* he was furious that the Navy had gotten such a jump on the AAF by using color and he wondered why the AAF was not using it too. No doubt diplomatically, Craig reminded his boss that when he had requisitioned color film Arnold had personally disapproved it.[100]

Arnold immediately sought to remedy the situation by ordering the formation of *ad hoc* photographic teams with first priority on equipment and shipping to go overseas on "Special Kodachrome Projects" that would do for the AAF what *The Fighting Lady* had done for the Navy, only better. Four of these projects, technically known as Special Film Projects #186, #193, #194, and #195, commenced in early 1945, with #186 devoted to Europe, where the war was winding down, and the other three to the Pacific, where Japan still seemed a formidable foe.[101]   Craig himself led the advance unit for #186.[102]   The AAF's CCUs suddenly found so many of their personnel and cameras being snatched away to shoot color that they could not continue normal black-and-white coverage; some even received orders to suspend all black-and-white photography and to shoot only color. Filming the AAF's role in defeating the Axis powers in color and for public release became an all-consuming passion. In late March the first Kodachrome footage for #186 began arriving in the States, and by mid-May the 4th CCU alone had exposed 120,000 feet of color for the project. Work continued apace on the Pacific color projects.[103]

But the AAF ran out of war before it could bomb and strafe the Navy with its new-found photographic weapons. Shortly after Japan surrendered, the AAF canceled three of the four Special Film Projects. The only one completed for public release was #193, titled *The Last Bomb*. Shot in 16mm Kodachrome and blown up to 35mm Technicolor, it told the story of the XXI Bomber Command, the organization that commanded the B-29s based on the Mariana Islands and conducted the strategic bombing campaign against Japan, including the dropping of the atomic bombs. The film contains one spectacular sequence after another—dogfights between American P-51s and Japanese fighters, bombs being dropped and exploding far below, the strafing of enemy installations, the charred remains of Tokyo after the March 1945 firebombing attack—that attested to "our relentless, expanding air power" that "had all but obliterated the enemy's ability to make war" by July 1945. Alas for the AAF, this brilliant documentary was not ready for public distribution until long after the war ended and thus lost much of its luster.[104]

Like the AAF, which became an independent Air Force and a full-fledged, coequal rival of the Army and the Navy only in 1947, color photography did not come into its own until after the war. Symbolic of color photography's limited role in World War II was the story of George Stevens. He was one of Hollywood's most famous directors with, among other noteworthy movies, A *Place in the Sun, Gunga Din, Shane, Giant,* and *The Diary of Anne Frank* to his credit. At the request of General Dwight D. Eisenhower, who like so many others was disappointed with the photographic coverage in North Africa, Stevens assembled a special unit to photograph the Allies liberating Europe. From D-Day to V-E Day Stevens' unit roamed the Continent with the troops, shooting the action for official purposes in 35mm black-and-white. But Stevens also carried a personal 16mm camera, and whenever circumstances permitted he shot the photographic equivalent of a personal diary in Kodachrome.

After the war Stevens put his "diary" in fourteen metal film cans and plunked them down in a storeroom in North Hollywood. After he died thirty years later, his son discovered the film, made color stills from some of the movie frames, wrote a brief introduction, engaged the eminent British military historian Max Hastings to write a commentary, and produced a book commemorating the fortieth anniversary of D-Day that became a best-seller. Many books have been written about the European campaign and almost all of them contain photographs. But so unusual was color photography in those days that only the book by Stevens' son can include in its subtitle the phrase *In Full Color*.[105]

VII

The U.S.S. *Monticello* was formerly an Italian luxury liner, converted to use as a military transport vessel and docked in San Francisco. By the evening of March 4, 1944, when the AAF's 6th CCU filed into its hull, all traces of its former luxury had long since disappeared. Next morning the ship passed under the Golden Gate Bridge and for more than two weeks alternately led and chased the sun westward before dropping anchor at Noumea, New Caledonia, where the 6th escaped from its "nautical prison." But things were not much better in sunlight's freedom. While waiting to engage in the combat photography for which it had been trained, the unit "became the regular labor detail for the 13th Army Air Force Supply Depot, adept at pulling slings around 1000-pound crates and getting the hell out of the way as the crane operator jerked them at our heads with maniacal abandon."[106] Thus did the men of the 6th CCU sweat out one of the great administrative and organizational problems that many photographic units encountered: few nonphotographic officers knew what to do with photographers and so gave them inappropriate assignments, although the 6th CCU's was an extreme example of unit mal-placement.

As might be expected, when the CCUs were first deployed, overseas AAF commands "had no idea of the possibilities or limitations." But this regrettable situation persisted well into the war. As one CCU officer said, the "main difficulty which had to be overcome was lack of understanding of the function of the unit...." Overseas commands often placed CCUs under photo-recon or photo-mapping officers "who did not understand the technical difficulties we encountered. It meant being sent on assignments that had no value, or were photographically impossible in some instances."[107] The SPCs (Army) and CPUs (Navy) could commiserate with their aerial brethren since they were also experiencing the demoralizing stranglehold of ill-informed officers.[108] So severe did the problem become in the Navy that one CPU OIC suggested creating "Demonstrators," experienced photo officers who would move from ship to ship dispensing information and explaining the "importance of *making* more photographs of important events...."[109]

Another administrative difficulty was slow decision-making. After describing the complex Navy motion-picture organization prevailing in the Pacific, a photo officer told Carleton Mitchell that he had "made a number of attempts to simplify the overall system, and to set up a more efficient procedure." In so doing he had "often caused a near riot" but had never effected any reforms. He continued to encounter "extremely irksome" situations "where an obvious decision should, and could be made promptly," except for those perpetual anti-motion devices known as proper channels and procedures, which guaranteed that the decision would be dropped into the lap of someone who could not even understand the question.[110]

Also ensuring frequent organizational tangles was the problem of coordinating the multiple and often-competing photographic agencies to secure adequate stills and movies while avoiding the wasted film associated with duplicated coverage. In Italy, who had paramount authority over Signal Corps photography? In conflicts among APS, the Bureau of Public Relations, and other War Department agencies, who was to prevail? In the Southwest Pacific, how was MacArthur to coordinate the Australian press representatives, the American movie and still pools, and the services' photo units when all of them were clamoring for equal opportunities? There seemed to be a "multiplicity of agencies" everywhere, all "making essentially the same type of material, that suitable for public dissemination."[111]

Complaints regarding administrative battles were numerous. A 2nd CCU officer believed that the unit achieved only about 40 percent of its mission, with one of the biggest difficulties being administrative confusion. As that unit's monthly history for August 1945 put it, "The battle for administration, etc., constantly seemed to supersede the importance of actual photographic operations." The 8th CCU also found itself engaged "in one administrative struggle after another" and "invaded by administrative inspectors." As the bureaucratic absurdities piled up, CPU #5 found that "the battle we went forth to was not always with the enemy." The unit became "immersed in fathoms of 'chain of command,' 'temporary additional duty orders,' and endorsements running from 1 to 17."[112]

Practically every photo unit could have echoed these lamentations.

3

"Jeez, This Is Just Like in the Movies"

Real War Versus Hollywood War

Determining whether Secretary of War Henry L. Stimson was just angry or both angry and frustrated is hard to do so many years after the event.

But in May 1943 Stimson was certainly acutely unhappy, as he confided to his diary. Both a British and an American documentary film on the North African campaign had recently hit the movie houses; the British version, entitled *Desert Victory* and produced by Colonel David Macdonald, was far superior to America's *At the Front in North Africa*, produced by Signal Corps cameraman Darryl Zanuck, a Hollywood mogul who had been one of the founders of Twentieth Century Fox. The North African campaign was the first important test for Allied World War II combat photography, and while the British received an "A+" their American colleagues had barely earned an "F–." *Desert Victory* was a smash hit—"that rare thing, a perfect movie, has been made," gushed one reviewer—while the most enthusiastic word *The New York Times* used to describe *At the Front in North Africa* was "deficient."[1]

The United States, Stimson wrote in his diary, was "just beginning to wake up to the importance of such efforts" in enhancing home front morale. But *At the Front in North Africa* was not going to inspire anyone. Stimson believed he knew why the film was so feeble and uninspiring: American cameramen were not trying hard enough, they were not out there—truly *at the front* where they could get themselves hurt. The British "lost four photographers killed and more wounded" in getting their pictures but Army Signal Corps cameramen "do not seem very anxious to be killed." Something had to be done about this, and Stimson was "prepared to take the matter up vigorously now" because the United States "must get it done better," and he was perfectly willing to expend photographers' lives for improved results.[2]

What Stimson did not know, though he should have since the April 5, 1943 issue of *Life* ran a story on it, was that *Desert Victory* looked "realistic" and "war-like" because Macdonald had staged many of the most dramatic scenes. The result was a bastardized film that blended commercial-studio war sequences with genuine documentary footage. *At the Front in North Africa* seemed "deficient only because it is 100 percent honest," incorporating nary a shot that was not authentic.[3] Zanuck's crew had operated under a War Department policy that prohibited mingling genuine and staged combat footage. Though he and his cameramen were constantly in the thick of the action being shot at, strafed, and bombarded, Zanuck had already had doubts about the results. "I don't suppose our war scenes will look as savage and realistic as those we usually make on the back lot," he wrote several months before the public saw the movie, "but then you can't have everything."[4]

Macdonald, Zanuck, and Stimson, each in his own way, revealed a great truth about World War II combat photography: real war and the Hollywood image of war bore scant resemblance. Macdonald fused the two, producing a film that was partially shot like a typical studio war movie with "realistic" acting in "realistic" settings. Zanuck stuck with genuine war footage but realized it would not be very impressive on the big screen. And Stimson thought Macdonald's work superior to Zanuck's because he did not comprehend the difference between real war and Hollywood war.

I

"I saw them World War II movies," a Vietnam War-era soldier said. "I thought war was glorious, I thought it was glamorous. Why didn't someone tell us different? Why didn't someone tell? War is *shit!*"[5]

World War II soldiers shared these sentiments, for they understood the limitations of celluloid war when it tried to portray real war. They loathed those too-numerous Hollywood movies depicting a stupid enemy easily beaten by heroic Americans moving forward, upright amidst an inferno of artillery shells spewing dirt (but apparently not metal) in every direction, their guns blazing, killing dozens of the enemy but somehow rarely getting shot by their inept foes. As one GI said, "Stuff like Humphrey Bogart whipping a whole German armored-car column practically singlehanded gives us pains in the pratt, because that kind of crap gives the folks at home the wrong kind of idea about what we are up against."[6] Real war was so different from studio-made war that when something occasionally occurred that seemed Hollywood-like, soldiers almost automatically commented on it: "Jeez, this is just like in the movies."[7]

The problem that the cameramen faced was not simply to photograph combat but to do it so that it looked like Hollywood war. Only then would it grab the attention and emotions of the homefront audiences, who were so accustomed to seeing Tinseltown's vision of warfare that they "knew" what war looked like and were disappointed when images appeared on the screen that did not measure up.

Although cameramen regularly risked their necks, even their best results were seldom as spectacular as those conjured up in Hollywood on a daily basis. Why was this? The explanation goes something like this. Combatants did not make massed daytime charges, save for the occasional Japanese banzai attack. During the daylight hours, all military forces were purposefully unphotogenic as they stayed hidden, shielding themselves from their enemies' accurate long-range weapons by resorting to dispersion and camouflage, including wearing drab uniforms. As the Chief Signal Officer observed, "the most striking feature of the battlefield is its emptiness." No one saw anybody—friend or foe—for very long, and bullets and artillery shells were invisible to both the human eye and the camera.[8]

When daylight action did occur troops moved forward in small units, with individual soldiers either belly crawling or scampering in short, irregular sprints from one sheltered position to another. Tanks moved forward with the soldiers but were widely separated; they dodged and weaved along erratic paths so that in spite of their size they were no easier to photograph than infantrymen. One enterprising member of the 163rd SPC, Morris Schimmel, tried to film tank action by running alongside an advancing tank, but he "was shot and badly wounded for his trouble, and almost lost his arm."[9] Filming air or sea battles was equally difficult. "When the bombs are released," wrote the 13th CCU's Jack Stirling, the plane "jumps, then zigzags so much to duck ack-ack that it's almost impossible to get motion pictures. I have shots of Zeros coming in for an attack, but they travel pretty fast—300 to 320 mph." Or, as MGM movie idol Clark Gable put it after flying five combat missions in Europe, an enemy plane "doesn't exactly come in so that you can photograph him. He seems to have another job to do."[10] Writing about a fleet was easier than conveying it photographically. The ships sailed in a dispersed pattern over five or ten miles so that "no possible camera position or lens will enable you to put more than two or three ships—half a dozen at most—on the screen at once. And on the screen the images of the ships will be small—too small to convey the desired impression of actuality—and generally hidden by atmospheric haze, as well."[11]

Daylight combat usually transpired at long range and when the fighting was closeup cameramen had to find shelter or die. If a photographer could see the enemy, the enemy could see him and as a general rule to be seen was to be shot. "So much action takes place just beyond the limits of even a telephoto lens," complained the CPS's Carleton Mitchell. You rarely saw the enemy, said Ignatius Gallo of the 166th SPC, but even when you did, "the distance is too much for the equipment you have." Gallo's colleague, Fred Mandl, went ashore on Omaha Beach on D-Day—a morning assault so that the troops had hours of sunlight to consolidate their position—but was so busy seeking protection that he did not take a single picture. Frederick W. Gerretson of CPU #8 was also at Normandy on D-Day. He "had imagined that our end of it would be much more dramatic than events proved." Things were plenty exciting but getting the action "on film so that it would look like something proved to be pretty tough" because he and his partner had to spend most of their time "looking over the top of foxholes or frantically trying to burrow down into one."[12]

The situation was no different in Italy, where Don Morrow spent more than four hours at the front trying to photograph dead and wounded soldiers being brought in. For most of that time he was flat on his face. "I was down so much," he wrote in his diary, "that when I stood up the altitude made me dizzy, and I was so low to the ground snakes would crawl by and say 'Hi, Shorty!'" And in the Pacific a Marine cameraman suddenly found himself facing two Japanese jumping out of a pillbox and running at him, firing machine guns in all directions. "Unfortunately, I didn't take pictures of this because I wished to take some pictures tomorrow."[13]

Much combat occurred at night. A member of CPU #5 swore that he was going to write a book entitled "It Happened at Night, or Over on the Horizon." Numerous sea engagements accompanied the land campaign for Guadalcanal but only one of them, the daylight Battle of Santa Cruz, received much photographic coverage; all the others took place at night. Marine cameramen cursed that the "Japanese themselves cause considerable annoyance" because of their uncooperative "habit of hiding by day and counterattacking by night...."[14] In Europe the Germans were equally unsporting; German cameramen undoubtedly felt the same way about Americans.

Bringing an artistic touch to a real battlefield was a lot more difficult than on a set. In Hollywood, with its carefully choreographed scenes and the ability to shoot multiple retakes, almost every scene could have superb lighting and composition. But in battle the cameramen had no control over light conditions or the speed at which events took place, and little ability to affect composition.[15] Foregrounds, backgrounds, the main subject's placement in the frame, all were difficult to compose in advance because "the one prediction that can be made about operations against the enemy is that they are unpredictable." The 162nd SPC's Jerry Kahn wanted to get some shots of an enemy artillery barrage—but every time he aimed his camera in one direction the shells exploded elsewhere. Artistic or not, action shots often depended on pure chance, though a cameraman had to be at the front in the first place even to give pure chance an occasional lucky break.[16] As a member of CPU #2 realized, sometimes the best philosophy was to "KEEP SHOOTING AND HOPE!!"[17]

Some situations increased the chances for luck to prevail, most notably amphibious landings and their fresh-water equivalent, river crossings. These often occurred during daylight, so all the ingredients for a photogenic battle were visible, except for the enemy. The photographer had a panoramic view of the terrain, the front line was clearly defined in his viewfinder, shells burst in the water and along the shore, and if he could not see the enemy, he could photograph the backs of Americans as they debouched from the landing craft and surged landward.[18] Cameramen who went ashore with the first waves sometimes actually turned their backs on the firing Germans or Japanese to acquire frontal views of subsequent landing waves. In an astonishing scene from Omaha Beach that appeared in the documentary *The True Glory*, a cameraman who had done just that filmed two soldiers getting shot, one of the rare photographic records of men actually being hit. But in Hollywood, such scenes, replete with dramatic gestures, profound dying words, and fake blood, were staples.

Equally rare in real life and equally common in make-believe were sequences of the enemy actually fighting back. *Attack! The Battle for New Britain* was a superb documentary about the island fighting in the Pacific Theater but it "did not satisfy the men who worked on it, for the enemy appeared only as dead or prisoners of war; there were no sequences of countercharges although many had taken place, there was no wide-angle shot of an American mass attack." The cameramen were brave and resourceful but no amount of heroism and ingenuity could overcome the dense jungle that constricted vision to a few feet and a clever enemy who attacked only at night and remained under cover by day, when the adversary could "be felt and sometimes heard, but seldom seen."[19]

It may be that only two sequences from nearly four years of war in the Pacific showed enemy infantrymen fighting back. Marine cameraman Norman T. Hatch made newsreel history on Tarawa when he "captured scenes, for the first time, showing Jap troops & Marines at combat in the same frames of film." And Marine Paul Peters was photographing an American on Peleliu when a Japanese soldier suddenly appeared on a ridgeline in front of him. Peters continued filming as the enemy spotted him, hesitated a second, and then threw a "yardstick" torpedo (similar to an American bangalore torpedo) at him. Peters *still* continued filming as the torpedo landed directly in front of him and exploded, knocking the camera from his hands and burying it in mud. The next day Peters recovered the camera—with the film intact.[20] Other sequences depicted live enemy troops who were not prisoners, but they were not engaged in combat.[21]

So unusual was *any* authentic scene of Japanese soldiers that the few good ones appear repetitively in various films in different contexts. As just one example, a Marine cameraman on Okinawa recorded in color a dramatic sequence of a Marine throwing a grenade into a cave followed by a dazed and burned enemy soldier staggering out of the hole and keeling over. Parts of this sequence appear in black and white in a historical film entitled *7th Infantry Division*, as if one of its photographers had filmed the scenes on Okinawa, but parts of it also appear in a similar film on the 27th Infantry Division as if the events had occurred on Makin atoll in the Gilbert Islands. In fact the *27th Infantry Division* movie is a virtual compilation of footage shot by other photographers in different locales.

II

Cameramen working on *Attack! The Battle for New Britain* shot 55,000 feet of movie film and a large number of stills. But in editing the motion-picture footage they realized they lacked certain "tie-in" shots to give continuity to the documentary. These few scenes could have been easily and safely posed in any number of places but the photographers had explicit orders to use only "actual battle scenes without any reenactment of any action." Orders were orders, not pleas, requests, or suggestions. So a five-man photographic team went back to New Britain, where some Marines were still in contact with the enemy. For seven days of additional filming Marines guided the team "to whatever action they needed." Several times, to get just the right tie-ins, the cameramen advanced as far as 400 yards *ahead* of the front lines and then had the Marines purposely initiate combat. Although the resulting footage might be considered "controlled" to a certain extent, the photographers had complied with the spirit, if not exactly the letter, of their orders not to include staged scenes.[22]

The photographers on New Britain were not unusual in their scrupulous regard for reality, for authorities discouraged reenacting or staging scenes for the camera's (and the audience's) benefit. "Absolute accuracy and absolute truth must never fail to govern the preparation of *all* photographic and news material" was the policy of the Marine Corps' Division of Public Relations. As the CPUs deployed overseas, the prevailing belief was that staged material "would not only be useless, but might be dangerous to public morale" because it would be misleading. "At present," wrote a high-ranking official, "Navy photographic policy is to secure documentary film, and it is felt that the Hollywood formula has no place in a military service." When Dewey Wrigley of CPU #10 wrote to his superior, Lieutenant Commander Carleton Mitchell, Jr., from Italy that he "had the engineers here explode some TNT that looked like shell fire," that the explosions "certainly looked like the real thing," and that "we were only reenacting what has actually happened," Mitchell replied that he understood the strong temptation "to duplicate something that happens frequently and cannot be properly photographed." However, "the whole matter is dynamite," so Wrigley should "be extremely careful about any reenactments," and must inform Mitchell "if any action is simulated" so that he would not release material under false pretenses.[23]

The AAF allowed only very limited reenactments. "DO NOT FAKE PICTURES," insisted an AAF document. But if a combat picture showed a plane's number or insignia, "it would be permissible to photograph the crew the following day boarding their plane or [at a] briefing, and cut it in the picture," making it seem as if "this part of the picture was taken in regular sequence."[24] SPCs also operated under a stringent no-staging policy, and adopted the practice of stating it on the caption sheet if scenes had been reenacted. In Italy, for example, no reenactments could be photographed without the specific approval of the Fifth Army Signal Service APS headquarters, and all such scenes had to have captions saying "REENACTED SCENES." These rules were mandatory and photographers knew that "Any violation of this directive will result in immediate disciplinary action."[25]

Staging scenes did not necessarily mean safety for the cameraman. Authorized reenactments frequently had a genuine flavor to them because they occurred near the front lines. After writing in his diary that he had photographed some reenactments of machine gunners in action, one cameramen noted that "though the stuff was staged Jerry was shelling on both sides of us. Many of them much too close for comfort."[26]

To presume that no photographers ever succumbed to the temptation to sneak in occasional reenactments under the guise of actual combat would assess human nature too generously. For two days during the Battle of the Bulge a photo team from the 166th SPC allegedly carried a dead German around in its jeep and "propped him up in the foreground of action shots to give 'atmosphere.'" Another team reportedly placed "smoke bombs in knocked-out tanks" and then had soldiers run by them to make it look like combat. Still a third team supposedly directed men to duck in and out of doorways, simulating street fighting. And the OIC of one detachment, which "DID NOT set up pictures," knew of "a couple of characters that I am sure would not have hesitated a second to do it—even to going out of their way to connive the shots."[27] But reenactments seem to have been remarkably few, and knowledgeable people were adept at spotting them. A Hollywood shell explosion, for example, usually looked more impressive than a real explosion. The former sent up photogenic clods of dirt in a symmetrical pattern while the latter pulverized the soil and showered it not only up, but also forward.[28]

In a sense, *all* war pictures—stills or movies, genuine or Hollywood—are deceptive. Corporal Samuel Fuller hit Omaha Beach on D-Day with the First Infantry Division (nicknamed "the Big Red One") and won a Silver Star for his exploits. As a postwar director and screenwriter, he made *The Big Red One*, a movie about "his" division. Though he succeeded better than many Hollywood directors, he knew that he had not portrayed war accurately. The problem was "you can't see anything in actual combat. To do it right, you'd have to blind the audience with smoke, deafen them with noise, then shoot one of them in the shoulder to scare the rest to death. That would give the idea," he said with wry wit, "but then not many people would come to the movies."[29]

Like Fuller, Robert L. Lewis, who commanded the 163rd SPC, understood film's crucial limitation: it affected "only the visual sense of the audience thousands of miles from the scene of action."[30] A movie with a sound track engages a second sense, hearing, but no photographic medium engages the other senses. An audience does not smell the rank odors associated with the involuntary defecation and urination that fear induces, or the charred remains of tanks and trucks and tents and people. As Norm Hatch narrated in *I Was There: Tarawa*, a "camera tells the truth but it doesn't give you an idea of how it smells, and the smell on that island was *bad*." The stench from rotting men and animals could be sniffed miles from the battlefield, and at close range induced gagging.[31] Audiences do not get the tastes of war either; they do not sup on cold rations and cold coffee in a frigid hole on a frozen day, or nervously lick salt-laden perspiration from their lips in the dank rottenness of a Southeast Asian jungle. When a soldier clutches his wounds, movie-goers are spared the sensation of touch, of warm blood, of entrails or brains. Even the vision and sound in a movie theater bear false witness to the battlefield. Perversely, movie patrons see and hear things *more clearly* than combatants do. As Fuller knew, soldiers were usually nearly blinded, since smoke and dust obscured their vision and stung their eyes. And no sound track captured battle's thunderous cacophony. Real combat was deafening, as Fuller said, and the noise did not conveniently stop or fade into the background so that soldiers could hear themselves and one another talk.

Some people who should have known better never did understand how extraordinarily difficult photographing genuine action was. In

February 1945 a Signal Corps colonel in the 26th Division, probably weaned on too many doses of Hollywood blood, confronted Joe Zinni and "asked me why we weren't able to take pictures of American soldiers bayoneting Germans, pictures of our machine-gunners mowing down groups of the enemy, pictures of our mortars landing on enemy installations & other fantastic, impossible & unobtainable pictures!!" As tactfully as he could, Zinni explained "just why these pictures couldn't be obtained but he can't be convinced—he wants blood!!— My blood & my men's blood!!"[32]

Considering the travails that hampered the cameramen and the difficulty of "shooting" real war, the war's photographic record is remarkable—incomplete and imperfect, but nevertheless astonishing in light of the prevailing conditions. The wonder is not that genuine combat scenes were so few, but that cameramen recorded as many as they did.

And the wonder is that so many cameramen resisted the temptation to engage in large-scale staging in an effort to make real war appear like war as Hollywood knew and loved it.

One man who did not resist the temptation was John Huston, who produced *San Pietro*, a documentary about the battle for, and liberation of, a small Italian town by that name.[33]

III

Released in the spring of 1945 for public theaters, *San Pietro* received rave reviews; it has since become a highly-praised classic documentary. The *New York Post* reviewer gushed that the film "dwarfs all fiction versions of modern war and nearly all the rival documentaries." Although few theatergoers would have heard of San Pietro, after leaving the theater they would never forget it. "This, you can see, is war, not by diagram, not in reenactment, not with smoke bombs and leadless blanks, not with telephoto lens." Cameramen advanced right with the troops to record the battle as it happened! The *Motion Picture Herald* praised the "utterly realistic camera which follows the foot-soldier as faithfully as his shadow through the campaign...." *Time* was equally enthusiastic, declaring that Huston's handiwork "is in every respect as good a war film as any that has been made; in some respects it is the best." The magazine praised *San Pietro* for "its remarkable honesty and excellence" and commended Huston for leading his cameramen "into no-man's-land hours ahead of an attack" and for constantly moving "from man to man of his small crew, guiding them to the best positions, the best shots." *Time* predicted that history was likely to recognize *San Pietro* as not just a good film, but a great one.[34]

Time's prophecy came true. Authorities on World War II films have considered it "an engrossing chronicle of savage fighting between American and German forces," a "moment-by-moment depiction of a real battle from inside" with a "searing and inescapable" truth to it, and "a poignant on-the-spot account of Allied attempts to capture a German-held Italian village." They have acclaimed the film for exhibiting "the persuasiveness of the true documentary film in the hands of a master" and for providing "an accurate sense of what [war] looked like."[35] The cameramen received praise for being "right on top of the fighting" in order to get "close-in combat photography" with "the camera constantly shaken by the bombardment." The film profoundly affected everyone who saw it.[36] Novelist Herbert Gold recalled that it had "an immediacy" not found in other documentaries since "Huston and the others were there, no shit, really right there under fire while men were dying." And David H. Hackworth, America's most highly decorated post-World War II soldier, showed the film to units he commanded. "It was a brilliant picture that showed on-the-ground, real-life infantry in combat," he wrote. Hackworth especially loved the movie because "it dispelled all myths of war as a cops-and-robbers game; I always felt they should have given salty old John Huston the Blue Max just for making it."[37]

Huston's biographers have uncritically accepted the film for what it purports to be—a genuine portrayal of a brutal battle filmed under real combat conditions. Huston never said anything to discourage them from perceiving it that way, claiming that he and his crew filmed it during the actual battle and therefore exposed a great deal of film "because we never knew what we were going to get. We just photographed." In a 1960 interview he maintained that *San Pietro* was "the first time real Infantry combat conditions, involving Americans, had ever been seen on the screen."[38]

His autobiography, titled *An Open Book* and thereby implying complete honesty, again omitted even a hint of the truth, which was that he staged most of the action *after* the battle.[39] In many ways the only differences between *San Pietro* and Hollywood war films was that Huston used real soldiers as actors and reenacted his scenes at the battle's location instead of on a back-lot set. Essentially he used the same techniques in *San Pietro* that he had employed while directing

Humphrey Bogart, Peter Lorre, Sydney Greenstreet, and Mary Astor in *The Maltese Falcon*, released in 1941.

IV

The battle for San Pietro was a significant engagement during the Allied struggle to liberate Italy. In the Army's multivolume official history of World War II it received an entire chapter in the volume that chronicled the fighting from Salerno to Cassino.[40] The small, ancient village sat at the mouth of the Liri Valley astride Route 6, a main north–south road running from the Volturno River toward Cassino and on to Rome. To get to the Eternal City the Allies had to get by San Pietro. Knowing this the Germans converted the village and the surrounding hills into a strongpoint in their Winter Line. An attacking force entering the Liri Valley had to run a gauntlet, fighting through dense olive groves in front of San Pietro while under fire from defenders dug in on the valley floor, on Mount Lungo to the west, and on Mount Sammucro, consisting of twin peaks known as Hill 1205 and Hill 950, to the northeast.

The primary American unit hurling itself against the tenacious Germans defending this treacherous terrain was the 36th Division, composed primarily of Texans and frequently called "The Texas Army," at least by people from the Lone Star State. Commanded by Major General Fred L. Walker, the 36th was a typical World War II "triangular" division consisting of three regiments (the 141st, 142nd, and 143rd) with each regiment divided into three battalions. A full strength regiment had 3,257 officers and men. The 36th also had both "organic" and "attached" units. The former, such as the 111th Engineer Combat Battalion and four Field Artillery Batteries, were permanently detailed to the division, while the latter were only temporarily assigned to it. Among the most important attached units were the 3rd Ranger Battalion and the 753rd Tank Battalion.

Supplementing the 36th Division in the attack was the 504th Parachute Infantry, the 1st Italian Motorized Brigade (the first liberated Italians to fight against their former German allies), and the 1st Special Service Force, composed of carefully selected Americans and Canadians who had been trained in mountain warfare, paratroop operations, and long-range sabotage missions. After encountering the 1st

Special Service Force in combat the Germans called it "The Devil's Brigade."

As with all World War II battles, San Pietro was a series of separate engagements each consisting of multiple smaller actions. In mid-December 1943 the Allied force made two direct assaults on San Pietro and the surrounding heights, hoping to push at least two miles due north up the Liri Valley to the village of San Vittore. Lasting from December 8th through 11th, the initial assault resulted in the 1st Battalion of the 143rd Regiment capturing Hill 1205 and the 3rd Rangers holding Hill 950; reinforced by the 504th Parachute Infantry, they held Mount Sammucro's peaks against furious counterattacks. But the Germans pulverized the 143rd's 2nd and 3rd Battalions in the olive groves on the valley floor and the 1st Italian Motorized Brigade took horrendous casualties in an unsuccessful effort to capture Mount Lungo.

The second attack began on the 15th and ended on the 17th. Although the 753rd Tank Battalion suffered severe losses the 142nd Regiment drove the Germans off Mount Lungo and elements of the 141st and 143rd fought their way into San Pietro. However, a northward attack down the back slope of Mount Sammucro spearheaded by the 504th Parachute Infantry failed to reach San Vittore.

The battle for San Pietro is a case study of a Pyrrhic victory, since the Allies achieved minimal gains at an enormous cost both to the fighting forces and to the villagers. With San Vittore and the high ground immediately beyond it in enemy hands, no easy breakthrough to Rome along Route 6 occurred. Germans retreating from San Pietro soon improvised a new defensive line running from San Vittore to Mount Porchia, still blocking the Liri Valley. Allied casualties were staggering. The 36th Division had approximately 1,200 battle casualties, the 504th Parachute Infantry 280, the 1st Italian Motorized Brigade 375, and the other units also had high losses. Of sixteen tanks committed to the attack only four returned. Nonbattle casualties resulting from disease and accidents swelled the totals. For example, the 36th had 2,200 nonbattle casualties during December, a month of deplorable weather during which soldiers could rarely escape the rain, snow, mud, and cold. General Walker agonized about his troops, admitting that he did "not understand how the men continue to keep going under their existing conditions of hardship." Many of them could not. A report from the Division Headquarters showed that battle and nonbattle casualties had reduced the 141st to 57 percent of full strength, the 142nd to 63 percent, and the 143rd to only 21 percent.

For the people of San Pietro the situation was no better. During the battle an estimated 1,000 villagers—mostly old men, women, and children—huddled in caves and cellars. As many as 300 of them may have died in the fighting. Those who survived emerged into a devastated landscape; toward the battle's end each new round of high explosives delivered by air or artillery simply rearranged the rubble. San Pietro was so shattered that the inhabitants did not even try to rebuild it. All but a few families, no more than forty people, moved into the new village of Campobasso. Ironically, one of the few upbeat sequences in *San Pietro* is when the villagers greet their liberators. Huston's narration implied that a rebirth occurred as the townspeople quickly started rebuilding the village and planting the nearby fields. When writing the script he had no way of knowing that San Pietro would be virtually abandoned or that this liberation had few happy immediate consequences.

V

Huston's film emerged out of a specific context shaped by a presidential decision regarding the difficult question of exactly what to show the home front about the nature of warfare.

The belief that Pearl Harbor instantly inflamed all Americans to support the war unanimously and wholeheartedly is a myth. During 1942 public opinion polls by a variety of private and public agencies showed that a substantial minority of the population—perhaps as many as 30 percent—disagreed with President Franklin D. Roosevelt's "no compromise" policy, especially toward Germany, and was reluctant to wage total war. Many people were passive, indifferent, complacent, and unwilling to endure great sacrifices. Instead of committing themselves to the war no matter what the cost to themselves, many civilians selfishly sought to make sure that the sacrifices and inconveniences fell on someone else's shoulders.[41]

Part of the problem was that the home front had no firsthand knowledge of the war. Unlike the people of Poland, France, Britain, Russia, Germany, China, Burma, and elsewhere, Americans were isolated geographically and psychologically from hunger, violence, pain, and death. They had the luxury of viewing the conflict from afar; their country was a safe haven, a refuge of tranquility in a tumultuous world. Civilians only experienced the war vicariously through the newspapers and magazines, on radio, and in still photographs and motion-pictures. But even this vicarious experience was muted, especially during the war's first eighteen months. Although officials such as Archibald MacLeish, the head of the Office of Facts and Figures, and Elmer Davis, chief of the Office of War Information, advocated a "strategy of truth," the *whole* truth rarely emerged. Authorities shielded the home front from bad news about production bottlenecks and shortages and presented a superficial, romantic view of combat, emphasizing its heroic aspects and virtually ignoring its horrors. In World War I the government had imposed a ban on showing any pictures of American dead, and an identical policy initially guided World War II photographic coverage.[42]

Providing only good news nourished the prevalent complacency and fostered an optimistic outlook bordering on overconfidence, which deeply concerned President Roosevelt. Throughout 1943 he struggled to unite and inspire the home front and to harden it for the long, costly war he believed the country faced. And he vented his frustrations when civilians did not respond to his appeals. The president emphasized that the United States waged total war not because it wanted to but "because our very existence is threatened. Without that supreme effort we cannot hope to retain the freedom and self-respect which give life its value." Although inevitable, victory would not be easy. When Russian victories in the winter of 1942–43 prompted "thousands of Americans to throw their hats in the air and proclaim that victory is just around the corner," he warned against premature celebrations. The age of miracles was over and "there is no Joshua in our midst. We cannot count on great walls crumbling and falling down when the trumpets blow and the people shout." "I state only a blunt fact," he said later in the year, "when I tell the Congress that we are still a long, long way from ultimate victory in any major theater of the war." Casualties were going to be heavy. Every military operation entailed grave risks of "severe losses of men and materials" and many operations lay in the future.[43]

Total war was a "grim reality" requiring complete dedication by all Americans. Repeatedly Roosevelt tried to erase the distinction between the fighting front and the home front: "you can't take a piece of paper and draw a line down the middle of it and put the war abroad—or the war front—on one side of the line, and put the home front—so called—on another side of the line, because after all it all ties together." Sacrifices in blood made by soldiers must be matched by civilian sacrifices, including the cheerful acceptance of increased taxes, higher costs, fewer consumer goods, and especially of long hours of hard work and sweat because "it is becoming more and more evident that this is essentially a great war of production." The fastest path to victory with the fewest casualties was through ever-greater production of food and armaments. "More cooperation, more teamwork, and more production, all the way from the farms and mines through the assembly lines," he told the nation's businessmen, "will enable us to win the war more quickly."[44]

To both inspire and embarrass civilians into complaining less and sacrificing more, in the spring of 1943 Roosevelt decided that the home front should have a more accurate picture of the hardships endured by soldiers, sailors, airmen, and Marines. No matter how difficult conditions were at home they paled compared to those in the war zones. But exactly how realistic should the picture be? Battle is a ghastly, grisly ordeal and portraying it too vividly might sap morale and undermine support for a war that occasioned so much intense misery.[45] "In these affairs," wrote William L. Chenery, a highly-respected journalist and the long-time editor of Collier's Weekly, "there is no simple precise rule to be worked out." Although believing a democracy could function only if its citizens were intelligent and well informed, he opposed fully informing them about combat. His friend, Secretary of the Navy Knox, invited him to a private screening of "an unedited film of an island landing attack," which "was not pleasant to see." Afterwards Knox asked him what the Navy should do with such footage and Chenery replied that it should be shown only "to discreet editors and publishers who ought to be informed of the realities so that they might govern their own news policies intelligently in the public interest." But ordinary civilians should be spared the psychological burden of seeing what war did to their husbands, brothers, fathers, and sons.[46]

The administration agreed with Chenery that a policy of what might be called "restricted realism" was necessary. In mid-May the AAF CCUs received a memorandum entitled "Release of Pictures" setting forth the new policy. The president desired "that the public be shown the grimness and hardness of war through still and motion-pictures." However, such shots should be judiciously selected "inasmuch as we must not pass the line beyond which such exhibition does more

Although they were ubiquitous in the combat zone, wielding their cameras as weapons, armed forces photographers were unknown to the public because they were not given individual credit for their photos. For example, *Newsweek* credited its May 22, 1944 cover of a 155mm "Long Tom" at Anzio to "U.S. Army Signal Corps Photo" but the 163rd SPC's Fred Bonnard took it. *Photo provided by Bonnard. Photo published courtesy of* Newsweek.

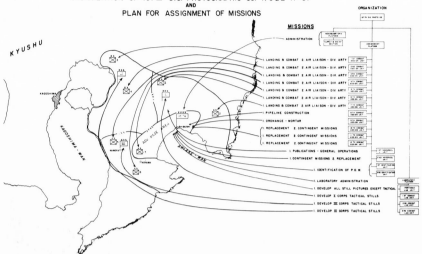

An indication of photography's importance was the detailed planning for photographic operations, as indicated by this chart prepared for the projected November 1, 1945 invasion of Japan. *Photo courtesy of the Combined Arms Research Library, Fort Leavenworth, KS.*

The caption for this drawing, which appeared in the records of the 168th SPC, sarcastically illustrated the pressure photographers felt to get dramatic photos. A cameraman, the caption explained, "might expect to receive a telegram such as this at any time: 'Your island invasion stuff good but shows only backs and profiles of troops landing Stop Can you arrange hereafter to land ahead of troops and get pictures of them onrushing Japs.'" *Photo by John F. Sanders.*

The workhorse cameras were the 35mm Bell and Howell Eyemo with a three-lens spider turret, held by William H. Ettinger (left), and the Speed Graphic, nestled in the lap of John Moore (right). *Photo provided by Ettinger.*

Unlike the other services, the Marines frequently used 16mm movie cameras like the one Martin Friedman is holding. Note that Friedman mounted his camera on a gun stock to get added stability while hand-holding it. *Photo provided by Friedman.*

Burdened with photo equipment, cameramen ordinarily could not carry a rifle and were nearly defenseless at the front. The 163rd SPC's Fred Bonnard, shown here at his "home" in the entrance to a wine cellar at Anzio, carried only a .45 automatic and a knife, which were typical weapons for cameramen. *Photo provided by Bonnard.*

Because of their need for mobility cameramen had ready access to transportation, as depicted in this shot of a typical 163rd SPC Combat Assignment Team, consisting of James A. Cuca (left), George J. Cipra (center), and Del Ratick (right). *Photo by Allan Smith. Photo provided by Cuca.*

Like many other types of units, photographic outfits often had distinctive insignia, patches, and stickers. The top photo is of the 6th CCU's shoulder patch, designed by a Walt Disney artist. By 1943 Disney Studios had five artists working full time producing insignia for various units. *Photo provided by Joe Longo.* The middle photo is the 832nd SSB's logo, also designed by Disney. *Photo provided by William A. Avery.* The bottom photo is of a Pacific Fleet Combat Camera Group sticker. *Photo provided by Earl F. Colgrove.*

Here is the 163rd SPC's headquarters building in Caiazzo, Italy, soon after American planes bombed it by mistake. The arrow points to the room where Gordon F. Frye was resting when the planes struck, badly injuring him. *Photo provided by Frye.*

This shot of the rubble in Caiazzo after the bombing was one of the author's first clues that not all of *San Pietro* was filmed in or near San Pietro during the battle. A movie sequence showing the same scene appeared in *San Pietro,* supposedly depicting the results of German sabotage in the village. *Photo provided by Samuel T. Tischler.*

The top photo, though seemingly not very exciting, is quite unusual. It shows the 163rd SPC's John Vita *in combat*. Usually cameramen were too busy photographing the action to take pictures of themselves. A shot like the bottom photo was all too common—that's Vita in a hospital after being wounded when a mortar shell hit his jeep. *Photos provided by Robert L. Lewis.*

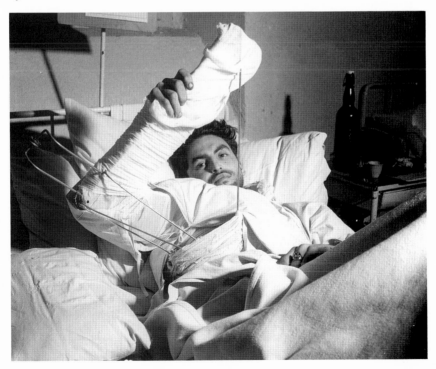

While making routine shots of troops advancing on Luzon, the 165th SPC's Robert C. Reinhart captured a rare moment—an *enemy* shell exploding. Getting a picture like this on purpose was next to impossible. As Reinhart admitted, "It was one of those 'lucky shots'—also lucky in that I didn't get hit at the time!" *Photo provided by Reinhart.*

Somewhat easier to photograph was an exploding *American* shell because a cameraman could coordinate his activities with the artillerymen. Here a shell explodes near a battered house that German soldiers were using for cover. *Photo by Jerry Rutberg. Photo provided by Joseph D. Boyle .*

harm than good. It is not desired that horror pictures should be released, but special effort should be made to find those photographs which accurately depict the terrible strain of wartime conditions." A high-ranking Office of War Information official explained the policy to a newspaper association meeting by saying that "I'm not arguing for stories that will chill the blood of a mother or sweetheart, but we do want to know what our sons are really enduring."[47]

By late May the policy had been publicly announced and put on display. *Newsweek* alerted its readers that "plenty of stark photos will be appearing soon" and gave them a foretaste of what was coming. Under the headline "Photo With a Message," its May 24th issue published the first photo released by the Navy in the campaign to harden home-front morale by "letting civilians see photographically what warfare does to men who fight." It showed a bleeding and powder-burned Marine who had been wounded on Tulagi receiving emergency medical treatment.[48]

But the revised policy only limped along during the summer of 1943 because the Army was reluctant to release realistic photos. A direct appeal to Army Chief of Staff Marshall finally resulted in the release of three photos in September that *Newsweek* labeled "unbelievably stark." It ran the most gruesome of the trio, one of the few publications with the nerve to do so: a head-on shot taken in a hospital that focused on the stump of a soldier's amputated leg. Another showed dead paratroopers in Sicily, and the third three dead Americans lying face down in the sand along the beach at Buna, New Guinea. Taken by *Life* photographer George Strock, the latter is one of the war's most famous pictures and is oftentimes erroneously considered the first one showing American dead. But in early August *Life* had already published a shot of a dead soldier covered by a blanket, with only his right boot and left elbow visible.[49]

The new policy touched off a prolonged controversy between those who applauded it and those who were aghast. Despite impassioned opposition from some editors and citizens, once committed to greater realism the government never reverted to its "see no evil" policy. In early November *Newsweek* noted "the recent increase in the number of photographs of American wounded and dead" and such pictures were soon commonplace.[50]

Out of concern for family and friends and for the overall impact on home-front morale, photos during the war's last two years were never completely honest. Shots of wounded men, like the one of the wounded Marine published in May and the amputation scene in September, invariably showed them getting help—being assisted or carried to the rear by fellow soldiers, tended by battlefield medics, or surrounded by white-garbed doctors and nurses. The implication was that prompt medical attention was always available for wounded Americans. And the wounds shown were usually neat and clean. Photos did not depict gross mutilations or show the wounded lying between the lines, untended, thrashing in agony, bleeding to death, or slowly dying of dehydration. As with wounds, so with death: photos did not tell the whole truth. They avoided acute nastiness (no indistinguishable lumps of smoldering flesh or scattered and shattered bodies), were often artistically composed, and rarely showed the faces of dead men. While understandable, these restraints tended to depersonalize death.[51]

By late 1943 the new policy was evident not just in still photos but also in the newsreels and documentaries. "Grim realism will stalk the screens," the *Motion Picture Herald* announced in its preview of *The Price of Rendova*, which told the story of that Pacific island battle "with no punches pulled." By mating motion and sound to pictures, newsreels and documentaries made combat seem much more realistic than the best still photographs could. A still picture is static but a motion-picture, like life itself, moves. Bob Lewis of the 163rd SPC understood still photography's limitations in portraying action. "All cameramen know the disappointment and let-down," he wrote, "in viewing a shot made at the time all hell may have been letting loose—since bullets don't photograph, and shells aren't visible, and the noise of battle is missing—the rain, the dust or the mud—all this has been reduced to one dimension" that affects only the viewer's visual sense. He implored his still men "to inject MORE ACTION!" into their shots but knew that conveying "to anyone who wasn't there, the impression of actually being on the spot" was an extraordinary challenge for someone with a Speed Graphic.[52]

Research revealed that although movies were "not fully 'real' they approximate reality more nearly than do ordinary photographs and pictures or verbal descriptions. By moving, they become animated, i.e., alive.... the tendency to adopt the attitude of reality is much more striking in motion-pictures than in any other form of pictorial or photographic representation." By maneuvering the camera in appropriate ways a viewer "can be made to identify himself with an active participant in the situation and to do what he does, firing at an enemy fighter or even fighting in hand-to-hand combat." The experience was still vicarious but it *seemed* real, creating the empathic bonding between the home and fighting fronts that Roosevelt was so anxious to achieve.[53]

As the war continued the home front received an increasingly graphic portrayal of what fighting entailed, despite the limitations on complete disclosure. Critics of wartime censorship have berated the home front's sanitized, innocent war but perhaps the emphasis should be on the realism rather than the restrictions.[54] With immediacy and force, particularly in the movie theaters and on movie screens set up at home, civilians witnessed at least some of battle's horrors while a narrator stressed that casualties had been high, gave relatively accurate casualty figures, and said as a matter of fact rather than as a prediction that "before it's over there'll be more dead on other battlefields."[55] Although the influence of a single movie or newsreel would have been limited, the constant repetition of casualty scenes accompanied by a sobering narration meant that people on the home front, no matter how far removed from the actual carnage, could not pretend to themselves that winning the war would be painless.[56]

VI

When the Italian campaign began in September 1943 the Signal Corps was under intense pressure to acquire realistic battlefield coverage. A radio message from the War Department to Colonel Melvin E. Gillette, the highest-ranking Signal Corps photographic officer in the North African Theater of Operations, expressed the president's dissatisfaction with the prevailing still and motion picture coverage of combat operations. "Production of first-rate pictures of this type is essential to give the American people a visual accounting of the accomplishments of our soldiers overseas." The president wanted combat action "filmed as it happens" so that "the dangers and grimness of war" could be conveyed to the home front. Photographic personnel *must* accompany the front line troops; only fill-in and background shots could "be made either after or before an operation." If Gillette needed additional personnel or equipment to carry out his mission he should send a radio request. After carefully analyzing the message, Gillette concluded that its emphasis was primarily on motion-picture coverage for the newsreels and feature-type films for public consumption, especially one that "should be completed for release almost coincident with the close of any significant phase of the [Italian] campaign."[57]

Gillette hoped to alleviate Roosevelt's dissatisfaction by providing superb coverage of the Italian campaign, but he confronted severe personnel and equipment shortages. The lack of experienced motion-picture cameramen and film directors was acute. Although part of the 163rd SPC had arrived in the theater, none of its officers had professional motion-picture experience and most "had received only a few weeks' hurried training in Eyemo camera operations." The situation was no better with the enlisted men. As for equipment, fewer than twenty motion-picture cameras were available for covering the invasion of Italy; since the 163rd's equipment had not yet arrived no immediate improvement was in sight. Additionally, the Signal Corps barely had enough film for the few cameras it had. Even if more men, cameras, and film magically materialized, the only ground transportation consisted of weapons carriers and two-and-a-half-ton trucks that were too large for frontline use.

Undaunted, Gillette radioed for fourteen qualified motion-picture cameramen, more cameras, and a supply of 35mm film. And he asked that "two qualified directors and two recognized motion-picture writers" be dispatched immediately by air transportation. The War Department responded that directors Major Herbert A. T. Freeland and Major George Stevens and writers Major Linden Rigby and Captain Charles Grayson would be sent by air and the other men and equipment by slower water transportation. For unknown reasons Gillette requested a substitute for Stevens; in late September he learned that Captain John Huston would be sent as a replacement.

With qualified directors and writers en route and competent cameramen and ample equipment following in their wake, Gillette hurried to Fifth Army Headquarters in Italy to supervise the full-fledged photographic effort he had organized. Getting more cameramen into the front lines would improve "the chances of obtaining transitory material of a spectacular nature," which would be essential for a feature-length campaign film. Since the Italian operation was an Anglo-American venture, Gillette also arranged with the British for the film's joint production.

When Freeland, Rigby, and Grayson arrived at Fifth Army Headquarters on October 11, 1943, Gillette sent Freeland and Rigby to the front with six-man or seven-man teams, equipped with studio-model Mitchell or Wall cameras, and riding in weapons carriers.

Grayson stayed behind to coordinate incoming film and do creative planning for the campaign film. Complaints soon arose that the two big field units riding in large vehicles and carrying huge cameras mounted on tall, heavy tripods "invited enemy artillery fire on our troops and installations, and interfered with essential forward area traffic." Having no Eyemos available to re-equip these teams, Gillette temporarily diverted them to other duties. Since the campaign's earliest operations had not been adequately covered he sent the teams back to the areas already captured to make connecting material; he also put them to work photographing prisoner-of-war camps, chaplains' activities, and other human-interest material. Importantly, just before the battle for San Pietro began Freeland's team returned to the front.

Meanwhile the 163rd SPC moved into the Fifth Army sector in mid-November. Gillette had visited the unit in late September relaying the president's message regarding better combat coverage and telling the cameramen that "we are expected to produce in order to justify our existence."[58] Now he scrounged for jeeps, violated the unit's Table of Organization and Equipment(T/O&E) by forming three-man teams, and filtered them into the front. The additional fourteen officers and men Gillette requested did not reach Italy until mid-December. Although they immediately became part of the 163rd they required a two-week training course in such things as camouflage, scouting, map reading, basic tactics, and field sanitation before they joined their colleagues at the front in January 1944.

A week before the 163rd began deploying into the forward areas, Huston reported to Gillette. Accompaning him were Captain Eric Ambler, who was a famous British mystery writer, and Lieutenant Jules Buck, who had worked with Huston on *Report From the Aleutians*, a documentary filmed during the fall and winter of 1942 about the campaign to oust the Japanese from the Aleutian Islands.

San Pietro was not the film Huston intended to make. On the way to Italy he stopped in Washington, London, and North Africa and consulted with representatives of the Army's Public Relations Office, the Office of War Information, the Psychological Warfare Branch, and the British Ministry of Information. Collectively they decided Huston should produce a propaganda film for liberated areas entitled *Welcome to Italy*, which emphasized the difference between Allied and Axis ideals and behavior and "would be an excellent complement to the combat film now in production." Huston informed Gillette that he would make "a separate film for propaganda use, completely apart from film on the Italian campaign," demanded that the best equipment and personnel be placed at his disposal, and requested that his exposed film be reserved for his exclusive use—that is, kept out of the Signal Corps film pool.

The colonel had a rude surprise for him. As far as Gillette knew, Huston was there as a result of his request for two directors to assist in covering combat operations. He would *not* divert personnel and equipment for Huston's proposed project without specific War Department authorization, which had not arrived, or treat his film any differently from any other Signal Corps film. While Gillette awaited clarification of Huston's status he told the director "that whatever he did here must be material that would fit into a general story of the campaign." But Gillette was not unreasonable. He arranged for Huston to work with the Counter Intelligence Corps as it entered a newly occupied town, an assignment that meshed with either an overall campaign film or a liberation/propaganda movie if authorization for it came. And he assigned Huston five men from the 163rd: Wilbur Bradley, Philip Falcone, Leonard Ryan, Sam Tischler, and Gordon Frye. Because of poor health Bradley did not film any of the San Pietro battle. Later two other members of the 163rd, Roland K. Meade and Abraham Morochnik, also worked with Huston.[59]

The partnership between Huston and the 163rd was uneasy. Combat cameramen resented the temporary-duty status of Hollywood types like Huston and Buck, who whizzed into the war zone for a few months and then returned to clean sheets and soft pillows. Huston gave company headquarters nothing but headaches by disrupting normal operations with demands for scarce manpower and equipment. He also endangered the lives of his crew since he, Buck, and Ambler had only minimal military training and took unnecessary risks. In at least one instance some cameramen refused to follow Huston in what their training and experience told them was a foolhardy venture.[60]

A War Department message dated November 17, 1943, clarified Huston's status. The Army had gone to a great deal of trouble to get Huston to Italy to obtain "actual combat coverage," could not understand why anybody presumed he would do something else, and wanted him in the combat area to perform "the mission to which he was originally assigned." When the battle for San Pietro began Huston's team was on the front lines.

VII

The combat scenes in *San Pietro* do not show real war. As with all documentaries, it omitted battle's most gruesome aspects; and in an actual engagement no narrator explains and clarifies events. Huston added the sound effects in the editing room, and aside from being conveniently loud or soft as the narration required the sound track does not include any pained screams from the frightened, wounded, and dying. The music is artificial—the Army Air Force Orchestra, the Mormon Tabernacle Choir, and the St. Brendan's Boys Choir are not ordinarily heard on battlefields. Watching a video of *San Pietro* with the sound turned off is a supremely dull experience.

Huston also did some clever editing by manipulating scenes at the editing table. *San Pietro* contains an extraordinary number of left-handed riflemen and grenade throwers. In real life these men were right handed, but to achieve certain effects Huston turned the film over, converting the soldiers into southpaws. He also used some scenes twice, but in at least two cases they look different because he again flipped the film. In one instance a right-handed rifleman leaps into a foxhole, coming from the right of the screen; when flopped the same scene shows a left-handed rifleman jumping in from the left. In another example, a grenade explodes on the right of the screen and the camera pans that way to catch the puff of black smoke; later the grenade explodes on the left and the camera pans leftward. A close-up of a white phosphorus shell exploding appears twice—or perhaps Huston had two cameras side by side recording the staged explosion. Some of the editing was also shoddy. A medium shot shows four soldiers carrying a wounded man on a stretcher. The next scene, supposedly a close-up of the same action, has a different background and three soldiers and a civilian toting a stretcher.

Whether stills or motion-pictures, all photography is only an illusion of reality. A famous documentary filmmaker called film the "creative treatment of reality," but perhaps Oliver Wendell Holmes best defined photography as an illusion with the "appearance of reality that cheats the senses with its seeming truth."[61] Although the fundamental nature of photography has been the subject of much philosophical speculation, most commentators agree that a photograph is merely an artifact or token, a piece of special paper, "a material product of a material apparatus" created by complex mechanical, optical, and chemical processes.[62] Cameras do not record all that the eye perceives but only what the cameraman sees through the viewfinder. Humans have peripheral vision, cameras do not. An elephant herd could be standing one millimeter outside a camera's tunnel-like field of vision and no one would know it. Human-eye movement is extremely rapid and the eyes constantly dart hither and yon, yet a person's vision does not blur. But the human "process of scanning or looking around has no real counterpart on the screen."[63] A camera must move slowly or a scene becomes fuzzy and disorienting.

Most fundamentally *San Pietro* does not accurately depict the battle that occurred in December 1943 because Huston stage-directed most of the action later, in January and February of 1944.

Although the film contains some footage shot under real combat conditions, just watching it provides minor hints that *San Pietro* is not completely authentic. In a few instances different scenes in the same sequence contain wide variations in light from bright sun to heavy overcast. Usually the camera shakes after a nearby artillery explosion but occasionally it remains rock steady. The battle occurred in winter but some soldiers wear summer uniforms. Even the winter uniforms are suspicious: they are much too clean for troops engaged in ferocious combat. So are the soldiers. Revealingly, after the battle the 36th Division went into a rest area near the village of Alife where the men set up tents, took showers, went through a delousing process, and received clean uniforms.[64]

What about Huston, whom one biographer labeled the "Maker of Magic"? He probably knew that parts of *Desert Victory*, the acclaimed British documentary about North Africa, had been restaged. And he had reenacted combat scenes before he went to Italy. About the time Huston returned from the Aleutians, Roosevelt asked to see Signal Corps footage of the North African invasion. Unfortunately only one small team photographed the invasion, and all its film had been lost when the Germans sank the ship carrying it. To avoid admitting that no footage existed, the Signal Corps ordered Huston and Colonel Frank Capra to manufacture some footage and do it quickly. One of Hollywood's premier prewar directors, Capra headed the 834th Signal Photographic Detachment based in Hollywood and was then working on the famous *Why We Fight* propaganda-film series to solidify support for the war. Huston and Capra staged scenes in the Mojave Desert and Florida but the "material was so transparently false" that Huston was somewhat embarrassed. By the time they finished the president had apparently forgotten about his request, but someone (exactly who is unclear) suggested combining British and American film on North Africa to produce a documentary. Since the British had excellent footage (some of it reenacted), the poorly done Huston-Capra fabricated scenes did not appear in the resulting documentary, entitled *Tunisian Victory*. From this affair Huston knew that the Signal Corps sanctioned reenactments under certain conditions, but that any faked combat must be carefully crafted or it would look counterfeit.[65]

More compelling than either the film's minor hints or Huston's previous experience is testimony from some of the participants. In his autobiography Eric Ambler claimed that during the battle "San Pietro was reluctant to yield footage of any kind," that Huston "was reluctant to pull out empty-handed," and that most of *San Pietro* was reenacted footage "of a fairly impressionistic kind."[66]

By itself Ambler's testimony would be suspect. He considered Huston pretentious and did not particularly like him; moreover, he also left Italy before most of the reenactments occurred.[67]

But more persuasive than Ambler's account is the testimony of Gordon Frye and Sam Tischler. Frye worked with Huston's team until being wounded at company headquarters in late January; Tischler was with Huston until the latter left Italy and "shot about 19,500 feet reenacted and whatever." One of Tischler's favorite sayings was that "the best combat pictures were made in Hollywood," and at one point after watching Huston's team stage a sequence the GI-beloved journalist Ernie Pyle smiled and said, "Well, here we have Hollywood up in the mountains of Italy." Frye and Tischler attest that Huston staged all the action in the olive groves and on Mount Sammucro, all the scenes of soldiers throwing grenades, and all the white phosphorus shell explosions. When the camera supposedly quakes from artillery fire, "that was our astute, experienced, and ever-present Hollywood director John Huston 'bumping' the magazine of our 400-foot Bell & Howells [Eyemos]." One of the film's most dramatically composed scenes was a low-angle shot with a dead German in a foxhole in the foreground and American soldiers advancing in the background; the "dead" soldier was a live GI attired in a German uniform.[68]

Tischler kept a wartime record of the film he shot that precisely dates the restaging in January and February 1944 and proves that the 36th Division's 143rd Regiment provided the actors. Between January 4 and 15 Huston's team worked for nine days with squads from the 143rd sent from Alife, where the division was refitting and getting clean uniforms after the battle for San Pietro. The team also spent one day filming antiaircraft artillery and another shooting tanks. From mid-January until mid-February, when the 36th Division was fighting along the Rapido River and near Cassino, Huston's team worked in San Pietro and the nearby valley, at an Infantry Replacement Depot in Caiazzo, and with litter cases at the 111th Field Hospital, where Huston even staged some casualty scenes. From February 12 to 15 the cameras again photographed soldiers from the 143rd, with the reenactments on Mount Sammucro occurring on the 12th and 13th. Shortly thereafter, Huston left Italy.[69]

Others in the 163rd not directly involved with Huston either knew about the restaging or guessed it. "My viewing of Huston's production almost automatically told me that not every scene was shot in actual combat," wrote Ned Morehouse, the 163rd's commanding officer at the time. "You just can't photograph some of those scenes in actual combat and live to get the film back to the lab. As a matter of fact, you wouldn't live to even photograph them."[70] Further confirmation came from Captain Joel Westbrook, who facilitated Huston's reenactments by, for example, making sure that the soldiers tossed concussion grenades rather than the more dangerous fragmentation grenades.[71]

Even some of the scenes of the liberation and rebirth of San Pietro did not occur in that village, since many events included in the film's last third transpired before or after the battle or in other locations. Tischler filmed villagers receiving food in Prada-Sannita in early December and children in San Pietro on February 16. In July 1944 Frye made "a few last shots" that Huston requested after he began editing the film. The scene of a dead woman being dug out of the rubble after a German booby trap supposedly exploded was actually taken at Caiazzo after *American* planes accidentally bombed it, wounding Frye and killing many civilians.[72]

Reinforcing the participants' testimony are *San Pietro*'s camera outtakes. Located in Record Group 111 in the Motion Picture Branch of the National Archives, these are the unused portions of the film shot for a production. The card index contains forty-six cards, each corresponding to a reel of 35mm black-and-white film from Huston's team; nine are either undated or contain ambiguous dates, four are dated during the battle, and thirty-three are dated *after* the battle. Twenty-eight cards specifically indicate that the film was completely or partially reenacted. For example, the card for reel ADC 546 says "Partly reenacted," for ADC 562 "Reenacted in part," for ADC 575 "Majority of this footage is reenacted," and for ADC 584 "All footage is reenacted."[73]

The Signal Corps practice of explicitly identifying staged footage was not perfect and some reels that do not indicate reenactment obviously are. Since the card for reel ADC 587 does not indicate any reenactment and is dated "Dec 1943," it theoretically could be genuine combat footage. But the reel contains multiple retakes of scenes supposedly shot during combat and other clear indications of staging. Four takes show a "direct hit" on a tracked vehicle, the "hits" being set charges. Two left-to-right pans show five "dead" GIs—but in the first take one of the "dead" men moves before assuming a "dead" position. In an "assault" on a stone house a soldier steps out of a doorway, looks directly at the camera, and points to himself as if to say "Me?" Many virtually identical scenes show patrols cautiously probing through the rubble of San Pietro. In one of them the camera caught two soldiers at ease, one smoking a cigarette; then somebody yelled "Action!" and the men suddenly looked "on the alert" and moved warily forward.

Even without knowledge about Huston, the participants' testimony, and the camera outtakes, a memo from Major Freeland proved, albeit indirectly, that Huston staged *San Pietro*. Dated just days after Huston allegedly filmed the battle, the memo explained why obtaining genuine combat footage in Italy's mountains was impossible.[74] The teams headed by Freeland and Rigby took Roosevelt's injunction to photograph war's grim dangers literally. Their units, "augmented by the arrival of Captain Huston, have been busy in the field—particularly at or near the front—securing a very wide range of material for a story of the Italian campaign, as well as material which we deemed suitable for newsreel consumption and for War Department record and usage." They had been striving to obtain combat material "often at the risk of life and limb, even to the point of drawing enemy fire upon ourselves and the troops around us" and had "even gone ahead of the infantry in our desire to secure something that could be photographed with telling and dramatic effect."

The teams acquired "plenty of footage showing dead and wounded, both our men and the enemy; of burials; of surgical operations and first aid in the field and at evacuation and field hospitals; of the devastation of towns and villages; of uprooted humanity fleeing the battle; of pathetic refugees along roads or digging in the ruins of their former homes." Getting film of blasted and sabotaged railways, roads, bridges, farms, utilities, industries, docks, and warehouses was easy. Also plentiful was "human interest" material that would "lend necessary warmth, vitality, and humor" to a film by showing "how the ordinary soldier lives, works, rests and relaxes, fights, suffers" and "the various national and racial types of the men under arms in this theater." But Freeland asked—rhetorically, since he knew the answer was "No"—whether such scenes were "adequate for consumption by a public that has been educated to expect and demand excitement of the 'studio war' variety?"

What the cameramen could not get were "actual combat scenes of an exciting nature" that would be "necessary in creating a telling picture." Even under direct enemy fire "we were unable to see, let alone photograph anything that is usually accepted as combat material." They had recently "spent three days with cameras set up behind rocks on the slope of Mount Lungo" overlooking San Pietro and San Vittore with the battle lines less than half a mile away, yet all they recorded were American shells landing in San Vittore and German shells in San Pietro. As Freeland admitted, "mere striving for combat material is not enough." Actual combat was invisible. They could never see the "perverse and unaccommodating" enemy soldiers who held the high ground, firing on anything that moved below them. Since camera crews acted like magnets in attracting enemy metal, they could rarely see Americans either; GIs developed an "allergy" to cameramen and did not want them anywhere in the vicinity. Both sides relied on high-explosive artillery shells rather than the more photogenic white phosphorus projectiles, and anyway most infantry attacks occurred in darkness or fog when photography was impossible.

Frye, Tischler, and the other members of Huston's team were at the battle for San Pietro, repeatedly risking their lives as they strove to film genuine combat. But Freeland's memo was correct: under the combat conditions prevailing in Italy, striving, no matter how heroically, was not enough. Only reenactments could provide dramatic scenes that would impress home-front audiences versed in Hollywood-style war. In any event, San Pietro achieved "the stamp of authenticity," not authenticity.

VIII

San Pietro was far different from the film Huston envisioned when he went to Italy, and the publicly released version was not the film Huston originally edited. Accompanied only by Benjamin Hibbs, editor of the Saturday Evening Post, General Marshall viewed the original version, which was fifty minutes long. The General feared it "might be too heavy a picture to be shown to the American public" and that the movie was too long. But Hibbs argued that the film "was just what was needed to awaken the American people, and that this reason out-weighed other considerations." Persuaded by the force of Hibbs' argument, the Army Chief of Staff agreed that the picture should be made public, but only after being shortened.[75]

Responding to Marshall's concern regarding the film's length, the Signal Corps demanded that Huston, assisted by Capra, cut the initial production by approximately twenty minutes. They had to eliminate all shots showing mangled bodies and recognizable American dead (in accordance with the "restricted realism" policy), repetitious shots of artillery barrages and GIs throwing hand grenades, and some liberation footage, because scenes of Italian children conveyed little information to the home front about the American soldiers' combat ordeal. Capra also suggested that Fifth Army commander General Mark Clark give a short introductory speech, which was added to the movie long after the rest of it had been completed.[76]

San Pietro was an aberration. Although other Hollywood directors serving in uniform incorporated some show-business techniques into their documentaries only John Ford's *December 7th*, depicting the Japanese assault on Pearl Harbor, used massive restaging. Since few cameras recorded the surprise attack he had no choice but to resort to model ships and actors.[77] But Ford's *Midway*, about that epic June 1942 battle, contained much genuine footage and William Wyler, winner of multiple academy awards, made *The Memphis Belle* and *Thunderbolt* primarily from genuine air-war footage. The armed forces also produced legitimate and stunning documentaries without the assistance of famous Hollywood personnel, such as *Attack! The Battle for New Britain*, *With the Marines at Tarawa*, *The Battle for the Marianas*, *To the Shores of Iwo Jima*, *Fury in the Pacific*, *The Fleet that Came to Stay*, and *The True Glory*.

Superimposed on *San Pietro's* last scene is a statement saying that "All scenes in this picture were photographed within range of enemy small arms or artillery fire. For purposes of continuity a few of these scenes were shot before and after the actual battle of San Pietro." At best this is disingenuous, at worst a blatant falsehood. When Huston staged the fighting the battle line was ten miles or more to the north, and his team filmed more than "a few" scenes after the battle.

In extenuation and mitigation, the rugged terrain made the Italian campaign quite extraordinarily difficult to photograph with dramatic effect. Although it utilized a small amount of Huston's staged footage, Gillette's campaign film, *The Liberation of Rome* was more genuine than *San Pietro* but also much duller. It covered the nine months from the invasion of Italy until Rome's liberation in June 1944. Ironically, it did not even mention San Pietro as it skipped directly from the fighting along the Volturno River in mid-October 1943 to the struggle along the Rapido River and at Cassino in January and February 1944. Compared to the fighting in Italy, ground combat in other theaters, and sea and air warfare in general, were easier to photograph, giving cameramen at least an occasional opportunity to record a few breathtaking scenes that pumped excitement into the best genuine documentaries.

A few men in the 163rd SPC gloried in rubbing elbows with a famous Hollywood director, but many felt aggrieved when Huston's team staged fantastic scenes while they abided by Signal Corps injunctions against reenacting events and turned in comparatively unexciting footage.[78] Some were angry when *San Pietro* finally played in the theaters and Huston got all the credit; he never shared the praise with Frye, Tischler, and the others from the 163rd who were by his side during combat, did the superb camerawork on his staged scenes, and remained in harm's way in Italy after he left. Still, they had reason for profound self-satisfaction. As Frye wrote to his wife on the last day of 1943, "if the pictures we make help the effort back home by showing how tough a job the boys have in this war, well then I guess I've done my job well."[79]

4

"We Shoot 'em with a Camera—Only"

The Army's 163rd Signal Photographic Company

Had Gordon Frye been more prescient he undoubtedly would not have gotten married in mid-June 1943.

He was still expecting to stay in the States for the duration; after all, he had remained Stateside since he joined the 103rd Field Artillery of the Rhode Island National Guard in November 1940, and all indications were that he would remain at the Signal Corps Photographic Center (SCPC) in Astoria, New York, until Germany and Japan capitulated. Even though Frye was twenty-six and going prematurely bald when he entered the Army, he was simply a "big kid" in his optimism and naiveté about his fellow human beings. Although he had grown up on the wrong side of the tracks in Newport, Rhode Island, he was an ambitious lad, intent on making at least a million dollars so that he could live like the aristocrats who dwelled along Newport's spectacular Cliff Walk. At age eight he began working as a caddy for the wealthy. But Frye soon demonstrated an artistic bent, which might make him happy but would never make him rich. While attending Rogers High School he edited the school's yearbook; and as a graphic arts major at the Rhode Island School of Design in Providence, from which he graduated in 1939, he worked part-time for the head of Brown University's

art department, learning a great deal about still pictures and the preparation of slides. Employment with the Chrome Art Motion Picture
Company taught him how to shoot 16mm motion pictures.[1]

The National Guard's train trip from Rhode Island to Camp
Blanding, Florida, began the process of hammering "man-soldiers out
of boys." Once there, the before-dawn roll calls, vigorous physical con-
ditioning, discipline, and "eternal inspections—inspections, inspections, inspections" hastened the transformation. But all was not
exertion and tedium. In the spring of 1941 Frye became a photograph-
er-reporter for the *Grapeleaf*, the newspaper for the 43rd Division.
With a jeep and driver at his beck and call and a front-row seat on all
the division's activities, Frye found that military service could be fun.

A year later Frye departed the 43rd, then stationed at Camp Shelby,
Mississippi, to attend Officer Candidate School (OCS) with a specialty in engineering. But he had also been trying to get a job with *Yank*,
which was still in the planning stage. His brother Arnold had friends in
the advertising business in New York and they knew the men who were
setting up the GI magazine. After just a few weeks at OCS opportunity
knocked, and to the utter astonishment of the OIC at OCS Frye
resigned, turning his back on the possibility of becoming an officer
(and a gentleman) to return to the enlisted ranks![2] But though Frye
had walked through opportunity's door, the new enterprise had "considerable labor pains." Becoming disenchanted, he entered a new doorway at the Signal Corps Photographic Center (SCPC), where Army
Pictorial Services (APS) trained cameramen and produced training
films.

While at SCPC he and six other men formed a special newsreel
unit. As part of their training the men went to the Fox-Movietone
newsreel company to watch a newsreel being put together and shot a
story in 16mm Kodachrome (color) on the launching of two cargo ves-
sels. By December 1942 the unit had become a close-knit group that
looked forward to working together. Instead, SCPC disbanded the unit
in the aftermath of Zanuck's experience in North Africa with 16mm
color film, which had proved less than successful and had poisoned the
War Department's attitude toward 16mm color. Two of the men, Frye
and Willis "Bill" Winfred, formed a mini-team that continued working
at SCPC, shooting scenes for training films and for the *Army-Navy
Screen Magazine*, a job that SCPC promised them they could have for
the rest of the war.

So Gordon Frye married Oleta. Then the SCPC sent him and

Winfred to North Africa on a brief "special" assignment, to shoot footage to insert into a training film based on the American combat experience in North Africa, especially at Kasserine Pass. Two and a half years later, by way of Casablanca, Oran, Algiers, Salerno, Naples, San Pietro, Cassino, Anzio, Rome, Corsica, St.-Maxime, Grenoble, Lyon, Luxieul-Les-Bains, Epinal, and many places in Germany, Frye saw Oleta again.

Sometimes a SNAFU (Situation Normal: All Fucked Up) is so bad that it becomes a FUBAR (Fucked Up Beyond All Recognition), and for Frye this was certainly a FUBAR situation. He was quite unhappy to be in North Africa in the first place and now things were getting worse. The trip across the Atlantic had been fine—playing cards, spreading rumors, singing, publishing the *Bilge Water News*, and listening to an inspirational message from the President about defending "freedom under God." And the traveling in northern Africa had been delightful. "In fact, if it were not for seeing uniforms of all nations, and talking with men who fought in the Tunisia and Sicily campaigns," Frye wrote, "I would feel as if I was just on a tour of North Africa. So far so good—here's hoping my luck continues."

But Frye's luck did not continue. After disembarking at Casablanca he and Winfred traveled to Algiers. There they met with Colonel Melvin E. Gillette, the head of Army photographic operations in North Africa, who had some unexpected and unwanted news. The 163rd SPC had recently deployed to North Africa without all its motion-picture equipment. Frye and Winfred would have to help fill the gaps in the upcoming invasion of Italy in September 1943. Gillette assigned Winfred to work with the paratroopers while Frye went to a small photo unit led by Lieutenant Wilbur Bradley, formerly a longtime Hollywood cameraman. Bradley's team went ashore at Salerno more than a week after the invasion, arriving just in time to endure a ferocious German counterattack that nearly destroyed the beachhead.

Contrary to all his expectations of just a few months earlier, Frye was now "touring" Italy with the Fifth Army. After several months of roaming, "living more or less the 'outdoor' life of the soldier," Bradley's unit finally found an official home in early December. "We are now full-fledged members, in good standing I hope," Frye informed Oleta, "of the newly arrived 163rd Signal Photographic Company."

I

Mention amphibious assaults and people generally think of the United States Marine Corps's island-hopping campaign in the Pacific, but some Army personnel made more amphibious assaults in the Mediterranean and European Theaters than did most Marines.

Before the war was over the 163rd SPC compiled an illustrious record by, among other things, engaging in five amphibious assaults—Casablanca (November 1942), Sicily (July 1943), Salerno (September 1943), Anzio (January 1944), and Toulon (August 1944)—as it photographed its way from North Africa to Sicily and Italy, where it participated in the torturous fighting up the boot, and then northwest to the French Riviera, through France, into Germany, and on to Austria.[3] Some "lucky" members of the 163rd, such as Fred Bonnard, participated in all five D-Days (every invasion, not just the one in Normandy in June 1944, had a D-Day). He went ashore at the base of the old fort at Port Lyautey, French Morocco, and at Gela Beach in Sicily, crossed the Straits of Messina with a British unit to the tip of the Italian toe, was at Anzio, and landed with the French near St.-Tropez on the Riviera. After twenty-six months in the combat zone he returned to the States in December 1944, while the rest of the 163rd stayed on to finish off the Nazis.[4]

The 163rd SPC was one of eleven such companies mentioned in the records—the 161st through the 168th, the 195th, 196th, and 198th. Initial planning called for one company to be an organic part of each field army, but as the war progressed not every army received a SPC because too few skilled cameramen and lab technicians were available to form that many companies.[5] As the United States edged closer to war in 1940–41, the War Department activated the 1st Signal Company, Photographic, at Fort Benning, Georgia, in February 1941. Five months later the Army redesignated the 1st Signal Company as the 161st SPC, and by August the 162nd had also been activated. By Pearl Harbor both were ready for overseas assignment. However, neither deployed as an entire company. For more than a year the 161st and 162nd served as a "training ground, a school of military photography" from which officials drew small detachments to accompany divisions heading overseas or to became cadres for new SPCs being formed in the States. Detachments from the 161st went to Ireland, Iceland, Hawaii, Australia, and Chungking (now spelled Chongqing), while those from the 162nd scattered from London, Newfoundland, and

Algiers to Puerto Rico, Panama, and Trinidad, and to New Caledonia in the Southwest Pacific.[6]

On April 9, 1942 Special Orders No. 87 at Fort Benning designated First Lieutenant Ned R. Morehouse and twenty enlisted men from the 161st as the cadre for the 163rd SPC, which soon moved to Fort Sam Houston in San Antonio where it received a steady influx of additional men. While at Fort Sam Houston the men shot pictures "of everything that would hold still" and "a lot of film was going thru the camera, into the lab and out to the trash file." Detachments also trained with troops in the field. Four officers and thirty-two enlisted men, for example, served with the Third Army during the Louisiana Maneuvers in the summer of 1942 and another detachment went to Fort Huachua, Arizona.[7]

Two vital War Department documents affected the 163rd and all the other SPCs, one providing their Table of Organization and Equipment (T/O&E) and the other their Standing Operating Procedure (SOP). The relevant T/O&E was No. 11-37, which went through several modifications during the war with the February 12, 1944 edition being illustrative. It set the authorized strength for an SPC at one captain, sixteen lieutenants, one warrant officer, and 135 enlisted men, for a total of 153, only about half of whom were photographers; the rest were clerks, cooks, mechanics, and camera repairmen.[8] SPCs were often below authorized strength; by the fall of 1944 the 161st SPC was five officers and twenty enlisted men under strength, the 164th lacked an officer and seven enlisted men, the 167th had all its officers but was short five enlisted men, and the 163rd was missing two officers and ten enlisted men.[9]

Under T/O&E No. 11-37 the officers and men formed three platoons (or sections). A Headquarters Platoon handled all matters pertaining to administration, supply, camera repair, vehicle maintenance, and the mess. Processing still photographs was the responsibility of a Laboratory Platoon. Subdivided into two Identification Units, two Newsreel Assignment Units, and twelve Combat Assignment Units, an Assignment Platoon did the actual photographic work.

Three problems arising from the T/O&E bedeviled the SPCs. One was that "the allocations of the grades and rating is the reverse of what should be provided. Men performing combat-area photography should be given at least a grade higher than any photographer performing rear-area work." But the T/O&E rewarded safety more highly than danger. Second, the officers' ranks were arbitrarily low. Considering "the importance placed upon photographic work coming from the combat areas, especially, and of the work done by laboratory superintendents," an SPC should have had a major and four captains, not just a single captain.[10]

The third difficulty was that an SPC's organization was too inflexible and impractical. The T/O&E did not provide for a liaison officer between an army headquarters and its corps headquarters, making it hard to administer the photo teams attached to divisions. With their bulky sound cameras, Newsreel Assignment Units were totally unsuited for combat work. Each of the twelve Combat Assignment Units consisted of one officer directing six men, usually two still photographers, two motion picture cameramen, and two drivers, toting all their equipment in a jeep and a weapons carrier. As the number of divisions in the combat zones increased, a dozen units per SPC could not adequately cover them all. Moreover, a Combat Assignment Unit was so large that cameramen invariably turned in duplicate coverage, with several cameras recording the same event. And the units were visible and lucrative targets that almost automatically drew enemy fire near the front, which made the job more dangerous than it already was— and alienated any nearby American soldiers who were the unintended recipients of the hostile fire.[11]

To perform their mission effectively SPCs were obliged to violate their T/O&E, with the 163rd paving the way. It developed Corps Photo Liaison Officers to serve as an intermediate administrative level between an army headquarters and its divisions, used the Newsreel Units only for rear area work, and most important, evolved smaller front line units. Through trial and (costly) error in North Africa, Sicily, and the beginning of the Italian campaign the 163rd discovered that a three-man unit was ideal: a still photographer, a motion-picture cameraman, and a driver, all fitting snugly into one jeep. Under this *ad hoc* system many of the company's lieutenants ceased being the executives that the War Department intended and became working photographers. Late in the war, when photographic coverage was spread ever thinner across ever-wider fighting fronts, the 163rd even resorted to a few two-man teams, converting some of the drivers into photographers, and then having one of the photographers doubling as the driver. Instead of a dozen teams the 163rd could now deploy at least twice that many, and a lone jeep with two or three soldiers usually seemed so innocuous that the Germans did not even bother to fire at it.[12]

In February 1945 the 163rd's third commander, Robert Lewis, consolidated these new arrangements in a document entitled "A Standing Operating Procedure for Combat Assignment Teams (SOPCAT)," which outlined a revised chain of command running through a Corps Photo Liaison Officer, who supervised a number of photo teams working down at the division level. Instead of the Combat Assignment Units specified in T/O&E 11-37, the 163rd used a Combat Assignment Team (CAT) composed of three men and a jeep. The driver would get the photographers to and from their assigned missions, perform minor maintenance on the jeep, and guard the vehicle and equipment while the cameramen were at the front. Each team was to "Maintain a mobile state at all times, prepared to meet any demands put on the team for Photo Coverage."[13]

In practice the 163rd eventually fielded CATs #1 through #24. A CAT was "the smallest integral part of the company, and the principal operating unit. All other operations of the company revolved around the CATs." The 163rd's commanding officer would select a CAT from among a pool of photographers and drivers at Headquarters and dispatch it to a Corps Photo Liaison Officer, who then assigned it to a specific division or, in some cases, to a specified area such as a town that Allied forces were attacking or a river they were crossing. After procuring pictures of the unit or area the CAT delivered its exposed film to the Corps Photo Liaison Officer, who in turn insured its delivery to the Lab.[14]

Since the 163rd was the first SPC with substantial combat experience, it was the first to understand the necessity for more flexible arrangements than those embodied in the T/O&E. But all the SPCs came to essentially the same conclusion, developing local variants and terminology. In China the 164th, for instance, used various-sized "Detachments" and identified them with letters. In late December 1944 Detachment A was in Ledo with two officers and fourteen enlisted men, Detachment B was in Kunming with four officers and forty-three enlisted men, Detachment G was in Chungking with just three enlisted men, and so on. These detachments divided into smaller subunits for specific assignments.[15]

The hard-learned emphasis on flexibility found implicit expression in the second important War Department document, Pamphlet No. 11-2, *Signal Photography: Standing Operating Procedure for Signal Photographic Units in Theaters of Operations*, published on April 20, 1944. The pamphlet began by discussing the "Function of Photographic Units," stressing that "combat photography is the first duty of all units," and described the "Responsibility for Signal Photographic Activities," emphasizing the need for close contacts between photographers and staff officers to insure combat coverage. Then followed six sections on subjects ranging from "Photographic Operations" and "Handling and Shipping Film" to "Captions" and the "Care and Operation of Equipment." But perhaps the most significant section was the "Introduction," which acknowledged the need for flexibility depending on different conditions when it said that "Theaters of operations and subordinate units will supplement this with local SOPs."[16]

Many local SOPs appeared. Issued in March 1945, the Seventh Army's SOP defined "methods of establishment, operation and maintenance of Signal photographic activities ... *based on experience* gained in the operations in Africa, Sicily, and Italy and guided by War Department policy." And the "Handbook for Motion Picture Photographers" frankly stated that photo units in the European Theater did not necessarily adhere to the T/O&E because "operational methods cannot be standardized, due to the fact that there exists a fluid condition dependent on the availability of supplies, camera equipment, and personnel which varies from time to time."[17]

II

The 163rd, said Joe Boyle, was "totally fragmented," a description that also applied to other SPCs.

The unit's fragmentation was so complete and occurred along so many fault lines that some men in the company quite literally did not know other members of their unit. How and why did this splintering happen? Even before the company deployed overseas it permanently lost a substantial element. A detachment composed of two General Assignment Units spent about three years in the Aleutians, Hawaii, and other, less congenial Pacific Ocean islands such as Japanese-defended Kwajalein, Guam, and Tinian.[18]

The remainder of the company deployed to the Mediterranean Theater, but it went in three stages over the span of nearly a year. After receiving orders in late September 1942 to pack up its equipment the entire 163rd moved from Fort Sam Houston to the East Coast in preparation for overseas duty. The first stage of the movement overseas consisted of an advance detachment of only two dozen men who participated in Operation Torch, the invasion of North Africa in November. Few of these men ever rejoined the unit. A month later, in the second stage, the Laboratory Platoon, led by Lieutenant Brooks C. Noah, departed for North Africa where Joe "Shorty" Boyle greeted it.[19] Like Frye, Boyle was not one of the unit's original members. Along with about 15,000 other soldiers, he had been sent to England aboard the *Queen Elizabeth* in August 1942. His military specialty was photography but no photo units were in England yet, so he busied himself helping to string telephone wire. Three days after the North African landings he showed up at Oran, again with no photographic responsibilities, but he made himself useful by helping different types of newly arrived units get settled. Noticing that the 163rd SPC Lab Platoon was on its way, Boyle made a special effort to get permission to meet it. He "mothered" the Lab upon its arrival and since he was a photographer and a lieutenant with no "home," and Lieutenant Noah was short one officer, the Lab adopted him in early 1943.[20]

Not until August 1943 did the third-stage movement occur, when now-Captain Ned Morehouse shepherded the Headquarters Platoon and the remainder of the Assignment Platoon to North Africa aboard a converted Italian liner sailing in a huge convoy. The 163rd was so deep in the ship's hull that the men had no portholes or air circulation, so they endured a perspiration-soaked voyage. The sojourn not only brought physical discomfort but also had a tragic moment when a generator exploded, killing one sailor and badly burning several others. With the convoy's flags at half mast, the dead sailor was buried at sea that evening. "Our first taste of violent death in the the theater of operations," noted the 163rd's Warren Kieft in his diary. Unfortunately, this was not the 163rd's last taste of untimely death.[21]

The Italian liner docked at Oran, French Algeria, on September 2, and as the 163rd disembarked the men boarded trucks that took them to a nearby bivouac area where they set up pyramidal tents in a "barren, sun-drenched dust bowl without even a tall weed for shade." But the unit's equipment did not arrive for several weeks, which is why Gordon Frye visited misnamed "sunny" Italy.[22]

The fragmented deployment continued even though the entire company was now located in North Africa. By the time the Headquarters and Assignment Platoons arrived in Oran, the Lab had moved to Mostaganem, and the Lab and Headquarters remained separated for the next year. The Lab departed North Africa for Italy in mid-September 1943, landing at Salerno on D+5 and then moving to

Naples and on to Caserta, where it remained from late October 1943 until June 1944 before moving to Rome. Finally the Lab traveled back to Naples in September where it linked up with Headquarters Platoon, which had been on its own odyssey. From its bivouac near Oran it went to Bagnoli, Italy, arriving in late October when the Lab was at Caserta. Then Headquarters moved to a location four miles northwest of Caiazzo, to Caiazzo, San Marco, Ninfa, Tuscania, Roccastrada, and to Naples in late July 1944. The day when the Lab joined Headquarters there marked the first time since the Lab had left the United States almost two years earlier that the 163rd's Lab and Headquarters sections were in the same place at the same time. The two platoons moved in tandem thereafter, but even though they were often in the same town they sometimes billeted in separate buildings in order to have enough space for efficient operations.[23]

The Lab–Headquarters separation was not capricious. The former needed considerable space in a relatively secure area where it had access to a decent water supply, which meant it could not be close to the battle lines. Processing film, making and drying prints, writing captions, and filing negatives required so much room and equipment that the Lab could not be moved easily or often. It also had to remain close to Army Headquarters to supply urgently needed prints on short notice. On the other hand, the Headquarters Platoon had to be as near the fighting zones as possible "to serve its function as a base for [photo] teams, a supply point, a service agency for the repair and maintenance of transportation and equipment and as an administrative unit." The closer to the front Headquarters was, the less traveling the photographers had to do, which facilitated their combat-coverage mission and helped keep the roads unclogged so that fighting units could move expeditiously wherever and whenever commanders needed them.[24]

The final aspect of the company's fragmentation was the far-flung dispersion of the photo teams along the forward edge of the battle zone. Some General Assignment Units went ashore at Salerno with the invasion, thus arriving five days before the Lab and a month and a half before the Headquarters Platoon. By the winter of 1944, all the CATs were on the move so much and at such a great distance from Headquarters that the cameramen rarely saw either the Lab or Headquarters. Consequently, the 163rd began publishing a weekly information sheet, the *Foto-Facto*, "to provide a tie between the 'family' at headquarters and the breadwinners in the field."[25] Holidays such as Christmas and Thanksgiving had special meaning for the company for on those days most CATs made a special effort to visit Headquarters, uniting much of the 163rd for at least a few hours. Despite being scattered like ragweed pollen riding a summer breeze, through the *Foto-Facto* and holiday reunions the men developed a strong cohesion, and their bonds of affection and respect have reasserted themselves in periodic reunions for more than four decades after the war.

III

As the war pulled him first this way and then that way, Gordon Frye's morale ebbed and flowed in an almost rhythmic pattern, like the tide responding to the moon's gravitational influence. By late December 1943 after near-continuous frontline duty since landing at Salerno in mid-September, his emotional and physical reserves were ebbing rapidly. Shortly after joining the 163rd in early December he and two other men (photographer Sam Tischler and Leonard Ryan, a former Philadelphia taxi driver) had been assigned to work with Hollywood director John Huston on a project that eventually resulted in *San Pietro*, one of the war's most famous documentaries, described in the previous chapter. While they were filming for Huston the weather had been dismally cold and damp and the fighting utterly brutal, as Allied forces battered against the German Winter Line, a defensive system spanning the Italian peninsula.

On December 25 Frye "worked to-day, as usual on a Christmas story for the newsreels, but finished in time to go to the company [headquarters] in the afternoon for a big turkey dinner," which he thoroughly enjoyed. But the merriment was only momentary and on the last day of the year he wrote his wife that he was "hoping for a rest in a few weeks, as I'm becoming very tired and grouchy. I haven't had a real rest or day off in over three months here in Italy and I'm getting to be a mighty grim gent."

Fortunately for Frye, in January 1944 Huston learned that his good friend Humphrey Bogart was coming to Naples with a USO show. Just before the War Department called Huston to active duty he had been directing Bogart in a movie. Now the director turned army officer just *had* to see Bogie and so he gave his cameramen a few days off, a welcome development indeed. Unfortunately for Frye, American bombers hit company headquarters at Caiazzo and so he ended up getting his much-needed rest in a hospital.

After returning to duty in March and with the arrival of spring, Frye felt much better. Despite lingering aftereffects from his wounds his health was much improved. The injured shoulder and arm still bothered him "when the weather is damp, but then it only gets stiff without paining anymore." He was also promoted from corporal to sergeant, resulting in a substantial pay raise (an important consideration with a new bride at home) and an opportunity to command his own three-man team. Frye was not only "right back in the groove again" as far as photography went, he was also at peace with himself regarding the decision to leave *Yank*, which had brought in its wake such a wholly unexpected train of events.

Frye's soaring spirits continued throughout the summer. He was on the move a great deal and was trying to spend as many nights as possible "in the woods, just in case ole kraut-face tried to find us ... ever since I got caught in that house when I was injured I've been leery of houses to stay in." His journeys took him to the Anzio beachhead in time for the breakout, where he not only photographed British Army commandos but actually *fought* for the only time. Snipers holed up in a building were holding up the commandos, so they asked Frye's team to "try to apply a little more pressure." For maybe fifteen minutes the three men blazed away "without really knowing what we were shooting at" and the commandos got by the snipers. From Anzio, Frye, his still-picture cameraman Jack Harris (a baseball fanatic and exquisite violinist who lugged his violin around for most of the war), and driver Lennie Ryan moved northward and liberated Rome. They entered the Eternal City with the first troops "and instead of the Germans waiting for us, there was nothing but mobs of overjoyed Italians, who cheered us and threw flowers at us." Now, he said exactly two weeks after Rome's liberation, "if I can just get to do the same job soon in Paris or Berlin...."

It looked like he might get that opportunity, for Frye participated in Operation Anvil, the Seventh Army's invasion of Southern France on August 15, and it seemed as if the Nazi regime would soon expire. In preparation for the operation the 163rd was reassigned from the Fifth Army, which it had been covering in Italy, to the Seventh Army, turning over its Fifth Army photographic duties to the 3131st Signal Service Company—"an ignominious name if there ever was one," said Sam Tischler, who left the 163rd, became a member of the 3131st, and eventually won a Bronze Star for heroic actions in Italy in 1945. The 163rd also developed a detailed "Operation Plan for 'Anvil' Photographic Coverage" so that it could provide the initial Assault Convoy with appropriate units and deploy the rest of the company to France in a timely manner between D + 1 and D + 45. For the initial invasion the 163rd assigned approximately ten officers and fifty men to combat units, including the the assault waves and the glider and parachute elements of the First Airborne Task Force.[26]

Among those assigned to the initial assault was Frye, who was in a team with Lieutenant Noah and a driver. None of them knew where the assault would occur—only that it would. Frye was not happy about making another invasion but he dutifully readied himself and his camera, which he had affectionately nicknamed "Oleta" after his wife, for the task. Waiting for the operation to commence was the toughest part—far harder, at least in retrospect, than the actual invasion. Making the time crawl by even slower was the knowledge that he was going aboard an LCT (Landing Craft, Tanks) that would be in the third wave hitting the beach on "D-Day."

The voyage from Italy "was unexpectedly gay." The LCT was British and Frye liked the "Limeys," as the GIs called them, especially the young chef who gave Frye one hot meal a day in the galley. Hot food made Frye feel guilty since the other GIs aboard had nothing but thrice-daily cold C-rations, but he rationalized the special treatment by arguing that "after all, in the army one has to take care of oneself or no one will." Frye also met the LCT's captain, hoping that he could learn the invasion site and finagle better sleeping arrangements. Although the skipper was friendly, he was tight-lipped and "could do nothing for me in regard to sleeping facilities naturally on such a small craft." But the captain did promise "that if all went according to plan, he would land us on the beach without us getting our feet wet." As an experienced soldier Frye was wary of such a promise, recognizing that the phrase "*if* all went according to plan" rendered it meaningless. He understood that uncertainty was a central feature of warfare. "But the unknown element," observed Frye, "is always—how will the enemy react, and what surprises did he have in store for us that our very up-to-the-minute intelligence reports did not give us[;] that was what we would have to wait and see for ourselves."

Despite the gaiety and friendships the voyage to the Riviera had two especially frightful aspects, one mental, the other physical. "The worst things take place in your mind, only," Frye realized. After staring at the horizon and at the sky for a few days, imaginary periscopes popped up near the LCT from below and hallucinatory Luftwaffe planes dove down on it from on high. But "dame nature, not the enemy attacked us." A violent storm with lightning and thunder bombarding the convoy "like a creeping artillery barrage," thrashing the LCT to and fro and hurtling men out of their bunks and into the bulkheads. Frye "wasn't scared; I just couldn't control myself." He lay in his bunk shaking "like a milk-shake in a mixer" and received a nasty gash on his head when he slashed it against the bulkhead.

The Riviera's D-Day dawned so foggy that Frye had a dreadful feeling his LCT alone was making the invasion. But as the sun battled its way through the haze, the huge invasion fleet materialized. All of a sudden Frye wished for something to conceal the fleet from the Germans' prying eyes, but "the invasion stage was being set up without even a smoke screen for a curtain. I was amazed. In all my experiences in Italy, it was always SOP to lay a smoke screen over any attack to be made when we were in full view of the Germans." Yet things remained quiet—too quiet for Frye, who felt sure the Germans were concocting a surprise. While the infantry-laden assault craft formed up, Frye put "Oleta" on a tripod on the deck and waited, chain-smoking, lighting the next cigarette off the burning butt of the last one, and pacing "the crowded deckspace of the bridge like an expectant father."

As Frye watched the shoreline, a German star shell arced over the water, driving out the lingering remnants of darkness and fog with its luminescence, then another, and then the enemy batteries and machine guns opened up. "THEN—a half hour before H-hour we opened up with our attack from the air and sea." Zooming in from all directions, planes bombed and strafed the shore defenses. Although the LCT was several miles offshore the concussions shook the deck and made Frye's ears pop. As the planes departed, the battleships, cruisers, and destroyers unleashed their heavy guns, supplemented by "thousands of flaming rocket shells that were sent ashore just ahead of the infantry assault." Frye was filming all the while—"the big guns firing, the rocket ships firing in the distance in front of me, and the movement of the assault craft around us."

Suddenly the pre-invasion barrage halted, the silence now as stunning as the bombardment had been. The first wave of Higgins boats went in, then the second, and now Frye's LCT moved forward with the third wave and with "the whole panorama of invasion before me." Frye was going ashore on the sector allocated to the 45th Division; in front of him the soldiers moved onto the beaches virtually without opposition. But off to his right, where the 36th Division was landing, the enemy was more stubborn. Frye felt badly for the 36th, which had already been savaged at Salerno, San Pietro, the Rapido River, and Cassino back in Italy, but admitted that "it made for great pictures for me." As usual, the best pictures were at the expense of somebody going through hell.

And the miracle happened. As promised, the British LCT captain got Frye ashore without even getting his feet wet. With excellent pictures already "in the can," with hardly a shot having been fired in anger on his section of the beach, with dry boots and socks, and with "Oleta" caressed in his hands, he went merrily on his way photographing dead Germans, the damage, the first liberated towns, the initial German prisoners, many of them dazed and wounded—"and during the whole day I did not see one American soldier wounded!!" Other nearby cameramen, such as Ed Newell, also marveled at their good fortune that day on that particular beach.[27] As darkness descended on D-Day, Frye delivered his film to a courier who got it on a plane. As it turned out, his motion pictures were the first ones to reach England from the invasion and, being timely and dramatic, the newsreels used them extensively.

After completing his D-Day mission Frye visited a Naval Aid Station to have the deep cut he received during the pre-invasion thunderstorm looked at, for it "hadn't been cleaned up for a couple of days and needed a little attention." The medic who gave him first aid asked if he wanted to fill out the form for a Purple Heart. "No thanks," Frye replied, "I already have one." He later regretted this decision since a Purple Heart was worth five points, and the men with the highest point totals went home first after the war ended.

Within a few days Frye, along with Noah and two enlisted men, Sidney Blau and Fred Bornet, had been assigned to cover Task Force Butler, a 1500-man, lightly armored group that raced up the Durance River Valley, taking advantage of the disorganization that temporarily prevailed among the Germans, liberating one French town after another. The task force had soon penetrated well inland toward Grenoble. Along the way liquor that had been hidden from the Germans magically appeared and cascaded down the throats of the liberators. As the task force neared Grenoble it suddenly veered to the west through the town of Die and then attacked German defenses near Montélimar in the Rhone River Valley from the rear, helping to open up a second vital route inland. As the narrator for the documentary entitled *Invasion of Southern France* said, "Task Force Butler really paid off."

By late August, the pervasive euphoria that accompanied Germany's seemingly inevitable and imminent demise gripped Frye. In late July the forces that had landed in Normandy in June broke out of their beachhead at St. Lô, racing almost effortlessly to the Seine River and liberating Paris by the end of August. Now a second invasion had smashed the enemy, and as German forces reeled eastward toward the Reich, it did not appear they could continue resisting much longer. "Keep the chins up," Frye wrote to his parents on August 30, "and the factories working—we'll all be hearing of the end of Germany in a few months!" Other photographers felt the same way. Warren Kieft noted that optimism prevailed everywhere, that "the discussion now centers on not when the war will end but when we go home. The conclusion of the war seems to be a foregone conclusion because everything points to the difficult spot Germany is in and it seems to be only a matter of time before they get rid of Hitler and ask for the cessation of hostilities."[28]   Like many others, Frye bet that the European war would be over by Christmas.

Frye lost his bet. By mid-September the Germans, who just days earlier seemed completely routed, were fighting back. "Apparently the damn Germans don't know when they're licked," he informed his parents, "so we'll just have to knock hell out of all Germany to make them surrender." On virtually the same day Kieft made the same point: "For some reason or other the feeling of optimism is much less than it was three weeks ago and that is a very general feeling."[29]

As enemy resistance stiffened and euphoria yielded to realism, Frye's spirits ebbed, his health deteriorated, and by midwinter he languished in the tidal mudflats of near despair. In November he was hospitalized for two weeks with a bad hacking cough, being released just in time to enjoy Thanksgiving dinner with a smaller-than-usual holiday contingent at headquarters. Most of the cameramen were too busy in the field to make the event. One who was not was Jerry Rutberg, who had recently been shot in the head by a sniper. Luckily, when the projectile hit his helmet the liner diverted it around his head, so the bullet burned his ear instead of killing him. Still, Rutberg was not "feeling too good" and "he didn't really enjoy his Thanksgiving dinner." The Christmas season was more joyful—at least as joyous as might reasonably be expected in the midst of a world war. Most of the cameramen, including Frye, who was working then with the 36th Division, made it to headquarters for a turkey dinner on Christmas Day, and a few lingered on to play poker on New Year's Eve when a "disgustingly SOBER" Frye won ten bucks. But since he had lost fifty dollars on Christmas he was still in the hole.

And he was deeper in the hole psychologically, suffering from acute nervous and physical exhaustion. He had had too many close calls— only recently a piece of shrapnel had cut the legs off a pair of pants that had been hanging over his bunk—and he had "worked and walked through rain, mud, waded streams, climbed steep rocky mountains, hiked through snow and woods, have flown in big planes (C-47) and little ones (a Cub), and have ridden in and climbed all over every damn type of landing craft and ship that our Uncle Sammy owns!" Calls came in the middle of the night for him to go out on assignments, and the constant packing and unpacking of equipment got on his nerves as he kept pace with the fighting front. "I've averaged a good fifty miles (I don't know what's good about it) a day," he complained, "over the goddamndest roads in Africa, Italy, and France."

Early in 1945 he wrote Oleta that "the damn grim business of war has me down." His sustaining zest for photography had diminished "because this damn war recording on film gets terribly monotonous in its repetition of material—poor civilians, homeless, hungry kids, blasted ruins of once beautiful little villages, blasted twisted forms that were once human beings." Everything, he lamented, "is uncertain, only the bloody war is definite." Ten days later he wrote again, saying that "at times, I become sort of numb, indifferent, tired and just plain goddamn sick at heart from it all." Another three weeks and he admitted that "I'm sort of punch-drunk I guess from seeing too much of the ravages of war."

Yet Frye was tough and determined. In January 1945 he was hospitalized again, this time for pneumonia and bronchitis aggravated by damage to his windpipe during the headquarters bombing a year earlier. The doctor who treated him told Frye that he probably qualified for a medical discharge but Frye refused, saying that having come this far he "wanted to be in on the final kill!"

By March 1945 Frye was thirsting for the kill, pounding ever deeper into Germany with the 36th Division, to which his CAT #18 was still assigned. So refreshed was Frye that he took out pen and paper and began drawing cartoons. One showed a jaunty trio riding in a winged jeep labeled CAT #18 of the 163rd flying over the countryside. In the middle, easily recognizable because of his conspicuously bald head, was Frye; on one side was driver Stanley Ross and on the other side was still photographer Budd McCroby (known as McPorky, and the caricature of him in Frye's drawing makes clear why). Frye has a modest half-smile in the self portrait, McCroby is showing all his teeth, and Stan Ross is saying, "It ain't SOP—but it's SURE fun!!" A nearby bird tweets, "Gee—what a breeze!"

As March gave way to April the personnel in Frye's CAT #18 changed. Al Gretz replaced "McPorky" as the still cameraman and Luther "Tex" Luper took over as driver. These three were together for the rest of the war, which was not quite the breeze Frye's cartoon indicated. As CAT #18 accompanied the 36th Division across the Rhine and then southeast to Worms, Mannheim, Stuttgart, Munich, and the outskirts of Innsbruck, Frye considered them "the *toughest* and *roughest* days" of the war because of the fast pace and wild events. But "with the certainty of victory within our reach, all the moving and hauling to make pictures has not been too tiresome." Frye reveled in seeing at first hand "the terrific results of all the bombing our airforce has been doing the last year or so," gloried in the "sweet music" made by wailing German civilians and soldiers, and fantasized about the job he really wanted: "making pictures of the German surrender or us meeting up with Russian troops—wow, what a pic that will be, when we meet the Russians!!" On those occasions when his nerves started to go ragged again, Tex Luper was there, "always cheerful with a never-say-die attitude." The alert jeep driver also saved Frye's life. In late April Frye was filming a prisoner-of-war story and, with his eye glued to the camera's viewfinder, was very vulnerable. Luper noticed a "Hitler-Youth type edging up on me from behind. Tex, a tall, lean and mean forty-five year old gent jumped the kid, pinned him down and disarmed him." The teenager had a knife. "*That* knife," Frye wrote forty years later from his home in Vermont, "still hangs in my home here with other prized souvenirs."

The European war's last morning found CAT #18 alone, five miles beyond the last American outpost in the camp of a surly group of SS troops who were not happy about surrendering. After filming for an hour amid these "Nazi butcher boys," CAT #18 departed "feeling mighty good when 'WHAM,' a big hole appeared in our hood about a foot in front of the windshield. That did it. We were doing about forty when they shot at us but Luper really shoved down on the gas and we reached the outpost on the double." An hour later they photographed those same Nazis surrendering, a "terrific finish of a terrific war."[30]

"Amen—it's over, over here!!" Frye informed his parents on May 14 from Germany. "Believe me it is hard to realize it—but it is finished— thank the Good Lord for bringing me safely through."

———————

"I'm not kidding when I tell you that the things I've seen and done, but can't write about [because of wartime censorship], would fill a book—and by God, it would be a good one—maybe I'll write one when I get home—I think I'll call it 'War Kibitzer' because that's what we photogs are—we see it all, make a record of it, but never really do any of the fighting—we shoot 'em with a camera—only." Gordon Frye never wrote his book, but he was right. By God, it would have been a good one.

5

"Sticking Their Necks Out Doing Their Weird Things"

The Army's 166th Signal Photographic Company

Two seemingly unrelated circumstances—catching pneumonia in the fall of 1943 and speaking imperfect English—almost got Arthur Herz summarily executed in the winter of 1944.

Herz had been born in Berlin in the early 1920s but his family, which was Jewish, fled to Italy to avoid Nazi persecution. Within eighteen months conditions in Italy for Jews had deteriorated so badly that Herz moved on to Switzerland, England, and Cuba before finally arriving in the United States in 1939. He began studying photography at the Rochester Athenaeum and Mechanics Institute (now the Rochester Institute of Technology in Rochester, New York). But as soon as England and Germany went to war in September of that year, Herz was ready to suspend his studies. Knowing the evils of Nazidom firsthand, he queried the British Consul General in New York City about joining the British forces; that august official referred him to Canada's Ministry of Defence. "My military qualifications," he wrote to the Ministry, "consist of an excellent health, a strong body power, a good education and training and the will to do all and everything in my power to help winning this war for the Allies and the world." Less than a week later the Department of National Defence replied with bad news. Only British subjects or "Aliens of Allied or Neutral countries who were resident in Canada on 1st September, 1939" were eligible for duty in the Canadian active service. Since he was still a German national Herz could not enlist.[1]

So Herz continued his studies until first thing Monday morning, December 8, 1941, when he appeared at the Rochester Navy Recruiting Office, as eager as any of the thousands of potential recruits who swarmed into recruiting offices across the country that hectic morning. Alas, he met the "same stuffy attitude" the Canadians had displayed regarding his nationality. Frustrated again in his quest to fight the Nazis he continued with school, graduating a year later with a degree in Photographic Technology. After he worked briefly as a lab technician at the Eastman Kodak Research Laboratory, "the U.S. Army finally relented and took me in." Basic training was at Camp Croft in Spartanburg, South Carolina, where he was taken off duty to be sworn in as a naturalized United States citizen.

Herz volunteered for the paratroopers but the Army had other plans. With trained photographers in short supply it assigned him to the 166th SPC at Camp Crowder, Missouri. As part of its training the unit covered the Army's Tennessee Maneuvers in the fall of 1943. Herz contracted pneumonia during the maneuvers and was still in a Nashville hospital when the 166th shipped overseas in the early 1944. When he finally arrived in Europe, Herz was with the 583rd Signal Depot Company and the 166th was with the American army approaching the German border. On December 16, 1944 he departed the Signal Depot Company to rejoin the 166th, heading eastward from Luxembourg toward the front lines as a passenger aboard a supply truck.

Several events now conspired to confront Herz with the possibility of instant death. Before dawn on December 16th the Germans launched a massive surprise counteroffensive through the rugged Ardennes region of Belgium and Luxembourg. Code-named Wacht am Rhein (Watch on the Rhine), the attack by three German armies resulted in the Battle of the Bulge, the largest pitched battle ever fought by the United States. To sow confusion among the Americans a special unit commanded by one of Germany's most innovative officers, Lieutenant Colonel Otto Skorzeny, helped spearhead the assault. Composed in part of soldiers who spoke at least some English, drove Allied vehicles, and wore American uniforms, this elite force did little actual damage but made American MPs hyperzealous about exposing these intruders. On several occasions even General Omar Bradley, commanding the American Twelfth Army Group, had to answer questions about football teams, state capitals, movie stars and their spouses, and other things that only a good American would know. Bradley could not identify Betty Grable's husband—but his GI inquisitor recognized the general, told him the answer (Harry James), and then let him pass.[2]

General Bradley might not know the answers to all the trivia questions that a suspicious MP could concoct, but at least he spoke like an American. Private Herz, however, had not been in the United States long enough to lose his deep guttural German accent.

Herz learned about the German attack when the supply truck he was on encountered heavy, disorganized traffic heading the other way. At a crossroads near Echternach the truck driver learned that the Germans had broken through, turned his vehicle around, and joined the retreat. But before the truck began retracing its route Herz dismounted, deciding to continue on foot in search of the 166th even though nearby positions were coming under enemy fire. He naturally asked nearby troops for directions. In retrospect, this was not a wise thing to do. The soldiers were immediately and properly suspicious. Here was a man who was obviously not 100 percent American! He spoke English with a Teutonic ring, did not know the password, did not understand baseball scores, had no idea which team had won the pennant, and was carrying some newfangled signal equipment that he had "confiscated" from the 583rd. As Herz recalled, he "had a chance to ask questions or directions and troops locations only once before being jumped by our troops with guns at the ready."

The MP sergeant who took charge of Herz was sure he had captured a "Kraut-bastard in a GI uniform who wants us to believe that he comes from Upstate New York." As the noise and confusion of the fighting intensified, Herz feared summary conviction and execution. But he convinced the sergeant "that there was more glory for him in receiving a medal for uncommon vigilance in apprehending a cleverly disguised bona fide German spy, than by shooting a man in a GI uniform whose accent and treacherous activity could then not be verified." The MP sent Herz back to Liège with a group of German prisoners, a fate that did not necessarily ensure salvation since the Germans, unlike the GIs, believed he was indeed an American. After nine anguishing days "when it was uncertain whether I would be finished off by my former or my present compatriots," authorities finally verified Herz's story.

On Christmas Day 1944 in the city of Metz he rejoined the 166th SPC as a member of Detachment #4, a three-man team that now consisted of OIC Adrian J. Salvas, motion-picture man Bernard J. Caliendo, and still cameraman Arthur Herz.

I

Unlike the 163rd SPC, which the Army raised directly, the 166th was one of five "affiliated" companies that traced their roots to Hollywood. Like most elements of the armed forces the Signal Corps had been slowly mobilizing for possible war since the late 1930s. As part of its preparation in May 1940 it adopted an Affiliated Plan, which was based upon the Signal Corps' World War I experience, when the Operating Telephone Companies of the Bell System supplied the officers and men for twelve telegraph battalions and the Western Electric Company supplied two radio companies. As in World War I, the purpose of the 1940 plan was to procure skilled communications personnel who would perform essentially the same technical tasks in the military that they did in civilian life. The Signal Corps applied the Affiliated Plan to obtain trained personnel from companies such as Bell Laboratories, American Telephone and Telegraph, Postal Electric, Eastman Kodak, the International Federation of Associated Pigeon Fanciers, and the Research Council of the Academy of Motion Picture Arts and Sciences.[3]

Hollywood had developed a working relationship with the Army in 1930, when the Signal Corps began sending one officer a year to the West Coast to study film production, a skill the Army needed as it moved into the training-film era. After its formation in the mid-1930s the Research Council coordinated the Signal Corps-Hollywood program and assisted the Army in producing training films. When the Affiliated Plan went into effect, Darryl Zanuck, the Research Council's chairperson, immediately agreed that the Council would sponsor the Signal Corps Photographic Laboratory, GHQ; in late 1942 the personnel from this unit transferred into the 1st through 8th Signal Photographic Lab Units. Meanwhile, two months after Pearl Harbor the Signal Corps asked the Research Council to sponsor the 164th and 165th SPCs under the Affiliated Plan; subsequently it sponsored three more companies, the 166th, 167th, and 168th.

The Affiliated Plan produced 5,427 officers and men who formed the cadre for 404 affiliated units of all types. Out of all those who entered the Signal Corps through this program, 105 officers and 610 enlisted men recommended by the Research Council went into photographic units. Of these, 56 officers and 347 enlisted men served in the five affiliated SPCs.[4]

Like many others in the affiliated companies, the 166th's Billy A. Newhouse believed that Hollywood had cut a shady deal with the War Department, agreeing to recruit and train cameramen if the Army would hold off drafting the industry's talented filmmakers. Keeping most of the really good cameramen stashed away in the studios meant that the Research Council "was signing up anybody that came along that had any idea which end of a camera the lens was," said Newhouse. "That's how I happened to get into it." His 166th SPC colleague, Ralph Butterfield, was a teacher both before and after the war, not a photographer. He had taken the necessary tests to apply for a Navy commission as a way to avoid being drafted. Just before signing on the dotted line, he made the rounds of the Los Angeles enlistment offices one last time—and noticed a small sign saying the Army was seeking photographers and that anyone interested should dial a certain phone number in Hollywood. He called, had an interview, and enlisted in the Army—all within ninety minutes![5]

Although most of the affiliated officers were experienced photographers, rank amateurs like Newhouse and Butterfield filled the enlisted roster. Of the eight second lieutenants commissioned on the Research Council's recommendation and scheduled for activation with the 166th SPC, all had at least four years of relevant experience and some had worked more than twice that long for MGM, Columbia, Walt Disney, or other Hollywood studios. But apparently none of the enlisted men even approached this level of expertise.[6]

To train the large number of unqualified photographers it had recruited, the Research Council established a two-month training program in motion-picture and still photography. Working with the American Society of Cinematographers (ASC), the International Photographers Local 659, and the Hollywood-based technical staff of the Eastman Kodak Company, the Research Council's training effort commenced in June 1942. ASC members representing all the major studios taught moviemaking, the local union coordinated instruction in camera maintenance and still photography, and Eastman's technicians enlightened students on basic photographic theory and technology. The chairperson of the committee responsible for motion-picture training admitted that eight weeks of instruction, even by the world's foremost experts, would not yield polished cameramen. But he hoped that by stripping the classes of nonessentials the amateurs could become serviceable, if not brilliant, photographers.[7]

Those who took the Hollywood training course had mixed feelings about it. Eastman's technicians received rave reviews. As Butterfield put it, they "gave us a very good and very thorough theoretical training or instruction upon many, many phases of photography. They emphasized cameras, the basic nature of lenses, of optics, of films, of papers, of densitometry, of speeds of films. It was a very, very good course in such basics." But at MGM the practical training in photography that Butterfield received "was really token." That studio seemed primarily interested in lending its name and prestige to the training effort and "could have done a great deal more than [it] did." Others agreed with Butterfield's assessment.[8]

Fortunately for the Army's pictorial effort the Hollywood course was only a beginning, not the end, of photographic training. The War Department activated four of the affiliated companies at Camp Crowder, Missouri, where each company's Hollywood cadre was fleshed out to authorized strength with drivers, clerks, cooks, a few cameramen trained at the SCPC, and additional officers who had graduated from the Signal Corps' Officer Candidate School (OCS). While at Camp Crowder cameramen received training that filled the void left by Hollywood. Providing especially valuable additional instruction were photographic officers from APS, including Captain Arthur Lloyd, a longtime Hollywood cameraman whom the 166th remembered with reverence.[9]

Through lectures and practical experience Lloyd taught the neophyte motion-picture men the necessity of pictorial continuity, created by changing lenses and angles to acquire a variety of different types of shots. A typical movie sequence (that is, a group of related individual scenes) might commence with an establishing shot, followed by a mixture of long shots, medium shots, and close-ups, and then conclude with a re-establishing scene. For example, a sequence on an artillery piece in action might be edited together in this order: a medium shot from the right side showing the gun and its crew, which is the "establishing shot"; a close-up of the shell being loaded; a close-up taken from a high angle looking down the gun barrel's mouth; a head-on extreme close-up of an officer yelling "Fire!"; a medium shot from behind the gun as an artilleryman yanks the lanyard and the gun fires and recoils; a long shot of an exploding shell on a distant hill; a re-establishing medium shot from the left side as the crew begins to load another projectile. These seven scenes required quite a bit of activity. To get the different focal lengths, the cameraman either had to change lenses several times or else pick up the camera and move it closer to or farther from the subject. And the photographer would definitely have to move at least four times from his initial position on the gun's right side: to the top of a truck or some other elevated perch to get the high angle scene; to in front of the officer; to behind the gun; and to the left of the artillery piece. Of course, these scenes could be shot in any order, even on different days if the light matched, and then reorganized during editing.

Without diverse camera angles and a balance among long, medium, and close-up shots, editing a motion picture is extraordinarily difficult. Motion-picture footage simply "becomes a group of stills that cannot be tied together" unless the cameraman has provided a combination of different shots.[10] To drive this point home, Lloyd dispatched camera-men to nearby communities and farms to photograph stories involving action and equipment, such as railroad station operations and milk production. Although these subjects may have seemed rather unmili-tary, Lloyd selected them wisely since warfare consisted in large part of movement of men and machinery. Then he critiqued the material—usually scathingly. Through trial and error and to avoid acute embar-rassment the men improved rapidly.

Even more realistic experience came when units covered huge army maneuvers or accompanied particular divisions as they trained in the rain and mud and snow, with artillery and tanks, and with squads and platoons learning how to move cautiously and stay alive, which meant remaining unphotogenic. Most of the 166th participated in the Tennessee Maneuvers but some detachments went to Wisconsin, South Carolina, Colorado, and Oregon to train with individual divi-sions. Other affiliated companies also covered the exercises in Tennessee and scattered their units across the nation to work closely with divisions in stateside training.

Since the men were soldier-cameramen, specialized photographic training was not enough. The affiliated companies also underwent physical toughening and learned essential military skills. The 164th took a series of practice marches, starting with just a few miles and a mere overnight bivouac and gradually increasing distance and time. The company history religiously noted the weather on these exercises:

very hot, rainy, rain and sleet, but never delightfully comfortable. The bivouac areas usually matched the weather. Few in the 164th ever forgot "Stoney Acres," the camping spot that inflicted a sleepless night on the men in late July 1943. Along with the marches the soldiers ran obstacle courses, shot rifles and Thompson submachine guns on the rifle range, took combat intelligence and basic medical courses, and endured inspections.[11]

Suddenly, however, "all that remained to be done was to pack up that old duffel bag" in preparation for movement overseas.[12]

II

When Lieutenant Harvey Weber led Detachment #1 of the 166th SPC ashore on Utah Beach in Normandy about a week after D-Day, the company's history stretched back more than six thousand miles from Hollywood to Camp Crowder, then to New York harbor where the 166th boarded the U.S.S. *Susan B. Anthony*. After it had crossed the Atlantic and landed at Belfast, Northern Ireland, authorities assigned the 166th to General George Patton's Third Army. It remained with the Third Army until the war's end, joining it in England in early May and deploying into combat with it on the English Channel's "Far Shore." Organized according to the dictates of T/O&E 11-37 and assigned to the 79th Infantry Division, Weber's seven-man unit, which included Billy Newhouse and Ralph Butterfield, was the first 166th SPC detachment to go into action. Others soon followed, landing in France with each Third Army division.[13]

On July 22nd the 166th had its first battle casualties when an enemy artillery shell killed two men and wounded two others, an event with both immediate and long-term consequences.[14] As with every novice unit engaged in battle, news that the adversary had drawn the blood of friends and colleagues was a shock. Especially unsettling was war's capriciousness, its sheer random nature. One explosion, one microsecond, two men dead and two others badly hurt! Why them and not us? The loss of trained personnel also reduced the company's ability to perform its mission. The 166th SPC had trouble getting replacements, so that fewer and fewer personnel covered an ever-expanding campaign. As more and more divisions, corps, and special forces poured into Europe, the only way the 166th could provide adequate coverage was to emulate the 163rd SPC's experience: ignore the T/O&E, fragment into smaller detachments, use clerks and drivers as photographers, and convert officers from executives into active cameramen. By early 1945 two- and three-man teams were the norm. Not until the war in Europe was over did the 166th get its initial replacements. Because the War Department had slated the company to redeploy to the Pacific, this was not an altogether idle gesture; many prognosticators believed the war against Japan would last into 1947.[15]

Other photographic units in the Army and in the other services could empathize with the 166th's plight. Although the 163rd SPC received a few manpower transfusions during its lengthy combat ordeal, a study of "lessons learned" during the Italian campaign revealed that many of them "arrived only semi-trained as photographers, and with no combat training whatsoever. This lack of training has proved both costly and tragic in failures and casualties."[16]

Remaining near authorized strength was particularly hard for the AAF's CCUs. Flying frequent combat missions exacted a terrible psychological toll, grounding many aerial cameramen because of "combat fatigue." And late in the war in at least a few units (though never all of them) a photographer was eligible to return to the States after a certain number of missions. In August 1944 the 6th CCU had twenty officers and men qualified for flying duty, but a year later it had fewer than half that many. Occasional replacements had arrived but they were usually not aerial cameramen, "our neediest category." Finally in September 1945 the 6th received seven flight-qualified replacements who, as the unit history noted, "are not of much use to us now."[17] The replacement problem was so acute in the 10th and 12th CCUs that they established their own schools to train aerial cameramen overseas rather than wait interminably for replacements from stateside.[18] So scarce were good photographers that the 9th CCU gloated when it acquired Gerald Marshall from the 1st CCU. The 9th's war diary noted that the prized acquisition "was a neat bit of 'looting' as Marshall is an excellent motion picture man" with extensive aerial photographic experience.[19]

The mobilization and overseas deployment of the armed forces during 1942–1944 had already absorbed most of the military-age photographers who were either prewar professionals or avid amateurs. Training cameramen from scratch was a difficult and time-consuming process, since learning photography—in and of itself a sophisticated technical specialty—was not enough. Like infantrymen or aerial gunners, they also had to master military skills if they were to have a reasonable chance of survival in a combat environment. The training process could barely keep up with the demand for vitally-needed new photographic units, much less provide replacements for those units already overseas.

Efforts to photograph the war with quickly and inadequately trained cameramen could yield miserable results. When the 11th CCU departed his area the Commanding General of the 11th AAF complained that motion-picture activities came to a complete standstill. Personnel from several air-base photo labs tried to carry on, but the results were unsatisfactory. "Without trained men, men with motion-picture imagination—'movie conscious'—it is next to impossible to get the type of pictures" the AAF needed.[20]

With well-trained cameramen in great demand around the globe, Arthur Herz's return to the 166th SPC was indeed welcome. Herz's new unit was Detachment #4, consisting of himself, OIC Lieutenant Adrian J. Salvas, and Bernard J. "Calley" Caliendo. And nobody was happier to see Herz than Calley.[21]

III

Art Herz, said Calley, "was like an angel sent to me from Heaven." The two were instant friends, each a "character" in his own right, and their interacting charisma was evident to those who knew them. Billy Newhouse recalled that Herz and Calley had great reputations because of their irrepressible personalities and because "they were always kinda sticking their necks out doing their weird things."[22] Driven by an exceptionally conscientious attitude toward their duty, a hyper-curiosity, and Lieutenant Salvas' constant perusal of the war-room maps so that he always knew where the action was the hottest,[23] they relentlessly pursued the fighting front. As Herz put it, "self-discipline and peer pressure" prevented them from dogging it, "and because the best picture opportunities arose wherever the action was, we sought out places where shells and bullets had to be dodged."

The war was "a little scary but always interesting," according to Caliendo. One of its most intriguing features was how much it differed from what he thought it would be like. Forty years after the war he still vividly recalled his first day in combat. Having seen many Hollywood productions "where three and four hundred men were charging across a field and there were explosions and all that," he expected life to replicate cinema. Instead he found himself deafened by the noise from shells, rifles, and machine guns, and yet when he looked around he could not see a thing. Learning the wary ways of World War II-style warriors, Calley was soon thankful when he could shoot as much as one hundred feet of usable film while covering hours of action. Deep in Germany a few months later, a Hollywood-like panorama actually materialized before his eyes, with the planes strafing in front of advancing artillery and armor thrusting down a road strewn with burned vehicles and charred bodies, and with a burning town in the background. He wrote about it in amazement. Having encountered real war he knew how rare such scenes were—about one per war in his case.

Even before linking up with Herz, Calley's real war experiences had earned him a Bronze Star and an Oak Leaf Cluster (which a recipient wears in lieu of a second Bronze Star). He received the Bronze Star for filming direct artillery hits on a German machine-gun position followed by dramatic footage of American infantry crossing the Mosel River in the face of withering enemy fire. To get these shots Calley had to reach a forward observation post by dashing down shell-drenched roads and then literally crawling across open terrain raked by German rifle and machine-gun bullets. The cluster recognized an earlier exploit, when he recorded superb scenes of the 35th Infantry Division during the fighting around St. Lô. For good measure, in late August 1944 when Allied "advances have been by leaps and bounds, and we really have the Jerries by the balls," he, Salvas, and an artist from the Army History Section actually captured fifty-six Germans. Seeing half a dozen of them on a hilltop the trio, using fractured German, persuaded them to put their hands up and come down the hill. As the Americans advanced to meet their captives, Caliendo almost fainted as dozens of Germans appeared from behind the hill's crest. But putting on a fierce mien and "waving my little .45 in the air," he helped the others shepherd the prisoners to the rear, where they turned them over to the infantry. Calley was especially pleased with this affair because he acquired a Luger, which was worth about $75.00 when sold to someone in the rear who had never had a chance to acquire such loot firsthand.

Herz matched Caliendo's inquisitive and adventuresome spirit. In early March 1945 he was with elements of the 11th Armored Division and 4th Infantry Division to the northeast of Prum, Germany, as they did "their bit in following Gen. Eisenhower's order to destroy all the German troops this side of the Rhine." Among other scenes he recorded that day were shots of the men hugging the ground to avoid enemy shrapnel. Herz was vulnerable to the same shrapnel; yet to take pictures he could not lie flattened on the ground like the infantrymen he was photographing.

Three weeks later Herz was near Oberwesel with a regiment from the 89th Division when it crossed the Rhine. A chemical-warfare unit spewed artificial fog, clouds and rain made the early morning light even worse, his camera had a busted range-finder, and the Germans maintained a steady drumbeat of machine-gun bullets and mortar fire from the river's far side. While infantrymen choked the roadside ditches seeking protection, Herz remained exposed taking stills. Then DUKWs waddled up the road and the infantrymen and Herz scrambled aboard as the amphibious vehicles slithered down the riverbank and into the water. The troops crouched low to avoid whizzing bullets and mortar explosions; Herz continued his picture taking. On the far shore the soldiers disembarked and sought cover; Herz stayed with the DUKW to go back across the river and bring reinforcements. Despite the difficult conditions his negatives were "superior from every standpoint, and the resulting prints rank among the best action pictures made in this Theater."

A month later he was with elements of the 99th Division trying to cross the Danube near Neustadt. "At the very moment that the first assault boats were launched, Jerry commenced a murderous fire from the other side," wrote Herz. "From that moment on the situation got confused—photographically as well as militarily." He did the best he could, but the situation was desperate as infantrymen frantically "tried to plug holes in their boats with little sticks and handkerchiefs." Using his Speed Graphic, Herz exposed only two film packs before resorting to his 35mm camera. He actually submitted only one of the two film packs because the other was drowned in the Danube—the 4 × 5 Graphic was so cumbersome that Herz pitched it overboard, film pack and all.

While Calley and Herz had their individual exploits, the Germans were in real trouble when the two worked side by side. "Herz and I really had a[n] excitable time," Caliendo wrote to a friend, "besides shooting pictures." For one thing, they "were taking prisoners right and left. They were all scared to death, and many times we didn't even pull our pistols out." In one instance they got into a town first and had eighty-two prisoners in tow before the first infantrymen arrived. In the last helter-skelter days of war they also acquired "all the souvenirs we could carry."

But their double-daredevil demeanor came through most clearly at Eisenach when the 89th Infantry Division had a German unit virtually surrounded. To avoid unnecessary loss of life the American commander sent a staff officer into town under a white flag—accompanied by Caliendo and Herz, who did not want to miss this photo opportunity! The Germans were so astonished when an American jeep pulled up at Wehrmacht Headquarters that they permitted the photographers to take shots of the headquarters building and nearby soldiers. After overcoming their initial bewilderment the Germans tried to confiscate the cameras, but the photographers refused to surrender them and finally made it to the conference room where surrender negotiations were in progress. Even though the staff officer insisted that at 1900 hours American artillery would subject Eisenach to a terrific bombardment, the Nazi commander wanted to fight it out. Just twenty minutes before the impending artillery assault the negotiations broke down, so the Americans were anxious to be on their way. But as they left the conference room the Germans *insisted* that Herz and Calley give up their cameras and film. This time "the grabby SS characters" would not be put off, so after a quick discussion between the two cameramen Caliendo offered to destroy the film if the Germans would let them keep their cameras. At 1850 hours the Germans agreed and the photographers ceremoniously opened their cameras and unraveled the film. At 1858 hours the jeep skittered into American lines with Caliendo and Herz grinning from ear to ear because of the trick they had pulled on the Germans. Just before leaving the conference room they had unloaded the exposed film, tucked it away in their uniforms, and reloaded their cameras. The destroyed film had been blank![24]

IV

Herz and Caliendo were such expert photographers that their work remained noticeably superb decades after the war. The former was an unusually sensitive and gifted photographer-artist whose work often incorporated a juxtaposition of war and peace. "I remember," he wrote, "that I often attempted to show pictorially the incongruity of battle and its aftermath, e.g., wounded men being treated in a Battalion Aid

Station in a crypt decorated with trumpet-blowing angels; a dead soldier in a burned-out tank with a church in the background; a little girl cradling a kitten in the smoking ruins of her farm."

Because of his sensitivity and intense humanity Herz engaged in self-censorship by refusing to shoot pictures of dead Americans. During the Battle of the Bulge he saw "a uniformed arm sticking heavenwards out of a pile of snow but since this stark scene involved the body of a fellow GI" he did not photograph it. Instead, he "shot a much less dramatic picture of some Grave Registration men doing their duty among unrecognizable snow-covered lumps in a wooded clearing." Such self-limitations were unusual but not unique. Harvey Weber's detachment "did not usually try for corpses in the pictures. While nobody ever mentioned it (not to do it), we did shy away from GI stiffs and only shot the Kraut stiffs if it was important to a picture." Out in the Pacific, Marine cameraman Martin Friedman took only one shot of a dead Marine showing the outline of a body wrapped in a canvas bag, and one of the Navy's most eminent photographers, Edward Steichen, tried not to depict war's most brutal ugliness.[25] Others felt no such compunction and photographed the war as it really was, with bodies blasted into debris hanging from nearby trees, the surrounding snow drenched in crimson. But censors prevented the publication of such graphically real photographs.[26]

When *Time* wanted a dramatic photo as the lead illustration for a story commemorating the 40th anniversary of D-Day at Normandy, it selected a Herz picture, which is not surprising since he was always in the heat of the action and his photos were excellent in terms of composition, lighting, and dramatic form. Supposedly taken in the dull morning light of June 6, 1944, the scene showed taut-faced infantrymen riding in an assault craft, clutching their weapons as they approached Omaha Beach and hunkering down against enemy artillery shells exploding in the water nearby. The shot conveyed the action so vividly that today a viewer can still sense the fear, taste the vomit rising in the throat, feel the chill spray soaking the uniforms and splashing against bare skin, and hear the roaring of artillery and boat motors.[27] Making someone far removed from the scene actually feel that he or she was there was "the test that separates snap-shooters from cameramen, and makes good combat cameramen rare specialists."[28]

Although the acuity of *Time*'s picture editors in selecting such a brilliant photo is commendable, their historical knowledge warrants no praise. Herz was not even in Europe on D-Day. The shot is his; but it depicts soldiers from the 89th Division in a DUKW crossing the Rhine River near Oberwesel, an action that Herz photographed in late March 1945.

Inadvertently Herz had been a party to the pictorial misidentification of World War II that occasionally occurs in the late twentieth century and that will undoubtedly get worse in the twenty-first century as those who knew World War II firsthand bequeath its history to subsequent generations. More recent examples occur in *American Image* by Martin W. Sandler,[29] wherein an an Iwo Jima scene is labeled as Guadalcanal because the Defense Department agency that supplied the photo provided the wrong information, and a picture of a medic in Sicily shot by Lieutenant John Steven Wever is miscaptioned as "Photographer unknown/Italy, 1943." Identifications of movies as well as still pictures are often faulty. The Army's 1953 documentary entitled *The 36th Infantry Division* is doubly deceptive, since it not only uses Huston's staged footage but incorporates it into sequences on the Salerno landings, the battle along the Rapido River, and the attack at Anzio. Few documentaries about D-Day omit a daylight scene of the accompanying airborne assaults, even though those actually occurred at night, and oftentimes scenes shot during rehearsals for an upcoming operation were intercut with genuine combat action.[30]

Pictorial misrepresentation of warfare dates from the Mexican War when the camera was less than a decade old, so such mistakes, though regrettable, are not surprising.[31] However, such errors demonstrate that still photographs and motion pictures are historical records that can be misused and abused as easily as written documents. As one scholar put it, "They may be lifted out of context, chosen as representative when they are not, incorrectly labeled, placed out of sequence, cropped, and doctored."[32] Viewers must be cautious, for they do not always see what they think they see.

If Herz's great strength was the ability to freeze a dramatic instant in time and instill it with extraordinary emotive powers, Caliendo's most noteworthy accomplishment was that even under the stress of combat he not only performed all the fundamentals soundly but also remained a master of motion-picture story building, a near-genius at maintaining continuity as he filmed a sequence.[33]

Aside from the ability to maintain continuity, several other factors distinguished marvelous motion-picture cameramen like Caliendo from mediocre ones. Excellent photographers had mastered the fundamental mechanical aspects of their craft. The automatic features that grace contemporary movie and video cameras were unknown in World War II. Getting a motion-picture camera properly loaded was a challenging task even under ideal conditions. The photographers loaded their cameras by hand, which could not be done in daylight without ruining the film. On the battlefield the men often resorted to a changing bag, a black bag with two light-proof armholes. Inside the bag the cameraman placed the camera, black paper to wrap the exposed film in, a metal can for the exposed roll, adhesive tape, a new roll of film, and a spare take-up spool. Working blind, he opened the camera, removed the exposed film, wrapped it, sealed it in the can and taped the can shut, inserted the new roll, and then threaded the film through gates and apertures, over and under notched rollers, and onto the take-up spool. Then he hoped that he had not made even a single slight mistake.

When ready to shoot, a cameraman focused by turning a ring on the lens, set the proper exposure, and if he was a still-picture photographer, set the proper shutter speed to stop the action so that the photo would not be blurred. He also had to make sure the lens was clean and the camera level. A cameraman carried a light meter to get proper exposure, but since holding one up to get a "reading" was an invitation to get shot, the photographer often just estimated the correct exposure. Constant practice at judging light values eventually resulted in near-perfect estimates almost every time, but until then a lot of film was either under- or over-exposed.

A photographer had to hold the camera absolutely steady, because the slightest movement was magnified a hundred times when projected onto a movie screen. Using a tripod eliminated the unsteadiness but, as Harry Downard phrased it, "Where the hell were you going to stand to set up [a tripod] to shoot combat when everybody's digging a hole?"[34] Hand-holding ruined many scenes because the human body, being a bipod rather than a tripod, is ill designed for holding a camera steady. Still, a hand-held camera could be reasonably steady if a cameraman practiced it, braced himself against a tree, rock, or wall, or used a special camera mount such as a modified rifle shoulder stock. Even with these precautions hand-held scenes were often readily apparent.

Even worse than a shaky scene was a shaky scene where the camera panned (that is, where the cameraman remained in one spot but moved the camera either vertically or horizontally). Carleton Mitchell told all his Navy CPU officers that "Panning ranks second to hand holding as a major evil. Occasionally the two are combined to produce results too terrible for description." Inexperienced cameramen panned too often and too fast and for no apparent reason except to be "artistic." It took training and experience to restrain the panning urge, to pan only when following movement and not on stationary objects, to pan with the action and not against it, to pan left to right (the way the American eye reads) instead of right to left, and to let the film run for a few feet before beginning a pan and then for a few more feet after completing it.[35]

Good photographers never confused quantity with quality. As Mitchell emphasized to his CPUs, "Better less film carefully made than a lot of poorly done [film]—material is judged by quality, not quantity. Over-shooting is the hallmark of the amateur." When the 2nd CPU submitted 25,000 feet of film for one project, Mitchell complained that the coverage was "too complete" and that more than 10,000 feet on any one subject was "frankly an embarrassing amount."[36] This problem also afflicted still photographers, many of whom simply aimed and fired without considering the picture's composition.[37] Experienced professionals understood that careful attention to the foreground and background as well as the main subject often made the difference between a compelling photograph and a mere snapshot. Not the least of the problems associated with shooting too much too quickly was that cameramen occasionally ran out of "ammunition" at the critical moment.

Once deployed overseas, motion-picture cameramen rarely saw the pictures they took, which was a severe handicap in trying to improve their mastery of the mechanics, artistry, and continuity essential for excellent work. Processing still photos was a comparatively simple procedure that could be done quickly and close to the action, but virtually all motion-picture film required processing in specialized labs in Hawaii, the United States, or the United Kingdom. Thus, still pictures could be studied, critiqued, and praised within hours after being taken but motion-picture men packaged up their exposed film, shipped it off to be developed, and then usually never saw it again.[38] Virtually all commentators agreed that correcting errors and maintaining enthusiasm and morale were difficult because movie cameramen never saw their film. "It's difficult to help a photographer improve his work, and keep him interested in it," wrote the OIC of CPU #6, "without ever showing him results. That's been one of our chief difficulties all along."[39]

Instead of seeing the film, motion-picture cameramen received written critiques, but these were "inadequate and sketchy," provided little technical data about such things as focus and exposure, did not take into account the hazards that the cameraman had endured, and often lumped the work of several cameramen together so that evaluating an individual's skill was almost impossible. "A cameraman can 'talk' a good case, may write a fine 'dope sheet', in wordy fashion perhaps, and still be a very, very poor cameraman and we have no means of proving his worthlessness," lamented one high-ranking Signal Corps officer. Unless units received detailed individual reports followed by 16mm work prints (crude but serviceable copies) of all exposed movie footage, not much qualitative improvement was likely because officers lacked "all the necessary information on which to weed out incompetents and build up the better men."[40]

Only occasionally did units receive work prints. In May 1944 the 12th CCU received about 9,000 feet of work print that unit personnel avidly viewed and critiqued. The unit history noted that the work prints were "excellent for the boys who take the pictures and for correcting mistakes in techniques." And in early 1945 the 164th SPC was overjoyed to get 50,000 feet of work print showing more than a year's work.[41] The AAF finally decided to send each CCU work prints of all the film its men had taken. "This will be of great benefit to the cameramen," commented a CCU history, "for they will now be able to see, within a reasonable amount of time, the results of their own work, and thereby be able to improve their techniques or correct their mistakes." The AAF's decision came just one month before Japan surrendered.[42]

Fortunately, the armed services mobilized enough motion-picture cameramen like Gordon Frye, Sam Tischler, and Barney Caliendo— men who were so good that they compensated for those who were inadequately trained and inexperienced when they went overseas and never had the opportunity to get much better.

V

Arthur Herz's war ended a week before V-E Day while he was photographing the crossing of the Isar River near Landshut. One of his greatest assets was his fluency in German, a linguistic skill that had been useful in locating specific sites in towns the Americans were attacking, translating and evaluating captured documents, interrogating enemy prisoners, and in persuading German soldiers to surrender rather than die fighting. But a surrender request was "an invitation which sometimes was not received with raised hands but with a few rounds from a burp gun." Such was the case along the Isar when a sniper put a bullet in Herz's side.

Bernard Caliendo watched in horror as his friend fell but resisted the temptation to attempt a foolhardy rescue since he, too, would be an easy target. Unlike Herz, Caliendo did not know a single word of German. Nonetheless he grabbed a nearby German civilian, "pulled out my little .45 and I put it in his back and pointed out there and he knew exactly what I wanted him to do and so he went out there and picked up Arthur and brought him back and then we put him in the jeep and took him to an aid station." Calley's quick thinking probably saved Herz's life—and his own.

6

"It Seemed Like a Lifetime"

The Army's 832nd Signal Service Battalion

"Nowhere in the world today," a correspondent told *Time* in December 1942, "are American soldiers engaged in fighting so desperate, so merciless, so bitter, or so bloody."

The reporter was referring neither to Guadalcanal, where the First Marine Division went ashore in August as part of Operation Watchtower, initiating a fierce six-month battle against the Japanese, nor to North Africa, where Operation Torch first sent American troops into combat against the Nazis in November. Instead the reporter was referring to the eastern tip of New Guinea, known as Papua. Commencing in late July 1942 and ending in January 1943, the Papuan campaign was the first Allied victory in the Southwest Pacific Area (SWPA) and the initial step on the arduous road back to the Philippines for SWPA's commander, General Douglas MacArthur.[1]

Places like Buna, Gona, Sanananda, Sinemi, Giruwa, Oro Bay, and Dobodura are all but forgotten now, but to men serving in Papua they meant death at worst and acute misery at best. Although MacArthur's headquarters issued one of its typically less-than-accurate press releases at the campaign's end saying that losses had been low, more Allied soldiers were killed or wounded in Papua than on Guadalcanal. Worse

135

places to fight may exist on earth, but if so mankind has yet to discover them. The burning equatorial sun made New Guinea seem hotter than the lowest level of Hell. When the sun did not shine, torrential rains of ten inches a day or more drenched the region. Combined with intense humidity that rarely dipped below 85 percent, the deluges ensured that muck and mire were a soldier's constant companions. The battlefield was a maze of swamps and jungles, sporadically broken by patches of shoulder-high, razor-sharp kunai grass. When not wading through neck-high swamp water, combatants hacked through tangles of trees and vines so dense that sunlight could not filter through to the ground. Assault waves moving through the jungle were "like a hand stretched out in a dark room, feeling their way."[2]

Soldiers did not flourish under these conditions. While their uniforms rotted off, leeches and various types of fungi, collectively known as jungle rot, latched on. Fifty years after the war veterans still visited their dermatologists to receive prescriptions to control fungus-related ailments acquired in New Guinea. And if the terrain and climate were inhospitable to transient human visitors—"this is no place for man not even fit for a Jap," an American noted in his diary[3]—they were paradise for snakes, lizards, spiders, rats, maggots, and mosquitoes, and for dengue fever, scrub typhus, dhobie itch, ringworm, skin ulcers, acute dysentery, malaria, and a host of other ills, many of them unknown to Western medicine.

Naturally Signal Corps cameramen were with the American forces throughout the entire SWPA campaign, commencing in Papua and ending in the Philippines. Along the way they learned that although "civilization makes a softy out of a person" they could adapt to primitive conditions, endure, and perform their mission.[4] The most noteworthy expression of their perseverance and skill, and their greatest collective gift to posterity, is *Attack! The Battle for New Britain*, a documentary of ground combat in SWPA that starkly revealed the tough physical labor and sheer misery involved in jungle fighting.

The initial SWPA Army photographic contingent was the 832nd Signal Photographic Detachment, consisting of approximately eighty-five officers and men detached from the 161st SPC at Fort Benning. As additional photographers trickled into SWPA the unit was twice redesignated and reorganized, first as the Photographic Detachment, 832nd Signal Service Company and then as the 832nd Signal Service Battalion (SSB). For convenience, this chapter refers to the unit as the 832nd SSB during the entire SWPA campaign. The 832nd was one of eight SSBs organized under T/O&E 11-500, which was promulgated in July 1943 and which dealt with all Signal Service organizations, including radar, radio, wire, signal intelligence, signal security, and photographic units. A fundamental aspect of T/O&E 11-500 photo units was that they were more flexible than the SPCs organized under T/O&E 11-37. Not only did T/O&E 11-500 provide for eleven different types of photo outfits, but these could be tailored to meet specific needs under differing conditions.[5] Consequently they varied tremendously in size. In June 1944 the 832nd SSB consisted of 204 officers and men, while the 3117th was less than a tenth as large; in May 1945 the 3119th SSB was only twenty-four strong but the 3908th contained 365 officers and men.[6] Although they were organized differently and more flexibly, like the SPCs all T/O&E 11-500 photo units were subject to the SOPs contained in War Department Pamphlet No. 11-2.

I

Shortly after arriving in Melbourne in late July 1942 the Army's 832nd SSB moved to Brisbane, where it set up and staffed a photo lab and divided the photographers into nine detachments, each consisting of one officer and from five to seven enlisted men. These soon deployed into the field. For example, in mid-September Unit #3 went with the 41st Infantry Division to Rockhampton and Unit #4 joined the 32nd Infantry Division, which was then in training just outside Brisbane. In late 1942 the 32nd Division moved northward to New Guinea, where it became the primary American unit involved in the Papuan campaign. Shortly thereafter Unit #4, commanded by Lieutenant Frederick A. German, arrived to photograph the division's desperate struggle against the enemy and the environment. Among German's photographers was William A. Avery.[7]

Before the war Avery had worked in the still picture laboratory at Columbia Pictures Corporation and as a free-lance still photographer. In March 1941 he tried to enlist in the Navy as a Photographer 2nd Class, but despite glowing recommendations from those who knew his work, the seaborne service rejected him because he wore glasses. Having no such qualms about a man whose eyesight was imperfect, the Army drafted him three weeks after Pearl Harbor. Although his letters of recommendation failed him with the Navy, when he flashed them around the Army induction center they were impressive enough to send him to the Army Photographic School at Fort Monmouth. There he underwent basic training and took photo classes in which the students learned about Speed Graphics and Eyemos. Since Avery owned and used a Speed Graphic in civilian life and had learned about Eyemos while at Columbia Pictures, he yawned his way through the classes as best he could. After he had completed the course the Army assigned him to the 161st SPC at Fort Benning. Soon he was off to Australia—and the war. Nowhere along the line had he received even a single hour of genuine combat training.

When Avery's unit arrived in New Guinea the Papuan campaign was in its final phase, with the battle centering on the strongly fortified Japanese position near Buna. Since the Australians and Americans lacked sufficient artillery, tanks, and air support to break through the enemy's defensive perimeter, the battle resembled a prolonged siege, with almost constant fighting as the Allies probed at the dug-in defenders, squeezing them into an ever-smaller area. Avery photographed action at Dobodura, Buna, Buna Mission, and Sinemi. Just one week before the campaign ended, he, Frederick German, and photographer Benjamin H. Burton performed so heroically at Giruwa that Captain Edwin C. Bloch of the 32nd Division's 127th Infantry Regiment recommended each of them for a Silver Star.

For a week the Japanese had compelled Bloch's battalion to cling desperately to a defensive position along the beach at Giruwa while other Allied units were organizing an enveloping movement against the enemy. To coordinate action between his battalion and the enveloping force, Bloch had to establish contact with an Australian unit only a mile to the north. But that intervening mile was enemy-held territory and any patrol advancing northward would have to hug the beach, which afforded no cover against the Japanese hidden in the dense jungle rimming it. Bloch called for five volunteers to accompany him on this dangerous assignment. In their eagerness to compile a complete photographic record of the battle, German, Avery, and Burton also volunteered, and a light machine-gun crew followed somewhat to the rear to provide covering fire for the patrol.

"Not knowing the strength of any Japanese forces we might encounter," said Avery, "the going was very slow and careful." It took three hours to cover one mile. Much of the way the men were in water and mud over their knees and sometimes up to their waists, in full view of concealed Japanese soldiers, and subject to intermittent but intense machine-gun and rifle fire. When the patrol finally contacted the Australians it established a defensive perimeter, which it held for several hours until the main force moved up. Bloch not only praised the cameramen for volunteering in the first place but also for taking "many pictures while under enemy fire with utter disregard for their personal safety." He also made an admission few officers ever make: his men had been suffering from poor morale. The photographers' bravery "was an inspiration to the members of my command," Bloch wrote, and it raised their spirits.

As sometimes happened in the confusion of war, Bloch's Silver Star recommendations got lost. In early 1944 the Army's Chief Signal Officer, having learned of the recommendations, wrote Bloch asking him to resubmit them, which he did. Alas, somewhere in the stupendous paper flow that accompanied this stupendous war the new recommendations were also lost! All efforts to trace them failed, and the war ended without Avery getting a Silver Star.

Silver Star or no Silver Star, Avery still had more of the war to cover. Shortly after the Giruwa action he had a dreadful experience: he saw— and photographed—evidence of Japanese cannibalism. Well before the battle ended Allied soldiers had encountered horribly emaciated enemy corpses. Now in the campaign's waning days Avery entered a Japanese hospital just inland from Giruwa and "photographed a butchered corpse in the kitchen area. One leg was still boiling in a pot on the stove. There was absolutely no other food to be found, but a canteen cup was full of [human] meat." The hospital patients "were starving. One man, barely alive, was lying next to a body-shaped mass of maggots." As historians now recognize, starvation was a major factor in the Japanese defeat at Buna because the Navy and AAF had severed their supply lines. Had MacArthur not rushed the battle's pace, the Japanese would have been defeated in only slightly more time and with many fewer Allied dead and wounded.[8]

A month after the battle ended Unit #4 returned to Australia where the 832nd SSB's units were reorganized. Avery became a member of Unit #2 commanded by Lieutenant Daniel G. Mason and including Frank J. Goetzheimer, Walter Drexler, and Francis H. Tichenor. In October 1943 Unit #2 joined the 503rd Parachute Infantry, which was to make an airborne assault as part of the Cape Gloucester invasion. To cover the 503rd's activities Mason, Avery, Goetzheimer, and Drexler volunteered to take jump training. They spent a weekend tumbling and falling, getting up, and then tumbling and falling again until, said Avery, "I was never so SORE in all my life." Glasses may have kept Avery out of the Navy but, with a liberal use of tape, they did not prevent him from leaping out of an airplane. Although Drexler broke his ankle on the first jump, the other three made the requisite five practice jumps.[9]

Avery never got to put his airborne training to the test, or even to photograph combat again. The para-photographers did not participate in the Cape Gloucester campaign because higher authority canceled the 503rd's role. Unit #2 then went to Goodenough Island, where it linked up with a 32nd Division regiment for the Saidor invasion. But Avery had been briefly hospitalized several times during the Papuan Campaign for various illnesses, and had contracted malaria soon after his heroics at Giruwa, which put him in a hospital for almost a month. On Goodenough he got a serious case of typhus fever that again sent him to a hospital. There the attending surgeon recommended that he be withdrawn from combat-related missions. So severe were the aftereffects from his multiple diseases that he could have received an immediate medical discharge. But Avery chose to remain on duty in a noncombat capacity, working for the Photographic Division Supply Division, Signal Section, Headquarters of the Army Service of Supply.

By early 1945, however, Avery was suffering from such "a marked somnolent condition" that he could not stay awake for more than twelve hours a day. After examining him, the head of SWPA's Typhus Commission recommended that he be discharged and warned him that he might never recover, which was an accurate prognosis. Despite this potentially crippling condition Avery had a remarkable postwar career. He returned to his old job at Columbia Pictures before moving to MGM and finally to Paramount Studios, where he became the first Hollywood studio photographer to shoot promotional still pictures with a 35mm camera. While working on the sets of more than 130 feature-length films he took such stunning portraits of movie stars—including Audrey Hepburn, Steve McQueen, Alfred Hitchcock, Woody Allen, Anthony Quinn, Henry Fonda, and Kirk Douglas—that in 1988 the Academy of Motion Picture Arts and Sciences held a champagne reception for an exhibition of his photographs. Avery thus enjoyed the rare distinction of being an honored still photographer in the world's motion-picture capital.

II

"I was just four calendar years older when I got out," said Bill Ettinger about his World War II stint in the Army, "but it seemed like a lifetime." The problem was that while growing to adulthood in the Midwest he had always said he wanted to go West. But as he half-seriously, half-humorously recalled decades after the war, "I failed to say how far." He had thought in terms of California or Oregon, but the Army exceeded his wishes and sent him much further westward than the West Coast. By the time the Army honorably discharged him just six weeks before Hiroshima he had spent almost three years in SWPA, where service seemed to accelerate the aging process. Fighting the slime, muck, kunai grass, fungi, leeches, rodents, and mosquitoes—not to mention the Japanese—made days seem like weeks, weeks like months, months like years, and years like decades.[10]

After being drafted in August 1941, supposedly for only one year, Ettinger went to training camp at Camp Grant in Illinois. Since he had been a prewar newspaper photographer, when officials there asked him what he could do he answered that he could take pictures, a response that got him assigned to the Fort Monmouth Photographic School for the thirteen-week class. Ettinger graduated on Friday, December 5, looking forward to eight months of easy stateside duty before donning civilian garb again. But on Monday, December 8 he was on his way to the 161st SPC at Fort Benning knowing that "our one year of service had just vanished."

At both Monmouth and Benning the most important things he learned had little to do with photography and everything to do with that special trait that confounded the officer-photographers: how to avoid normal soldierly duties. In more than three months at Monmouth he stood guard only once and got nailed for KP duty but thrice. In six months at Benning he never ran the obstacle course, never went to the firing range, and never walked anywhere because he always had access to a vehicle. However, he did learn to treat his camera with religious reverence. As one of his buddies stressed, "it's the only thing between you and the infantry."

Ettinger was with Avery in the original photographic detachment sent from Fort Benning that became the nucleus of the 832nd SSB. The enhanced velocity of his nonchronological aging really began in January 1943, when he deployed from Australia to New Guinea as part of Unit #3 to cover the 41st Infantry Division. Unit #3 went first to Port Moresby on the southern Papuan coast, where a sign greeted them that read: "Through these portals pass the best damn mosquito bait in the world." From Moresby the photographers sailed to the deepwater port at Oro Bay on the northern Papuan coast and then traveled to Dobodura, a grassy plain fifteen miles south of Buna where the Allies had established an air base. The "road" to Dobodura was "the only place in the world where you could be stuck in the mud and have dust blow in your face at the same time." On a good day it took four hours to drive the eighteen mile route even if you were in a hurry, because vehicles inevitably bogged down in soupy mud the color and consistency of a chocolate milk shake.

Dobodura, said Ettinger, "was to be our new home for the next several miserable months." Here the men learned all too soon and all too much about living in the bush—that fevers, dysentery, and leg ulcers were the norm rather than the exception, that it could rain twelve inches a night, that it often seemed literally hotter than Hades, that the Army's standard-issue jungle pack held more than a man could carry very far, and that "hardtack doesn't have the same consistency as a glazed donut." And that the Japanese knew about the place. Air raids occurred almost nightly. On February 20–21, for instance, enemy planes arrived at 10:00 p.m. and left at midnight, only to return at 2:00 a.m. for another half hour. They were so low the men could hear the "click" when the bombs were released. As the bombs came closer and closer to his tent Ettinger "lived a lifetime in a few minutes.... You really pray then of all times." Dawn saw him hard at work digging his slit trench longer and deeper just in case Someone Up Above did not hear or heed the prayers. Aside from the fear, "you can't sleep when you have to keep both ears open." The cameramen lost sleep every night until they became so exhausted that they slept right through the raids or, worse, simply ceased caring whether they lived or died and remained on their cots rather than fleeing to their slit trenches just a few steps beyond the tent flaps.

With diligence and hard work Ettinger photographed a great deal of military activity, except for actual fighting. Using an Eyemo he recorded events leading up to a battle, such as building roads, bridges, and hospitals, unloading supplies, laying iron matting for a new airstrip, antiaircraft batteries preparing for action, frontline machine gun emplacements, and barbed wire entanglements. And he photographed

Your receipt

Items that you checked out

Title:
Armed with cameras : the American
military photographers of World War II
ID: 0030301439573
Due: Wednesday, May 29, 2019

Total items: 1
Account balance: $0.00
5/1/2019 8:55 AM
Checked out: 1
Overdue: 0
Hold requests: 0
Ready for pickup: 0

Thank you for using the bibliotheca
SelfCheck System.

battle's aftermath, including closeups of a burning ship where oil drums and antiaircraft shells were exploding, damaged planes and cratered airstrips, medics at work, award ceremonies, burials, and bodies blown apart ("you want to stand upwind when you take that kind of shot"). Like many other cameramen Ettinger "hoped they would publish more [pictures] of dead Americans just to show the people back home that American soldiers do die." But when it came to genuine combat not much could be preserved for posterity. Although Ettinger often *saw* bombing attacks and dog fights, the planes were so far away they looked like dust specks through the lens, and he rarely saw enemy soldiers at all.

By June 1943 the war had swept northward beyond Papua, leaving little for the cameramen to do except take personal pictures of and for high-ranking officers, lie around wasting time, and bitch about the lack of promotions. "We are the original sad sacks," wrote Ettinger amidst the boredom, cursing, and self-pity. Finally on August 7 the unit left for Australia. After eight months in the bush the men celebrated their return to "civilization" by gorging on ice cream and Cokes, luxuriating in hot showers, donning clean khakis, walking on sidewalks, and being awestruck at the moon's beauty when it was not lighting their camp up for an air raid.

After six months of comparative ease Ettinger went back to New Guinea in a reorganized unit that joined the 41st Division in preparation for the late April invasion at Hollandia, two thirds of the way up the New Guinea coast toward the Philippines. Although he soon developed such a severe case of jungle ulcers that he looked like a leper and medics suggested he be hospitalized, Ettinger insisted on participating in the invasion. He went ashore in the second wave carrying 1,500 feet of film and accompanied by a soldier who was packing an additional 2,000 feet for him. As soon as he hit the beach Ettinger deposited his jungle pack next to a command radio car and spent the day photographing events. Nightfall caught him inland from the beach so he did not return for his pack. That evening a lone Japanese bomber appeared over the beach and dropped a single bomb, which hit a gasoline dump right next to "his" command car. "I think my pack is still up in the air," Ettinger wrote thirty-five years later. Fortunately he and his film-carrier companion were lugging all their film with them, and when Ettinger left Hollandia several weeks later he had shot it all.

Ettinger did not know it at the time, but Hollandia ended his fighting war. He remained in SWPA for another year carrying out a number of photographic assignments, always under adverse conditions, but saw no further sustained combat.

Heat, rain, mildew, arachnids, dysentery, jungle rot, skin ulcers, ringworm, malaria, too little sleep and too much mud, Japanese bombs and bullets. Such was Bill Ettinger's life in SWPA. Yet from his perspective every other theater and service had worse drawbacks. Europe was too cold and snowy and the AAF would have been too hard on his stomach since he got air sick almost every time he flew. Bad as conditions were, he would not have traded places with any other cameraman.

III

An essential aspect of the duty performed by Avery, Ettinger, and their photographic colleagues around the globe was writing captions, a task they performed almost daily while the scenes they had photographed were still fresh in their minds.

A story related by Mark Twain emphasized the significance of a good caption (or label). While visiting New Orleans, that southern terminus of life on the Mississippi, he studied a Civil War painting by E. B. D. Fabrino Julio done in the late 1860s. The canvas was of Confederate generals Robert E. Lee and Thomas J. "Stonewall" Jackson. But what exactly did it depict? Was this the first meeting of the two men? Was Jackson reporting a victory, or a defeat? Was Lee inviting his corps commander to dinner? Or said Twain, perhaps Jackson was asking Lee for a match. Fortunately little such confusion existed there. Almost everyone knew that Julio's artistry portrayed the meeting between Lee and Jackson on May 2, 1863, their last war council, because later that same day a hail of "friendly fire" mortally wounded Stonewall. But if an onlooker, by some stroke of ignorance, did not *know* this, the painting lost its dramatic significance; the most that could then be said with certainty was that here were Lee and Jackson together, immortalized smaller than life.

After musing on all this Mark Twain concluded that like most historical pictures, the painting meant nothing without a label: "A good legible label is usually worth, for information, a ton of significant attitude and expression in a historical picture."[11] As usual Twain was correct even when he was not necessarily being humorous. Without a title or caption a picture loses much of its importance. By itself a photograph often explains very little and invites multiple interpretations, some of which can become sheer fantasy. A caption allows a picture to speak to the viewer, to tell him or her exactly what the photograph or painting depicts. As one scholar put it, "the meaning of the photograph is too imprecise in itself and needs to be anchored by a caption, if it is not to drift into ambiguity."[12]

Authorities in the armed services recognized the value of full, accurate captions. "Captions are nearly as important as the picture which they describe," intoned an SPC SOP. "Too much emphasis cannot be put on correct and complete captioning." The "Handbook for Motion Picture Photographers" implored cameramen to remember that personnel handling their "film may be miles away and know nothing about the subject matter submitted by the cameraman. They depend on the cameraman to supply them with all the detailed information vital to the film, otherwise, this film will have no value."[13] After all, the Army distributed copies of Signal Corps combat-footage caption sheets to about twenty government agencies, some of them not directly or intimately involved with actual combat operations. As an AAF newsletter put it, "No one knows as much about the film as the people who made it, and if they don't tell us, all the research in the world won't compensate for what is lacking. The caption sheets are your voice in editing and commentary."[14]

Each service devised elaborate captioning procedures to follow and forms (often called dope sheets) to complete. War Department Pamphlet 11-2 provided an example. "Photographic coverage is valueless unless the pictures are completely identified by properly documented supplementary notes," it said. "Such notes, called captions, must contain all the information necessary for analysis or for the writing of commentaries." At a minimum captions contained the photographer's name and unit and answered these questions: Who? What? When? Where? Good captions also explained how an action portrayed on film "is performed, and under what special circumstances" and "why the subject was thought worth photographing." Whenever necessary, cameramen were to include maps, charts, or other documents to supplement the standard caption data. For still pictures the War Department insisted that captions be typewritten or printed in triplicate and shipped with the negative to the APS in Washington. Every print developed in the war zone before the negative went to the

APS was to have a copy of the caption pasted on the back. Motion picture cameramen had to make caption sheets in quadruplicate; one copy stayed in the war zone and the original and two copies went with the film to the processing lab.[15]

As an additional measure to ensure adequate information, officials also wanted movie photographers to slate their film. On a pocket-sized standard movie slate or on an improvised substitute a cameraman wrote his name, organization, subject, date, place, and assignment number. Then he briefly photographed the slate, preferably at the beginning of each roll of film. If the cameraman knew his subject in advance, slating at the front of the roll was easy. When roving the forward areas in combat the policy was for a cameraman "to slate whenever possible, but not to allow slating to hinder his work."[16] Generally movie photographers considered slating "a pain in the ass." A few simply would not do it, and some had the slate so out of focus or off center that film editors could not read it, but others slated quite well even under dangerous circumstances.[17] Several members of the 10th CCU received praise for their excellent slating and captioning during the battle for Myitkyina in Burma, and a Signal Corps cameraman who photographed an attack on a Japanese pillbox "slated every roll made under fire, thus showing fine professional discipline."[18]

Despite these precautions, captions could lie or at least not tell the whole truth. Sometimes captions were inadvertently inaccurate. Navy photographers lacked training in ship identification and in the long-range confusion of naval engagements they were not always accurate in identifying which ship was which.[19] Other miscaptioning was less innocent. Barney Caliendo was in Mortain, in France, after the battle there; he saw some engineers about to demolish a building. He asked them to give him a long fuse and then as soon as they lit it to "just run down the road and hit the ditch. So I back off and I get behind a big cart wheel and I shoot through the spokes and they light the fuse and they take off." Caliendo's film showed the engineers sprinting down the road and hitting the dirt as the building erupted in the background. He sent in a caption saying the scene showed a direct hit on the structure by a German artillery shell and received back a glowing report on such a fine shot.[20]

Caliendo's colleague Herz did not exactly lie but failed to provide a complete caption when he sent in a still picture of a group "of pathetic, frightened, tearful half-grown 15–16 year old German boys in Volkssturm uniform; they had been brutally commanded by a dapper, well-decorated Norwegian SS officer." Although the shot graphically showed and the caption explicitly explained that "the Nazis were scraping the very bottom of their manpower barrel, my caption failed to indicate that following a brief interrogation, the boys were sent to the rear as POWs whereas the Norwegian SS man was summarily executed."[21]

The armed services placed an extreme emphasis on identifying the soldiers, airmen, sailors, and Marines who appeared in every shot and scene. Some scholars believe that the foremost aspect of wartime photography was its anonymity. "Because the war was a common cause," one commentator has argued, "no one in it has a right to appear as anything but anonymous."[22] The anonymity argument rests primarily on national publications and a few famous photographs, such as Joe Rosenthal's picture of the second Iwo Jima flag raising. But this argument ignores the vast number of local publications, especially newspapers, that allowed the local folk to share the war with "their" boys overseas.

The armed forces strove to reduce the anonymity, to make the war personal. Confronted by World War II's dehumanizing aspects—its sheer massiveness, the reliance on sophisticated technology, the importance of overwhelming numbers of machines, the capricious nature of death and maiming—those directing the photographic effort emphasized the individual. Although one historian believes that this effort occurred only late in the war as the war's impersonal nature became especially pronounced,[23] the individual emphasis was present from the first campaigns. Photographic authorities recognized from the start that Americans did not want nameless images; they wanted to *know* their heroes and to identify with their exploits.

"In combat and out," wrote Bill Avery, "if we were photographing an individual, his name and home town was always included in the caption." And when a photo showed an individual soldier the Army wanted his face to be recognizable.[24] The AAF told its cameramen to "personalize men with enough details of background mode of life, rigors they endure, and their reactions." Edward Steichen urged his naval cameramen to "photograph the man, the little guy; the struggle, the heartaches, plus the dreams of this guy." Of course Steichen's men had to shoot some battleships and carriers, to please the brass if nothing else, but they should spend most of their time on individual sailors.[25] Marine Corps Combat Correspondents received repeated urgings to photograph individuals, not things, and to tell *"the story of action through the part taken by one man."* Hence *"Every* caption for *every* picture must be complete in itself, with full names, addresses, and information. . . ."[26]

If an important picture arrived in the States without this personalized information, the armed forces made a concerted effort to identify the individuals. In Rosenthal's Iwo Jima photograph five of the six men in it are not anonymous at all. Soon after the shot appeared on the front pages of the Sunday newspapers in late February 1945, people began asking who the flag-raisers were and the Marine Corps hastened to find out. In short order the three who were still alive—John Bradley, Ira H. Hayes, and René Gagnon—had been identified and brought back from the war zone to participate as living heroes in the 7th War Loan Drive, which began less than two months after the flag had been raised on that desolate isle. Those who died in the fighting before fame could rescue them were Michael Strank, Franklin R. Sousley, and either Henry O. Hansen or Harlon Block. Despite intensive efforts to identify the sixth man, including a Congressional investigation, the dispute as to whether it was Hansen or Block has never been resolved.[27]

Another such quest for identification involved a photo taken by the 196th SPC's John S. Wever that appeared on newspaper front pages from Baltimore to Los Angeles on September 2, 1943. Taken in an alley in Sant'Agata, Sicily, less than half a mile from the German lines and while under constant bombardment, Wever's picture showed Private First Class Harvey White of Minneapolis administering blood plasma to a wounded soldier. Though Wever's caption noted White's name it failed to identify the GI receiving the plasma. People wanted to know who the wounded soldier was. It took a concerted effort by the 3rd Infantry Division Headquarters but the man was finally identified: Private Roy W. Humphrey of Toledo.[28]

Rather than being exclusively one or the other, the photographic record was a mixture of the anonymous and the known. The war was a team effort, but teamwork did not require the submersion of every individual's identity.

IV

With his tiny stature, sparkling eyes, and almost impish look, he seemed a mere child among grown men. But like race, gender, or religion, size is no indicator of competence or courage; and five foot four and one half inches-tall Frank Goetzheimer repeatedly matched even his biggest colleagues in both competence and courage, especially during the reconquest of the Philippines. As with Avery and Ettinger, Goetzheimer attended the Photo School at Fort Monmouth, joined the 161st SPC at Fort Benning, and arrived in SWPA with the 832nd Signal Photographic Detachment. Unlike his two fellow photographers he missed the Papuan campaign because he stayed in Australia photographing army maneuvers. Only during the fall of 1943 did his war become more exciting.[29]

Goetzheimer was one of the Unit #2 photographers who earned a paratrooper insignia with the 503rd Paratroop Regiment. Following the cancellation of the planned jump at Cape Gloucester, the unit was attached to the 32nd Division on Goodenough Island for the Saidor invasion. At this point Avery and Goetzheimer parted, the former going to a hospital and the latter making the amphibious assault at Saidor in the first wave. For three months Goetzheimer covered combat operations in the Saidor-Madang region, the start of his superb combat photographic record. The critique of the film shot by Goetzheimer and Tichenor commended both men. "Extremely good attention to detail under obviously difficult circumstances," it read. "A fine choice of camera angles. For hand camera work, the material was also remarkably steady. All in all, a praiseworthy job." During the advance to cut off the Japanese route of escape to Madang, Goetzheimer accompanied the spearhead of the attack, which "met quite a bit of enemy resistance." He "had a damn tough go" of it dodging grenades and negotiating hills "standing up like a ladder and as slippery as hell." Under such circumstances "an Eyemo camera and 12 rolls of film is impossible to carry—but I did it."

After the Saidor-Madang campaign, Goetzheimer returned to Australia, where he worked in the 832nd SSB lab for several months and then photographed the naval bombardment of Morotai Island in the Dutch East Indies from the decks of a destroyer. Although the capture of Morotai placed Allied forces on the Philippines' doorstep, Goetzheimer was disappointed because he "wasn't getting much excitement" in the lab at Brisbane or from the deck of a ship. So he volunteered to serve with the 6th Ranger Infantry Battalion, which spearheaded the Philippines invasion.

Most people believe the attack on Leyte Island on October 20, 1944 marked the culmination of MacArthur's pledge to return to the

Philippines, but this is not true. On October 17 and 18, amidst heaving seas and driving rainstorms, the 6th Rangers assaulted three small islands guarding the entrance to Leyte Gulf. Goetzheimer accompanied the first wave attacking Homonhon Island on the 18th. Although the Japanese did not oppose these mini-island invasions, the Rangers had not known in advance that they would be so fortunate. Once ashore they set up harbor lights, which were essential in guiding the main invasion convoy on the 20th.

Following the landing on Homonhon, Goetzheimer covered combat on Leyte for six weeks before transferring back to the 503rd Paratroop Regiment, which was to air drop on Mindoro in advance of the amphibious assault on that island. But once again, like the aborted Cape Gloucester jump, his paratroop training went for naught. Because of an aircraft shortage the jump was canceled and the paratroopers went to Mindoro on ships, wading ashore like amphibians slithering in from the sea, not alighting like birds from the sky. As he had done at Saidor and Homonhon, the pint-sized cameraman went in with the first wave. Ground combat on Mindoro was relatively light so Goetzheimer soon rejoined the 6th Rangers for his fourth amphibious assault, the invasion of Luzon at Lingayen Gulf on January 9, 1945.

To photograph Luzon operations the Signal Corps committed one hundred ten photographers, most of whom, like Goetzheimer, went ashore on D-Day at Lingayen Gulf. As elsewhere during this war, the cameramen were invariably ahead of or with the lead combat units. Lloyd W. Halter, the OIC of a combat assignment unit, joined an eighteen-man patrol from the 43rd Division that scouted San Jacinto. Just outside the town they encountered a Japanese defensive position, and before the battered patrol escaped thirteen men had been killed or wounded. Halter was one of the fortunate six who escaped unscathed, and the next day his unit's jeep was the first vehicle to enter San Jacinto. Shortly thereafter he and Milton Snyder were ten miles behind enemy lines, riding in a captured Japanese staff car driven by Filipino guerrillas who took them to Guimba so they could photograph guerrilla activities. The exploits of Halter and Snyder were not unusual. Two other photographers entered Bambean with a patrol that was several miles ahead of the main force. Another photographic unit outdistanced the infantry to San Marcelino to record the liberators' triumphal entry, and then moved into Olongapo behind the first tank and even captured a Japanese garrison flag there.[30]

In the Central Luzon Valley several photo teams raced "not to keep

up with, but to get ahead of, the assault troops so that they could photograph the entry into Manila." There they covered the savage urban
fighting that left the Philippine capital one of World War II's most
heavily damaged cities. The suicidal, seemingly senseless month-long
Japanese defense virtually leveled the once-beautiful city and inflicted
a terrific toll on its civilian population. "Many of us had tears in our
eyes, and hatred in our hearts," wrote one cameraman, "because that
day we saw the Japanese policy, 'If we can't have it, no one shall.'
What many of us had referred to as the 'enemy' that day changed to
'the dirty little murdering yellow bastards.'" So extraordinary was the
coverage of the Battle for Manila that a cameraman serving in Italy
who saw the footage considered it "the best job of the war."[31]

Although Goetzheimer missed the fighting in Manila he participat-
ed in two dramatic actions elsewhere on Luzon, the raid on
Cabanatuan and the airborne assault on Corregidor. Initially "things
were pretty quiet" in the Rangers' sector on Luzon. Neither a mid-
January landing in a rubber boat with a Ranger patrol on nearby
Santiago Island nor the subsequent invasion of that island, which was
Goetzheimer's fifth amphibious operation, yielded much action. But
when Goetzheimer left Calasiao, Luzon, in late January with Company
C of the 6th Rangers he was embarking on one of the war's most dar-
ing operations: the raid on Cabanatuan, a town twenty-five miles
behind enemy lines where the Japanese had more than 500 men,
including more than 400 Americans, interned in a prisoner-of-war
camp. As the raid's leader, the 6th Rangers' Lieutenant Colonel Henry
A. Mucci, told his men, these prisoners were "what's left of our troops
who held out on Bataan and Corregidor ... and if we don't free them
now, you can bet they'll be killed by the Japs before our front reaches
their area."[32]

The Cabanatuan raiding force consisted of 120 Rangers, fourteen
members of a special Sixth Army reconnaissance unit known as the
Alamo Scouts, several hundred Filipino guerrillas and volunteers led by
Captains Juan Pajota and Eduardo Joson, and four men of the 832nd
SSB's Combat Photo Unit F: Goetzheimer, John W. Lueddeke, Wilber
B. Goen, and Robert C. Lautman. No one knew the precise number of
Japanese in the vicinity, but intelligence estimates put it at thousands of
soldiers with tanks at their disposal. "You had better get down on your
knees and pray," Mucci told his men with good reason. "Dammit, don't
fake it. I mean PRAY! And, I want you to swear an oath before God,
swear you'll die fighting rather than let any harm come to those POWs!"

On the night of January 28 the raiders passed through American lines. Moving only at night and sometimes bypassing enemy positions barely forty yards away, they arrived at their destination late on the 30th. The men of Combat Photo Unit F had a reputation for their "propensity to forget pictures for a more aggressive part in the fighting, but this time they were able to abandon their cameras with impunity, for most of the action took place after sunset." Goetzheimer accompanied the Ranger who crawled up to the prison gate and shot the lock off. Then he burst into the camp with the first liberators, running through the prisoners' quarters and shepherding the bewildered inmates out the gate. Within fifteen minutes all the prison guards were dead, the prisoners were free, and thousands of Japanese were converging on the area. Many of the captives were in such poor physical condition that the raiders had to carry them three miles to the rendezvous point where Filipino volunteers had assembled water buffalo carts to expedite the retreat. Filipino guerrillas, occasionally aided by some of the Rangers, established strategically-located blocking positions to keep the enemy at bay, buying time for the slow-moving column to reach the carts and then make the dangerous journey back to the American lines. As Goetzheimer told a reporter, "We owe our lives to the Filipino guerrillas, I guess; they protected our flanks on the way in, and covered our withdrawal."

By all but one standard of judgment the Cabanatuan raid was a resounding success. While Japanese casualties were heavy, Ranger casualties were only two dead and seven wounded, and the Filipinos had no dead and only twelve wounded. Although one prisoner died of a heart attack just as he was being ushered out the prison gate, 516 others were now enjoying freedom. But from the photographic viewpoint the raid was a failure. Darkness prevented coverage of the actual attack and during the daylight retreat the column never remained in one place very long. "I've been carrying this equipment for two days and haven't been able to take a single foot of film," Goetzheimer complained to one of the liberated Americans. "Every time I'm ready to set up the Rangers are on the move again!"

Goetzheimer had better luck two weeks later when he participated in the recapture of Corregidor, known as The Rock, where the last organized American units in the Philippines had surrendered to the Japanese in May 1942, completing the national humiliation that had commenced at Pearl Harbor. The bulbous head of tadpole-shaped Corregidor was known as Topside, the highest part of the island.

Nature had cleaved the 550-foot summit into deep jagged ravines and jutting rock outcroppings, and surrounded it with sheer cliffs. Strong and unpredictable winds wafted across Topside. Three years of war had splintered trees and shrubs that had become hazardous stakes that threatened to impale descending troops, battered concrete buildings, gouged deep bomb and shell craters, and strewn a liberal icing of debris on two small level areas, a nine-hole golf course and a parade ground.[33]

Astonishingly, the Americans planned to retake The Rock with an airborne attack by the 503rd on Topside followed several hours later by an amphibious assault by a battalion from the 24th Infantry Division along the tadpole's tail. No one, American or Japanese, thought Topside had even relatively decent drop zones. Airborne commanders preferred long, wide, level, and uncluttered areas, but the parade ground was only 325 yards long and 250 yards wide, the golf course was even smaller, and neither was in mint condition. Everyone agreed that an air drop on The Rock would be the war's most difficult airborne operation. However, strategists believed retaking Corregidor by amphibious assault alone was even more risky, and an airborne assault would have two advantages. Intelligence reports indicated that only 850 Japanese were defending Corregidor so the paratroopers would outnumber the defenders by more than two to one. And the assault would achieve surprise. Conditions were so unfavorable for paratroopers that American planners believed the Japanese would consider such an attack insane and be unprepared to defeat it.

To cover such an important operation the 832nd SSB committed substantial resources. Five cameramen comprising Combat Photo Unit Q participated in the first day's airborne drop. Unit Q consisted of Goetzheimer, who was *finally* going to put his airborne training to the test, Richard Williams, George W. Woodruff, and two of Goetzheimer's colleagues from the Cabanatuan raid, Goen and Lautman. Other than Goetzheimer, none of these cameramen had ever made even a practice jump before. Combat Photo Unit A covered the amphibious assault at ground level and five men photographed the operation from a transport plane and Piper Cubs. Two more cameramen originally scheduled to arrive by parachute on the following day had to make an amphibious landing instead because conditions atop Topside had become too hazardous.

The air drop on February 16 came close to disaster. Jumping from less than 500 feet and into the teeth of stiff gales, the men rarely hit the drop zones and, since their parachutes provided no more than a few seconds of support, they *slammed* into the rocky, rubble-strewn terrain. Out of 2,050 jumpers, 280 were immediate casualties—210 suffered broken legs and arms, crushed collarbones and ribs, and bashed-in faces while landing, fifty received wounds in the air or on the drop zones, three died when their chutes malfunctioned, two were killed when they smashed into buildings, and Japanese fire killed fifteen more.

Among the injured were three out of the five Unit Q cameramen. Arriving in the first stick (a unit of airborne troops jumping one after another) of the first plane of the first wave, George Woodruff won his wings on his very first jump. When he hit it seemed as if "every bone in my body was broken, every muscle and fiber torn from its roots." But luckily he only "flipped my ankle in landing." However, since he had never bothered to ask how to get *out* of a parachute, the wind caught it, yanked him down a deep bomb crater and up the other side, across a pillbox, through masses of debris, and toward the precipitous cliffs before it finally snagged on some steel girders and then held him "so tight I couldn't release myself from the silk trap." He felt "like a fool and a sorry soul" as enemy gunfire increased in intensity all around him. Fortunately another paratrooper came by and cut him free, and despite his damaged ankle he shot all his movie film before collapsing. Richard Williams hit half way down a cliff and received burns on an arm and a leg as he bounced against flaming rubble, while Wilber Goen tore his right knee apart when he hit.

Frank Goetzheimer was in the nineteenth plane and was the 153rd man to hit The Rock. Having received airborne training, he not only knew how to gather his chute but also carried a razor blade to cut himself free. Within minutes he was photographing subsequent paratroopers leaping from the planes, gliding earthward, landing or crashing, and then if physically capable beginning to fight. Two hours after he arrived on Topside, Goetzheimer had inched his way to the cliffs overlooking the landing beaches and photographed the battalion coming ashore into the teeth of heavy opposition. At day's end he had exposed 660 feet of film that made officers back at the SCPC marvel. The footage "was of such excellent photographic quality that not one frame had to be removed for technical imperfections," said the critique sheet. "His presence of mind supplied magnificent shots of paratroops coming down, and close-ups of men helping each other, besides graphically illustrating the rocky, jagged nature of the landing place. It was magnificent coverage."

"Nothing much to tell about the rest of the show," Goetzheimer told a reporter two months later. That was undue modesty, since the airborne assault was actually the easy part in recapturing Corregidor. Instead of the estimated 850 Japanese, 6,000 were on The Rock, so they outnumbered the 3,800 Americans who fought the battle. Digging the enemy out of pillboxes, tunnels, bunkers, and caves was savage and deadly, and before completing the task 700 more Americans became casualties. Goetzheimer photographed the ugly business for more than a week. The material he submitted on the second day was sharp and clear, "fine coverage as follow-up for this cameraman's excellent D-Day material." The next day his footage was "very good coverage" with "plenty of action," and his subsequent film continued "to be excellent both in quality and interest of action photographed. It clearly shows advances made by troops." Finally, after demonstrating "amazing tenacity in undergoing superior physical hardship," suffering from combat fatigue, and developing a temperature of 103°F. Goetzheimer was evacuated to Australia for recuperation.

Although he returned to Luzon in May and remained in the Army until late July, Goetzheimer's war was essentially over. He came home wearing a Bronze Star for Cabanatuan and an Oak Leaf Cluster (for a second Bronze Star) for Corregidor. He also had the personal satisfaction of learning that the SCPC's Combat Films Reviewing Section considered the motion-picture footage he and his fellow photographers shot on The Rock to be the "greatest coverage to come out of this war, or very close to the greatest."

Goetzheimer's friend Wilber Goen also received two Bronze Stars, one for Cabanatuan and the other for Corregidor, and in addition had a Purple Heart for his injury on The Rock. A proud Texan, he carried a Texas state flag with him that bore an inscription wishing good luck to any enemy soldier who was man enough to take it from him. But Goen was not as fortunate as Frank Goetzheimer. After his knee healed he returned to action in northern Luzon, and was mortally wounded there in early June. No one knows what happened to his flag.

7

"Some Incident of Danger to Maintain Their Good Humor"

The Army Air Forces' 9th Combat Camera Unit

As a young child Jerry Joswick hammered his piggy bank open, hurried to the corner drugstore, and invested a precious saved dollar in a box Brownie, a purchase that "headed me straight for the Army Air Forces as a combat cameraman."[1]

By the time Joswick left high school he owned a Speed Graphic, knew how to use many other cameras, and did his own developing, printing, and enlarging. Upon graduation he opened a commercial photographic studio and when the Japanese attacked Pearl Harbor he was happily, though not very profitably, taking pictures of weddings and babies. Joswick immediately closed his studio, sold his equipment, and enlisted in the AAF, emphasizing his photographic background on every form and in every interview.

From basic training Joswick went to Bolling Field outside Washington, where he and four other photographers formed a Special Photographic Unit, which became the advance detachment for the 9th CCU. Joswick's unit was one of five such detachments that General "Hap" Arnold hastily created shortly after the Allies invaded North Africa. The AAF Chief of Staff was "peeved" because of "an extreme shortage of motion-picture and still picture coverage" of AAF activi-

157

ties. By contrast, Signal Corps cameramen seemed to be everywhere and the Army was reaping much favorable publicity. Arnold "wanted the American people to know what the Air Forces were doing, so he was in a little bit of a hurry to get the project started." The commanding officer of Joswick's unit was Sanford E. "Sam" Greenwald, a friend of Arnold's who had been the Marine Corps' first aerial photographer.[2] In mid-November 1942, after a personal meeting with the Chief of Staff, the Special Photographic Unit departed for Cairo. There it was attached to the 9th Air Force. Greenwald activated the 9th CCU's headquarters in late November 1942 and the next month John D. Craig arrived with twenty-one additional personnel. Upon Craig's arrival, confusion ensued over whether Greenwald or Craig commanded the 9th CCU. Higher headquarters settled the issue in the former's favor; when Greenwald returned to the United States in the spring of 1943 John E. Felton temporarily assumed command, but later that year Craig succeeded him.[3]

Joswick, known as "Mr. Happy-Go-Lucky" because of his irrepressible personality, was the first man in the Special Photographic Unit to fly a combat mission, which was to Naples. At the time he was nineteen years old, unmarried, and a first-class, hell-raising prankster. "He was a trouble-maker," acknowledged one of his most cooperative colleagues in the trouble-making department. "I mean, you'd go out with Jerry and before the night was over, why, you were going to be in some kind of trouble."[4] On his first combat flight, however, trouble found him. He was aboard the *Witch*, a B-24 Liberator in Colonel John R. "Killer" Kane's 98th Bombardment Group, whose activities Greenwald decided his men should photograph. This mission was a rough one in two respects. First, Joswick as yet had no "feel" for the air war's rhythm and conditions. So, for example, he not only ran out of film at critical moments but also suffered severe frostbite after shedding his cumbersome mittens to operate the camera. Second, the German defenses were fierce. Piloted by Major Julian Bleyer, the *Witch* arrived back at its airfield speckled with holes from bullets and flak. In summarizing the flight Joswick noted that photographing combat "sure isn't like making portraits of brides in Chicago."

Soon Joswick was in the air again, this time in the *Vulgar Virgin* heading for Palermo. With his previous experience he did a better (though still imperfect) job of photography, but he could do nothing to lessen the Germans' ferocious defense, as was evident from Joswick's description of the plane's return to North Africa: "One engine gone, another smoking, a 12-inch hole in our starboard wing, bullet-drilled from nose to tail, half a stabilizer shot away, two crewmen due for Purple Hearts, on a bleak emergency field *Vulgar Virgin* belly-landed with a mighty crash."

From then on Joswick flew mission after mission, often in "tail-end Charlie" of the "Purple Heart" section—that is, in the last plane in a bombardment formation's last section. Although an excellent vantage point for photographing fighter attacks, colorful popcorn bursts of deadly ack-ack, and bombing runs, the tail plane was doubly dangerous. Not only did swarming enemy fighters try to pry it away from the formation, but by the time it arrived over the target the antiaircraft gunners on the ground had adjusted their fire to just the right altitude. Intent on getting superb pictures, Joswick repeatedly accepted the extra risks, though he always oozed fear-induced perspiration even in the frigid temperatures at 20,000 feet.

"Every bomber you rode on a mission got more or less shot up," he said, "but if she brought you back you called that mission routine."

Although trying to keep a brave front between and during these "routine" missions, Joswick began to show signs of "combat fatigue," which usually involved such physiological signs as severe weight loss, a rapid heartbeat, and blood pressure changes, as well as emotional disturbances, including anxiety, apprehension, and frustration. An airman suffering from combat fatigue often drank heavily, used excessive profanity, was insubordinate, and had premonitions of his own death— which sometimes became a self-fulfilling prophecy when he simply gave up if his plane was hit. In acute cases a man simply would not or could not fly despite his superior officer's most dire threats and doleful entreaties. Driven by the necessity to get the maximum number of planes into the air for each mission, operational commanders had little sympathy for such individuals, frequently accused them of LMF (Lacking Moral Fiber), and sometimes court-martialed them for the offense.[5]

But combat-fatigue victims were usually not cowards. Instead of being an absolute quality—either you have it or you do not—courage is like money deposited in a bank. Some individuals are richer in it than others but all can eventually deplete their accounts. When combined with the normal unpleasant vicissitudes of wartime service, the air war's special stress and strains tested the mettle of even the stoutest heart. These peculiar difficulties included the agonizingly long wait between mission briefing and takeoff; false starts and sudden postponements caused by bad weather over the target; long and ener-vating flights under cramped, cold conditions; pain from aero-otitis (a middle ear inflammation common among bomber crews); dread knowledge of the skilled enemy fighters and dense flak belts that lay ahead; and long casualty lists. Nothing shattered these men's morale more than heavy casualties, especially since the AAF, unlike the British Bomber Command, bombed during the day rather than at night. American aircrews *saw* what happened to their comrades. "Our air-plane was endangered by various debris," wrote Lieutenant Colonel Bierne Lay, Jr. (coauthor of the novel that served as the basis for *Twelve O'Clock High*, a superb Hollywood movie about the European air cam-paign). "Emergency hatches, exit doors, prematurely opened para-chutes, bodies, and assorted fragments of B-17s and Hun fighters breezed past us in the slip-stream."[6]

To reduce combat fatigue, AAF surgeons argued that heavy-bomber air crews should have an operational tour of no more than fifteen mis-sions. Bomber crews certainly agreed with this recommendation; based on a "conservative" estimate of 5 percent loss per mission, crewmen believed they would be dead by their twentieth mission. Airmen were poor mathematicians (a 5 percent attrition rate meant that 35 percent of them would survive twenty missions), but their general perception was correct: the air war could be murder. A study of 2,051 heavy-bomber crewmen showed that after twenty-five missions only 559 were still available for duty. The 8th and 9th Air Forces ultimately pre-scribed a limited tour of duty, initially of twenty-five missions but then raised to thirty.

Unlike the B-17 and B-24 crews, the CCUs never had an explicitly limited tour of duty, and by midsummer 1943 Jerry Joswick had already flown thirty missions, almost all of them desperately hard. As he wore down mentally and physically his once-healthy "courage account" neared bankruptcy. He cursed the North African desert life with its searingly hot days and icy nights and its powdery red sand that made the food gritty, colored the water, and gummed up his watch and cam-eras. Even with the aid of alcohol he slept only fitfully, and during his waking hours memories of home became disturbingly intense. He longed to sit on the back steps and feel the morning sun, to wolf down his mom's cake, to take a girl to the movies and then for a long, slow drive. Would he ever enjoy such pleasures again? Pessimistic thoughts nagged at his consciousness: "Is my number up?" "How long will I get away with it?"

John Craig, by then the 9th CCU's commanding officer, could not help but notice that Joswick no longer exhibited his normal ebullient personality. Although realizing Joswick needed a break from combat Craig also knew that two important missions were forthcoming, so he proposed a deal. "You've piled up more combat hours than anyone else," he told Joswick. "I'm going to get you a ticket home if you'll do just two more missions." "Sold," replied the cameraman.

The thirty-first mission was to help pave the way for the upcoming invasion of Italy by destroying Rome's railroad marshaling yards. Perhaps reflecting his deteriorating mental condition, Joswick made potentially fatal mistakes. For the first time he operated a 70-pound Bell & Howell studio camera instead of an Eyemo. By shooting through a trap door he hoped to utilize the Bell & Howell's 400-foot magazine and three lenses to get dramatically different shots of "Bombs away!" As the plane approached its target he knelt down beside the trap door and opened it up. The camera's weight and the fierce suction from the prop wash almost yanked him out of the plane. With his ankles on one side of the door and his elbows on the other, his body bent "almost like a chicken wishbone into the trap door opening. Any instant my back would snap." Fortunately an alert waist gunner grabbed his ankles, hauled him back on board, and slammed the trap door shut. Although seemingly safe, Joswick soon lost consciousness because he was kneeling on his oxygen tube. Again the gunner rescued him in the nick of time. Joswick's back ached for weeks but at least he "was one mission nearer to getting that ticket Stateside."

As it happened his last venture was one of the war's greatest air raids.

Just thirty-five miles to the north of Bucharest lay Ploesti, the Rumanian city whose oil refineries produced such a high percentage of the Nazis' petroleum products that British Prime Minister Winston Churchill referred to it as "the taproot of German might." In an effort to cripple the enemy war effort, thirteen B-24's bombed Ploesti in June 1942, a feeble raid that did little damage but spurred the Germans into strengthening the city's defenses. Within a year these included an early-warning radar and radio-intercept system, four Luftwaffe fighter groups, two hundred forty 88-millimeter antiaircraft guns, hundreds of smaller-caliber artillery pieces, a superbly trained fire/police unit, and a well-designed program to restore production quickly in case a few bombers penetrated the defenses. The Germans even had a train-mounted flak battery so that they could pursue fleeing bombers by rail.

Unaware of these extensive defensive preparations, the 9th Air Force decided to strike Ploesti again, this time in great strength and using novel tactics. Code-named Operation Tidal Wave, the plan called for the planes to fly extremely low so as to avoid the enemy's radar and thereby achieve surprise. Under tight security procedures five B-24 groups assembled at Libyan air bases and began practicing low-altitude level assaults despite the AAF's doctrinal emphasis on high-altitude precision bombing. Hugging the earth at only fifty feet off the ground in planes designed to fly four miles high and knowing nothing about the target or takeoff date, the crews were ready to believe rumors that they were going on a one-way suicide mission. Joswick doubted that. Still, things were mighty strange ... and "the conviction gnawed that maybe this mission was one too many."

Finally on the morning of August 1, 1943 more than 170 Liberators skimmed low across the Mediterranean heading toward their distant target. Joswick was the only trained cameraman on the raid. He was aboard the *Witch*, the same B-24 he had flown on his maiden mission, which was not just coincidence. He had selected *Witch* for his swan song because Julian Bleyer's flying skills were "unsurpassed by any pilot I knew." Although other 9th CCU photographers were scheduled to participate, they had been ordered off the planes before takeoff. Since each B-24 carried additional fuel tanks and two tons of high explosives, most pilots undoubtedly believed that their planes were overloaded enough without the weight of an extra passenger. But Bleyer did not have the luxury of ordering Joswick to stay home, since Colonel "Killer" Kane had personally requested that he accompany the 98th Bombardment Group. For still pictures Joswick installed cameras on specially designed mounts on the fuselage of a dozen different bombers. Pointing downward at a 45-degree angle, each camera was aimed at a mirror that acted as a windscreen and provided a rearward view. Special equipment installed in the cockpit controlled the camera, which automatically took a picture every five seconds after the pilot flipped a switch. Joswick carried two Eyemos to record the raid in motion pictures.

But the German defenders received forewarning and the raiders did not achieve surprise. For staggering numbers of planes and men the attack was a one-way death mission. Approximately 1700 crewmen participated in Tidal Wave; almost 450 died and another 100 became prisoners of war. Of the 164 B-24s reaching the target area, the defenders shot down forty-one and fourteen other succumbed to causes other than enemy action. Many planes that survived were fit only for the scrap heap. *Witch* nearly fit that description. The B-24 limped home badly shot up, with two wounded crewmen, flying at a tipsy angle, and laboring on only two healthy engines (out of four) that gulped at fumes in the near-empty fuel tanks. But events confirmed Joswick's judgment about Bleyer's skill, for he gently and safely landed the stricken Liberator at its home base. Only the pilot's great stamina under prolonged stress and exquisite mastery of the controls brought the *Witch* back from its seventeen-hour, 2,700-mile round trip.

Although a few crewmen carried personal cameras and took some snapshots, all the official photography was Joswick's handiwork. Amidst the *Witch's* harrowing experiences, which included flying through a curtain of smoke and flame so intense that the heat scorched his skin and burned off his exposed hair, Joswick shot 520 feet of film. Out of his dozen camera-toting bombers, only half returned.

The enormous casualties shocked the survivors. "So many had not come back that we could not comprehend," wrote Joswick. "We could not believe those men would never again sit chatting at mess, never again wave from a pilot's seat." Despite the high cost the attack inflicted little damage.

"After thirty-two missions I had had enough of war for a while," Joswick recalled. "I collected the promised leave and headed Stateside."

But he would be back.

I

"How was the shooting, Lieutenant?" asked Ralph Edwards on his "Report to the Nation" radio program in the fall of 1943.

"Excellent!" replied cameraman Jim Bray who, like Joswick, went to North Africa with the Special Photographic Unit. "I got 20,000 feet over Sicily and Italy and I was credited with two enemy aircraft."[7]

Downing those two German Messerschmitt-109 fighters was instrumental in solving a fundamental problem that OIC "Sam" Greenwald's men confronted in working with "Killer" Kane's Bombardment Group: the crews were initially hostile to photographers, whom they considered interlopers. When individual pilots, navigators, gunners, and bombardiers arrived at an Operations Training Unit or Replacement Training Unit, they were formed into a crew, which became much like a family or team. Shared training and then combat forged tight bonds of trust and affection among the crewmen, and any stranger intruding upon this close-knit family threatened its harmony. Photographers were strangers. Since most of Kane's B-24s had ten-man crews and only ten oxygen outlets, carrying a cameraman meant leaving a family member at home; the only airman who could be bumped was a gunner, which potentially made the plane extremely vulnerable. Cameramen "felt like excess baggage," wrote a photo officer. "Pilots wanted gunners, not motion-picture cameramen, and nobody was happy."[8]

When Jerry Joswick made the unit's first flight he "felt like a pariah" and experienced a "crushing, frightened loneliness" as the crewmen made their dislike and distrust of him clear by excluding him from their banter over the intercom. Perhaps he felt his friendless position so acutely because it mingled with a sense of guilt, for Joswick had lied to get aboard the *Witch*. When asked if he could handle its .50-caliber machine guns Joswick had said yes. Actually he could not "recall ever touching a gun except the few times at home when I hunted rabbits with my brother's .22 rifle. And we'd never had a *hassenpfeffer* dinner." Serving as left waist gunner, Joswick had been slow to respond to enemy fighters and then missed them by such a wide margin that he simply wasted ammunition.

Bray did not have to lie when asked if he knew how to use the guns. Although only in his mid-30s he had already had a long photographic career. After working with Pathé News for a few years, Bray moved on to Twentieth Century Fox for almost a decade. He photographed the 1932 Olympics and was the first official cameraman for the 1939 New York World's Fair. Upon joining the AAF in May 1942 he "knew most things about movie and still cameras, nothing about guns. I never had fired a sporting gun or taken a pot shot in a shooting gallery." But as most CCU cameramen would do throughout the war, Bray took an aerial gunnery course as part of his training, "and when I arrived in North Africa in November, 1942, I at least knew what a .50-caliber gun was for." Still, as he eyed one of the guns he felt "a bit scared. Would I ever have to use it, and how soon? The answer wasn't long in coming."

Bray flew more than two dozen missions with pilot George Groff, who had extraordinary composure amidst even the most violent madness. During one of their first flights "the placid brown-gray earth underneath shouted hell" as the plane approached the target. "The antiaircraft guns threw up so much flak that as it burst underneath us it looked like a thick black carpet you could walk on." As the plane bounced and rolled from the concussions Groff came on the intercom. "Don't mind that, fellows," he drawled. "That's nothing. It's not even coming near us."

Now on April 11, 1943 Bray was with Groff again, flying a mission to Messina in *Penny's from Heaven*, which was tail-end Charlie. As antiaircraft bursts shuddered the plane and tore gaping holes in the fuselage, Italian Macchis fighters circled just out of range, acting as decoys while German fighters maneuvered in for the kill. Suddenly out of nowhere an Me-109 "came weaving in like a crazy mosquito to keep us from getting a shot." Bray grabbed the .50-caliber machine gun from a wounded waist gunner and waited, "excited as hell," for the enemy plane to make its head-on run at the B-24. When it flew past, Bray squeezed the trigger, saw a tracer strike the fighter, then a plume of black smoke, and watched in triumph as the plane "rolled over, hung in the air for a minute, and fluttered oddly" before beginning a long downward spin. Bray had just become the first AAF cameraman to shoot down an enemy plane.

Air crews remained skeptical, wondering if Brey was merely lucky. A little more than two weeks later Bray quashed the skeptics while aboard the *Arkansas Traveller* on a mission to Naples.[9] George Groff was again at the helm; he normally piloted *Penny's From Heaven* but that Liberator was having mechanical problems, so for the first and only time he was flying the *Arkansas Traveller*. Since they were again in the Purple Heart section the flak and enemy fighters were thick. Bray exchanged his camera for a machine gun after spotting a fighter a thousand yards out, which soon "came in at us in a long straight run. I gave him three bursts, the last when he was so close that he seemed to be under the wing. I fired again, and he went down with smoke streaming from the cabin."

But the *Arkansas Traveller* was also smoking. A flak burst put a huge hole in the plane's skin right next to Bray's position, an enemy fighter "sewed a seam of bullets and shells smack through our fuselage," the starboard inside engine was aflame, the hydraulic system was wrecked, two tires were flat, and the aileron cable had only two strands left. As it limped homeward the *Arkansas Traveller* quickly lost height and speed. "Each minute we seemed to be getting lower and lower and going at a funeral pace," Bray recalled, and Groff silently wondered "what it'll feel like to die." Knowing he could not possibly make it back to North Africa the pilot headed for British-controlled Malta, where at one time or another practically every member of the 9th CCU made an emergency landing. As they neared the island Groff suggested that the crew bail out before he crash landed. But the crewmen decided to stay with Groff, who had always brought them through alive before. "There was a bump—another, and we were down," wrote Bray. "Then we were up, on our nose, as the front wheel buckled and the tail went and stayed at an angle of 70 degrees." After scrambling to safety the men stared at the plane's remnants, marveling that all of them had emerged unscathed. With typical equanimity Groff acknowledged that "I guess we'll need a new ship, boys," and then headed off for a few stiff drinks before visiting the debriefing room.

Bray's confirmed kills—in subsequent actions he added two "probables" to his record—brought two rewards, one personal and the other collective. On May 1, 1943 he received a field promotion from sergeant to lieutenant. More important his performance demonstrated that carrying a photographer who was cross-trained in gunnery did not necessarily endanger a plane, and the bomber crews' hostility to cameramen all but evaporated. Perhaps more than anyone else he had paved the way for the 9th CCU's widespread acceptance.

By July Jim Bray had flown thirty-two missions, the same number as his good buddy Jerry Joswick, and he needed a rest. On Independence Day word came that he was going home. But like Joswick he would return.

———————

"The daily life of each of them was incomplete and irksome without some incident of danger to maintain their good humor," a home-front essay exulted about the 9th CCU's cameramen. "Dangerous missions were the tonic experiences necessary to their well being and mental comfort."[10]

Well, not quite. Craig admitted that the conditions were so primitive and the dangers so dreadful that few cameramen were "physically and mentally suited for combat flying." Rarely did he have more than six men who could regularly endure the rigors of aerial photography without suffering chronic combat fatigue, and even those stalwarts would have gladly accepted a reduction in the hazards of combat flying.[11] They may have disagreed vigorously on whether they most feared flak or fighters, but neither Joswick, Bray, nor any other member of the 9th CCU complained about too little flak, too few enemy fighters, or too many in-flight amenities.

III

While the 9th CCU, which was one of the first CCUs deployed overseas, garnered hard-learned experience, General "Hap" Arnold was organizing a full-fledged photographic effort. Within months after Pearl Harbor an AAF staff study recommended establishing a Motion Picture Unit that would include a Combat Units Division to produce motion pictures "under actual combat conditions" in every war theater.[12] The five Special Photographic Units were only a first step in that direction; the day after creating them Arnold instituted a more comprehensive program by ordering "that combat motion picture units be organized and dispatched to each Air Force." Their paramount mission was to record conditions in the combat zones on 35mm motion-picture film.[13]

By late 1944 fourteen CCUs had been organized; twelve were overseas, one was being disbanded, and another was being reorganized in the United States. At the special request of the 9th Troop Carrier Command (TCC), the AAF also established the 9th TCC CCU (Provisional), which was in Europe. In addition, three experimental 16mm CCUs were in northern Europe and three were deploying to the Mediterranean.[14]   Unlike the other CCUs, which returned their exposed film to the United States for processing, the 16mm units had portable processing equipment, so they could process their film for immediate screening overseas. Organized under T/O&E 1-707, each 16mm unit had an authorized strength of two officers and eight enlisted men. On the whole the 16mm experiment failed. Although a few units made movies in the field, most did little more than process Gun Sight Aiming Point (GSAP) camera film (for more on the GSAPs see Chapter Eight).[15]

Compared to the Army's SPCs the CCUs were small. Initially a CCU operated under a Manning Table that permitted nine officers and twenty-three enlisted men comprising a headquarters (three officers and one enlisted man) and two field detachments (three officers and eleven enlisted men in each). Out of these thirty-two people, at least fourteen were supposed to be aerial photographers. Although the cameramen believed their units were too small—some drafted plans for revised units more than twice as large—in April 1945 the AAF promulgated T/O&E 1-708, which decreased a CCU to eight officers and twenty-two enlisted men.[16] However, the number of qualified photographers increased to twenty, including fourteen trained in aerial gunnery, since experience demonstrated that cameramen often had to man the .50-calibers. But the CCUs rarely conformed to either the Manning Table or the T/O&E. Ordinarily they were undermanned, though occasionally they exceeded authorized strength. In May 1944 the 4th CCU in England had sixty-four officers and men as it prepared for the Normandy invasion.[17] However, even a surfeit of aerial photographers did not guarantee adequate coverage. Many CCU personnel were ill trained, units rarely had enough cameras, and combat fatigue constantly depleted the ranks of those qualified for flight duty.[18]

The CCUs emulated the Army's SPCs by operating in small detachments that neither the Manning Table nor T/O&E 1-708 envisioned. The 4th CCU's splintering began in January 1944; at times it had as many as eleven teams in the field. So great was the distance between headquarters and these teams that the unit acquired an A-20 light bomber to transport film, supplies, and men.[19] With its detachments scattered all over the South Pacific covering the 13th Air Force, the 6th CCU's communication problems were equally bad or worse. "Our situation, therefore," lamented the unit historian, "is comparable to that of trying to run a business in Los Angeles with an office in Chicago, no telephone connections and only indifferent mail service." It regularly took more than two weeks for exposed film to arrive at headquarters; in a few instances the commanding officer did not hear from a detachment for *months*.[20] The 9th CCU's clerks "proceeded into quiet hysteria trying to work out the orders on departures and returns. With all this movement, their job has become a paper war of no small proportions."[21] Although the clerks won the war, they lost many battles along the way.

IV

No one knew for sure where Ken Chaney was but everyone in the 9th CCU assumed he was dead, his body floating somewhere in the Gulf of Corinth.

Chaney had arrived in Egypt with John Craig in late 1942. Young, single, and convinced that he would never come out of the war alive, Chaney was soon torching the candle at both ends "both in working and also in having fun." He and Joswick enjoyed "some hellacious alcoholic escapades in Cairo and Alexandria," Chaney wrote decades after the war, "and it is more through good luck than good sense that we are not both still in an Egyptian jail." But when the alcohol wore off or boredom reared its noxious head he took to the air again and again. A fellow cameraman considered him "one of the keenest daredevils" in North Africa and a "man absolutely devoid of the sense of fear." Through forty-two missions Chaney skimmed along with peril at his side, usually riding in Mitchell B-25 medium bombers over German-occupied positions in North Africa, but occasionally crossing the Mediterranean with the heavy B-24s to bomb targets in Italy and Sicily.[22]

After Italy's surrender in September 1943 (which did not end the fighting there, since Germany continued the war on Italian soil) the 9th CCU was detached from the 9th AAF and attached to the 12th AAF in Italy. Chaney's station was with the 321st Bombardment Group (B-25s) operating from a muddy little strip on Italy's heel twenty miles from Bari.

Before departing on his forty-third mission Chaney got good news. Pilot Joel Hartmeister assured him it would be a "milk run," little more than a sightseeing tour with a momentary interruption to drop bombs on a German airfield near Athens. Intelligence reports indicated that only a few flak batteries and a handful of Focke-Wulf 189s guarded the airstrip. And forty-eight P-38 Lightnings were escorting the mission, more than enough to handle the 189s. When Hartmeister's B-25 left Italian soil on the morning of October 8, 1943 Chaney felt safe even though their plane was tail-end Charlie, that dangerous position favored by cameramen determined to bring back great pictures.

The milk run went sour because the intelligence reports were inaccurate. "In addition to more than normal antiaircraft fire," Chaney wrote, "shortly after leaving the target we encountered heavy and totally unexpected fighter opposition; namely, an entire group of Me-109G's," which were superb fighters. The P-38 pilots "were a bunch of inexperienced yahoos and were flitting around like a flock of barn swallows two miles above and ten miles ahead of us. Consequently the fighters chopped us up pretty good." When a 20-mm cannon shell mangled one of the B-25's engines the plane lost speed and spewed dense smoke that brought half a dozen Messerschmitts closing in for the kill "like wolves dragging down a crippled deer." Cannon shells tore into the Mitchell, including one that exploded directly under Chaney, peppering him with shrapnel and breaking his right ankle. When the plane burst into flames "it became sickeningly apparent that we were not going to make it back to Italy or anywhere else."

Considering the circumstances, Hartmeister made a near-textbook water landing in the Gulf of Corinth. Nonetheless to Chaney the initial sensation "was that of all of my muscles being hammered flat," then it seemed as if thousands of gallons of cold water were sloshing over him. Although the three gunners were dead, Chaney, Hartmeister, copilot Ernest Frey, and bombardier Tommie Flynn were still alive. Alas, all but Flynn were injured, Frey did not know how to swim, none of the others was a strong swimmer, the Greek coast was ten miles away, and as the B-25 sank with a soft, sobbing hiss it yielded only one substantial piece of floating debris. During a brief nautical war council the men cautioned each other against panic, then floundered shoreward. Progress was slow and tiring. They encountered a school of glutinous jellyfish that was so thick it took fifteen minutes to paw their way through and that left painful stings all over their bodies. Storm clouds appeared, making the water seem much colder, and breezes kicked up, churning the ocean's surface. Then the rain began. After three hours in the water, with his stamina waning and his body thoroughly chilled, Chaney "felt an almost tearful regret that I had never until this moment properly appreciated hot coffee."

Miracles, or at least seeming miracles, do happen. Through salt-blurred eyes Hartmeister and Chaney spotted a tiny white triangle— a sail! Fifteen minutes later "a couple of heaven-sent Greeks in a smelly fishing boat" of nearly prehistoric design pulled alongside them. Only Frey had enough strength to raise his arm and wave hello. Despite language difficulties the airmen learned that the Greeks lived in a nearby coastal village, had seen the B-25 ditch into the water, and had braved the oncoming storm to search for survivors. As the ship tacked a zigzag course back to the village and the thankful survivors huddled under tarpaulins "that smelled mightily of ripe fish," Chaney had a few words for Hartmeister. "Just one thing before I forget it," he said. "*If* we ever see Italy again, and *if* we do any more flying, kindly don't invite me on any more milk runs. From now on I'll stick to the tough ones."

It would be almost a year before Chaney saw Italy again, and he never flew another combat mission, neither a milk run nor a tough one. Nor did he do any more photography. When OIC John Craig learned from the other B-25s on the "milk run" that Hartmeister's plane had been shot up by enemy fighters and then crashed in the ocean he believed that no one had survived. Weeks later, however, he got a message from Chaney in Greece.[23] He and Hartmeister had linked up with a small group from the Office of Strategic Services (OSS), the forerunner of the Central Intelligence Agency, and had transferred into that outfit. Now they were busy "doing various dastardly deeds to annoy the Germans," such as putting explosive coal in railroad tenders and laying mines on train tracks.

When Chaney developed an intestinal tumor requiring skilled medical help he boarded one of the DC-3s that occasionally landed on a clandestine airstrip in the Greek mountains and flew across the Adriatic Sea to Bari. Dressed in Greek civilian clothes and a British battle jacket, sporting a long mustache, and without any identification, he ambled into OSS headquarters in Bari and asked for assistance. What he got was a jail cell crowded "with a bunch of sick and drunk AWOL soldiers, Italian collaborators, and what not. Terrible place." The OSS wanted to check out his "story" about belonging to the 9th CCU. Chaney thought this would only take a few hours, but he was unaware that Major Craig and nine other original members of the unit—those who could most readily verify his account—had returned to the United States in March 1944.[24] So for three days he curled up in pain on the jail floor until the OSS finally confirmed his identity and rushed him to a hospital.

After a month-long recovery Chaney temporarily returned to the States. He wrote OSS propaganda in Washington and served as a demolitions instructor on Catalina Island before being sent to Calcutta to analyze prisoner-of-war interrogations, "a very, very dull job" entirely unsuited to his personality. Fortunately salvation was soon at hand. Learning of a planned paratroop drop behind enemy lines for a Greek-like venture in Thailand, he immediately volunteered, made six jumps during training on Ceylon, and then deployed to Burma, where he whiled away the days playing bridge and drinking whiskey, waiting for the moon to reach the proper phase to provide appropriate light conditions for the jump.

"And then," said Chaney, a twinge of disappointment still coloring his voice thirty-five years later, "all of a sudden they dropped the atomic bomb."

V

Like Operation Market-Garden, the combined armored and airborne offensive in September 1944 that tried to capture a bridge over the Lower Rhine River at Arnhem, Operation Varsity was a mighty effort by armored and airborne forces to cross the Rhine River. Yet while Market-Garden is famous, Varsity is virtually unknown—even though it included the greatest single day's airborne operation of the war, even larger than Market-Garden's airborne component. Varsity's objective was Wesel on the Rhine's east bank. To aid the ground forces in crossing the river and capturing the city, the British 6th Airborne and the American 17th Airborne Divisions would capture the Diersfordterwald, the high ground behind Wesel. About 9:00 a.m. on March 24, 1945 the IX Troop Carrier Command (TCC), utilizing almost 1,700 transports and 1,350 gliders, began delivering almost 22,000 paratroopers and glidermen on the target area. There to photograph the action were Jerry Joswick and Jim Bray.

When Joswick and Bray had returned to the United States from North Africa they were heroes. The former already wore a Distinguished Flying Cross for his photography at Ploesti and the latter soon received one for having shot down the two enemy fighters; both men also sported an impressive array of other chest ornaments. Joswick spent three days in the Pentagon, where he narrated his Ploesti film for a select AAF audience; then he participated in bond drives by making radio appearances and speaking at defense plants. He ended up at the AAF's First Motion Picture Unit (FMPU) in Culver City, just outside Hollywood. Here he trained future CCUs in the vagaries of high-altitude photography and mingled with FMPU's employees, many of them former Hollywood bigwigs whom Joswick viewed with ill-concealed contempt. "My impression that few of these gentlemen wanted to hear guns go off had a strange effect on my eyesight," he wrote. "Six inches away I could not identify rank in a Hollywood and Vine major.... I made it plain that I'd be a fast man to salute anyone back from hell in the South Pacific, but at the Brown Derby or Mike Romanoff's I couldn't tell an oak-leaf colonel from a doorman." He was in such elite establishments often, since his hero status brought more social invitations than he could fulfill. "Two months of furious living it up," he recalled, "with not too much time taken up instructing movie people how to take pictures, left me as worn out as the day after Ploesti."

Orders to head to England provided a respite from the draining social schedule. In February 1944 Joswick departed FMPU in a reorganized 9th CCU commanded by Sam Greenwald. However he soon transferred to the 4th CCU.[25] After photographing the build-up for D-Day, Joswick went ashore with the assault troops at Omaha Beach to photograph close air support from the infantryman's viewpoint. From then until late 1944 he was in almost continuous action. Among other things he covered the fighting in the Normandy Beachhead, the capture of Cherbourg, the St. Lô breakout, the capitulation of Brest, the gruesome fighting at Aachen (the first German city captured by the Allies), and the penetration of the Siegfried Line.[26]

Meanwhile Bray had followed much the same stateside pattern, the biggest difference being that he got married shortly after arriving home. Following a brief honeymoon he toured East Coast war industries, made public relations appearances in Detroit, recounted his gunnery exploits on three different national radio programs, and ended up at FMPU as a photography and aerial gunnery instructor. In early October he received the Distinguished Flying Cross at an FMPU ceremony. Looking on from the front row was one of those Hollywooders so loathed by Joswick, AAF Captain Ronald Reagan, future President of the United States. But Bray soon received orders directing him to England and by midsummer he had teamed up with Joswick in France, where they worked primarily on the ground trying to film close air support.[27]

By mid-December 1944 Joswick and Bray were in England as members of the IX TCC CCU (Provisional), a unit of four officers and about a dozen enlisted men commanded by Captain John W. Steger and formed in late 1944 at the insistence of Major General Paul L. Williams, the IX TCC's commanding general.[28] In June 1942 General Arnold had created the TCC to provide transportation for paratroopers, airborne infantry, and glider units, and to conduct local air-transport missions. Assigned to the 9th AAF in England, the IX TCC had inserted (landed in France) the 82nd and 101st Airborne Divisions on D-Day and some 35,000 men over the course of several days during Market-Garden. Since General Williams believed that his organization was not getting enough publicity, he requested a photographic outfit to make sure IX TCC received more recognition during the next major airborne operation. In December 1944 Joswick and Bray visited the IX TCC's wings to explain the new CCU's function, the officers and men met with the IX TCC's Public Relations Office so the organizations could coordinate their efforts, and unit members made numerous flights to acquaint themselves with the TCC's activities.[29]

For the the first two months of 1945 it appeared that no other big air drop would transpire, and the cameramen spent their time photographing routine (and sometimes mundane) matters, such as a IX TCC basketball game, the new C-46 Curtis Commando Troop Carrier Airplane towing a new glider model, promotion and award ceremonies, and the TCC's dental clinic. Perhaps the most unusual photo opportunity was when Joswick, Bray, and another cameraman filmed the IX TCC delivering "war dogs to the front to be used as sled dogs to haul troops and supplies over the snow-clad battlefields." But in the "Combat Operations" section of the IX TCC CCU's monthly narratives for January and February, the compiler simply noted that "a negative report is submitted."

Late in February 1945 two hints of future action appeared: the CCU obtained a B-17G as a photographic plane and an advance echelon deployed to the IX TCC's forward headquarters on the outskirts of Paris. And in March action—plenty of it—finally occurred during Varsity. Learning of the operation three weeks in advance, Captain Steger divided his unit into four teams. Team #1, Captain Steger's, remained in England to process film and carry out administrative duties. Flying in the B-17G was Team #2; Team #3 covered the 53rd Troop Carrier Wing; and Team #4, consisting of Bray, Joswick and Fay N. Steele, photographed the 50th Troop Carrier Wing. Unlike Teams #2 and #3, which used 35mm black-and-white film, Team #4 shot color because it had been commandeered for Special Film Project #186, the effort to make a color film that would be better than the Navy's *Fighting Lady*.[30]

Although Teams #3 and #4 experienced no serious mishaps Team #2 had a rough time. Flak near Wesel set the B-17G aflame and the entire crew, including the three cameramen, had to "hit the silks." Despite the imminent possibility of a midair explosion in the burning plane, cameraman Frederick W. Quandt delayed parachuting "until he had finished his roll of film, carried the roll with him on his descent, and then refused medical treatment after landing in order to return his film to headquarters." His still photos, the first pictures of the airborne landings east of the Rhine, soon appeared in the British daily newspapers and were wire-photoed to the United States, where they received widespread display.

Team #4's clever planning ensured the broadest possible color coverage. As Joswick filmed the operation from a C-47 transport, Fay Steele actually landed aboard a glider. For two days he photographed infantry action on the ground and on one occasion he "further risked injury and possible death by going back nearly 100 yards under fire to obtain a container of whole blood in an effort to save a seriously injured glider pilot." Bray employed the team's most imaginative photographic approach. While doing a story on P-38 pilots in Belgium he saw a special P-38 with a glass nose. Each P-38 squadron had one of these modified planes, called a "droop snoop." The glass nose normally accommodated a bombardier with a Norden bombsight. Especially during bad weather, the droop snoop would be the lead plane and all the other P-38s would drop their bombs on its signal. Bray suggested that the droop snoop would be ideal for aerial photography and after a little administrative pushing and pulling, one was assigned to him on March 14.

The P-38's pilot was Lieutenant Malcolm E. "Hank" Henry, a young hotshot from the 9th AAF's 429th Fighter Squadron who eventually became a Brigadier General in the Maryland Air National Guard.[31] Because the mission presented a novel challenge Henry welcomed the assignment. But during practice flights Bray had his doubts, for Henry "enjoyed scaring the hell out of me" as he made barrel rolls and steep dives, buzzed so low over the landscape that farmers jumped from their tractors, and played aerial tag with an RAF pilot by literally tapping the Spitfire's wings. By the time Varsity began, however, they had become good friends. On the big day they took off after all the transports and gliders were in the air, creating a formation ten miles long and four miles wide. "We, of course," wrote Henry, "were able to fly much faster than these troop carriers and we flew over the top of them, underneath them and on each side of them shooting film." The P-38 went right into the combat area with the transports. "Pictures from the nose of paratroopers bailing out were quite exceptional," Bray recalled, "and when we made our final passes over the drop zone, the ground looked like a huge crazy-quilt blanket."

Henry expected to return to his unit immediately after Varsity, but because another secret mission was supposedly imminent he stayed with Bray. Rumor had it that the new operation involved a plan "to fly special assault troops to Hitler's retreat at Berchtesgaden and capture Hitler." Whatever the truth of the matter no other secret mission occurred. Instead after flying Bray on a few noncombat photographic assignments Henry "went back to my fighter unit and flew a few more missions and the war was over."

The war was over for Bray and Joswick, too. Arriving in the States shortly after V-J Day, Bray joined his wife Kathryn in San Francisco, where "I saw my thirteen-month-old son Patrick for the first time." Even before the war in Europe ended Joswick had been in England assembling and editing footage for Special Film Project #186, and when he received orders to return to America he had mixed emotions. "Like everyone else," he wrote, "I was interested in going back to the States and civilian life, but after so long an investment of time and effort in making my part of the camera record of the war, I was more interested in staying on to finish our Project 186." But being a good soldier he smothered his disappointment and boarded the *Queen Mary,* heading westward across the Atlantic from Southampton.

Two street fighting scenes, the top one genuine and the bottom one staged. Thanks to the Signal Corps policy of labeling staged material, the original captions reveal the difference. The caption for the top photo reads: "American infantrymen patroling section of Metz in search of snipers." *Photo by Billy A. Newhouse. Photo provided by Newhouse.* The bottom photo's caption reads: "A typical combat mission shows a combat photo team on assignment. . . . Recording the fast action keeps the cameramen busy (*staged*)." *Photo by Irving Leibowitz. Photo provided by Robert L. Lewis.*

Because many World War II photographs look similar to each other, they are often misidentified. Here troops crouch in assault boats as they cross the Rhine River in March 1945. The May 28, 1984 issue of *Time* misidentified the photo as troops heading for Omaha Beach on D-Day. *Photo by Arthur H. Herz. Photo provided by Herz.*

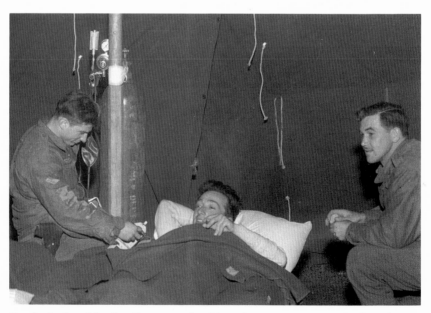

On the banks of the Isar River near Landshut, Germany, Herz met the fate of many cameramen: a bullet. Before being evacuated to France Herz received a visit from some of his 166th SPC colleagues, including Robert Brill (right), Theodore Halkias (left), and of course Bernard J. Caliendo, who took this photo. *Photo provided by Herz.*

The 832nd SSB soon discovered that the hostile environment and determined Japanese resistance in the Southwest Pacific Area placed a terrific strain on combatants, as evidenced by these photos of William A. Avery before he went into combat (left) and after he returned (right)—gaunt, haggard, and suffering from malaria. *Photos provided by Avery.*

Frank J. Goetzheimer (third from the right) may have looked like a child among men, but his small stature did not diminish his competence or courage, as his numerous exploits demonstrated. *Photo provided by Goetzheimer.*

The top photo shows James M. Bray on the right, pilot Malcolm E. Henry next to him, and Henry's crew chief and assistant crew chief. They are standing in front of the "droop snoot" P-38 that Bray used as a camera plane. The bottom photo is a closeup of the logo painted on Henry's plane. *Photos provided by Henry.*

The top photo is of the original nine CPUs before they scattered around the globe. The head of the Combat Photography Section, Carleton Mitchell, is on the extreme left in the first row. Earl F. Colgrove, who commanded CPU #1, is next to him. Photo provided by Colgrove. The bottom photo, based on a map in Colgrove's possession, shows CPU #1's route to Camp One in China. *Map prepared by Donald E. Robinson.*

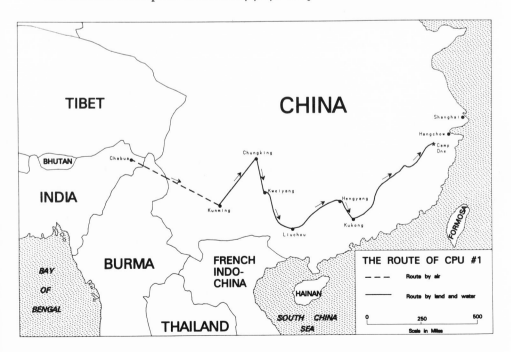

Here is Earl F. Colgrove's shot of a kamikaze just before it smashed into the carrier *Essex*. Colgrove's colleague in CPU #1, Douglas B. Jones, filmed the kamikaze attack in motion pictures. *Photo provided by Colgrove.*

Although suffering from combat fatigue the 9th CCU's Jerry J. Joswick went on the low level Ploesti bombing attack, the only professional cameraman on the raid. As with the kamikaze scene filmed by Colgrove and Jones, Joswick's dramatic movies and still pictures, such as this one, have been staples in World War II books and documentaries. *Photo by Joswick. Photo published courtesy of the National Archives (14652-FO).*

The Marine Corps cameraman in the top photo is Harold L. Watkins, shown working with John Wittingham (standing on the truck) and Art Sarno (kneeling). Watkins was later severely wounded on Saipan. *Photo provided by Watkins.* The bottom photo shows Watkins' friend and fellow Marine cameraman Federico Claveria in later years holding a famous picture of himself, at an internment camp on Tinian, giving candy to a child. *Photo provided by Claveria.*

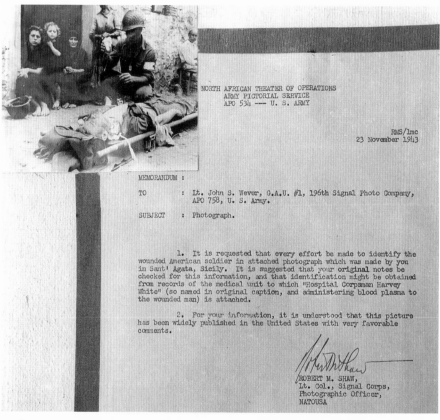

John S. Wever's photograph, widely used in Red Cross blood drives, demonstrated the wartime emphasis on reducing anonymity by identifying individual soldiers, sailors, airmen, and Marines. Who was the wounded man? Army Pictorial Service wanted "every effort" made to find out. *Photo provided by Wever.*

8

"The New Battlefront, the Air Front"

The Making of *The Memphis Belle* and *Thunderbolt*

The tedium of noncombat duty drove Karl H. Maslowski to distraction, but his wife Edna was "very thankful that you are being bored to death rather than shot to death. It's so much easier to recover from."[1]

"I must confess," she wrote, "I don't understand your *perfect willingness* to be in one of the more hazardous positions when you consider the responsibilities you leave behind you." The hazardous position Karl H. Maslowski sought was that of an AAF combat cameraman, and the responsibilities he left behind included an infant daughter and a pregnant wife. A successful prewar wildlife photographer, he entered the Army in May 1943 as a thirty-two-year-old draftee who was determined to become a military cameraman. Haunted by the knowledge that "one isn't always placed in the field he feels best suited for," he omitted everything but his photographic qualifications on all the forms he filled out and in all the interview questions he answered. But becoming a combat cameraman in an overseas unit required an epic odyssey through the military bureaucracy. Referring to the *Know Your Enemy* series of government information-propaganda movies produced by Frank Capra, Maslowski became so exasperated with authorities for

177

keeping him stateside that he suggested they "produce one more film in this series and title it 'Know Your Enemy—Army Red Tape.'"

A patriot's patriot, Maslowski believed that World War II was a struggle for democracy against tyranny. Consequently he "could never live with myself if I tried to crawfish out of the Army" and would "always feel proud that when my time to be drafted came along I went, asking only for enough time to see my [first] child born." He urged his agitated wife not to worry about him getting hurt or killed because "I've made up my mind that I'm coming back, now you do the same." Explanations and reassurances did not appease her. She simply could not comprehend his "crazy eagerness to get into combat photography.... I do feel very strongly about your leaving no stone unturned to get into it! And I mean I don't like it!"

The last stone finally kicked loose in mid-July 1944. Maslowski was playing third base in a pick-up baseball game at a replacement camp near Naples when a message arrived with the great news: He had been assigned to the 12th CCU. Finally!

I

Maslowski's maneuvering for front line duty began during basic training at St. Petersburg, Florida. Only rarely did the trainees do something he considered useful, such as "sneaking around behind bushes and trees and crawling snake-like over the hot white sand" as they learned how to take enemy strongpoints. Overall, however, the sun, the sand, the numbing routine of drills, parades, and K.P. and guard duty bored him. Fortunately he devised a way to keep his mind active. Although *loathing* mathematics, he devoted his spare time to studying it because the qualifiying test for photography school emphasized math.

After he easily passed the math test, the classification office assigned Maslowski to an AAF photographic school. However, authorities first shipped him and a thousand other St. Petersburg soldiers across the state to Miami Beach. For more than a month Maslowski endured "the grim monotony of moronic tasks" and railed against the seeming stupidity of wasting the time and energy of so many men. Deciding which affliction pained him the most was not easy: the physical agony of prickly heat, which felt "like a porcupine with heated quills is rolling around inside my undershirt and shorts," or the mental misery of "being assigned to help in the Financial Department!"

Finally, in early September the world again turned for Maslowski's gratification, spinning him from Miami Beach to the AAF Technical Training School (Photography) at Lowry Field near Denver. Each class of forty students spent four weeks on photographic fundamentals with an emphasis on still pictures. Based on their performance in this course, every student then graduated into a specialty, such as darkroom work or photo-mapping. Only one man from each class went into cine-matography. "I'm going to try my damndest to see that I'm that *one*," he said.

The Army assumed that the students knew nothing about photogra-phy, so Maslowski whisked through the preliminary class, for he already knew how to operate a Speed Graphic, mix chemicals, develop film, and make prints. But to cinch the motion-picture assignment from his class he arranged to show one of his wildlife documentaries, *Our Heritage in the Rockies*, at the Lowry Field Service Club on October 7th. The public lecture went so well that he then had to give a private showing, because "some of the men in the Cine Department who couldn't come last night want to see it." So impressive was the private presentation that he had to do an encore, this time for the "Director of the School and a couple of other brass hats. They liked it too." However, this scheming did not secure Maslowski the motion-picture assignment. The day *before* the Service Club performance the news arrived that he had already been selected for the motion-picture class.

Since Maslowski had used 16mm cameras and projectors exclusively in his prewar career, the cinematography training taught him a great deal. He learned about the AAF's bomb-spotting camera, the 35mm Akeley and the Eyemo, a new 16mm sound camera called an Auricon, and the 35mm DeVry projector. All of this was exhilarating. Even watching *Desert Victory*, which "opened with the cheerful note that 4 photographers lost their lives, 7 were wounded & 6 captured during the making of the feature," did not dampen his enthusiasm. Although he realized that a cameraman "would be entering hostilities with two strikes on him what with shooting *film* instead of bullets at his oppo-nents," his determination to get to the front armed only with a camera never wavered.

After graduating in mid-December and enjoying a brief furlough with his wife and daughter in Cincinnati, Maslowski did what soldiers have done since warfare first developed as a social practice: he waited. First he went to Mitchel Field, on Long Island, New York, where he did guard duty, guard duty, and then more guard duty. Then he received

orders to Westover Field, Massachusetts, where the classification officer "just shook his head and mumbled, 'What the Hell'd they send
you here for?'" Officials put him to work in the darkroom, which he
disliked, but since the lab was already overstaffed they converted him
into an instant Military Policeman, which he despised even more. "My
feeling of utter discouragement has plumbed new depths of despair,"
he moaned. At least he discovered why he had not been sent to FMPU.
Stamped on the bottom of his classification record was a notation that
he was too tall for combat crew training. He demanded a remeasure-
ment, and had the dreaded remark removed from his record. But the
classification office soon notified him that he was being reclassified
from cameraman to laboratory technician, a genuinely odious
prospect.

Salvation appeared to come when "a special request for a cameraman" arrived from the Charleston Field. But no, an Army SNAFU had
nailed Maslowski to another cross. Charleston did *not* need a motion-
picture cameraman. So he became a projectionist there, showing such
glittering titles as *Quartermaster—1753—Cooks—Part 1—How to Cut
Up a Quarter of Beef*. Fortunately on March 10, 1944 he was called to
the classification office and shown a letter from FMPU, where the
CCUs were formed and assigned to overseas duty, requesting his
immediate transfer to FMPU. Alas, four days later he discovered that
his transfer request had "traveled a mere 400 yards. It's still stuck in
headquarters. At this rate of travel I calculate we'll be fighting the
Sixth World War before I see service as a combat photographer. My
papers have to span the continent twice!"

When orders finally arrived they sent Maslowski to Seymour
Johnson Field in Goldsboro, North Carolina, which "just about broke
my heart." Three weeks later he was on the move again, all of one hundred and thirty miles to Greensboro, North Carolina, which was "like
stepping from the frying pan into the skillet." Here he repeated the
overseas processing he had just completed at Seymour Johnson Field,
sat through more lectures and movies, and kept his bunk bed warm.
On the first anniversary of his induction he glumly concluded that "If I
had it all to do over again I think I'd join the other side this time."

But he was soon at a Point of Embarkation, with hope waging a
valiant battle against skepticism. By way of Gibraltar, Oran, Algiers,
and Sicily, he arrived at the replacement center near Naples on July 3,
1944, fearful that "that's how the war will end—I'll replace a replacement in a Replacement Center." Luckily the earth was still rotating on

his behalf and a week later he joined the 12th CCU. His wife was "none too pleased about my getting assigned to any outfit with the word *combat* in its title," but he told her that "After fourteen months of the stuff I had to put up with I'd still think I had a good deal even if I got killed tomorrow."

Maslowski's arrival delighted the 12th CCU, if for no other reason than he was the unit's first replacement in its eighteen months overseas covering the North African campaign and the invasions of Sicily and Italy. It had "lost men in various ways but this is the first one that we have picked up."[2] As Allied forces moved onto and up the Italian peninsula the 12th CCU deployed from North Africa to Italy, initially establishing headquarters at Foggia but then moving to Caserta in March 1944. While there Maslowski joined the unit, which he immediately liked for its informality. Roll calls, parade ground formations, bed checks, guard duty, yes-sirring, saluting, "and all the other petty annoyances which make a GI's life miserable" were absent.

II

Like all CCUs the 12th operated in small detachments. Maslowski was soon on detached service on Corsica, working on a 16mm Kodachrome project directed by Lieutenant Colonel William Wyler, an acclaimed Hollywood director whose *Mrs. Miniver* had won the 1941 Academy Award for best film. Wyler was fresh from producing one of the war's great documentaries, *The Memphis Belle*, which told the story of a B-17 Flying Fortress with that name and its crew as they flew their twenty-fifth and final mission before returning to the United States. The raid was against Wilhelmshaven; getting there and back took the *Memphis Belle* through a gauntlet of flak and fighters. As the film's narration emphasized, the *Belle* was "just one plane and one crew in one squadron in one group of one wing of one Air Force out of fifteen United States Army Air Forces," so Wyler treated the Wilhelmshaven raid as representative of all strategic bombing missions. Photographed primarily from *inside* the plane, the movie made theatergoers vicarious participants, not merely observers, in an air battle over Germany. As a *New York Times* reviewer put it, "every last taxpayer can literally climb aboard a Fortress and find out for himself how it must feel to plow through a curtain of deadly flak over the target area, at the same time playing a desperate game of tag with the Luftwaffe."[3]

Wyler's dramatic story line developed by accident. When he arrived in England in 1942 he "had no idea I was going to make a picture about one plane."[4] He simply began filming all phases of the strategic bombing campaign, trusting that an appropriate story line would emerge. In particular Wyler was looking for a story that revolved around people. Like most great filmmakers he realized, as one of his friends and fellow directors said, "that if you want to put across meaningful material you've got to do it in some form of story telling, some form that will grab people's intellectual interest, their curiosity, and their feelings for things, and what people feel most about is people."

Wyler and his small hand-picked crew (RKO Studios cameraman William H. Clothier and RKO soundman Harold Tannenbaum) did some of the photography. In addition, just as John Huston had used cameramen from the 163rd SPC, so Wyler utilized film shot by the 8th CCU. For example, the men of Detachment B were in the air constantly shooting color sequences for Wyler, and having a fearful experience. On Daniel A. McGovern's initial mission German bullets knocked off his helmet, the first in a series of close calls that culminated in a bizarre episode: his crippled plane limped back to its base in a formation of German bombers raiding the English coast! The plane flipped over when it crash-landed. "It had hit a tree and the wings were sheered off from the fuselage, the engines had torn themselves free of the wings and plowed up mud for yards," reported McGovern, who eventually suffered such a severe nervous collapse that he had to be hospitalized. Things were no easier for the detachment's other men. In rapid succession George E. Gamble was wounded; Tony Edwards was killed in action; William Wood was shot down and missing in action (it took six months, but he walked to freedom through France and Spain and returned to the unit); David Barker was missing in action and probably dead because his plane had exploded in flames after being hit by flak; and Irving Slater was killed in action.[5]

As for Wyler's little crew, Tannenbaum, a forty-seven-year-old World War I veteran, died on his first mission when the Germans shot down his plane. Clothier, who later commanded the 4th CCU and then had a distinguished postwar career as first cameraman on dozens of Hollywood films including many John Wayne westerns, flew twenty-eight missions. Wyler flew five, with the fifth being crucial. After four missions he thought he had enough film to produce a documentary even though no story line had yet emerged. But he learned that if he went on one more mission he would get an Air Medal. By happenstance he flew aboard the *Memphis Belle*, piloted by Robert K. Morgan, "who was kind of annoyed, thinking 'Oh shit, there's another guy coming with us.'" Wyler did not know this was Morgan's twenty-fifth mission until the plane was safely over the North Sea on its way home, when the crew began celebrating. Reflecting on the significance of completing twenty-five missions, the director realized "Jesus, that's the thing!" The film's original title was *25 Missions*, which Wyler changed only at the last moment because he thought *The Memphis Belle* sounded more "commercial."[6]

Like *San Pietro*, *The Memphis Belle* was not exactly what it seemed. Although its combat scenes were genuine, only a handful actually occurred during the *Belle's* twenty-fifth mission; William Clothier shot much of the film's combat footage and he was never even on that plane. "But it doesn't matter," said Wyler. "The missions, they're all alike." Ground-crew scenes were filmed on a day when no mission occurred, and shots of the plane's crewmen were staged *after* the last mission. Wyler and Clothier actually debated about which plane and crew to feature, with the latter preferring *Invasion II* piloted by Oscar O'Neill, the father of future actress Jennifer O'Neill. The King and Queen of England did not just happen to inspect Morgan and his men at film's end. "Dear Heaven," Wyler implored the air base commander when he learned the royal couple was visiting, "tell them to inspect the *Memphis Belle*." And the movie does not contain a scene Wyler desperately wanted: a flak burst. "I could never get one explosion," he sadly recalled, "because how the hell do you know where one's going to explode? Once the cloud is there it's too late. All that flak so close to us, and I could never get the explosion."

Wyler returned stateside in October 1943 with approximately 20,000 feet of film, which he edited down to 3,700 feet. Publicly released in April 1944 by Paramount Studios through the War Activities Committee of the Office of War Information, *The Memphis Belle* was a hit with the public and the critics, winning a number of national awards. Considering the difficulties involved in aerial photography and the primitive equipment, the cinematography was gorgeous. The "plot" involved Hollywood staples that always packed the movie houses: human interest, terrific violence, and gripping suspense. The narrator introduced the audience to all ten crew members, giving their names, home towns, and occupations. Wyler used reverse psychology, avoiding false heroics by understating the crew's dedication and bravery. The script depicted the men as simply average Americans—a construction worker, a carpet-company clerk, a paint-company chemist, an industrial engineer, a washing-machine repairman, and so on—doing a nasty, dangerous job as best they could. As intended, the audience reaction was "What do you mean, they're not heroes?"

After the crew participated in a "26th mission" by making a nation-wide industrial tour to help inspire American workers, the *Belle's* pilot and bombardier returned to combat and flew in the first B-29 to bomb Tokyo, an event portrayed in the AAF documentary *Target Tokyo*. In the late 1980s the *Memphis Belle*, named for the pilot's girlfriend Margaret Polk, was restored and put on display at the Memphis Belle Pavilion along the Memphis waterfront. Although their romance did not survive the war, both Margaret Polk and veteran pilot Robert Morgan were on hand for the ribbon-cutting ceremonies.[7]

Having produced a film about strategic bombing in the European Theater, it seemed logical for William Wyler to make a companion documentary about tactical air power in the Mediterranean Theater.[8] In June 1944 he arrived at the 12th CCU's headquarters with a two-man crew: Lieutenant John Sturges, who had been making training films at FMPU when he met Wyler who was there putting the finishing touches on *The Memphis Belle*, and Hollywood script writer Lester Koenig.[9] Again having no storyline in mind, Wyler intended to film everything relating to P-47 Thunderbolt fighter-bombers "under the theory that we could then utilize it in assembling some kind of continuity line." But this time he had many more cameras at his disposal because he "sort of took over" the 12th CCU. Shooting began in late June and soon 80 percent of the unit was working on his project.[10]

In mid-July Wyler and most of the 12th CCU deployed to Corsica, where they concentrated on "all phases of the activities of the 57th Fighter-Bomber Group including aerial shots of P-47s in formation, peel-offs, diving, firing their guns and rockets." Maslowski joined them on August 11.[11] From Wyler's perspective he was undoubtedly a valuable addition. Most CCU cameramen normally shot with 35mm cameras but this color project was being photographed with 16mm Cine Special cameras. Since he had used these in his prewar wildlife photography, Maslowski was an expert with them.

On the night of August 14, Wyler briefed 12th CCU members on their role in Operation Dragoon, the invasion of southern France, which began the next morning. One team covered the invasion from LSTs, a second filmed the gliders and paratroopers, while a third was aboard the task-force flagship. A fourth team worked with the 27th

Fighter-Bomber Group, which was the first tactical air unit to support the invasion force. A lone photographer flew in a B-25 camera plane over the beachhead, John Sturges stood by to cover air–sea rescues, and Maslowski went to a specially built airstrip on Corsica "to cover any action that might occur."[12] He waited for "three days for something to happen that didn't," and then returned to the 57th Fighter Group.

While most 12th-CCU cameramen endured some tense moments as they followed the invasion troops through southern France for the next month, Karl Maslowski stayed on Corsica and was as safe as if he had been photographing mule deer in Glacier National Park. He often took a jeep into the picturesque Corsican hills to get footage of interesting local scenes, pausing to nibble on grapes and blackberries, gawking at "ancient ruins which must have been old when Columbus discovered the New World," and marveling at stone villages clinging so precariously to steep hillsides that they seemed to defy engineering principles. When he was at the 57th Group's airfields he filmed some ingenious devices that the GIs had rigged up, including a moonshine still. When asked if he allowed the product to age, the operator drawled "Yeah, about fifteen minutes." Equally intriguing was a GI who made, and fished with, TNT bombs. "There he sat," Maslowski wrote his wife, "utterly absorbed in his work, a cigarette dangling from his lips, and so much TNT that had it gone off they wouldn't even have been able to send you one of my dog tags."

Getting to view "about a mile of the first film shot on our present project" was an unsettling event for Maslowski. The astronomical amount of footage was appalling to him. In his wildlife work, when he had to worry about profits and losses with the latter coming out of his pocket, every frame had to count. William Wyler had personally shot a considerable portion of the material, but his footage "had the appearance of being exposed in a camera mounted on a rapidly revolving eggbeater held aloft at half a dozen different places in Italy. I've never seen a more disgusting waste of valuable film in all my days." John Sturges agreed that Wyler was a poor cameraman because he "just fired a camera like a water hose in all directions." Some of the 12th's cameramen did better, but even their scenes seemed amateurish compared to the work of many nature photographers Maslowski knew in civilian life.

In early September Wyler ordered two teams to photograph, from the ground, P-47s attacking enemy positions. As the days clicked by with no success he committed more of the 12th CCU to the effort.

Soon Wyler himself joined the enterprise, leading a small team composed of Maslowski and another cameraman up the Rhone River valley.[13] But they could not find a vantage point to photograph the action without getting killed in the process, and in any event the sun "seemed to have gone traveling to some new planet," making color photography impossible. Despite the cinematic handicaps, being a liberator was fun. "I know now how FDR feels," Maslowski wrote, "when he rides down Constitution Avenue on Inaugural Day and the crowds cheer him every inch of the way."

While almost the entire 12th CCU was in France struggling to get scenes of fighter-bombers in action, and with Wyler's project still incomplete, a cablegram arrived ordering the unit's return to the United States. By the end of September everyone was back in Italy awaiting transportation.[14] Maslowski's status was uncertain. Most of the 12th had been overseas about a year and a half *longer* than he had. Would he return to the states or be transferred to another CCU? With a one-year-old daughter whom he had known for only a month and a one-month-old son whom he had never met, he wanted to stick with the 12th so that he could visit home at least briefly before being redeployed. Authorities did not grant his wish, instead transferring him to the 9th CCU, which had recently arrived in Italy.

The transfer did not alter Maslowski's assignment; he remained on detached service with Wyler, who began substituting 9th-CCU cameramen for those of the departing 12th. Maslowski was soon on the Fifth Army's front, still trying to film Thunderbolts in combat from a worm's-eye view. While there he "heard enough guns fired in anger to last me the rest of my life. Those big German shells come over with a swish like a jilted blonde's skirt. Ours sounded just as mad when they went back the other way." With enemy shells detonating nearby he kept his head down, which meant he had no chance to film the P-47s that roared by in his vicinity. Even after Wyler left Italy, Maslowski worked on the color project, taking a few scenes needed to complete it, especially of wrecked German equipment cluttering the highways.

Wyler's second documentary, *Thunderbolt*, was like *The Memphis Belle* in many respects. As with *Belle*, people watching *Thunderbolt* saw most of the action from inside the plane; for about thirty minutes each member of the audience became a P-47 pilot. The film also had a "personal" touch to it. Scenes showed airmen doing laundry, brushing their teeth, gambling, swimming, cuddling puppies, playing checkers, and getting staggeringly drunk. Audiences individually "met" a few pilots, shown in close-ups on the screen as the narrator gave their names, ages, home towns, number of previous missions, and a nugget or two of personal information. And as in *Belle*, movie patrons did not see what they thought they saw. Wyler's storyline had nothing to do with Operation Dragoon but instead revolved around the 57th Fighter Group's role in Operation Strangle, an air interdiction campaign to pave the way for an Allied advance to Rome by severing the Germans' supply lines. It began in March 1944 and the Allies captured Rome in early June. Yet Wyler did not begin filming until two weeks *after* Rome fell, so little if any of the footage acutally occurred during the operation. And when the film purportedly showed P-47s destroying *a* bridge, Wyler edited together footage from attacks on at least four different bridges. Similarly an attack on *a* train used scenes from strafing runs on half a dozen trains. *Thunderbolt* also lacked a scene that obsessed Wyler: the intense effort to get ground-level shots of P-47s as they strafed and bombed enemy positions was futile.

Lurking beneath the personalized patina created by getting to know the *Belle's* crew and the Thunderbolts' pilots lay the random, impersonal, savage reality of machine-age warfare. "I never had any trouble getting geared up for that war and those bastards," said John Sturges in a statement that exemplified the filmmakers' attitude. "I would have been happy to blow more of them up." The B-17s' best operational altitude was 25,000 feet, up "in the lifeless stratosphere" where the planes could not be seen from the ground and where the crews never saw any of the more than 300,000 German civilians killed in the strategic bombing campaign. *Thunderbolt* reinforces the theme of distant, impersonal death. "From the air Italy is more remote," the narrator explains. "The airman never sees the face of the people, only the face of the country." In one sequence a P-47 sprays the landscape with machine-gun fire as the narrator, speaking the pilot's thoughts, says "Somebody in that field. Wonder who they are. No friends of mine." Perhaps they were women or children rather than enemy soldiers, but the fighter-bomber's speed and altitude did not permit fine distinctions. Kill them. In the next sequence the narrator-pilot thinks the "houses around here look kinda suspicious. Might be something in 'em." Maybe an enemy headquarters, but maybe sick people or harmless elders. Kill them.

Neither film ignored the war's high cost to American airmen. *Belle* contains stunning images of crippled Flying Fortresses plummeting to earth with only a few crewmen able to bail out. As the planes returned from Wilhelmshaven, the patients in the base hospital watched anxiously out the windows. "They know what it feels like to lie on a bouncing Fortress floor for hundreds of miles, through the frozen stratosphere, in great pain, with the other men in your crew fighting to keep you alive until they hit the field." Some of the wounded were "not a pretty sight." And the film shows a body wrapped in a blanket as the narrator says that he, too, will get a Purple Heart—posthumously. "That's a wreck. A P-47's cooking," says *Thunderbolt's* narration, "and there's a man in it." "All you know for sure is," it continues as a ground crew pulls the charred remains from the smoldering debris, "for some, the war is expensive. You wish the people back home could at least see it." In *Thunderbolt* they *did*.[15]

Like every AAF documentary, Wyler's films contained doctrinal statements as part of the AAF's campaign for postwar independence from the Army. The AAF doctrine emphasized that air power should operate in direct support of land or sea forces only rarely, and then always under the control of AAF officers, not of the ground or naval commanders. Starkly phrased, AAF leaders argued that warfare had entered a third, more immediately decisive dimension. Lengthy, large-scale land and sea campaigns were little more than relics from an obsolete past. In particular, AAF theorists believed in the efficacy of long-range strategic bombardment hundreds if not thousands of miles behind enemy lines. They argued that daylight pinpoint bombing of enemy industrial targets by aircraft flying in formation at high altitude could win a war without much help from the Army or Navy. If an army needed more direct support than that provided by long-range strategic bombing, that assistance should be a deep interdiction of enemy supply lines, not air attacks along the front lines.

The Memphis Belle's narration, delivered over scenes of the English countryside, explained that "This is a battlefront—a battlefront like no other in the long history of mankind's wars. This is an air front." Moments later it repeats these phrases almost verbatim. Then it makes the point a third time and elaborates on AAF doctrine: "And this is the new battlefront, the air front, from which we seek out the enemy, not his infantry or artillery, not his Panzer divisions, but the greater menace, the industrial heart of his nation ... the steel mills and refineries, shipyards and submarine pens, factories and munitions plants. Pinpoints on the map of Europe which mean rubber, guns, ball bearings, shells, engines, tanks. Targets. Targets to be destroyed." And they were destroyed, at least according to the film, which asked, "Who can tell the number of German torpedoes that will not be fired, the number of our convoys that will get through now, the soldiers' and seamen's lives that will be saved, or the battles that will be won instead of lost because of what these bombers and airmen did today?" *Target for Today, The Last Bomb, The Earthquakers, Combat America,* and other documentaries also explained strategic bombing doctrine and showcased its effects.

At the tactical level *Thunderbolt* argued that the AAF had done a magnificent job of bombing Cassino in February 1944 directly in front of the Fifth Army, but this did not break the stalemate in Italy because it misused "the airplane's greatest asset," which was "its ability to get behind the enemy. That's what the air planners wanted to do." Their plan, Operation Strangle, was to "isolate the battlefield," weakening "the entire German front by depriving it of supplies, fuel, food, ammunition, reinforcements." Over sequences of enemy truck convoys being attacked, the narrator emphasizes that "Those aren't just trucks and Germans. You're stopping ammunition before it's fired on the Fifth Army front, and you're doing it two hundred miles behind that front." During a montage of wrecked trains and bridges, the narration returns to this point. "How many German tanks went out of business because of the gasoline these trains never carried? How many German shells were never fired because they couldn't get across the rivers?"

Although postwar historians questioned the effectiveness of both strategic bombing and Operation Strangle, *The Memphis Belle* and *Thunderbolt* expressed no doubts about the success of the air campaigns they depicted. Through its documentaries the AAF made a strong "eyewitness" case for its mission as an independent service.

III

Since P-47s and other fighters were single-seaters with room for only the pilot, some spectacular footage in *Thunderbolt* and other AAF documentaries came from automatic cameras that combat photographers installed and maintained. One of the most important, called a GSAP, was an electrically-driven 16mm camera with a 50-foot film magazine and a lens set at infinity and heated against high-altitude cold. Mounted in a plane's wings and linked to the same solenoid that operated the machine guns, a GSAP began filming within an eighth of a second after the pilot fired. To record the effects of the machine-gun fire GSAPs had an "override" switch that kept them running for several seconds after the guns stopped. "With the touch of a finger on a stick," said the narrator in *The Fight for the Sky*, "a camera and eight machine guns are put into action. Small cameras set on the wings make the record; too often poor pictures [resulted] due to gun vibration." As shown in *Thunderbolt*, to get less fuzzy pictures than those from GSAPs, cameramen mounted some automatic cameras away from the machine guns: under the wings, in the wheel wells, in the instrument panel to photograph the pilot, and behind the pilot; often they mounted two here, one shooting forward the other backward.[16]

Since the CCUs' primary mission was to take 35mm motion pictures, personnel put much effort into developing 35mm automatics and designing appropriate mounts for both fighters and bombers. Despite many technical hurdles, late in the war and independently of each other several CCUs developed systems that were compact, simple, and dependable.[17] So vital was this enterprise that two 12th-CCU cameramen received the Legion of Merit for their success in motorizing and installing 35mm automatic cameras on fighter planes.[18]

Automatic cameras were the World War II equivalent of instant replay, showing a pilot's-eye view of exactly what happened: "how many enemy planes a pilot shot down, how good his shooting was, or why he missed, whether he wasted much ammunition, and how skillful was his approach to the enemy."[19] Officials regarded GSAP footage as conclusive proof of a "kill" even if no other visual confirmation was available. And they found that GSAPs were effective training tools. Using live ammunition in training was impractical, so trainees shot pictures instead of bullets. Then they studied the results, and usually dramatically improved their marksmanship as they saw both their mistakes and successes. Indicative of the GSAPs' value was the number of them that the armed forces used. The Navy ordered 50,000 of the 16mm models by the fall of 1943 and by the summer of 1945 the AAF was employing 175,000 of them.[20]

Pilots, who were after all technicians, became fascinated with the automatic cameras and sometimes delayed going into action until they double-checked to make sure they were working. Keeping the automatics in good operating condition could be aggravating duty for cameramen. In the spring of 1945 Maslowski spent several weeks maintaining automatic cameras in the 47th Bombardment Group. "If, when I return, I ever contemplate taking pictures of wildlife with an automatic camera I wish you would apply the nearest heavy object to my skull," he implored his wife less than a week after this assignment began. "Our little detachment is having one hell of a time with 'em. I never knew so many things could go wrong with cameras, motors, switches, relays and wires." When things worked correctly photographers could perform their duties quickly; then they simply killed time waiting for a mission equipped with their automatics to return. "Been sitting here for fifteen minutes trying to dream up a topic on which I might continue this letter for at least another paragraph," Maslowski noted between yawns, "but it seems as though I'll need a pipe-ful of Opium to accomplish that."

Fortunately other assignments were more exciting. Maslowski and three other cameramen filmed supply drops to partisans behind German lines, and he flew nighttime bombing missions hoping to shoot some spectacular pyrotechnics when the American bombs landed on a munitions train or oil dump. But every time he went aloft the bombardier "hit nothing more flammable than five acres of farmland or a masonry bridge." On another occasion he was in a detachment making movies of a new air-to-ground rocket. This assignment became a harrowing experience when a rocket went awry and, with a paralyzing hollow roar, thundered into the ground and exploded not more than 50 feet from the cameramen. Although hurled to the ground and splattered with mud, they were unhurt. The 9th CCU's war diary noted that "It's still a mystery why all three weren't killed instantly,"[21] but Maslowski had the answer: "The fact that none of us were scratched bears out the old saying that only the good die young."

IV

"If the sun shines I'll be so angry with the god damned solar system I'll become nocturnal," Maslowski threatened in October 1944. Strange sentiments from a cameraman who had recently cursed the lack of sunlight in Italy, Corsica, and France! But the next day he was taking his first Italian lessons and he had learned that his instructor was a pretty brunette. Good weather would require him to go on a mission and miss the anticipated ogling. Thankfully the sun did not appear, yet the lesson was disappointing. Maslowski's comely teacher had eaten garlic for lunch, and he would "rather try to knock off the Siegfried Line single-handed than parry a single zephyr of this pungent seasoning."

The irony of such a beautiful woman having bad breath symbolized the juxtaposition between the lovely European landscape and the blemishes inflicted by war. Maslowski found "something positively charming about the neat, orderly appearance" of the Italian countryside with its slow-moving ox teams and little gray burros, its blossoming fruit trees and tidy vegetable gardens, its shimmering wheat fields and picturesque mountain villages. Unfortunately war's marring ugliness sullied these pleasing panoramas. True, each liberated village brought victory nearer, "but it was also pathetic to walk through the gutted dwellings and shops. Broken china, bright red buttons, dead horses, children's toys, splintered furniture, and it seemed, even men's hopes were churned up in one grand mess of mud and dust amidst shattered masonry and twisted girders." So great and widespread was the devastation that "I shouldn't wonder if the people despair of ever rebuilding their country."

And who could truly enjoy the wonders of a foreign culture and magnificent scenery with death so omnipresent? Although the battle for France dominated the headlines, Maslowski reminded his wife, "the fight here is just as grim and deadly as it ever will be in France. Guys get killed just about every minute." He had usually been "in relatively 'safe' spots. But you and the others back home must remember that war can reach back and touch even these spots." Sometimes it was not even the enemy that did the reaching. In November 1944 three 9th CCU cameramen were photographing newsreel-type footage of four Brazilian Air Force planes flying in formation. For the final scene the Brazilians were to peel off close to the camera plane but the last plane came too close and clipped its wing. No one survived the crash.[22] Life-claiming accidental crashes were relatively common in the AAF and Maslowski brooded over these seemingly senseless deaths: "Each corpse was like a pebble dropped in a pool of water. The waves of tragedy that rippled outward would engulf wives, sweethearts, children, mothers, grandparents and friends."

V

Maslowski's military career ended as it began, with him awaiting an uncertain future for months and then suddenly being granted his foremost desire. When the Germans surrendered, first in Italy and then in

Germany itself, the 9th CCU did not celebrate very much since most unit members believed that "'tis an almost foregone conclusion that some of us will be sent to help in the battle for Rice Paddy 16."[23] Unless the war in the Pacific ended unexpectedly Maslowski thought he would still be in khaki in the spring of 1946.

Immediately after the German collapse Maslowski filmed the GIs' reaction and a memorial service, and then in late May joined a delegation that went to Russian-occupied Vienna for two weeks to select buildings and an airfield suitable for an American occupation force. Maslowski's part in the mission was secret.[24] His specific task was to photograph the airfields and (since he had learned German from his parents, who had emigrated from Germany) to make discreet inquiries about how much fog occurred in their vicinity. Officials could then select the best airfield for AAF use. Maslowski despised communism and did not like his Russian hosts. They were "too shifty and suspicious for my money" and severely restricted his photo opportunities. "Those babies might be our Allies," he told a friend, "but believe me we've got lots better friends in this World."

After he returned to unit headquarters, few photographic assignments interrupted the waiting and wondering. Shooting an occasional awards ceremony, WAC weddings, troops returning to the United States, a celebrity tennis match, and an Allied track meet were at best brief interludes in the daily boredom. Then in early August the 9th CCU received some good news and some bad news. The former was word that it had been ordered home; the latter was that "we are in Class 2—destined to come home for a thirty-day furlough and then go on to fight some more." Since he had more than enough points for a discharge, Maslowski questioned whether he would actually be redeployed to the Pacific; still "only time will tell what disposition will be made of the members of the 9th CCU."

Maslowski and his fellow cameramen had to endure the uncertainty for a shorter time than any of them had dared hope, for none of them had yet heard of atomic bombs. Although the bombs that destroyed Hiroshima and Nagasaki did not by themselves force Japan to surrender, they surely helped shorten the time necessary to resolve the issue and end the waiting.

Yet the bombs that did so much to speed Maslowski home to his family and back to wildlife photography did not make him especially joyous. "Of course I'm happy to know we've got such a weapon since it will surely shorten the war," he confided to his wife, "but its dreadful destructive power depresses me. With knowledge like that in existence no one can live in safety anymore."

"I must admit that since coming overseas I've had about as good a time as any soldier can have away from home," Maslowski reflected midway between the German and Japanese surrenders "I've never had to do a lick of really hard manual labor. Practically no discipline has been exercised over me and whenever I've wanted to use a car one has been at my disposal. Of course I've worked under highly dangerous circumstances at times but that only added zest to my life over here."

Getting into a CCU had taken longer than the impatient Maslowski liked. Once at the front he flew no spectacular missions like Joswick's Ploesti raid, engaged in no special heroics like Bray's fighter kills, and had no incredible adventures like Chaney's swim in the Gulf of Corinth and subsequent OSS service. But at least the armed forces had matched his skills and wishes with their needs. Perhaps the world did rotate on Maslowski's behalf.

9

"Frankly, I Wouldn't Have Picked This as an Assignment"

The Navy's Combat Photography Unit #1

Sleek and graceful, fifteen or sixteen inches long, with a gray and white body except for the blood red bill and and black head, the Arctic tern has no avian rival in the distance it travels on its annual migration. The bird nests in the Arctic regions as far north as Ellesmere and Bathurst Islands but winters in the sub-Antarctic seas.

The photographic equivalent of an Arctic tern was the Navy's CPU #1.

Working under orders so secret that even Lieutenant Commander Carleton Mitchell, the head of the Navy's Combat Photography Section (CPS), did not know its ultimate destination, CPU #1 undertook a journey unmatched by any other photo outfit. Commanded by Lieutenant Earl F. Colgrove, the unit began its peregrinations in Washington, D.C., heading westward through Chicago, El Paso, and Los Angeles; crossed the Pacific to Wellington, New Zealand and Melbourne, Australia and then doubled back to India, first to Bombay, then via train and boat to Calcutta, Dhubri, and Chabua; flew in a DC-3 over the "Hump" of the Himalaya Mountains to Kunming, China; went north by truck to Chungking; and then from there commenced a 2,200-mile journey to a secret camp ninety miles west of

Hangchow, a coastal city on the East China Sea deep behind Japanese lines in occupied China.

Less than a year later Colgrove was on the move again, completing a westward circumnavigation of the globe by returning to Washington through India, the Middle East, and North Africa and then across the Atlantic. After a brief respite, a reorganized CPU #1 virtually followed its original route as it headed westward. The destination this time, however, was not China but the Pacific Fleet, which the unit reached in time to photograph the largest naval engagement in history, the Battle of Leyte Gulf. In late January 1945, CPU #1 returned to Pearl Harbor, its wanderings completed because by early 1945 the naval photographic establishment was phasing the CPS out of existence.[1]

I

The war was already ten months old and naval photogaphy was a disaster, at least according to David O. Selznick, a Hollywood producer who had donned a naval uniform. The Navy's photographic activities were then so uncoordinated that "nothing approaching the maximum potential result is being obtained" and "the possibilities of the use of photography as an instrument of warfare scarcely have been touched." The longtime Hollywood insider believed, the Navy could do "an infinitely better job" of familiarizing the public with its executive heads, commanding officers, and heroes "through newsreels and magazine reels, and in short subjects especially created and produced by the Navy." Immediate action was necessary. "Other branches of the armed forces have enlisted important motion picture directors, writers and other creators, and are continuing to enlist them at an ever-increasing rate." If the Navy dallied much longer "it will find itself with third or fourth 'pickings.'" To sail the Navy out of the photographic doldrums Selznick proposed a Bureau of Photography with divisions responsible for "combat intelligence; strategic films; training films; Public Relations films; historical compilations and archives; and suggestions and directives."[2]

Responding to Selznick's critique the Navy's Director of Public Relations, Leland P. Lovette, made two points.[3] First, the question of a photographic bureau was moot. More than a year earlier Secretary of the Navy Knox had created a board to consider the service's photographic needs and to "examine into the advisability of pooling facilities where both economy and efficiency can be served." It concluded that the existing facilities were terribly inadequate and stressed "the desirability of greater use of photography for publicity and training." Especially deplorable were the slow, cumbersome procedures that hamstrung the Bureau of Public Relations. But the board rejected the idea of creating a separate photographic bureau. In April 1941 the Chief of Naval Operations assigned the development of photographic facilities to the Bureau of Aeronautics (BuAer), which had been actively engaged in photography for two decades. Rather than reverse this decision Knox's board recommended that BuAer's photographic program be expanded, and the secretary approved the recommendation.[4]

Second, even as Selznick was writing the Navy was overcoming its feeble start. A huge new Photographic Science Laboratory (PSL) was nearing completion at the Naval Air Station at Anacostia, Maryland, and a CPS was already being formed in the Office of Public Relations. The driving motive behind the formation of the CPS was the desire to generate better publicity for the Navy. Secretary Knox was distraught that pictures of "historical, news, and recruiting value have not been obtained on many occasions," such as a recent seaborne meeting between President Roosevelt and Prime Minister Churchill and the first convoy of American ships to cross the Atlantic, and news agencies were complaining about the "inadequate still and motion-picture coverage of Naval activities."[5]

The Navy's problems in generating material for public release were twofold. Although it had a large number of photographers, many of them were specialists in aerial reconnaissance, an indispensable function but one that yielded few pictures suitable for inspiring the civilian public. Even nonreconnaissance photographers shot little newsworthy material because they invariably had other combat responsibilities. So-called "photo officers," for example, were often aviators or gunnery experts and in battle these other roles took precedence.

Officially established on October 15, 1942 to alleviate these problems, the CPS was a cooperative venture between BuAer and the Office of Public Relations. All members of the section were BuAer personnel on "loan" to Public Relations and all the section's equipment and supplies came through BuAer, a rather unfortunate arrangement which meant that the CPS was "always in a requesting status, even down to such minor matters as the development of film and the procurement of one filter." Although BuAer was normally cooperative, occasionally the section received a curt "No" in response to what it considered an important request.[6]

Lieutenant Commander Carleton Mitchell, Jr., a reserve officer who had been a civilian public relations expert before reporting for duty in the summer of 1941, headed the CPS.[7] Since he was the "father" of the CPUs his vision molded their actions. The CPUs, he believed, should serve many constituencies. Most important, they must supplement civilian war correspondents and the existing naval photographic establishment to produce more film that could be publicly released, thereby generating favorable publicity by providing high-quality movies and photographs to the newsreels, magazines, newspapers, and other commercial agencies.[8] Because the Navy's foremost concern was publicity, Mitchell directed the CPUs to focus on actual combat, with all its enormous emotional and photogenic appeal. To facilitate the CPUs' combat mission, high-ranking Navy officers received instructions calling their attention to paragraph 3(b) of General Orders #179 issued by Navy Secretary Knox in August 1942: "Commanding Officers are directed to obtain photographs at times of emergency, disaster, and combat action."[9]

Mitchell also emphasized that the CPUs were not organized solely for the benefit of the Office of Public Relations. They could provide motion pictures and stills of a tactical, technical, and intelligence nature to other naval bureaus. CPUs carried extensive "wish lists" from virtually every bureau detailing the specialized subjects that they wanted photographed. Mitchell wanted his cameramen to work on these requests during lulls between battles.[10]

Mitchell initially organized each CPU as a four-man unit; with one officer and three enlisted men, all of them trained cameramen and with three of the quartet being motion-picture specialists. He thought four men was the minimum number necessary to do a thorough job and yet few enough to get transportation and quarters on warships, where space was always at a premium. However, neither Mitchell nor the CPUs were inflexible. One CPU dispatched to the Pacific late in the war had one officer and five enlisted men, and in the field CPU officers sometimes "borrowed" as many as three photographers to cover important events. The only rule, Mitchell explained to one of his officers, was not to "get saddled with too many people so that you destroy your mobility."[11]

To form the CPUs Mitchell and Colgrove sent out a request for officers knowledgeable about photography who would volunteer for a combat assignment. After scanning the volunteers' personnel records to identify likely prospects they interviewed the men, selecting those with extensive photographic experience. For example, the OIC of CPU #2, John P. Drennan, owned his own photo service and did free-lance work for the newsreels; the OIC of CPU #4, Harold L. Tacker, taught photography at the University of Oklahoma; and the OIC of CPU #5, John R. Munroe, was a supervisor with Fox Movietone News. In addition most officers were graduates of the Navy Photography School at Pensacola and all attended a special two-month-long motion-picture course that the five newsreel agencies and The March of Time (a company that produced "short-subject" movie documentaries on current issues) conducted in New York. Every selected enlisted man graduated from the Navy Photography School and many had additional prewar experience or further photographic schooling from the Navy, particularly at its Motion Picture (or Eyemo) School at Anacostia.[12]

Mitchell's organizational proposal for the CPS called for ten units, but only nine were in the original contingent that was on active duty by February 1943. He eventually organized four more units: #10 in April 1943, #11 in June 1943, and #12 and #13 in the fall of 1944.[13] Not all of these were always in the field at the same time. And as with the SPCs and the CCUs, even the tiny CPUs sometimes operated in smaller detachments. In late June 1943 CPU #5's OIC split his men between two destroyers and the OIC of CPU #6 divided his crew between a cruiser and a transport.[14]

Technically the CPS first covered combat even before the individual units had been formed. It was only a few weeks old when Mitchell learned of the upcoming North African invasion. So he hastily selected eight motion-picture cameramen (all enlisted men, since no officers were available yet), equipped them with Eyemos, and sent them to Norfolk, Virginia, where they joined fleet units engaged in Operation Torch. They shot 20,000 feet of film, of which 12,000 went to the newsreels. But not until mid-1943 did substantial amounts of CPU material pour into Washington. Between May 10 and June 30 the Navy released twelve "short subjects" to the newsreels; CPUs provided ten of them. Between May 1 and June 30 it provided 433 still pictures to the press, 70 of these coming from the CPUs.[15]

II

"It has been amusing to get your short notes from time to time as you progress toward an ever more distant point," Mitchell wrote playfully to Colgrove in mid-June 1943. "I think you have almost achieved some sort of record for remaining in a travel status." Eleven months later Mitchell was still writing with a light touch, trying to be humorously supportive. "Had you lived in biblical times," he told Colgrove, "your trials and tribulations would have made you famous rather than that gent Job." By then Colgrove was in no mood to be humored, and probably did not see anything remotely funny in the comparison between himself and Job. For him naval service was no longer a job or an adventure but a trauma.

Determining exactly where and when CPU #1's venture became an ordeal is not easy, but a likely benchmark would be its arrival in early July 1943 at Chungking. Getting that far had not been without its tiresome moments but, at least in retrospect, everything afterwards was worse. The roundabout voyage to Bombay that began in late March 1943 had not been too bad. Colgrove and the three men in his unit were good sailors who did not become seasick, and standing an occasional watch like "real seamen" was an interesting experience. Still, after an uneventful month at sea time began to drag. About the only item Colgrove thought worth recording in his diary was crossing the equator twice, first when heading to Wellington, New Zealand, and then again when sailing back toward India.

Despite being long and uncomfortable the train trip from Bombay to Calcutta had its intriguing aspects, such as the method of keeping a train compartment cool, which Colgrove explained in a letter to his wife and young daughter: "you wire ahead for a block of ice that is placed on the floor in the center of the compartment and then a fan is set to blow across it." At Calcutta he stayed in the Grand Hotel, which was fine except that the heat and insect life made sleeping nearly impossible.

On June 1 CPU #1 was heading toward Chabua in extreme northeastern India. When it reached Dhubri on the Brahmaputra River the initial monsoon rains forced the unit to take shelter in an abandoned bungalow. But the delay was only momentary, and later in the day the men headed upriver aboard an old sidewheel steamer. On the way CPU #1 had a modest but portentous encounter with deteriorating health. Colgrove "had a little infection on my leg" and cameramen Doug Jones and Edwin Perrigoue were "a little under the weather." Only the unit's fourth member, Thomas G. Phillips, Jr., was completely healthy. After transferring from the leaky steamer to a decaying train at Pandu, the unit arrived at Chabua on June 5. There, amidst the flies, mosquitoes, monsoons, mud, and seemingly endless waiting for a flight over the Himalayas, Colgrove wrote his wife that "when I get back to Burbank I'll sure be happy to stay there the rest of my life. People at home just don't know how lucky they are."

Flying the "Hump" from Chabua to Kunming was always dangerous, since Japanese fighter planes patrolled the vicinity in good weather and crossing in bad weather invited fatal accidents. Colgrove made the flight under deplorable weather conditions. "Shortly after we took off we heard on the radio that the Japs were raiding the field we had just left," he noted, "so we barged on across despite bad weather that might otherwise have turned us back." They arrived at Kunming toward evening and during the ensuing days tried to arrange air transportation to Chungking. None was available so they scrounged up a handful of trucks. They found that some minimal special training was necessary before leaving. Since bandits infested the road running northward from Kunming, "all hands were ready to 'repel boarders' and a hot reception would have greeted anyone foolish enough to try stopping us along the road." Poor-quality fuel and poorly-aligned wheels, failing brakes and bad clutches, broken springs and flat tires, dead batteries and leaking radiators, swollen rivers and landslides, droves of mosquitoes and herds of rats, and air-raid warnings were everyday occurrences for CPU #1 along the route, but the convoy encountered no bandits.

A sense of relief engulfed Colgrove when he reached Chungking. With its traveling completed, CPU #1 could look forward to its photographic work—whatever it might be, for Colgrove still did not know exactly what his assignment was.

Actually only the *easy* part of CPU #1's journey was over. And as Colgrove learned on Independence Day 1943, CPU #1's mission dealt only secondarily with photography.

III

"Frankly, I wouldn't have picked this as an assignment for a CPU knowing all the long months you spent training us if I had known all the job over here needed as I know it now," Colgrove wrote to Mitchell, "but as long as we are here we'll do the best job that we know how and hope that in the not too distant future we'll get a crack at some real action pictures." Such were his sentiments a few days after reporting for duty to a boss named Mary at a place called Happy Valley.

"Mary" was Commander Milton Edward Miles' nickname, and "Happy Valley" was his secluded headquarters in the hills north of Chungking. Miles wore dual hats, one as the head of the U.S. Naval Group, China (the so-called "Rice Paddy Navy," which ultimately numbered 2,500 officers and men from the Navy, Marines, and Coast Guard) and the other as the deputy director of the ultra-secret Sino-American Cooperative Organization (SACO), established in early 1943. Among other things, SACO (pronounced "socko" to imply a hard-hitting outfit) trained and equipped approximately 30,000 Chinese guerrillas, set up coast-watching stations and other intelligence units, and established clandestine weather stations to provide meterological data, especially for the Pacific Fleet. Since weather moved from west to east across China and over the Pacific, the Navy would always be fighting the Japanese at a disadvantage if it did not have accurate, timely land-based weather reports from west of its positions at sea. In addition, Major General Claire L. Chennault's China-based Fourteenth Air Force relied heavily upon SACO-generated intelligence regarding such vital matters as weather conditions, Japanese troop movements and supply depots, and enemy airfield construction.[16]

The meeting with Milton Miles had not gone as Colgrove anticipated. Instead of talking about photography, "Mary" pointed to a spot on the map labeled "Camp One," the first of a dozen camps he operated that stretched almost 1,500 miles from the Indochinese border to the Gobi Desert's northern limits. Camp One was far beyond a red line indicating the limits of Japanese occupation. This, he told Colgrove, is where your unit will deliver a load of equipment and then remain to help train guerrillas. When Colgrove asked about the unit's photographic mission "Mary" explained that "We are short of men and these Chinese need our help—your primary job is to teach those soldiers to kill more Japs—train them, and equip them and they'll do the rest." Only if time and circumstances permitted was Colgrove to make pictures of Camp One's conditions and training program.

After the Happy Valley briefing Colgrove wondered why he had not kept his mouth shut instead of volunteering for secret duty; he also now understood the purpose of a special school he had attended before departing the United States. Upon completing his basic training in

October 1942 Colgrove, a *New York Times* photographer who had covered prewar naval maneuvers off San Diego and Hawaii, thought he would become a photography instructor at Pensacola. At the last moment he received orders to report to Washington, where he became Lieutenant Commander Mitchell's executive officer and helped organize the first CPUs. As planning progressed for shipping the units overseas Secretary of the Navy Frank Knox told Colgrove that "there was one assignment of special hazard that he wanted my best crew to cover. I told him that my men were the best and after talks with the men I agreed we would all go." Each man received a tommy gun, a .38 revolver, two knives, machette, Marine field clothes, jungle-type medical kits, and innoculations against yellow fever, typhus, typhoid, plague, and tetanus. But only Colgrove went to Area D at Quantico, where all personnel wore civilian clothes, were known only by their first names, and learned Morse code, nighttime maneuvers, demolitions and other types of sabotage, close combat, and how to sneak up and strangle a sentry.

Camp One was 750 airline miles due east of Chungking but Colgrove traveled more than 2,000 miles getting there. When CPU #1 departed Chungking in mid-July 1943 it was in a convoy with twenty other Americans, sixty Chinese soldiers, and ten tons of equipment and supplies in half a dozen near-antique trucks. To avoid the Japanese the convoy, which went by train for part of the trip, took an erratic route, moving south to Kweiyang and Liuchou, then northeast to Hengyang, dipping south again for 150 miles to Kukong, and finally turning northeast in the direction of Hangchow. Japanese planes flying from Hangchow and Canton subjected the convoy to numerous air raids. The trucks were in no better condition than those that had transported CPU #1 from Kunming to Chungking. Demolished bridges, washed out roads, and rock slides were the daily norm. So the journey was dangerous, arduous, and slow. Sixty miles from their destination the road became so bad that they had to cache the trucks and make the final leg of their journey in commandeered sampans, which earned Colgrove the title of "Sampan Admiral."

CPU #1 arrived at Camp One near a mountain village called Chung Shuen, just five miles south of Hweichow and "surrounded by Japs or Japanese puppet troops," late on August 17, 1943. The average rate of speed during the month-long trip from Chungking was sixty-seven miles per day. It had taken the unit five *months* since leaving Washington to reach its destination.

By the time it reached Camp One, CPU #1's strength had been halved, and it never served as a complete unit in China. Suffering from "some mysterious fever," Perrigoue remained behind at Chungking and never rejoined the unit. By the time the trucks reached Kweiyang three days later, Phillips had to be hospitalized with malarial chills and fever. Months later he got to Camp One but by then Jones was already gone and Colgrove was about to leave. Only Colgrove and Jones arrived at Camp One and they were not in perfect health. En route the former had developed a severe heat rash and acute diarrhea, while a bad ear infection afflicted the latter. Neither was illness- or injury-free for the remainder of his China tour.

While inspecting the facilities with the camp commander, Major John H. Masters (whose men called themselves Major Masters' Mad Monks), Colgrove learned about the training plans for the first guerrilla class of approximately 300 students, which began within the week, and also investigated film-making possibilities. Meanwhile still cameraman Jones rigged up a darkroom. Having anticipated travel difficulties, Colgrove had brought smaller, lighter 16mm movie equipment. Before the war Jones had honed his skills as an Associated Press staff photographer and would, after the war, become a *Look* magazine cameraman who covered the Vietnam War in 1966–67; while in China he shot with less cumbersome 35mm still cameras rather than a Speed Graphic.

Among subjects taught to the budding guerrillas, some of them no more than thirteen or fourteen years old, were aircraft identification, infantry tactics, camouflage, sabotage, close combat, grenade throwing, and demolitions. Teaching the Chinese to hurl a grenade was challenging, since few had ever played baseball and most "threw like a girl." As a safety precaution the instructors had students hurl grenades downhill until they developed arm strength. Colgrove specialized in three areas. First, he taught students "secret methods of carrying weapons," sixteen of them in all, such as inside a fish belly or a melon or in the false bottom of a water tub. Second, he developed "rules to be observed when passing through enemy occupied areas." Individuals should go disguised as commoners; no more than five guerrillas should infiltrate enemy lines in one location at the same time; cover stories "should be carefully thought out and kept in mind, ready for the enemy's interrogation"; local civilians should be mobilized as guides; and so on. And finally, he explained methods for the "secret transportation of an enormous amount of explosives." For example, if carrying explosives or weapons aboard a ship, "huge stacks of wood or bricks or charcoal should be placed on the outside for purpose of concealment. Cigarettes or other stuff should be given to enemy soldiers as bribes so that they will be less careful when they investigate."

Between training assignments Colgrove also attended to his secondary mission, photography. Since no combat action was occurring in the vicinity he commenced a series of training films on the camp's activities, including "such subjects as Infantry Squad Tactics, Use of Small Arms and Grenades, Use of Natural Cover, Demolition Problems, etc." He used Chinese students and dialogue, believing that films of this type would help train new students at similar camps. Movie film could not be developed locally—in fact, nowhere in China—so Colgrove put exposed film in hollowed-out bamboo rods that Chinese recruits carried back to Chungking; from there it went to a Calcutta laboratory. Sometimes things got FUBARed. When Colgrove eventually returned to Chungking he found several bamboo containers that had never been opened! Jones not only assisted in the movie-making but also took approximately 5,000 still shots during his China sojourn.

Amidst their training and photography Colgrove and Jones unexpectedly discovered they had a third mission: as nurses. In mid-September a radioman had an appendicitis attack that required immediate surgery. Performing the operation was Dr. Victor Goorchenko (known as Doc Goo), a White Russian who lived in a nearby village. Luckily, although untrained as a surgeon he knew French. Immediately before doing the appendectomy he read a book, written in French, explaining the procedure. Working by the dim light of a still photo enlarger powered by a "one cylinder putt-putt generator," using rusty Japanese surgical instruments, and assisted by Colgrove as scrub nurse, Jones as surgical nurse, and other equally unqualified medical assistants, Doc Goo did his cutting and sewing, maintaining a steady hand even when his surgical nurse got sick while looking at the gory sight. Though it saved the radioman's life the initial operation was not entirely successful, and two days later the pickup team operated again. Fortunately the victim-patient was "so damn ornery that nothing could hurt him."

Just as Colgrove and Jones completed their initial training film project on infantry squad tactics and began scripting one on demolitions, a Japanese offensive compelled Camp One's hurried evacuation. Colgrove loaded all essential equipment and about two dozen

American and Chinese personnel aboard the sampans and drifted downriver to where he had cached the trucks. For six weeks they lived on the sampans with occasional forays ashore to wander through nearby villages where they met "a variety of odors, due largely to the numerous 'open air' privies that line the streets, the pig sties, and refuse that clutter up the scenery and, I suppose, the practice of leaving the dead in their coffins above ground in nearby fields." One village challenged the Americans to a basketball game. "Our boys in their khaki and heavy G.I. shoes, towered over the Chinese team in their snappy blue shorts and white shirts," Colgrove wrote. Superior size was of no avail in the absence of skill. At the end of the first half the Chinese led 35 to 12; the second half was not much better.

When the Japanese threat receded the sampans moved back upstream "at what might be called a good fast snail's pace," arriving at Camp One on November 9, 1943. The next day a new guerrilla-training class began and two days later Colgrove was again working on the demolitions script. But he never produced the movie. His remaining film was "so far out-dated as to be unreliable" and most other photographic supplies were exhausted. Worse, his good friend Doug Jones had to be evacuated to a base hospital for treatment of his ear infection compounded by malaria and spinal meningitis. CPU #1, Colgrove forlornly explained to Mitchell, "was now scattered over most of this country due to the various sieges of illness."

After mid-November Colgrove was lonely and unhappy. With further moviemaking out of the question, he tried to keep busy in other ways, including starting a Chinese-American language school and going pheasant hunting. But he was suffering from both eye and foot problems and longed to be out of China and into genuine combat photography. When he received a letter from Mitchell explaining that "other Units have been through a lot of battles and have turned in some very good stuff," Colgrove admitted that it "makes me envious in some ways." The isolation began to bother him, too. In December a camp member received a parcel mailed *one year* earlier and in February 1944 Colgrove finally got mail that had been postmarked in June 1943. Further eroding his morale was the cold, damp, snowy weather, which made "a fellow think of his nice warm home in good old Burbank."

To knock the edge off the dreary chill the men used charcoal fires that gave off carbon monoxide. With the windows cracked the fumes caused headaches, but if the windows were closed the noxious gas could be deadly. In late January 1944 one of the Americans forgot to open the windows in the radio shack while listening to messages from Chungking. He passed out and was well on his way toward death when Colgrove discovered him and raced to get the camp medic, Arthur J. Deegan, who had been a butcher before the war. While hurrying back Colgrove slipped and hurt his ankle. Initially he passed it off as a bad sprain, but Doc Goo diagnosed it as a broken bone just above the ankle. To give the injured leg support they "whittled out a wooden splint that looks like a three-sided box which we lined with cotton and then strapped to my foot—sure looks, and feels, clumsy." But the break got worse so they tried putting a cast on it using gypsum from the nearby hills. It took Doc Goo and Deegan the better part of a day to apply the full-leg cast. Alas, the gypsum was of such poor quality that, despite their toasting Colgrove and the cast for four hours in front of a stove, it would not harden. A week later they tried again but this time the cast became so hard and tight that his foot turned blue and they had to pound the concrete-like substance off with a hammer and chisel.

Like the other three members of CPU #1, Colgrove needed professional medical treatment and in late March 1944, almost exactly one year after departing Washington, he left Camp One heading for the base hospital at Hengyang. Since Colgrove could not walk he rode "in a covered 'chair' carried by two coolies who had quite a time making it over the several miles of hills to where our truck was waiting." The nearer he got to the hospital the sicker Colgrove became. On March 26 his diary noted he was "feeling very bad, temp[erature] 102." The next day he reached Hengyang, went to the hospital, and passed out as he entered its doors. Like Jones, Colgrove had a severe case of spinal meningitis. Although he lay unconscious for more than twenty-four hours a healthy dose of sulfa drugs saved him; he had severe headaches for several days afterward and it took more than a week for his temperature to return to normal. When he was well enough to have his leg X-rayed the results showed that the crack had started "to knit correctly and it should be all right in a month or so if I use a crutch and take it easy."

While recovering Colgrove wrote "Mary" Miles asking that CPU #1 be returned to Washington for re-equipping and reassignement. Miles agreed since the unit really no longer existed. Colgrove was incapable of active duty anytime in the near future, Jones was gravely ill in Calcutta, and Perrigoue had been sent to a SACO camp in Mongolia. Only Phillips was capable of further duty. Although not completely recovered from his malaria he had recently linked up with Colgrove at Camp One and would now remain in China to work directly for "Mary."

"Here's the news you've been waiting for!!" Colgrove wrote his wife and daughter immediately after learning of Miles' decision. "I'm heading for home!!" He went via Chungking, Kunming, and Calcutta (where he just missed reuniting with Jones, who had departed for the States the previous day), then through the Middle East and North Africa to Miami. Since his orders had assumed he would return the way he had come (across the Pacific) they directed him to report to the nearest West Coast hosptial. After a brief checkup in Florida, he traveled all the way across the country to the Long Beach naval hospital for a month-long recuperation. Along with his broken leg and the lingering effects from the meningitis, Colgrove received another memento of his China service: some false teeth—after the dentist had to pull his abcessed front teeth and impacted wisdom teeth.

"I feel pretty good so don't expect to be tied down long with the medicos," Earl Colgrove informed Mitchell even before he was out of India en route to the United States. By the time he reached American soil he was outlining a documentary for public release on "Mary" Miles' Naval Group. "This picture," he suggested, "should show: The planning, the hard work, the tough living, the fight against a numerically superior enemy, the friendships built up between our Navy men and the Chinese who worked with them; and a job well done!"

And Colgrove was itching to get back into the war and do some genuine combat photography.

IV

By September 1944 CPU #1 had been reconstituted—CPU #1 #2, as Doug Jones called it. While still hospitalized Colgrove began nagging Carelton Mitchell for a new assignment that would get him into combat, preferably in Russia, Turkey, or Norway, but in the Pacific Theater if need be. Mitchell ordered him to report to Washington to reorganize CPU #1 as soon as he could travel. Meanwhile after a long period of hospitalization at Annapolis, Jones "was released for duty with the recommendation that it be limited to the continental U.S., due to the danger of a recurrence of malaria." He received shore duty at the Navy's Photographic Science Laboratory (PSL) where, by coincidence, he bumped into Colgrove. Jones could not tolerate the prospect of prolonged shore duty any better than his old China commander, so he volunteered for combat duty with Colgrove's re-formed unit, which also included two new enlisted men, Lewis C. Cook and Robert B. Montague.

In mid-September Colgrove and his men departed PSL for the Pacific Fleet.[17] Arriving in Honolulu, they learned that cameramen heading for the combat zone had to go to aerial gunnery school. Two days after the school began they heard that transportation further westward was available *now*. Colgrove convinced the school OIC to write letters attesting that his men had *attended* gunnery school but omitting to say whether they had *graduated*. With these truthful but deceptive missives in hand CPU #1 #2 flew to Manus in New Guinea, boarded a tanker, and was soon aboard the U.S.S. *Essex*. Like most carriers the *Essex* had more than a dozen people assigned to its photo department but, said Colgrove, "they also had battle stations that demanded other duties besides their photographic work and seemed glad to have any help we could provide."

Colgrove and Jones agreed that compared to conditions in Camp One, clean sheets were one of the nicest features of life aboard the *Essex*. More than counterbalancing this amenity were the Japanese air attacks, including the kamikazes, who savaged the fleet for the first time during the Battle of Leyte Gulf in late October and then continued their attacks through the remainder of the war. During the liberation of the Philippines the enemy specifically targeted the carriers providing air cover for the various invasion forces. The incessant assaults ground down Colgrove's spirits to the point where at one point he thought he "had to get out of here or I'm going to go bonkers." Others in CPU #1 #2 also came perilously close to suffering battle fatigue.

With nothing obstructing the Americans' view of the Japanese aerial attacks, these presented extraordinary photo opportunities, and on October 24 Colgrove and Jones began taking advantage of them. On that date they filmed the death of the light carrier U.S.S. *Princeton* after a single bomb hit it and ignited an inferno. Firefighting crews struggled to save the burning ship while the cruiser *Birmingham* sought to take it in tow, but in midafternoon a huge explosion far below deck on the *Princeton* heavily damaged the supporting cruiser and so badly mangled the carrier that it had to be sunk. At one point during the day Colgrove earned a Purple Heart when shrapnel hit his arms and cheek. A month later Colgrove and Jones, standing virtually shoulder to shoulder, photographed a kamikaze at extremely close quarters. Trailing smoke after being hit by an antiaircraft shell, it plummeted out of the flak-filled sky directly toward the *Essex*. Using a still camera Colgrove snapped the shutter an instant before the plane hit while Jones recorded the entire dive in motion pictures, showing the suicide plane skim by the superstructure, narrowly miss the flight deck, and plow into the port side overhang where it exploded. Remarkably, the resulting fire only lightly damaged the carrier.

So extraordinary was Colgrove's still picture that Edward Steichen selected it as an illustration in his *U.S. Navy War Photographs: Pearl Harbor to Tokyo Bay*; since then it has been reprinted often.[18] Jones' movie scene has also been widely used both during and after the war. For example, it appeared *twice* in the Navy's wartime documentary *The Fleet That Came to Stay*, though the editing and narration made it seems as if the events occurred off Okinawa in the spring of 1945 rather than in the Philippines in late 1944. Through clever editing the film seemed to portray two separate kamikaze strikes. First the editors intercut other scenes into Jones' footage to make it appear as if the plane just missed a ship, then later in the documentary they used the entire scene uncut, showing it hit the *Essex*. In the postwar era both the *Victory at Sea* series and a segment on kamikazes in the National Geographic's "Explorer" television series also utilized the scene. As in *The Fleet That Came to Stay*, *Victory at Sea* used the scene twice, once in abbreviated form in the episode on the reconquest of the Philippines and then intercut with other footage in the Okinawa segment.

CPU #1 #2 was still aboard the *Essex* in early January 1945 when it steamed northward toward Formosa—whose northern tip was only 350 miles south of Camp One—to conduct air assaults against enemy positions on that island. Shortly thereafter the unit returned to Pearl Harbor. Colgrove continued on to the States, but Jones temporarily stayed in Hawaii to train newly-arrived photographers. In the spring he finally went Stateside, assigned to the Camel Project at China Lake in California where he took movies of enormous dummy bombs being dropped. Later he learned that these were mockups of "Fat Man," one of the atomic bombs detonated over Japan, and experts were testing its flight characteristics. Jones received an Air Medal for his China Lake work to go with the Bronze Star he wore for his valorous conduct aboard the *Essex*.

During its Pacific voyage CPU #1 #2 had been extraordinarily productive. It shot 3,300 feet of 35mm black-and-white film and 650 feet of Kodachrome during the Battle of Leyte Gulf; much of this footage appeared in homefront newsreels. And from November 1, 1944 to February 10, 1945 it "produced more releasable footage than all other navy photographers throughout the world combined." In that period Colgrove and his men supplied 13,594 of the 22,325 feet the Navy released to the newsreels.

Service on the *Essex* and the opportunities it provided to film combat partially consoled Colgrove and Jones for their long but photographically unproductive China sojourn.

V

Even as CPU #1 #2 was on its way to Pearl Harbor in early 1945 the CPS was being phased out of existence. Almost a year previously Mitchell began complaining that he could not get a clear policy statement regarding the CPUs' future and consequently could not make wise decisions. The siege of uncertainty endured for a year before he finally learned that CPUs had no future.[19]

To Mitchell the decision to eliminate the CPS was incomprehensible as it had achieved stunning results. Although the CPUs represented less than 1 percent of all naval photographic personnel they consistently supplied more than 80 percent of the Navy's publicly-released motion-picture footage and a smaller though its still substantial percentage of still photographs. Between May 1 and October 30, 1943, CPUs made 93 percent of the motion-picture film made by all Navy photographers throughout the world and 67 percent of the still shots. During the year ending June 30, 1944, CPUs supplied 84 percent of all naval motion picture footage shot outside the continental United States and released to commercial agencies. They had also provided quite a few magazine shots, including the October 3rd covers for both *Life* and *Newsweek*. As Mitchell explained to the Director of Public Relations, without the CPUs "there would have been periods of weeks on end during which no film would have been released by the Navy Department."[20]

Productive as it had been the CPS was on the decline. Opposition to its continuation stemmed primarily from common-sense considerations but also included an element of personal rivalry. As the European campaign increasingly became an air and land war, naval photography inevitably gravitated almost exclusively toward the Pacific. As of May 1944 Mitchell no longer contemplated sending replacement CPUs to Europe and sought clarification as to how many he should dispatch to the Pacific. By the fall of that year only four CPUs were there, far too few "to provide even basic coverage of Pacific Fleet activities."[21] Despite Mitchell's urgings no request for more CPUs came from Pearl Harbor, and he concluded that the Pacific photographic effort was in disarray. From his perspective no definite policy guided it; no proper liaison existed between photographers in the field and the staff of CINCPAC (Commander in Chief, Pacific Fleet); the relationship between those CPUs in the Pacific Theater and other photographers there was unclear; CPU OIC's received inadequate guidance as to what was expected of them; the handling of exposed film was uncoordinated; and long delays occurred in forwarding material to Washington. The result of this muddle was "duplication of coverage in some areas, while others have gone uncovered."[22]

Mitchell's solution to these perceived difficulties was threefold. First, saturate the Pacific with CPUs. Then, appoint a former CPU OIC (or someone familiar with and sympathetic to the CPUs) to coordinate their activities. As Mitchell noted, the Pacific Theater "was so vast and the Task Force relationships so complex that only someone who has the overall picture can hope to assign the various photographers so that complete coverage is secured." Finally, create a reserve "pool" at CINCPAC headquarters consisting of other photographers and equipment "that could be put under the temporary direction of any CPU officer for a special operation." If implemented, these proposals would make Mitchell a paramount influence in naval photography.[23]

The problem was that although having a Washington-based CPS had made sense when the Navy was fighting a two-ocean war, as Pacific operations became dominant logic decreed that someone more familiar than Mitchell with the Pacific Theater should now direct the photographic effort there. High-ranking officers who understood the situation believed that a CINCPAC photo pool was an excellent concept but that it should *absorb*, not supplement, the CPUs. Photo teams could then be farmed out from the general pool in accordance with the needs of the job. Some of those teams might have only two cameramen, others might require up to twenty.[24]

The concept of a general CINCPAC photo pool prevailed and it absorbed the few remaining CPUs. With nothing left to command,

Mitchell closed up the CPS office in March 1945 and became OIC of the Bureau of Public Relations' Still Picture Section, a position he held until September 7, 1945, his last day in uniform.[25]

Commanding the CINCPAC general pool was Edward Steichen, one of America's most eminent artist-photographers from the early 1900s until the 1960s. He had been active in Pacific Theater photography since 1942–43 and had cultivated the political power and personal connections that allowed him to outmaneuver Carleton Mitchell and dominate Navy combat photography during the war's brutal last campaigns.

VI

The bespectacled, kindly-looking old man could have been Earl Colgrove's father, or even that of Harold Tannenbaum, the forty-seven-year-old cameraman who died while working on *The Memphis Belle*. He should have been at home nurturing his curbside Victory Garden, figuring out how to squeeze a few extra miles from his monthly gasoline ration, and helping his grandchildren blow out birthday candles. And if the Army had had its way that is what would have happened.

Born in 1879, Edward Steichen had been of military age during the Spanish-American War. He did not serve in that conflict but did participate in World War I. In the years between 1898 and 1917 he had become a renowned artist and photographer who divided his time between America and France. When the United States entered World War I, Steichen was eager to become a photographic reporter in Mathew Brady's image. Commissioned a lieutenant in the Signal Corps, which had responsibility for Army photography, he was soon in France; there he became so intrigued by aerial photography that he transferred into the Air Service's Photographic Section, which he headed by war's end. Although his position did not require it Steichen personally flew many photo reconnaissance missions, some of them with General Billy Mitchell himself. There he quickly realized that the soft-focus techniques that had made him famous in civilian life were of little military value. What counted was the camera's ability to yield stark details. After retiring as a lieutenant colonel in 1919 Steichen pioneered in using sharp-focus photographs in advertising and became the world's highest-paid photographer.[26]

Although profoundly repelled by warfare, Steichen was eager to be a photographer-participant in World War II because he believed that "if a real image of war could be photographed and presented to the world, it might make a contribution toward ending the specter of war." Months before Pearl Harbor he went to Washington to see about being reactivated as an Army officer. An official politely recorded his name and address but when he learned Steichen's birth date, "he put down his pen with an air of finality and told me he was sorry, but I was beyond the age limit for induction into active service."

Discouraged in his effort to reenter the Army, Steichen seized an opportunity to be of service as a civilian. The Museum of Modern Art asked him to organize an exhibition and he "conceived the idea of doing a contemporary portrait of America, with the title 'The Arsenal of Democracy.'" While he was preparing the exhibit Japan attacked Pearl Harbor. Hastily retitled "The Road to Victory" and with a text written by Steichen's brother-in-law, the famous poet Carl Sandburg, the exhibit went on display to rave reviews in the spring of 1942.

As "Road to Victory" shored up morale in the war's bleakest months Steichen was again in uniform, but not the Army's. Out of the blue a telephone call came from the Navy Department asking if he would be interested in doing photo work. "I almost crawled through the telephone wire with eagerness," he recalled, and the next day he met with Captain (soon Admiral) Arthur W. Radford, who commanded naval aviator training. Steichen's advanced age surprised Radford, but the captain liked the photographer's enthusiasm and suggested that he create a special unit to photograph naval aviation training. Knowing that he was in competition with the AAF for recruits, Radford calculated that the resulting photographic publicity would help him get his share of the best talent.

Commissioned in early 1942 after receiving a special age waiver, Steichen soon assembled the Naval Aviation Photographic Unit, which he initially built around a half dozen hand-picked, talented young cameramen. Recognizing the importance of expert technical support he also established a separate laboratory facility staffed by specially recruited technicians, including a camera repairman, to serve his unit exclusively.

The unit's original formal mission, which initially did not seem all that important, was photographing aviation *training*. When the photographers began their work the shape of Pacific Ocean combat was not yet clear, since few people understood the paramount role that aircraft carriers would play. Most prewar observers believed that battleships would be decisive, but instead carrier-based aircraft put every battlewagon, even the Japanese super-battleships *Yamato* and *Musashi*, at risk. Carriers, not battleships, determined victory or defeat. Quite unexpectedly Steichen's unit was perfectly positioned to photograph the sea war's most vital aspect. As the Pacific war escalated the unit's role expanded to encompass all phases of naval aviation, and its size also increased, though only slightly, to match its larger mission.

Like the CPS, the Naval Aviation Photographic Unit was a small, specialized segment of BuAer's photographic structure. But while the former was "regular" Navy the latter was decidedly not. Stiechen and his photographers used Rolleiflexes, Medalists, and other small cameras instead of standard-issue Speed Graphics and shot 16mm color motion-picture film from the start. While the CPUs invariably had binding orders, Steichen secured "open orders" for his men. As one of them phrased it, his orders "were to go anywhere I liked, do whatever I wanted, and to go home when I felt like it."

Administrative duties kept Steichen in Washington much of the time, dispatching small teams to the Pacific for two or three months at a time before they returned to have their film processed. While in Washington Steichen took formal photographic portraits of Secretary Knox, Under-Secretary James Forrestal, and Chief of Naval Operations Ernest J. King, which helped build support for his work at the highest levels. He also made two tours aboard the U.S.S. *Lexington* to engage in combat photography firsthand. His initial voyage was between November 9 and December 23, 1943, during operations in the Gilbert and Marshall Islands. The Japanese kept his carrier under attack for several days, damaging it severely; a torpedo struck the stern and jammed the rudder on a sharp turn, so that the ship was forced to travel in circles during most of the trip back to Pearl Harbor for repairs. Steichen returned to the *Lexington* for the invasions of Iwo Jima and Okinawa in 1945. He went ashore on Iwo the day after it had been declared secure to photograph the men, sites, combat, and havoc.

Three great monuments resulted primarily from the work of Steichen and his Naval Aviation Photographic Unit, two of them consisting of still photographs and the third a movie. The exhibition entitled "Power in the Pacific" went on display at the Museum of Modern Art in New York in early 1945, began a nationwide tour in the spring, and appeared in book form before year's end. It featured 150 photographs that Steichen selected from among thousands shot by Navy, Marine, and Coast Guard cameramen. Printed by the unit's special lab, the photos were outsized, some of them as large as 6 × 8 feet. They pictured what the naval war was like, beginning with scenes of ships and their men at work and play and progressing relentlessly through combat. Steichen believed the photos demonstrated "how the camera can show what actually happened out there to those not present" and *Time*'s exhibit review agreed, proclaiming that the pictures provided "as close a secondhand view of war as most civilians are likely to get."[27]

The second monument featuring still photographs was Steichen's *U.S. Navy War Photographs: Pearl Harbor to Tokyo Bay*, originally published in early 1946 and reprinted several times thereafter in an expanded edition compiled by Tom Maloney, the founder and editor of *U.S. Camera* magazine. The book was the brainchild of Secretary of the Navy Forrestal, who assumed office when Knox died. As the war neared an end Forrestal thought about compiling a short but spectacular book of photographs and *giving* a copy to all naval personnel when they left the service. Six million copies would be necessary. However, Forrestal's budget did not include the money to pay for that many copies. So discharged sailors had to buy the 108-page softcover book with its Navy-blue-and-gold cover design. Thanks to generous paper companies, engravers, and printers who worked on a "no profit" basis, the book sold for 35 cents, perhaps the greatest book-buying bargain since the days of Johannes Gutenberg. "These pictures will go with you as a reminder of a job well done—a job of which you can be proud as long as you live," Forrestal wrote in a brief introduction, "because it gave mankind another opportunity to live together in peace and decency."

Supervised by Steichen, produced by Louis de Rochemont (the founder of The March of Time and of Twentieth Century Fox), and released in 1944 as "a newsdrama of the Pacific," *The Fighting Lady* was a stunning documentary depicting a carrier during operations against Marcus Island, Kwajalein, Truk, and the Marianas. The unnamed carrier, dubbed "the Fighting Lady" in the narration, supposedly represented all fleet carriers. Though cameramen shot much of the film on the U.S.S. *Yorktown*, the movie utilized footage from several different carriers and other naval sources as well. Lieutenant Dwight Long, one of Steichen's motion-picture specialists, directed most of the photography. In all de Rochemont received more than 60,000 feet of film, which he whittled down to one hour's worth (7,500 feet).

As Steichen knew and as Long and his cameramen showed the public, everything about carrier warfare was dramatic. To enhance the drama the photographers shot in 16mm color, utilized sunrises and sunsets as lavish backdrops, and mounted on the carrier aircraft numerous GSAP automatic cameras that put the audience in the pilot's seat—except, of course, that the theatergoers were safe and the pilots were not. With the vibrations from the airplanes' machine guns adding to the realism the GSAPs recorded one super-spectacular scene after another: of dive-bombing runs against enemy installations ashore; of Japanese Zero fighters bursting into flames, being blown apart, or nose-diving into the ocean with huge splashes and thunderous explosions; of enemy merchant ships and warships being strafed, torpedoed, and bombed by American planes flying through dense dark clouds of exploding flak. Supplementing these sequences were heart-stopping scenes of crippled planes crash-landing on the carrier deck and of crewmen bravely dragging injured pilots out of flaming wrecks, and heartrending shots of bleeding men on their hurried way to the sick bay for emergency treatment and of flag-draped coffins being committed to the deep. Almost every subsequent wartime or postwar documentary dealing with the Pacific incorporated some of these scenes, sometimes reproduced in black and white rather than color.

The film impressed both civilians and military personnel. *Time* concluded without too much exaggeration that the movie heaped "one astonishment so thickly upon another that the eye and mind can hardly keep pace. For violent air action and for pure visual magnificence, *The Fighting Lady* is not likely ever to be beaten." Other reviews were equally effusive.[28]   Admiral Chester W. Nimitz, commander of the Pacific Fleet, thought so highly of the film that he even contemplated "bombing" Japan with copies. If the Japanese "saw" the flood of American naval power crossing the Pacific it might sap their morale.[29] Perhaps most stunned by *The Fighting Lady's* visual and publicity impact was the AAF, which collectively cursed whoever "had the idea that we wouldn't need color photography when the policies covering combat photography were established" and immediately mobilized a considerable effort to make an even better film.[30]

Any skepticism regarding the film was rare, especially among those serving on carriers. But wherever thousands of hearts beat at least one, surely, will throb with a cynic's tune. "They keep showing us the picture 'Fighting Lady' to convince us that things are really going on," wrote Lee Blodget, a carrier-based photo recon pilot in March 1945. But, he continued, "I'll bet the Army and Marines get a laugh out of hearing that we Navy boys come 'right up close' to the enemy (anywhere between 80–300 miles of him) when they spend all their time talking to the enemy across a few yards of jungle."[31]

VII

"Steichen Heads Navy Institute ... and Assumes Command of ALL Navy Combat Photographers" proclaimed the headline for a story in the August 6, 1945 issue of U.S. *Camera* discussing events that had occurred almost six months previously.[32] The Navy had named Steichen to direct its new Photographic Institute, established to promote naval photography and to dispense annual Navy Day awards to deserving cameramen.[33] It had also placed Steichen in charge of the Pacific Ocean combat photo pool, variously called the CINCPAC Combat Photographic Unit or the Pacific Fleet Combat Camera Group.

Teams from the pool covered the first carrier planes to strike the Tokyo area (February 16–17), the invasions of Iwo Jima and Okinawa and the subsequent fighting on and around both islands, the final submarine and aerial onslaught against the enemy's merchant shipping, and the Japanese surrender aboard the U.S.S. *Missouri*.[34] Many cameramen photographed several of these events. Michael Abriola, for example, was on the Tokyo carrier strike and at Iwo and Okinawa. "Outside of the times that I was scared to death," he wrote shortly after the war, "it has been a lot of fun and very exciting and I wouldn't trade my experiences for a million dollars." Rick Rohde shot tens of thousands of feet of 16mm color film on sub warfare aboard the U.S. submarines *Sea Owl* and *Springer*, including a dreadful thirty-six hours on the latter while it lay on the bottom of the Yellow Sea enduring a depth-charge barrage. During the Iwo Jima fighting he was in a sub stationed offshore to pick up downed fliers, and at Okinawa he and seven other pool members set up a camp on Buckner Bay from which they not only covered kamikaze attacks but also accompanied GIs during the ground fighting.

Besides Abriola and Rohde, numerous other pool cameramen were at both Iwo Jima and Okinawa, since Steichen mobilized as many photographers as possible, some of them former members of CPUs, to cover these horrific battles. Much of their film appeared in two spectacular documentaries, the color production *To the Shores of Iwo Jima* and the black-and-white *The Fleet that Came to Stay*, which depicted the fleet at Okinawa as it endured a virtual kamikaze blizzard. Marion Cvitanovich, Marvin L. Paris, Wilber L. Granger, Lee M. Mark, Edward L. Racine, Wilton G. Hill, Guy P. Roberge, Walter J. Duggan, and others escaped unscathed, at least physically. Others, such as William C. Loewe and Hayes D. Thompson, were wounded in action. And still others were not that lucky.

Of the nine people employed by the *Antioch* (California) *Ledger* before December 7, 1941, five joined the military. The last to enlist was Harry Leo McGrath, who had done "a variety of tasks that included shop work, some reporting, some photography" and who went into the Navy in April 1944. His ambition was to become an international news photographer and he hoped naval camerawork would help him reach his goal. But as a member of the Pacific Fleet Combat Camera Group he died while filming the Iwo Jima pre-invasion offshore bombardment.

"It isn't very lengthy," Harry's distraught mother wrote when providing a brief biography for a postwar survey of the men who served in Steichen's photo pool. "You see, my son was not yet nineteen when he was killed. He was my one son, my baby." After he departed for Pearl in late 1944, she confessed, photo pool personnel "probably know more about his experiences than I." However, her "mother love and pride would like to add that I know that there was and is many fine and good boys in the navy but there was never a better boy."

Nearly sixty-seven years old, Steichen left the Navy in early 1946. The next year he became the Museum of Modern Art's director of photography, holding that position for the next seventeen years and doing some of his most creative work before retiring at age eighty-five. He was ninety-six when he died.

10

"Old Glory Was Raised and, Boy, Tears Ran Down My Cheeks"

The Cameramen of the Marine Corps

"It was a photographer's paradise—in hell!" wrote Marine Corps photographer John F. Leopold in describing Tarawa, the key to Japanese defenses in the Gilbert Islands. In that particular patch of Hades, like many similar patches the Marines discovered in the Pacific, combat was so relentless and ferocious that a cameraman had only to point his lens and "it was bound to cover action in any direction."[1]

The 2nd Marine Division's invasion of the Tarawa Atoll in late November 1943 marked the initial step in the Central Pacific campaign, which moved roughly in tandem with General MacArthur's complementary offensive through SWPA. As they did with each step along each axis of advance, the Japanese made the taking of Tarawa excruciating. During the seventy-six hours it took the Marines to capture the atoll's main islet, Betio, which was less than three square miles in area, the defenders killed or wounded more than forty Marines per hour.

One of the Marine cameramen in Hell during those sanguinary hours was Norm Hatch, who joined the Corps in 1939, endured the physical and mental abuse the drill instructors inflicted during basic training at Parris Island, served as the editor of the "Sound Off" column in *Leatherneck* (the official Marine Corps magazine), and was attending The March of Time's newsreel course in New York City when the Japanese attacked Pearl Harbor. After completing the course he stayed to help instruct the next class before joining the 2nd Division's Photo Section in September 1942.[2]

Unlike the other armed services the Marine Corps had no formally organized photo units equivalent to the SPCs, CCUs, or CPUs. However, every Marine division had a photo section assigned to the division's G-2 (Intelligence) staff. Depending on the magnitude of the operation, divisional photo sections varied in size from fewer than two dozen to more than three dozen. In addition the Marines had several other sources of combat cameramen. Divisional engineer sections always had a few photographers, primarily to take technical pictures; these were frequently "borrowed" for combat. Like the Navy, late in the war the Marine Corps established a Pacific Ocean photo pool (formally titled the Photographic Company, Headquarters and Service Battalion, Fleet Marine Force, Pacific) that furnished additional photographers "in sufficient number and correct composition to meet the requirements" of each operation. Pool cameramen could be attached to any unit from a company to a corps for temporary duty depending on the mission.[3] The Marines also had a few "roving" photographers, of whom David Douglas Duncan was the most famous. With his "open orders" he meandered through the Pacific, serving with Fijian guerrillas behind Japanese lines on Bougainville, flying in planes hunting Japanese merchantmen off the China coast, and photographing strafing runs on Okinawa from a modified P-38 belly tank.[4]

And in early 1942 the Division of Public Relations began organizing Combat Correspondents to secure more publicity for the Corps. Motivated by the dearth of news stories and photographs about the Marines' heroic defense of Wake Island in December 1941, Director of Public Relations Brigadier General Robert L. Denig proposed sending writer-photographer teams, perhaps accompanied by a motion-picture cameraman, into the field to write feature stories and provide appropriate illustrative material.[5] Vigorous recruiting brought in a number of newspapermen and commercial newsreel cameramen whose first task was to complete basic training at Parris Island. "These men are NOT civilians in uniform," Denig emphasized. Their job was "to report to the home front the sidelights and highlights of duty overseas, to inform and inspire America with tales of everyday deeds and of Marine valor and heroism on land, at sea and in the air," but they were also trained to fight if need be.[6] By early 1945 approximately 150 Combat Correspondents (not all of them photographers) were overseas.[7]

Marine Corps photography was similar to that of the other services in one respect: the Corps never had enough cameramen. So acute was the shortage that in the spring of 1944, after the armed forces began drafting previously-deferred married men with families, the Corps sent an open letter to photography magazines hoping to entice some of these draft-eligible men into enlisting for photographic duty. This letter alerted readers that the Marines needed "additional Combat Photographers for Divisions already overseas, as well as those units now forming." Although the work was "hard and strenuous" and would therefore "appeal only to a limited number of individuals," the letter-advertisement brought in several promising recruits.[8]

Before Tarawa the Marines' photography had been unimpressive. Wake Island had been missed entirely, and coverage of the six-month battle for Guadalcanal was sparse. The OIC of the 1st Marine Division's photo section at Guadalcanal, Karl T. Soule, Jr., had only a handful of cameramen. "We just plain and simple didn't have the equipment, didn't have the film, didn't have the people," he recalled.[9] *This is Guadalcanal* demonstrated that Soule's memory was accurate, for it did not contain a single truly exceptional ground-combat scene. But by late 1943 the Marines were well organized photographically and Tarawa displayed their new ability to compile an enviable record.[10] Of course during Tarawa and most subsequent campaigns they had two great advantages: Marine operations relied on amphibious assaults in which a great deal of action occurred in the open, and most (though not all) motion-picture men carried compact 16mm equipment.

Hatch and thirteen colleagues in the 2nd Division Photo Section accompanied the unit to its New Zealand staging area, where their OIC joined them. He was Captain Louis Hayward, the South African-born Hollywood actor who starred in such swashbuckling dramas as *The Man in the Iron Mask* and *The Count of Monte Cristo*. Hayward suffered from asthma so badly that a doctor nearly ordered him back to the States but relented after the actor begged not to be sent home since it would mar his manly screen image.[11]

In numerous ways the cameramen prepared for the forthcoming invasion. Trading in their carbines for .45 pistols, they took lessons from a sergeant who had attended the FBI school on pistol marksmanship. He emphasized the importance of firing first to startle the adversary, even if the shot missed. The cameramen also learned—and this was not completely comforting—that if they needed a rifle "all you have to do is bend down and pick up a weapon because there's usually one laying around some place." Motion-picture men like Hatch tried to think through an orderly sequence of events so that "everything I shot could be put together in one piece, and it would at least tell what the battle or story was about and, of course, it could always be intercut with anything anybody else shot." And photo personnel participated in the division's invasion rehearsal at Efate before going to Tarawa so they had some "feel" for an amphibious assault.

As they approached Betio, Hatch and fellow photographer William F. Kelliher were in a landing craft called an LCVP. Unfortunately almost every LCVP got hung up on the reef that fringed the isle and theirs was no exception. They had to wade ashore through 400 yards of bullet- and shell-swept water. Most of the Marines crouched low, making as small a target as possible as they moved shoreward, but because they had to keep their cameras and film dry Hatch and Kelliher walked upright holding their equipment overhead. All around them were swirls of bloody salt water where metal had crushed flesh, but to their astonishment both cameramen made it to shore unhurt. As they tumbled into a shellhole and peered over the edge, the reality of combat momentarily shocked them. Just a few feet away lay a Marine whose buttock had been torn away; he was bleeding profusely but remained stoically quiet, awaiting a medical corpsman.

After regaining their composure Hatch and Kelliher stashed their extra gear at a nearby command post and began filming. For part of the battle they had a unique arrangement, with Kelliher serving as Hatch's assistant. While Hatch shot a three-lens 35mm Eyemo, Kelliher wrote captions and reloaded the camera, thus letting the photographer concentrate exclusively on taking pictures. Perhaps the arrangment saved Kelliher's life. At one point while Kelliher was reloading the camera Hatch, contemplating his next scene, spotted a sniper taking a bead on his assistant. The photographer snapped off a pistol shot. "It's the only shot I ever fired during the whole war," Hatch said, "and I just aimed it in the general direction." The shot missed but it made the sniper hesitate and before he could recover two Marines killed him.

Perhaps that arrangement is also what permitted Hatch to make newsreel history by capturing an image of Japanese troops and Marines at combat in the same filmed scene for the first (and only) time during the war. In this remarkable scene, which initially appeared in *With the*

Marines at Tarawa and then in just about every subsequent film dealing with the battle, half a dozen or more enemy soldiers bolt from cover and run to the left, perfectly framed between two Marines shooting at them.[12] And working with Kelliher may explain how Hatch could shoot 2,000 feet of film with almost every frame good enough for newsreel use, for he never had to break his concentration to load film or write captions. Although the newsreels usually carried several stories, the footage from Hatch and the few other cameramen using 35mm black and white was so extraordinary that on that occasion they showed only Tarawa.

When the motion-picture photographers returned from the battle, many of them to participate in the Fourth War Bond drive by relating their experiences to audiences across the nation, the newsreel companies held a party for them to express "their appreciation for the finest newsreel coverage done in this war." Hollywood honored the men with an Academy Award, and Hatch, who provided the bulk of Tarawa's black-and-white footage, starred in the autobiographical mini-documentary *I Was There: Tarawa.*[13]

I

Bill Genaust and Howard McClue were good friends and fellow cameramen in the comparatively small Marine Corps photographic fraternity. They had received photographic training at Quantico, shipped out together in early 1944, and in mid-June stormed ashore on Saipan in the Mariana Islands as members of the 4th Marine Division Photo Section.[14] June 1944 was a memorable month. Not only did the Allies capture Rome and invade France but massive offensives on the Eastern Front crumpled the German lines as the Soviets pressed westward toward Vienna and Berlin. Now as the Americans, British, and Russians cracked open Hitler's Fortress Europe, the United States penetrated Japan's inner defense sphere when it wrested Saipan, Tinian, and Guam from enemy control.

Capturing the Marianas was nasty business. By day the Marines battled bluebottle flies as large as a man's big thumb joint. The huge flies swarmed over everything—exposed skin, food, drinking water. At night mosquitoes tortured the men with unceasing buzzing and biting, spreading malaria to those who had been too careless to take atabrine pills. (Rumor had it that atabrine not only turned the skin yellow but also made men impotent.) Compounding the misery were the nearly foot-long land crabs, which exuded a miasmic stench and annoyingly clacked their claws as they ambulated about from dusk to dawn. The weather changed quickly and erratically, alternating between stupendous cloudbursts and broiling sun. And always the Japanese were there, hunkered down in their camouflaged bunkers, caves, and tunnels, and selling their lives dearly except when they occasionally emerged above ground to make horrific banzai attacks.

Enduring these conditions together, Genaust and McClue worked side by side almost continuously, the only interruption coming shortly after they arrived on Saipan's beaches. Several mortar shells landed close to Genaust, stunning him so badly that his OIC wanted him returned to Pearl Harbor. But in a day or two Genaust pronounced himself recovered and rejoined McClue at the front. Early on the morning of July 9 they made coffee and had chow, McClue attended divine services while Genaust checked out the equipment, and then, joined by a Marine scout name Bob McNally, they made their "way up to the [front] line in time to join the advance which was to wipe out all organized resistance on the island." After pausing to take pictures at the recently captured Marpi airstrip, they reached the island's far end by early afternoon and advanced around Marpi Point to link up with the forces driving up the island's other side. "We three were out in front," recalled Genaust several months later, "and made the first contact with the other division, a tank which had advanced in front of their infantry." The tank driver asked for some infantrymen to go back with him to "clean out about a dozen Japs from some buildings he had just passed." Genaust, McClue, and McNally volunteered. When the tank hit a land mine a few moments later they went on alone, found the Japanese, and killed them.

The three men headed back to their command post to turn in their exposed film and get a little rest. On the way a group of at least fifteen enemy soldiers fired on them from nearby cliffs and "then charged us in one of their Banzai rushes." The Marines took cover behind a sugarcane railway embankment and blazed away, hitting several Japanese soldiers and causing the rest to take shelter only fifty yards away. During the ensuing sniping duel Genaust did not immediately realize that he was suddenly alone because McNally and McClue, independently of each other, had slipped away to get reinforcements. Even when Genaust discovered his predicament he continued fighting. He could have retreated through a cane field "but when I yelled to the other two I got no answers. I thought they might have been hurt so I stayed to make sure the Japs wouldn't get them."

After a desperate hour during which Genaust killed at least half a dozen Japanese soldiers, Marine reinforcements arrived, led by McClue, who had hastened to the rear for assistance and then back to the front as fast as human endurance and a modest concern for safety permitted. "When I saw help arriving," wrote Genaust, "I stood up and moved forward, directing the group toward the Jap position." But he took only a step or two before a rifle slug ripped through the fleshy part of his thigh. McClue saw him go down, called out to see if he was hit badly, and then pressed on toward the cliffs when Genaust answered that he was okay. A hospital corpsman soon reached Genaust, dragged him into the nearby canefield, administered first aid, and evacuated him at dusk. Not knowing that Genaust had been moved to the rear, that night McClue went looking for him. He never returned. The next day a search party found McClue's corpse, his heart pierced by a bullet.

Another 4th Marine Division photographer, Harrold A. Weinberger, commandeered a truck to take the body to the division's cemetery where McClue "was laid to rest with full military honors in the presence of his sorrowing friends and buddies." The grave site, Genaust wrote to Mrs. McClue in an effort to comfort her, "is near the shore where we first set foot almost a month before. It is a beautiful spot and time will soon erase the scars of war as I hope it will ease the pain in your heart."

The date Genaust was wounded and McClue died, July 9, was the day the High Command declared Saipan secure.

———

Genaust was utterly fatigued both physically and mentally and limping from his leg wound. Although his commanding officer, Lieutenant Colonel Donald L. Dickson, knew that the Marines had too few cameramen to cover the upcoming Tinian invasion adequately, he told Genaust "to take it easy. I was sending him back to Pearl Harbor. He left by air a few days later." Dickson had decided that Genaust really needed to return to the United States for a rest "and had started the ball rolling for his transfer when I, myself, was ordered back upon completion of my second tour of overseas duty." He asked his replacement to follow through on Genaust "but something unexpected must have turned up after I left, because Bill was assigned to the Iwo Jima operation."

II

Ten days after McClue's burial Hal Watkins was on Guam going through his death throes. Three times.[15]

Watkins had studied photography for four semesters under the tutelage of Clarence A. Bach, who had founded the country's first high-school photography class at John C. Fremont High School in Los Angeles, where he taught for thirty-four years. That one school furnished 146 World War II combat cameramen! By his senior year Watkins was so proficient that he was working as a photographer for a West Coast magazine. After graduation he enlisted in the Marines, went to boot camp at San Diego, and then attended the Hollywood studios' photo school. His baptism in combat photography came in the Bismarck Archipelago where he filmed bombing missions over Rabaul and Kavieng. Steichen's Photographic Institute judged some of this footage as among "the most dramatic film sequences of the war" and many of his scenes appeared in *The Pacific Milk Run*, a film on Marine Corps aviation.

Fungus nearly kept Watkins off Guam. It so hideously afflicted his hands and legs that a hospital corpsman tried to prevent him from boarding an LST bound for the island. But Watkins insisted that the medics give him some cotton swabs and a bottle of acid used to burn the fungus away and let him go.

Watkins should have listened to the corpsman.

As a member of the 3rd Amphibious Corps Photo Section attached to the 1st Provisional Marine Brigade, he was in the third landing wave. Amidst intense enemy fire he got ashore and began moving inland. "I went a little faster because most of the guys are taking shots at people and I'm not," he recalled. He was several hundred yards from the beach when it suddenly became "quiet as the devil, and I get a little nervous. And I look around and there's nobody around me. I'm alone." Spotting two big banyan trees nearby he headed for them hoping they would provide some protection. Just before reaching the trees he looked back over his shoulder and saw a picturesque shot of tanks moving up and troops following behind them. After shooting twenty-five feet he paused to rewind his camera, again noticed the unnatural silence, and turned his head to look around. As his head swiveled a sniper's bullet went through the base of his neck and exited into his backpack, igniting the jam-packed 100-foot rolls of film. Watkins did not immediately realize that he was afire.[16] Badly wounded, he struggled toward the banyan trees, but "began to get hotter and hotter, and so finally I reach around and burn my hand," which was how he learned he was aflame.

Taking out a knife that his sister-in-law had sent him, he began cutting off the pack. He had to sit up to do it, and before he could complete the task a grenade landed about three yards behind him. The explosion mangled his left arm and splattered his rib cage, shoulder, and head with fragments. When the grenade exploded Watkins knew he was dead. The movies had taught him what to do in such a situation, so he went "through a Hollywood routine and I die. I moan, groan like I'm dying." But he did not die. Instead a Marine lieutenant, whose name Watkins never learned, appeared out of nowhere and helped him shed the still-flaming pack, which left second-degree burns on Watkins' back. Moments later a bullet hit the lieutenant. He fell on Watkins, virtually blanketing him. The dying officer went through his death throes, loudly gasping, praying, calling for his mother. His voice attracted attention in the form of three grenades. Luckily for Watkins the lieutenant's body absorbed most of the iron, though one sizeable fragment penetrated his boot and damaged his right heel.

As Watkins rapidly lost blood and got progressively weaker, a firefight occurred practically on top of him but nobody paused to offer assistance and the sounds of combat soon moved beyond his position. With ebbing strength Watkins raised up on his right elbow to push the dead lieutenant's body off so he could crawl toward the rear for medical aid. A slug hit his already injured left shoulder "so I then die again." But death eluded him. Realizing he was still alive Watkins continued trying to extricate himself from the extra body. Another bullet—and for the third time theatrical death throes welled up in Watkins' throat. Then he lost consciousness.

When Watkins groggily awoke troops were stringing communications wire, using the the banyan trees as posts. "Look at this mess," one of the soldiers said pointing to the pile of gore represented by Watkins and the lieutenant. The soldier assumed both Marines had been killed in action, so imagine his surprise when one of the dead men spoke. "Jesus Christ, you assholes, give me a hand, will you!"

Two pints of plasma administered at a field aid station saved Watkins. From there he went to a hospital ship, the beginning of a fifteen-month recovery in various hospitals. Although doctors removed most of the grenade fragments, which Watkins displayed on his office desk after the war, about a fourth of a grenade in assorted shrapnel chunks remained in his body. The doctors discovered that the last bullet that hit Watkins was actually an American slug, part of the ammunition the Japanese seized when they captured Guam in December 1941.

Somehow in the midst of his hospitalization his records got FUBARed and despite a bad limp and useless left arm the Marine Corps had him scheduled to return to combat. Even Hal Watkins was not that tough.

Ten cameramen made *The First Provisional Marine Brigade on Guam*, and Watkins was unlucky only in a comparative sense. Claude Winkler died filming a dog platoon in action. Martin McEvily lost his life photographing infantrymen at the front. Howard Foss was moving alongside the lead tank attacking Guam's airfield when a fatal bullet struck him. "I guess," Watkins punned, "Old Man Death just didn't *focus* on me."

III

Of all the nether worlds the Marines encountered, Iwo Jima was probably the worst. Eight square miles of volcanic ash virtually devoid of vegetation, the island lay almost precisely midway between the Marianas and Tokyo, so the Japanese had converted it into a bastion, supersaturating its crevices, ravines, and cliffs with mini-fortresses in every cave and tunnel and on every hillside. When the Marines invaded on February 19, 1945 the resulting battle was unparalleled in its exterminatory savagery. For more than a month the Marines countered the suicidal Japanese defense with suicidal assaults. On average, each square mile cost 740 Marines killed in action and another 2,175 wounded, not to mention approximately 2,875 dead Japanese.

Overlooking the devastation and death from Iwo's southern tip was 550-foot high Mount Suribachi. Captured early in the battle on February 23, it would have been relatively insignificant in historical memory except that four cameramen were on its summit that day. In a pictorial paradox, although Iwo Jima was one of the war's most carefully planned photographic operations the historic images captured on Mount Suribachi occurred by happenstance.

Several weeks before the amphibious assault Lieutenant Commander John W. McClain, OIC of the operation's naval photography, received access to the attack plan. Because of this advance notice he called a conference in Honolulu to map out joint Navy-Marine Corps photographic assignments.[17] Representing the 5th Marine Division were Norm Hatch and Obie E. Newcomb, Jr., a still cameraman who had been in the first wave at Tarawa and who went through that battle with "death in front of him, at his side, and missing him only by fractions of inches."[18] Herbert Schlossberg was there for the 4th Division and Captains Karl T. Soule, Jr. and Raymond Henri for the 3rd Division. The meeting's purpose was to ensure complete coverage while avoiding duplication among the approximately sixty photographers assigned to the operation. A few cameramen were to shoot "anything they saw that looked like it should be covered," but most had specific assignments. For example, the 4th Division's Harrold Weinberger and Richard Tiernan were to concentrate on Japanese prisoners and Frank Cockrell was to stay with the division's medical battalion. In addition conference participants worked out a scheme to collect exposed film and have it sent to the labs as quickly as possible.

Along with the more thorough advance planning two other differences were apparent between Marine photography at Iwo and earlier in the war (at Guadalcanal, for instance). One change was in the amount of photographic equipment available. Even as late as Tarawa cameramen had not been well equipped. But according to Hatch, by 1945 "it was sort of like Christmas all over again to be able to walk into one of these big supply warehouses and say, 'I'll take two of those and three of that and four of those.'" The other difference was that the Marines had converted almost exclusively to 16mm color.[19]

When Lieutenant Harold G. Shrier's forty-man patrol from E Company of the 2nd Battalion, 28th Regiment of the 5th Marine Division cautiously advanced to the crater atop Mt. Suribachi on February 23, Louis R. Lowery was with it. As a *Leatherneck* photographer he was one of the Marines' roving cameramen who operated independently with *carte blanche* to go wherever and do whatever he pleased. Lowery was the only photographer to cover six major Pacific battles: Saipan, Tinian, Guam, Peleliu, Iwo Jima, and Okinawa.[20] Along the way he earned two Purple Hearts and came close to getting a third on Iwo because Suribachi's crest was still not secure when the patrol arrived, provoking a vicious mini-battle.

Even as the melèe continued two Marines found a long pipe and attached to it a 54-inch by 28-inch flag that Schrier had brought with him, not realizing that it was too small to be seen from the beaches below. At 10:31 a.m. several Marines raised Old Glory. Lowery preserved the moment on film, though not all Marines were happy about it. Eighteen-year-old Private First Class James Robeson had no desire to be a "Hollywood Marine" and refused to be in the picture, which was fortunate for Lowery. No sooner had he clicked his shutter than a Japanese soldier popped out of a cave and fired at him and Robeson, missing both of them. Robeson killed the enemy soldier with a blast from his Browning automatic rifle, but the gunfire attracted a hailstorm of enemy grenades from nearby caves. When Lowery leapt aside to avoid an explosion he tumbled fifty feet down the steep slope. Amazingly both he and his camera were unhurt.[21]

Meanwhile AP photographer Joe Rosenthal had arrived at the 28th Regiment's command post. Rosenthal's eyesight was so poor that he had been disqualified for military service, but during almost a year of duty in the Pacific as an accredited civilian correspondent he had shown that his courage was not deficient. He photographed action on Guam, Peleliu, and Angaur and then landed at Iwo early on D-Day. Now, four days later, soldiers at the command post told Rosenthal that a patrol had already started up Suribachi carrying a flag. He decided to ascend the mount anyway, but since civilian correspondents were unarmed he needed an escort. Bill Genaust and Marine Corps still photographer Robert Campbell, both carrying weapons and cameras, volunteered to accompany him.

Halfway up the hill the three photographers met four Marines coming down the slope. One was Louis Lowery, who told them the flag was already flying atop Suribachi and he had photographed it being raised. Nonetheless the trio continued uphill. Reaching the summit about noon the men saw a group of Marines preparing to raise a second, larger flag (almost five feet by eight feet) that could be seen from much of the island. Unlike the dangerous circumstances attending the initial flag raising, the area was now secure. To get a better angle Rosenthal backed off about ten yards and, because he was quite short, piled up some rocks and a sandbag to stand on so that nearby brush would not clutter his photo's foreground. Shooting 16mm color with a Filmo camera, Genaust took up a position about three feet to Rosenthal's right. With the courtesy normal among photographers Genaust asked if he was in Rosenthal's way, and as the latter shook his head "No" the Marines began hoisting the flag. Genaust started his motion-picture camera as Rosenthal turned, squinted through his Speed Graphic's viewfinder, and triggered the shutter. Campbell, who was also using a Speed Graphic but shooting from a different angle, captured the first flag coming down as the second flag went up.

Rosenthal took sixty-five photographs on Iwo (eighteen of them on February 23) and some are examples of skilled combat photography. But the picture that made him famous was the result of good luck more than skill. Rosenthal often contemplated "the things that happened quite accidentally to give that picture its qualities." Enough light filtered through overcast skies to "give the figures a sculptural depth," the flagpole was so heavy that the men strained getting it up and thus imparted "the feeling of action," the broken terrain and shattered shrubbery at their feet exemplified war's turbulence, and the wind swirled the flag over their heads. Out of twelve pictures in the film pack he used atop Suribachi, light streaks ruined two of his shots but not *the* shot. "GOD beamed on Joe Rosenthal that February afternoon," wrote Harrold Weinberger, who met him as he came down from Suribachi on his way to the U.S.S. *Eldorado* for the night. The *Eldorado* was the command ship that served as a base for civilian photographers, a place where they could get a hot meal, shower and shave, clean their equipment, package their film for transit to the labs, and get a good night's sleep.[22]

The evidence that Rosenthal's picture was not staged is overwhelming. Most obviously, he took only *one* shot of the event. As every professional cameraman knows, if a photographer goes to the trouble to stage-manage a scene, *one* shot is never enough. Had the scene been posed, Rosenthal would have taken more than one picture. He would have asked—begged if necessary—the Marines to raise the flag several times so he could take multiple shots from a variety of angles just to make sure he got at least one good picture. Photographers often jokingly comment that this type of logic has made Eastman Kodak rich. Second, given the wartime emphasis on identifying individuals, the faces of the men in the scene would have been recognizable. "Had I posed the shot, I would, of course, have ruined it," Rosenthal wrote, because he would have made the flag raisers "turn their heads so that they could be identified for AP members throughout the country, and nothing like the existing picture would have resulted."

Finally, Genaust's motion pictures, taken simultaneously from the same angle, confirm that Rosenthal's shot was genuine. The Marine's camera recorded the flag going up and then lingered on the scene, the flag flapping out to the right above the six men who raised it. Another

Marine stands in the foreground looking off to the right. As the flag raisers struggle to drive the flagpole securely into the ground, an eighth Marine moves into the scene. Rosenthal was forever thankful for Genaust's film since without it Marine Corps authorities and everyone else might have had lingering doubts about his picture's legitimacy.[23]

Genaust's movies appeared in the newsreels shortly after he and Rosenthal stood elbow to elbow atop Suribachi and they have been shown frequently ever since. Actually, the scene has usually been *misused*, invariably symbolizing final victory on Iwo, or in the Pacific, or in World War II as a whole. The misrepresentation began early. When the Navy Photographic Institute recognized Genaust's work at its first awards ceremony on October 27, 1945 the citation claimed that "His color motion picture sequence made of Marines raising the flag on Mount Suribachi stands as a symbol of Marine Corps courage and achievement in the Pacific. As a climax to the battle film 'To the Shores of Iwo Jima' it rallied the American public as no other sequence in war photography." The citation is erroneous. *To the Shores of Iwo Jima*, the marvelous documentary resulting from the Marine Corps' careful preplanning, was one of the few instances of the sequence being used correctly. It appeared not as a *climax* but *early* in the film, just as Mount Suribachi's capture occurred early in the battle. As the dramatically delivered narration explains, Suribachi gave the Marines "a toehold on the southern tip of the island. But ahead the main strength of the Jap garrison was entrenched in steel and concrete. The show was just beginning." The show—what a wonderful euphemism!—was just *beginning* that February 23rd when Lowery, Genaust, Rosenthal, and Campbell toted their cameras up Suribachi's slope.[24]

Joe Rosenthal left Iwo on March 2, arrived on Guam two days later, and went to the press headquarters where, for the first time, he saw the flag-raising picture. On that same day, March 4, 1945, Bill Genaust died on Iwo without ever having seen his motion picture-scene.

Visibility on the 4th was so poor that Genaust could not shoot much film, so he was doubling as an infantryman at the point of advance, fighting the Japanese in caves and tunnels amid the ridges and crevices along Iwo's western shore. The Marines threw grenades into a cave "and it was believed all the enemy were killed" but they "wanted to double check and asked Bill if they could borrow his flashlight." Instead of loaning it to them, Genaust went into the cave with them. "There were many Japs still alive and they immediately opened fire. Bill dropped without a sound. As the bearer of the light he had been the first target for a number of bullets." Rather than risk more Marine blood, "TNT charges were quickly planted at the cave mouth and exploded," sealing any remaining Japanese and Genaust's body inside. Since his body was not recovered, as the 5th Marine Division's chaplain explained to Genaust's widow, "his remains were not interred in a cemetery. A memorial service for all personnel of the Protestant faith of this command who died on Iwo Jima was held at the Fifth Marine Division Cemetery on 21 March 1945."[25]

IV

"OKINAWA," blared the *Life* headline. "Except For Japs It Is A Very Pleasant Place."[26] Perhaps so, but photographer Martin Friedman was too concerned about staying alive to discover anything pleasant about the island.[27]

Okinawa was Friedman's only campaign, but since the fighting rivaled Iwo Jima in its brutality and exceeded it in length by more than six weeks, one was enough. Serving in the G-2 photo sections of the 1st and then the 6th Marine Divisions, he was on Okinawa from the initial amphibious assault on April 1, 1945 until the fighting ended in late June. Throughout the battle he used an Eastman Kodak 16mm camera that he had bolted to a gunstock to make it relatively steady even when hand held. Although G-2 officers sometimes gave Friedman specific assignments, such as photographing enemy gun emplacements, captured weapons, or small submarine suicide boats, most of the time he free-lanced.

Although death lurked everywhere all the time on Okinawa, on three memorable occasions Friedman knew he nearly got killed or at least seriously injured, twice by the enemy and once by fellow Marines. Fulfilling the invasion plans, the Marine divisions initially moved northward from the landing beaches; no one then knew that the Japanese had concentrated their defenses on the island's southern third. For about a week the Marines advanced to the north without much difficulty. Suddenly one night "we had our first heavy barrage of mortar fire and this was right in the middle of cooking a dinner of a hand-caught chicken." Not only was Friedman using his helmet for a cooking pot, which made it too hot to put on, but the only handy entrenching tool was his spoon. Helmetless and frantically spooning out a foxhole, Friedman was lucky. The unexpected barrage caused "many casualties" but he was not one of them.

Having cleared Okinawa's northern two thirds the Marines turned south to help the army divisions, which had collided with the main enemy defensive positions, including Sugar Loaf, Half Moon, and Horseshoe Hills. After the Marines joined the battle they encountered heavy resistance, and Friedman was "out each day with the front lines in order to take whatever films I was able to get." At one point he maneuvered ahead of the front line to photograph American tanks with supporting infantrymen coming toward him. When Friedman raised his gunstock-mounted camera one of the tankers, peering through his tank's narrow aperature, thought he saw an enemy soldier pointing a weapon and was about to shoot the "Jap." Fortunately a photographer accompanying the advance noticed that Friedman was aiming a camera, not a gun, and persuaded the tanker not to fire.

Friedman's most narrow escape came on May 21. The day before he had shot 250 feet of film "of very close hand-to-hand fighting" on Half Moon Hill. On the 21st he was in almost the same spot, photographing Marines near the crest of a ridge throwing grenades at Japanese soldiers less than ten yards away, but out of sight, on the ridge's far side. Enemy soldiers were likewise hurling grenades at the Marines. During the morning he shot 200 feet of tense Marines engaged in this grenade-throwing contest, scenes that appear in *The 6th Marine Division on Okinawa* and just about every other documentary about this battle. At about noon, as he was intently focusing on events through the constricted view of his camera's eyepiece, Friedman did not see a Japanese grenade land right at his feet. "Look out!" yelled nearby Marines, pointing to the ground. Friedman looked down, saw the grenade, and jumped away at the same instant it exploded. For several moments, until he felt his side becoming warm and wet, Friedman did not know he had been hit. That afternoon he made it back to an aid station, got patched up, recuperated for twenty-four hours, and was back filming combat on May 23.

Despite these close calls, the worst part of Friedman's duty was not at the front line. More than anything he dreaded going back to a command post with his exposed film at day's end. "While returning I was all by myself most of the time and it was a harrowing experience, particularly," he remembered, "when you're going between our lines and enemy lines and they're taking sniper shots at you."

Like all soldiers wounded in action Friedman received a Purple Heart. He also got a Bronze Star—forty-five years after Okinawa. During the battle his OIC told Friedman he was being recommended for a Bronze Star, but when the war ended several months later nothing had come of it. Friedman forgot about the promised medal until he retired from the film industry in 1986, when curiosity got the best of him and he contacted the Marine Corps. It took four years of checking and rechecking, but in 1990 the seventy-nine-year-old Friedman finally got his medal. Appropriately, it came with a "V" for valor.

V

Federico Claveria was good to the United States, and the United States was good to Federico Claveria.[28]

Born in Mexico City in 1908 of mixed Spanish-Basque parentage, while still a child Claveria moved to Texas with his family to escape the Mexican Revolution's turmoil. As a young man he left home and went to California; there he began working as an apprentice in a commercial art studio, and when the studio established a photo lab he began dabbling in still photography. Eventually he worked for both RKO and Warner Brothers as a professional photographer.

Immediately after Pearl Harbor Claveria attempted to enlist in the Marines, but the Corps rejected him since he was not yet an American citizen. From the enlistment office Claveria hurried directly to the Los Angeles Federal Building, demanding to see the individual in charge of naturalization proceedings. Saying that he loved America and wanted to fight for it, he pled for instant citizenship. As it happened, the judge hearing his appeal was a former Marine who had fought at Belleau Wood in World War I. The red tape surrounding the citizenship process dissolved and a week later Claveria, now a United States citizen, was back at the Marine recruiting office, only to be rejected a second time because he was color blind. Dejected, he was leaving the office when a recruiting officer noted his interest in photography. Since the Marines urgently needed cameramen he gave Claveria a medical waiver.

After boot training in San Diego Claveria went to The March of

Time's school in New York and to Hollywood for additional motion-picture training. And then he was on his way to hostile shores in the far Pacific. Before each of his three amphibious operations he asked the ship's chaplain to say a prayer, not for himself but for his family so that his parents would "feel tranquility and peace of mind" if he died in action.

Kwajalein was his first assault. Carrying a three-lens Eyemo and shooting 35mm black and white, he went in with the third wave, seasick and scared. His pre-invasion steak-and-egg breakfast turned to vomit after he boarded a landing craft as its constant rocking and diesel fumes mingled with the burnt-powder smell permeating the landing area. And having been a boyhood hunter, he "could understand very well what a bullet hole could be." Once ashore the nausea ceased and his nerves calmed down. He first filmed subsequent landing waves arriving on the beaches, then turned and photographed the Marines' advance.

After Kwajalein the landings on Saipan, where he knew Bill Genaust and was in the same photo section with him, and on Tinian were easier for Claveria since he was never again quite so seasick or scared. However, he begged off going to Iwo Jima. "Look," he told his OIC, "I already had three operations, there are people here in our group who have had two, there's other groups who have only had one, and there's nine men who have just arrived today." One of the new cameramen went to Iwo in his stead.

In later years Claveria talked with the greatest animation not about Kwajalein, Saipan, or Tinian where death and dismemberment were constant companions, but about Wake Island. The absence of cameramen on Wake during the December 1941 Japanese attack had been instrumental in spurring the Marine Corps to mobilize a great photographic effort. And when Japanese forces returned the island to United States control Claveria was there. At the ceremony, when authorities lowered the Japanese flag he was shooting motion pictures, but "happened to look up and I saw a Japanese soldier saluting his flag coming down and tears were running clear down his cheeks to his lower jaw. Okay, that touched me. But then, by the same token, a little while later Old Glory was raised and, boy, tears ran down my cheeks, too. So I could understand that the Jap and I were two human beings in the same boat. He was doing his duty; I was doing mine." Decades later Claveria's eyes still became misty as he visualized and described the American flag's return to Wake Island.

To the World War II generation the American flag was a potent symbol. Knowing that scenes with the flag in it had enormous emotive impact, cameramen utilized the symbol in ways that, fifty years later, seem heavy-handed and hackneyed. But photographers were not necessarily exploiting the flag simply to nurture home-front morale. Their own devotion to the Stars and Stripes was extraordinary. Claveria, for example, first saw the American flag when he was four years old as his parents crossed from Mexico into Texas in October 1912. Ever after he *loved* Old Glory, considering it "the symbol of our liberty and our freedom, of this wonderful country God has given us." After the war he owned the La Tolteca Tortilla Factory in Santa Barbara; he ran color advertisements for his business that featured himself seated in front of a huge flag. Beneath the picture was the caption "HONOR IT!" No one who knew Claveria ever doubted this ad's heartfelt sincerity.

Unlike the Suribachi flag-raising, the Wake Island flag-raising never became famous. Yet in a sense the latter really *was* a climax to the war. Wake had been the second United States possession conquered by Japan (Guam was the first) and the scene that Claveria photographed occurred on September 4, 1945, two days *after* Japan signed the formal surrender document in Tokyo Bay aboard the U.S.S. *Missouri*.

11

"The Fringe Necessities"

Supporting the
Combat Cameramen at the Front

In military lingo photographic outfits, like all World War II combat units, had an unbalanced "tooth-to-tail" ratio. Maintaining small numbers of cameramen or infantrymen ("teeth") at the front required large numbers of people and organizations ("tail") to provide "the fringe necessities,"[1] including training, technological innovations, supplies, maintenance, and laboratory processing. "This homespun, if not humdrum work," noted an Army study, "is the starting point for all the more romantic Signal Corps photographic activity."[2]

Although each service mobilized as many professional photographers as possible, the supply of military-age pretrained experts soon dried up.[3] By necessity, the armed forces turned to enthusiastic amateurs or even to novices like the 163rd SPC's Joseph D. Boyle, who was a horseback-riding instructor, or the 166th SPC's Charles E. Sumners, who had "very little knowledge of anything other than farm, home, & family."[4] To convert such nonprofessionals into minimally competent cameramen each service expanded its training programs, and civilian photo schools often supplemented them as well.

As of mid-1941 the Army trained its photographers at modest facilities located at Fort Monmouth, New Jersey. To meet its expanding

241

needs the Army planned to locate its proposed Signal Corps Photographic Center (SCPC) there, which would require at least a year's delay for new construction before it could open. But before these plans progressed very far, the Army learned that the $10,000,000 Paramount studio on Long Island, New York, could be acquired at a fraction of its value. In late December 1941 the Army purchased the studio for $400,000. Not only was the cost reasonable and time saved, but this SCPC studio was close to numerous commercial labs in New York City, which could be utilized at particularly busy times. The SCPC grew dramatically from 445 officers, enlisted men, and civilians in late March 1942 to 1,258 total personnel on January 31, 1943. It leased additional space nearby, acquired branches in Detroit and Hollywood, and underwent several reorganizations as it struggled to reach maximum efficiency.[5]

None of SCPC's duties was more important than those conducted by its Photographic School Division. By November 1944 this division consisted of a School Equipment Branch, a Personnel Records Branch, and a Training Branch, with the latter subdivided into nine sections including basic school, still-picture school, motion-picture school, and lab school sections.[6]

Originally the photographic training course was only eight weeks long, but to compensate for the influx of men with little prewar experience the Army lengthened it, initially to twelve but then to seventeen weeks.[7] All students initially spent two weeks in the basic school, taking a combat refresher course to help them survive battlefield conditions. They studied map reading, first aid, camouflage, field fortifications, and basic photography, which included the mechanics of every type of camera the Army used. After assessing the students' prewar career and performance in basic school, officials assigned them to the still-picture, motion-picture, or lab school for the remaining ten or fifteen weeks.

At both the still and motion-picture schools the students next devoted four weeks to practical skills such as judging light values without using a light meter, estimating distance for a sharp focus, and carrying camera equipment over an obstacle course. During the remaining weeks of the course, training became more specialized. Still cameramen took an abbreviated lab course so they could develop film and make prints themselves, while motion-picture photographers cut and edited film to learn the importance of using different angles and lenses and developing continuity. Students received "field" assignments under simulated battlefield conditions, including going to a nearby tank school to work alongside tanks. They also critiqued battle-field still pictures and newsreels, had discussions with cameramen who had returned from overseas, and studied official reports of combat photo activities. During fiscal years 1944 and 1945 the Photo School graduated 1700 officers and men.[8]

The AAF, Navy, and Marines also had training programs. Individual AAF cameramen normally went to a technical photo school where they learned (or relearned) the fundamentals, and then to the AAF's First Motion Picture Unit (FMPU), where the CCUs were formed and underwent unit training. Out of the 4th CCU's original twenty-seven members sixteen graduated from the technical school at Lowry Field (now Lowry Air Force Base) near Denver and two more from another technical photo school; in the 3rd CCU twenty-four out of twenty-six attended a technical school.[9] At FMPU the Personnel Replacement Pool's Training Section stressed soldierly skills and photographic exper-tise. Although FMPU's headquarters were in the Hal Roach Studios in Culver City, the replacement pool operated out of the nearby Pacific Military Academy. There cameramen practiced on the rifle range, made field marches, learned defensive measures against chemical, air, or ground attacks, and attended an aerial-gunnery school; many went to a parachute school as well. They also flew simulated combat mis-sions, critiqued combat film, and heard lectures by veteran photogra-phers.[10] By 1945, 90 to 120 students were in training at any one time.[11]

For the Navy, BuAer's Photography Division administered the Training School (Photography) at Pensacola, where students received two months of basic still photography, one month of motion pictures, and one month of aerial photography. In July 1944, 337 officers and men were in attendance. After completing this standard course many graduates received additional training at more specialized photo schools, such as the Motion Picture School at the Navy's PSL.[12] Marine Corps cameramen trained at Quantico, the location of the Marine Corps Schools Photographic Section. Whether still or motion-picture photographers, Marines received no more than eight weeks of training.[13]

In addition to their own programs the armed forces also sent their photographer-trainees to civilian organizations, which offered classes free of charge to the military. Some of these organizations had been instructing small numbers of military cameramen since before Pearl

Harbor. In February 1941 The March of Time initiated a motion-picture course, the same summer *Life* instituted a still-photography class, and by the fall some of the major newsreels companies were offering courses. Before war's end Acme News, Associated Press, International News Service, the *New York Times*, and many other similar entities conducted classes.[14] On the West Coast, Hollywood studios provided training, especially for the Hollywood-raised SPCs but also for the other services. For young men thinking about joining the armed forces who hoped to do wartime photography, the New York Institute of Photography, the School of Modern Photography, and the Los Angeles Art Center School offered a head start by teaching courses in "pre-military photography."[15]

Carleton Mitchell of the Navy's Combat Photography Section illustrated the esteem some authorities had for civilian training. In early October 1942 he went to New York to arrange with The March of Time, the newsreel producers, and *Life* for a special course for CPUs, which began in mid-November. After a week of introductory lectures and screenings the officers spent two weeks with the newsreel companies and then four weeks with The March of Time, which included visits to the Associated Press, Acme News, and *Life*'s editorial office and labs. Meanwhile those enlisted still cameramen who had not been civilian news photographers went to the *Life* school, and the enlisted motion-picture photographers attended either The March of Time or the Movietone News school.[16] Much of the CPUs' success undoubtedly resulted from this experience with organizations that knew how to use stills and movies to attract the public's attention.

Amateurs or novices who graduated from the armed forces or civilian schools were not yet polished professionals but instead emerged with, at best, a passably good photographic foundation. Consequently their training did not cease with overseas deployment. The Army opened a school in Paris where cameramen rotated back from the front went to have experts critique their work. Some continuing education was less formal. After the Marianas campaign the 4th Marine Division Photo Section established an informal school to critique its performance.[17]

Despite these training efforts, amateurish mistakes, such as too much panning, hand held footage, under- or overexposed film, lack of continuity, and inadequate captions remained common. As with all professions—doctors, lawyers, accountants, even historians—so with photographers: nothing could substitute for years of education and experience in honing professional skills. Yet without the extensive bureaucracy dedicated to training military cameramen, World War II's pictorial record would have been far less impressive.

I

"An improved piece of photographic equipment can be as important as a new gun in winning a battle," claimed the author of a *Popular Photography* essay in one of many appeals for innovations. In another appeal, AAF officials urged the CCUs to "Report accurately and fully on improved equipment and machinery modifications in the field—as a result of working experience or unusual conditions that are encountered."[18]

Since many cameramen were experienced technicians with considerable ingenuity, ideas gushed forth. When their Eyemo batteries could no longer be recharged several CPUs adapted aircraft batteries for Eyemo use. CPU #8 built a .50-caliber machine-gun mount for an Eyemo that resulted in extremely steady film shot from a plane and CPU #6 improvised a special shoulder harness and shock-absorbing pad to steady a 20-inch lens used for long-range photography.[19] In the CCUs photographer-inventors converted spring-driven cameras into more efficient motor-driven models,[20] developed an array of mounts for GSAPs and other automatic cameras, and designed new types of automatics.[21] One of the most ingenious devices was a 16mm contact printer constructed by a 16th CCU lieutenant. The unit had tried for more than a year to requisition a printer through normal channels but without success. Beginning with only determination and extraordinary patience the lieutenant tinkered around for more than a year, scouting out useful contrivances and salvaging aircraft parts and then machining them down. "Finally," reported the unit historian, "on March 14 [1944] the last bolt was installed and test film put through for a preliminary run. It WORKED!"[22]

While field units improvised on an *ad hoc* basis the armed forces also undertook systematic programs for improving photographic equipment. An excellent example was the Army's Pictorial Engineering and Research Laboratory located at the SCPC.[23] Its duties included testing all equipment and making recommendations for modifications; preparing specifications and SOPs for equipment; and developing new equipment in response to requests from the field. By the summer of

1945 the research lab employed 130 officers, enlisted men, and civilians, had 250 projects in progress at any one time, and was completing about fifty projects per month.

Among the Pictorial Engineering and Research Lab's accomplishments were designing standardized repair kits for various cameras; modifying the Eyemo to alleviate several mechanical problems; inventing a jeep camera mount; devising a small, lightweight tripod to reduce hand holding; designing a helmet with a movable visor for motion-picture cameramen so they could film without removing their helmets; and perfecting a waterproof carrying bag to protect sensitive photographic equipment during amphibious landings, river crossings, and rainy weather. Other projects that the laboratory studied but rejected or had on the drawing board at war's end included a periscopic viewfinder to enable cameramen to photograph while protected from enemy fire; a spring-driven Eyemo that shot 100 feet of film instead of 50 feet before needing to be rewound; and an American-made 35mm Leica still camera.

"A cameraman without supplies is no cameraman at all," declared the 164th SPC's unit historian, who understood the crucial importance of logistical support.[24]

Indispensible photo supplies encompassed more than just film and cameras. The basic items issued to photo units, said an AAF technical manual, "include portable or mobile photographic labs, supply trucks, and motorcycles; developing, printing, enlarging, restituting, transforming, copying, and other laboratroy apparatus; photographic film, plates, paper, chemicals, and many small items of accessory equipment." Even this robust list is deceptively simple. Take chemicals. The manual listed sixty-four of them, ranging from acetic acid and sodium thiosulfate to paraformaldehyde and diaminophenol hydrochloride.[25] The Army's 1945 Signal Supply Catalog listed two dozen cameras, many with specialized accessories such as filters, batteries, lubricating oils, and lens. And each of the catalog's many different processing sets contained dozens of items—cable releases, cases, connectors, clips, cords, and canvas covers, and tanks, thermometers, timers, trays, trimmers, and tripods.[26] The Navy's 1944 standard photographic stock list filled almost twenty-three single-spaced pages, but cameramen in the field still suggested additions.[27]

Camera equipment and supplies were "highly technical, expensive, fragile, and require special care and expert handling by personnel familiar with their use," observed Colonel Robert B. Miller of the AAF's Motion Picture Services Division. "The average supply depot or sub-depot does not afford such facilities." As a result horror stories abounded. A Mitchell sound camera arrived at the 12th CCU without its lenses and a motor labeled "24-volt" that was actually 110-volt. Ten months later neither the lenses nor the correct motor had yet been delivered. Just before the 11th CCU undertook an assignment it received new equipment, but had to return twenty percent of the cameras as "hopelessly inoperative." To avoid these FUBARs Miller recommended that the Hollywood Air Depot Detachment be enlarged, staffed by qualified personnel, and serve as "the one centralized depot for assembly, testing, repair and shipping headquarters of all special and standard AAF motion picture equipment and allied supplies."[28] The other services also discovered that photo equipment required trained supply personnel and specialized procedures. Thus, for instance, the Navy established nine major photo supply depots and had five ships and several barges devoted exclusively to photographic supplies.[29]

"As I gently open the camera case," wrote an army camera repairman, "a large cloud of dust pours forth, out crawls every kind of insect known to mankind, and some unknown, and there, underneath it all, is the camera. The leather is half off, mold is half an inch thick, and it smells like a latrine. The lens, bless it, has the habit of growing a most cultivated and thick garden of moss."[30] Keeping such messes in working order required repairmen to perform miracles.

Even well-designed equipment, channeled through an efficient supply system, required routine maintenance and repair. Normal wartime wear and tear took their toll and severe shortages meant that equipment was virtually irreplaceable, so units either had to repair their gear or do without it. The armed forces organized repair and maintenance on an "echelon" basis, essentially involving three levels. Usually performed by the cameramen, first-echelon repairs delayed normal deterioration through preventive maintenance and simple on-the-spot adjustments. "THE CAMERA IS YOUR WEAPON, TAKE CARE OF IT PROPERLY," was the motto of the 163rd SPC's commanding officer. Second-echelon repairs required specialized tools and were done by skilled unit repairmen. Located far from the fighting fronts, third-echelon shops like those at PSL's Repair Division often involved complete rebuilding; sometimes the armed services even hired commercial firms to make major repairs.[31]

The repair hierarchy's most vital link was the second echelon. The 163rd SPC's repairmen were Chester E. Owens, Bernard Grubman, and Hugh Turner. In theory Owens was the OIC, Grubman worked on motion picture cameras, and Turner attended to still cameras. In practice each of them became adept at repairing all camera types, as well as virtually any other malfunctioning equipment. As one unit officer marveled, "Nothing was seemingly beyond their abilities," which was fortunate, especially in regard to cameras. Although the company commander declared that "cameras will be turned in for periodic checks at intervals of NOT LESS THAN ONE MONTH," cameramen rarely complied with the policy.[32] Usually by the time a photographer consented to be without his "weapon" even temporarily it really needed repair. Yet despite precombat predictions of camera losses in the 25 percent range, after more than a year of campaigning only one of the unit's 180 cameras had been declared unrepairable.[33]

Although Owens, Grubman, and Turner stayed at company headquarters and waited for cameramen to make their periodic visits, other SPCs employed repairmen, either individually or in small teams, who traveled to the detachments. These trips frequently took them close to the front. One of the 167th SPC's itinerant repairmen, Robert B. Stuart, received special recognition for voluntarily directing "an operation to procure valuable enemy machinery and tools from an enemy munitions plant. Working under enemy fire, he performed precision machine work in the field, making parts which kept photographic equipment of the Twelfth Army Group Photographic Companies in operation."[34]

Along with repairing photo equipment, automotive maintenance was an important support function since the SPCs could not operate their far-flung detachments without a well-maintained vehicle fleet. Like all the SPCs the 168th SPC had a motor pool that was such a "nerve center" that "at times it almost seems the primary mission of the company is to keep our vehicles in shape." William Markus, who had been born "with a silver wrench in his mouth," and others of similar mechanical aptitude took ailing jeeps and trucks and "nursed their various wounds and illnesses until they regained health and efficiency."[35] In one month in late 1943 the 163rd SPC's motor pool mechanic-soldiers made major repairs on twenty-eight vehicles and minor repairs and adjustments on 120 more.[36]

Photographers depended not only on vehicles but also on drivers, many of them trained to perform first-echelon vehicle maintenance. "Now that our drivers have left us," moaned the 166th SPC's Joe Zinni, "we are going to have to devote less time to photography than we were able to do before since we'll all have to chip in & service the vehicles & make necessary minor repairs."[37] Some drivers served as chauffeurs, transporting photographers to their desired location, dropping them off, and then waiting for them to return. Others acted as couriers who drove to and from the front daily to pick up exposed film and deliver new supplies. Being a driver was often dangerous, since jeeps and trucks regularly ventured into sniper-infested areas and within range of enemy machine guns and artillery. Snipers, for example, wounded two of Zinni's drivers and the 163rd SPC's Ben E. Karlgaard received a Bronze Star for heroic action when he rescued a wounded photographer amidst intense enemy fire.[38] And drivers may have been even more susceptible than cameramen to combat fatigue. A driver was "torn between getting the hell out of an area that is being shelled versus staying there and doing his duty and it started to wear on these people day in and day out," observed Robert Goebel, a 163rd SPC officer. "The photographer had a reason for being where he was. He'd have to go forward, maybe get shelled and everything else, but he had a reason for taking pictures. But the drivers just waited."[39]

II

Since processing still pictures was less complicated than processing motion pictures, the former could be done near the front lines while the latter usually went to rear-area laboratories. Along with the unit labs associated with SPCs, CCUs, and every major ship and shore station, for still-picture work the armed forces utilized an array of mobile and portable labs that came in boxes, tents, vans, and trailers. Eastman Kodak manufactured a portable darkroom that fit into a box of less than two cubic feet. The Signal Corps' Darkroom PH-392 consisted of a lightproof six-foot-high tent with thirty-five square feet of floor space. The 163rd SPC had a lab van, operated by four or five men, for use when time did not permit setting up the unit's regular lab. For example, at Salerno the 163rd relied on the van because the unit knew it would soon move to Naples.[40] One day after the Luzon invasion a 161st SPC lab came ashore, consisting of a two-wheeled trailer lab, a three-and-a-half-ton supply truck, and a seven-and-a-half-kilowatt power unit. Arriving somewhat later was the 832nd SSB's mobile lab, a specially designed thirty-four-foot semi trailer that had already done several weeks of duty on Leyte.[41]

For motion pictures the primary reliance was on military and commercial labs far from the fighting, although H. W. Huston, who built developing equipment for several Hollywood studios, did design portable 16mm and 35mm developing machines. Weighing 1,500 pounds and about the size of an office desk, the 16mm machines received relatively widespread acceptance, particularly in the AAF, but the larger and more complex 35mm developers were little used.[42] Most CCU 35mm film went to the AAF Combat Film Detachment in New York City, which farmed out the film to several commercial labs for developing. The AAF also relied on Olympic Laboratories and Eastman Kodak Laboratories in London, Laboratoire Cinematographique Moderne in Paris, four labs in Australia, and several more in India.[43] Navy movie film normally went to the PSL for processing, but that service also farmed out work to New York City labs.[44]

Even more than the other services, the Army utilized a variety of motion-picture-processing labs. By late 1944 it had eight Signal Mobile Photographic Lab Units capable of developing motion picture film, a huge APS Base Lab in London, and a somewhat smaller APS Lab in Paris. The Army also utilized commercial labs in London, Paris, Hawaii, and Australia, some of them with a huge capacity. Olympic Labs and the George Humphries Lab in London could each process 20,000 feet a day and the Denham Labs could do another 7,000 feet. If no overseas facilities were available exposed film went to the SCPC, the Signal Corps Photographic Laboratory at the Army War College, DeLuxe Labs in New York City, or the Eastman Kodak Labs in Rochester, New York.[45]

The number of labs reached enormous proportions, absorbing large numbers of trained personnel. Along with the APS labs at London and Paris, the Army operated eighteen smaller labs in the United Kingdom alone; by June 1944 the APS London Lab had 400 officers and men working in it, with many hundreds more manning the other labs in England. Up to four dozen officers and men staffed each of the Signal

Mobile Photographic Lab Units.[46] The Navy had 117 complete labs in July 1942, almost 400 a year later, and 700 by the summer of 1945.[47]

Labs often operated twenty-four hours a day, and field lab personnel in particular endured arduous conditions above and beyond the normal twelve-hour shifts. As Joe Boyle put it, the 163rd SPC's lab produced still pictures "under less than ideal conditions ALL the time."[48] Film processing depended on water and electricity, and neither was dependable in the war zones. Since functioning indoor plumbing was rarely available, lab workers often toted water from the nearest lake or river. But all sorts of problems arose. In China the water often contained so much mud that personnel had to filter it, and during the European winter of 1944–45 the labs had to melt snow to get water. As for power in war-shattered areas, labs resorted to generators, which were often under-powered and broke down. The proper temperature for processing solutions (called "soup") is 68°F. but in tropical darkrooms temperatures reached 120°F. More than once worries about temperature control had personnel "crossing our fingers and muttering brief but fervent prayers every time we dunked film and paper into the soup."[49] In humid regions prints that normally dried in a few hours would still be wet days later. Many labs lacked sufficient space since personnel rarely enjoyed the luxury of selecting ideal sites.

A picture was worth the proverbial thousand words only if it got into the proper hands in a timely fashion. Consequently nothing was more important in moving film from the front to the labs and then from the labs to the consumer than speed. The AAF documents stressed that exposed motion-picture film "will be shipped by the first available practical method" and that the authorized procedure for dispatching film was "by the fastest possible means."[50] Carleton Mitchell repeatedly reminded the CPUs that "In the event of actual combat film, days and even hours, can make a great deal of difference as to its usefulness here," and urged them to arrange for transmitting their material "by the quickest possible means."[51] As for the Army's philosophy, a beleaguered member of the 163rd SPC's lab best summed it up, perhaps only half in jest: "In one way of figuring, with the new decrease in time lapse, it will be possible to have the picture received in the States 2 hours and 53 minutes before it is taken."[52]

The evolution of special procedures to increase speed in the 163rd SPC exemplified the trend in most units. As late as June 1944, when the Allies captured Rome, the 163rd's methods for getting film to the labs remained haphazard. Photographers with the first assault troops entering the city returned film any way they could—via pigeons, a general's private Piper Cub, or motorcycles.[53] As the unit prepared for the Southern France invasion, one officer's sole assignment was to arrange to get pictures from the beachhead to the States as quickly as possible. "I had *carte blanche* from the Commanding General," he wrote, "to make any arrangements I thought were necessary." As a result he instituted more systematic procedures.[54]

By February 1945, when it was nearing Germany, the 163rd had inaugurated a jeep–airplane courier system. Each day couriers brought exposed film from the front to a rendezvous point where they loaded it onto a small plane that then flew to the airstrip nearest the company lab. At one point when the lab was alongside a road the company commander ordered trees lining the road cut down, converting the highway into a landing field. "Exposed film," recorded the company history, "could thereby be taken directly from the plane and processing started in a matter of minutes. Likewise film and pictures ready for delivery could be loaded onto the plane ... and flown direct to Paris and London." From there the film could be sent to the States, since APS had established a regular transcontinental air courier service just before D-Day. And a few carefully-selected still pictures could always be radiophotoed across the Atlantic. Either way, by using the 163rd's system pictures taken on the German front could appear in American newspapers within twenty-four hours.[55]

The rapidity achieved in getting film to the home front astonished contemporaries. Apparently the still-picture record was set at Iwo Jima. A photo taken from a Navy plane showing assault craft nearing the island was flown to Guam for processing, was then radiophotoed to San Francisco, and from there spread across the land over the AP wirephoto network. All this occurred in less than eighteen hours after the light reflected from the landing craft made its latent image on the emulsion.[56]

So remarkable was this feat that it sparked a *New York Times* editorial. "Even in these days of swift communications it seems almost incredible that newspapers reporting the first landing of Marines on Iwo Jima could simultaneously publish pictures of the landing itself...."

To watch a battle fought in mid-ocean, halfway across the world, almost from the moment it begins ranks among the miracles of modern transmission." In concluding, the editorial noted that "Television may accomplish something like this in the future, but it cannot do so now."[57]

12

"My Pictures Are at Least Doing a Little Bit of Good"

Combat Film on the Home Front

"American public opinion is notoriously mercurial," the British ambassador to Washington reported to the Foreign Office less than two months after Pearl Harbor, "and the problem of morale has given rise to many conflicting theories of how to deal with it."[1]

For several weeks after the United States entered the war the ambassador had assured his superiors that "there has been no rift in the front of national unity," but now he was becoming worried, as was the Roosevelt administration. Dissension was increasing and public opinion polls showed less than unanimous support for the war, especially against Germany. Old-style isolationism was making a comeback after the Pearl Harbor shock, labor unrest was on the rise, Republican Party leaders began criticizing President Roosevelt's policies, racial tensions threatened to sap the loyalty of some African-Americans, devout religious pacifists had not been cowed into silence, and virulent subversive bodies—the "criminal and lunatic fringe"—were being exploited "by more respectable anti-Administration groups." German- and Italian-Americans, linked by blood and culture to their former homelands, seemingly hesitated to embrace America's war. And if some segments of the population remained fond of America's enemies, other

255

citizens had little love for its allies: Irish-Americans were Anglophobes and many Roman Catholics despised the Soviet Union.[2]

Most authorities agreed that one way to counter the morale problem was to utilize combat film to solidify and galvanize the home front. The theory was that an informed and inspired public would endure inconveniences without complaint, produce more war materiel, buy war bonds, and participate in Red Cross blood drives. "On the morale-front," wrote one commentator, "photographs are bullets: a photograph is a thousand words and the message it packs across can go right to the spine of a million Joe Doaks," inspiring them to perform hundreds of tasks "each of which is one more nail in Hirohito's coffin just as surely as a two-ton bomb dropped on the Battleship Harakiri." A magazine essay echoed this sentiment, arguing that "propaganda is an even more important weapon than bombers. And pictures, as every photographer knows, are the spearhead of effective propaganda."[3]

I

Although the word "propaganda" has a pejorative connotation today, implying distortion and deceit, the article used it in a less sinister sense, meaning the systematic dissemination of information to encourage a supportive attitude toward the war.[4] In trying to build an enthusiastic consensus behind the war the administration followed a "strategy of truth," which was not the same as the *whole* truth. Fears about compromising military security and encouraging war weariness or defeatism were too strong for that. Military censorship overseas and the Office of Censorship and Office of War Information at home controlled what civilians read in the press, heard on the radio, and saw at the cinema. *Life*, for example, printed a title-page statement that "All photos and text concerning the armed forces have been reviewed and passed by a competent military or naval authority."[5] The media gracefully submitted to "censorship" and accepted "propaganda" because they embraced the war. As one editor admitted in early 1942, "our pages will be open to any way in which *U.S. Camera* can aid America's war effort."[6]

Despite the incomplete data available and the always-favorable interpretation that the propagandists placed on the information they were given, the official strategy of truth limited the extent of egregious deceptions and dishonesty. Expecting a long and arduous war, the government eschewed the potential immediate gains that falsehoods might provide in favor of nurturing long-term credibility. Making this strategy comparatively easy to pursue was a fundamental fact: after the war's darkest days in 1942 the United States and its allies were clearly on the offensive and winning. As a central part of its campaign to establish credibility and hence support for its policies, the government did less and less after 1943 to shield the public from the war's realities.

Even had the censors permitted complete honesty, no medium could perfectly replicate warfare for the folks at home. Nonetheless still pictures and motion pictures were more effective than newsprint or radio both in concocting a synthetic war and in conveying a sense of the war's reality to noncombatants. "Never before have the elusive realities of combat been recorded in this fashion," wrote one essayist about the work of armed-forces cameramen, "and perhaps not since the poetry of ancient wars have great events found a medium so eminently suited to convey their impact sharply and effectively to the people who had no part in the proceedings." Another commentator argued "that without pictures America would not have fought this war. For how otherwise could such an undertaking be made to seem worthwhile to the collective imagination of millions?"[7]

Photography informed the public about the war in three mutually reinforcing ways. Still pictures appeared in newspapers and magazines, bringing "the war into American living rooms with a far greater impact than any written description could." *Life's* July 3, 1944 cover showed a soldier helping a wounded colleague hobble back from the front. The caption explained that both were "effectively out of action, illustrating the military adage that it is more efficient to wound an enemy than to kill him," and also noted that the "wounded man is one of 225,382 U.S. casualties reported up to June 22." The magazine's readers had recently "seen" some of those casualties. Its June 19th issue featured two pictures containing about a dozen dead Americans, and the next week *Life* showed fourteen graves in Normandy with shrouded bodies in them. And the grim news continued. In mid-December it ran a picture of several stacks of paper, explaining that "piled in the Library of Congress are the typewritten sheets, twelve names to the page, that have announced war casualties to date.... Total: 544,056 dead, wounded, missing, prisoners." Several months later *Life* contained a pictorial essay on an American cemetery in Belgium where more than 15,000 soldiers were buried.[8]

None of *Life*'s pictures depicted grotesquely disfigured American bodies, but the wounded soldier's pained face, the large casualty figures, the shallow graves along the Normandy coast, and the rows of white crosses stretching to the horizon were, individually and collectively, troubling.

Reinforcing the still pictures were documentaries and newsreels. Because their images *moved* and thus simulated real life, these may have been even more instrumental than still pictures in molding the public's perception of the war. As with Hollywood's filmmakers, so with the documentarians: they were enthusiastic participants in the national mobilization. "Today, those of us who are making documentary films … have the added responsibility of making our films and the message they convey play a dynamic part in the War Effort," wrote one of them. Documentaries were "an important vehicle through which we can evaluate the quality and intensity of the fight for democracy as well as propagate its tested principles and urgent necessities."[9]

The War Activities Committee (WAC) of the Motion Picture Industry, serving as an agent for the Office of War Information, distributed combat documentaries as well as a variety of other government films. Formed in December 1941, WAC made a deal with the Roosevelt Administration. The government promised not to draft leading movie actors or compete with Hollywood in producing feature-length films. (Many actors, of course, *volunteered* for service.) In return WAC received pledges from the nation's 16,500 movie theaters to devote 10 percent of their screen time, free of charge, to government-sponsored films. This meant that theaters normally devoted up to twenty minutes to such topics as recruiting, war loans, economic stabilization, and the war's progress, rather than to entertainment. The government also reserved the right to present an occasional longer combat film. Consequently most documentaries were just under twenty minutes while only a handful, such as *The Memphis Belle*, *The Fighting Lady*, *San Pietro*, and *The True Glory*, were significantly longer.[10]

The result of this government–Hollywood bargain was "that a war message appears on every screen of the land every thirty minutes of showtime! It may be a ten–word plea to buy bonds; it may be a fifteen–minute visualization of a grave morale problem or a news flash of victory!"[11] Between 80,000,000 and 100,000,000 Americans (out of a population of 130,000,000) saw these messages each week, though many of the patrons were children and some people attended the movies more than once per week.

The first WAC-distributed combat documentary was *The Battle of Midway*, filmed by Hollywood director John Ford and his assistant Jack Mackenzie, Jr., and released in September 1942.[12] Long before Pearl Harbor, Ford had organized a Hollywood-based Naval Volunteer Photographic Unit, a reserve outfit analogous to the Army's affiliated SPCs. Although Ford's unit eventually transferred to the Office of Strategic Services, it was still in the Navy when military intelligence indicated that the enemy would soon attack Midway. Ford and McKenzie arrived there in time to photograph Japanese carrier aircraft attacking the island. Several bombs exploded near the cameramen, resulting in the film's most dramatic footage as the camera shakes wildly and the frame line jumps erratically before returning to normal.

The film won an Academy Award, but surely only because *Midway* was the first combat documentary and not for any intrinsic merit, for the movie had profound flaws. It misrepresented the battle by concentrating on Midway Island, whereas the significant action occurred several hundred miles away where American carrier planes sank four Japanese carriers. So disjointed was the editing that the film literally made no sense. And *Midway* was (at least in retrospect) almost unbearably maudlin, what with the flag appearing repeatedly, a sugary narration, and a sound track blaring patriotic and sentimental airs. For instance, one sequence depicts flag-draped coffins while "My Country 'Tis of Thee" swells forth.

After one other weak production (Zanuck's *At The Front in North Africa*, released in March 1943), the documentaries improved as the quantity and quality of combat footage increased. Documentary makers also learned the necessity of blending reporting with drama, fulfilling the government's desire to inform the public and the public's desire to be entertained through Hollywood-perfected techniques. *The Memphis Belle*, for example, taught a great deal about the air war's magnitude, complexity, and danger, but it wrapped this information in one of Hollywood's most conventional plot lines, that of disparate individuals being forged together in combat's white heat into a superb fighting team.[13]

Film editors rushed documentaries "to the screen before they could reach the awkward stage of being too old for news and yet too young for history."[14] Marines invaded Tarawa in late November 1943 and in early March 1944 the WAC released *With the Marines at Tarawa*; a mere five weeks after the Allies entered Rome *The Liberation of Rome* was on the screen; fighting in the Marianas did not end until August 1944 yet in mid-September Americans witnessed *The Battle for the Marianas*.

Considering the numerous procedures necessary to transform raw footage into a finished product, a lapse of only a few months was remarkable. Battlefield film had to get to the lab for processing, and from there to a censoring agency. Then the filmmaker screened tens of thousands of feet of film from the battle or campaign and selected the few thousand feet he wanted. After having a "work-print" copy made of this original footage the editor cut the work-print scenes to the appropriate length and arranged them in a logical sequence. Perhaps at this point the editor realized that the cameramen had missed a few vital scenes, in which case an assistant searched the stock film libraries for footage made at another time and place that could be utilized. Titles, maps, and perhaps animated sequences had to be prepared, photographed, developed, printed, and cut into the film. Meanwhile other specialists wrote a narration, selected music, and chose sound effects, recording a separate sound track for each of these audio elements; these then had to be coordinated with each other and with the images on the edited work print. After high-ranking officials checked the work print with its sound track for accuracy and to ensure that nothing in it violated military security, a few last-minute changes might be required. The approved work print had to be matched to the original footage, which was edited into a "master print" duplicating the work print. Finally, labs made copies of the master print for distribution. Since each of these steps by itself involved "a multiplicity of highly technical complications,"[15] this is a simplified account, but it does indicate the complexity of producing a completed motion picture.

With the assistance of the service that produced the film, special fanfare accompanied the release of most documentaries. After the AAF produced *Target Tokyo*, about the first B-29 raid on Tokyo, it provided a publicity brochure containing a movie synopsis and an effusive endorsement from Robert Lovett, the Assistant Secretary of War for Air. Helpful promotional suggestions included having a showing when Purple Heart veterans and Gold Star Mothers (those whose sons had died in action) would be featured guests, linking the showings of the film to bond sales, and building a lobby display with a map of Japan on the floor and a toy bomber overhead that could drop miniature dummy bombs. In addition the brochure showed the items theater-owners could obtain for publicity purposes: five ad slugs, a set of six "thrilling" black-and-white still pictures, and a "powerful and smash-ing" one sheet flyer available in any quantity required. The brochure also announced that "PUBLIC RELATIONS OFFICERS AT ALL ARMY AIR FORCES BASES AND INSTALLATIONS HAVE BEEN REQUESTED TO COOPERATE WITH EXHIBITORS IN THE PROMOTION OF 'TARGET TOKYO'!" A week before the official release the AAF held an advance showing for news and trade writers, who also heard an inspirational talk from Major General Haywood S. Hansell, Jr., who commanded the 21st Bomber Command when its planes delivered the "eggs" to Japan's capital.[16]

Theater owners went to ingenious lengths to publicize these war documentaries. William Egan of the Princess Theater in Sioux City, Iowa, held a special advance screening of *The Fighting Lady* for the press and radio, women's organizations, school officials, and business executives, leading "to the expected word-of-mouth advertising, plus the use of selected quotations in newspaper ads and radio spots." He also ran ads featuring glowing quotes about the movie from *Time* and other news and trade magazines. By chance two Sioux City servicemen appeared in the film, which "was good for further newspaper breaks." Navy recruiters aided Egan (and, no doubt, themselves) by persuading store owners to give them window space for promotional displays. Perhaps Egan's most innovative ploy was to tie the film's showing into the nationwide brownout. As a fuel conservation measure the Office of War Mobilization had forbidden all neon signs and ordered stores closed at dusk. So Egan built a "light machine" that used no electricity, and for a week prior to the film's opening it toured the darkened streets illuminating a traveling marquee. When the showings began the machine was outside the theater, beckoning patrons through the dimmed-out city. The imaginative Egan held a brownout party, lit his theater's canopy with lanterns, and set up curbside flares. He also "rigged up an old-fashioned kettle with tripod with a flare furnishing the fire. A sign alongside read: 'We are cooking up all sorts of fun, entertainment,' etc., etc."[17]

Aside from providing information about battles, the documentaries kept public morale on an even keel, navigating steadily between pre-mature over-optimism and faint-hearted defeatism. They did this by presenting a balance between the enemies' formidable military capabilities and America's strength and the righteousness of its cause. *With the Marines at Tarawa* explained that the Japanese were "savage fighters, their lives mean nothing to them" and *Fury in the Pacific* emphasized that enemy soldiers on Peleliu and Angaur were "smart, experienced veterans." In its review of *To the Shores of Iwo Jima*, *Time* told readers that "you will recognize if you never did before that the enemy is indeed tough."[18]   The European situation was the same. "The enemy," said *The Memphis Belle*'s narration, "is strong, skillful, determined to stop us," and the film contained enough scenes of German fighters, fields of exploding flak, and dying B-17s to underscore the point.

Enemy bravery and skill resulted in heavy casualties, which were no longer concealed after mid-1943. The War Department dedicated *Attack! The Battle for New Britain* "to those who now lie beneath wooden crosses marking the road to Tokyo." If *Attack!* was any indication the crosses were so numerous that wayfarers would have no trouble following the path. "Every step forward," the narrator said, "means some men coming back on stretchers. Sometimes it takes too long for the stretchers to arrive," in which case the soldiers died. Surgeons "worked together twenty-five hours out of the twenty-four" patching up casualties   Scene after scene contained dead and wounded Americans, "part of the price of a beach landing," just one more "day of American living bought and paid for." A high-ranking officer properly labeled the film "very frank" and "extremely gruesome."[19]

Fury in the Pacific followed in the same vein since Peleliu and Angaur typified "the fury and violence of war in the Pacific." One brutal shot after another paraded across the screen. One showed an American being shot: the camera was at a high angle looking down, with brush obscuring the view, and showed the man suddenly lurching backward, his arms flailing. Perhaps even more shocking was a scene of two soldiers evacuating a body through steep rocky terrain. As one lowered the corpse to the other, the dead weight was too great and the body slipped from their grasp, unceremoniously smashing head first into the rocks and knocking the lower soldier down. In still another scene, a bullet hits a stretcher-bearer, who drops his end of the stretcher and the wounded man he was carrying falls off, his head banging the ground. Reviews warned the fainthearted that the film contained a "terrible concentration upon men in the act of killing and being killed" and that it "is terrible to see, as terrible as the war."[20]

No one on the home front could have been unimpressed by the violence in *To the Shores of Iwo Jima* and *The Fleet that Came to Stay*. The former's end scenes were poignant reminders of war's cost: wrecked equipment littering the beach, a cemetery filled with seemingly endless rows of white crosses, and *huge* stacks of Marine helmets. "We stacked the helmets of our dead in neat piles," the narration explained. "Helmets of 4,000 men who died to take a tiny island somewhere in the Pacific." The latter documentary detailed the kamikaze assault against the U.S. Fleet off Okinawa, which was a "struggle between men who want to die, and men who fight to live." Although the film contained numerous scenes of kamikazes being shot down, it did not disguise enemy successes. Spectacular shots showed planes crashing into ships, followed by explosions, choking smoke, and searing flames. *Time* called the documentary "a shattering and dreadful record of the work of Japan's suicide flyers," which was unpleasant to see.[21]

America's cause justified the sacrifices. Its enemies, especially the Japanese, were barbarians, a theme that emerged in *Midway* and served for the duration. Near the end of that documentary, scenes showed a hospital that had been destroyed even though it had a large Red Cross on its roof, and another sequence of religious services being conducted next to a bomb crater where a chapel once stood. The implication was clear: the Japanese purposely attacked the symbols of civilization. *The Memphis Belle*'s narrator described the Germans as "those who invade and oppress ... the people who twice in one generation have flooded the world with suffering, suffering in such quantity as the history of the human race has never known, brought torment and anguish into countless American homes, gold stars, and telegrams from the War Department."

Almost every documentary implied that God had sanctified America's cause and asserted that the Allies would prevail because they fought for freedom. Scenes of pre-attack divine services, chaplains ministering to the dying and the dead, and religious burial rituals were commonplace. *To the Shores of Iwo Jima* summed it up best. "While we fought we prayed." *The Memphis Belle* explained how the English "have defended their island's freedom for over a thousand years" and were again preserving it from "the German lust for conquest." Wyler's other documentary, *Thunderbolt*, spoke of the Fascists' promise "to build a twentieth-century Roman Empire, conceived in tyranny and dedicated to the proposition that some men were meant to be slaves of other men."

No film spoke more eloquently about freedom than *The True Glory*, which detailed the victorious European campaign. In the film's introduction General Dwight D. Eisenhower emphasized that although the enemy "was strong, resourceful, and cunning," the Nazis erred when they underestimated the "spirit of free people, working, fighting, and living together in one great cause." Having defeated the Germans, that spirit "will likewise defeat that other great enemy of human freedom, even now in the far-off Pacific reeling under the blows delivered by our gallant comrades in arms." The general concluded by *praying* that "that spirit of comradeship will persist forever among the free people of the United Nations." At film's end the narration returned to the freedom theme. A soldier-narrator tells the audience that the spoils of victory included "only this, a chance to build a free world, better than before. Maybe the last chance. Remember that."

Complementing the documentaries were twice-weekly newsreels. An eight-to-ten-minute potpourri of news, sports, and entertainment, newsreels began in 1911 and endured until 1967 but reached their zenith from 1941 through 1945. Four of the five major companies—Fox Movietone, Paramount, Pathè, and Universal—made releases on Tuesday and Thursday while News of the Day's releases were on Wednesday and Friday. Under wartime pressures two other newsreels emerged. Produced under government auspices, United Newsreel was an overseas counterpropaganda instrument that appeared in sixteen languages. The government distributed it in friendly and neutral countries and dropped it behind enemy lines. The other newcomer was All American News, also government sponsored and crafted for use only in African-American theaters, which were segregated.[22]

Radio provided more immediate news and newspapers presented more detailed information, but newsreels allowed the home front to *see* the war. They familiarized the public, on a regular basis, with what "real" war looked like. Civilians became such avid newsreel watchers that some theaters, such as the Trans-Lux in Washington and Telenews in Cleveland, showed nothing but newsreels. Recognizing the newsreels' allure, theater owners undertook extensive promotional efforts, running newspaper ads, setting up special signs and placards, and offering a free still-picture enlargement from the footage if a customer recognized a family member. To aid these advertising efforts the newsreels sent "issue sheets," laden with bold type and exclamation points, to theaters giving a synopsis of the forthcoming newsreel.

"ADVANCE INFORMATION FOR NEWSPAPER PUBLICITY AND EXPLOITATION," was the way Universal billed its issue sheets, while Paramount urged theaters owners to "USE THIS DRAMATIC INFORMATIVE COPY FOR YOUR ADVERTISING!" and reminded them that "YOUR AUDIENCE IS MORE *NEWSREEL-CONSCIOUS* NOW THAN EVER BEFORE!"[23]

All the newsreel companies had access to a common pool of censored footage shot primarily by military photographers but often including scenes from accredited civilians. Military authorties submitted the material on a rotating basis to one of the five newsreel companies; that company then made copies for the other four companies. An overall description and detailed caption sheet accompanied the footage.[24] Each company was free to edit the footage as it wanted and to write its own script, though the narration often closely followed the military's descriptive guidance and captions.

Determining exactly what World War II audiences saw and heard is impossible. Many of the surviving releases do not include the original soundtrack, although for some a draft script exists. However, the final narration often differed from the draft. Both a draft script and the original soundtrack for Pathè's March 9, 1945 edition, which dealt with Iwo Jima, survive.[25] Here are just three changes between the draft and final version:

Draft: "An LCI is hit by Jap shells, that never stopped coming, until their gun posts were taken by frontal assault. There was no safety on shipboard for these brave men of the Navy."

Final: "A landing craft is hit by enemy shells, leaving wreckage and dead."

Draft: "To date, twelve thousand five hundred Japs have been killed on Iwo."

Final: "In the first sixteen days fourteen thousand five hundred were killed on Iwo."

Draft: ""The Marines push on in a battle that ouranks even Tarawa ... Kwajalein ... Saipan. Navy Secretary Forrestal, back from Iwo, announces that it has cost two thousand fifty American lives in fifteen days. But in the battle that still rages, a victory in proportion to the cost will be won."

Final: "Marines move ahead in a battle that outranks any fought in the Pacific. Iwo Jima in its first fifteen days has cost two thousand-fifty American dead, and the battle still rages."

Two factors accounted for these (and other) changes. One was more current information received between the draft and the final narration, which were often written several days apart. Thus the number of dead Japanese increased from 12,500 to 14,500. More important, the changes resulted in a *shorter* narration. Script writers know that to synchronize with the pictures a narration can average a maximum of four words per foot of film, although that rate cannot be sustained because it allows no time for the pictures alone, the music, or the sound effects to carry the story. Nonetheless even excellent writers frequently write "long" the first time through—that is, they write too many words for the available footage. When the words and images have to mesh, writers must cut their verbiage.

If entertainment features dominated the newsreels before Pearl Harbor, war pictures prevailed thereafter. In the twelve months after the Japanese attack almost 80 percent of newsreel subjects were war related, a percentage that did not change for the next three years.[26] During 1944, for example, Paramount allocated 77 percent of its time to the war, 8 percent to the 1944 elections, 6 percent to sports, 1 percent to fashion, and 8 percent to miscellaneous domestic topics such as floods, forest fires, and personalities.[27]

Newsreels changed over the course of the war. One change was the more timely release of material. Censors withheld Pearl Harbor footage for a year, and months elapsed before newsreels received film from North Africa and Tarawa, prompting complaints that "generally pictures of the war for the public have been too little and too late—while that same public has been indicted for being unaware of the war." But just two weeks elapsed between the Marshall Islands invasion in early 1944 and its newsreel coverage, and by D-Day the gap between event and newsreel was only ten days.[28]   Due to film shortages newsreels became shorter, shrinking from 900 feet (ten minutes) to 700 feet (less than eight minutes). Coinciding with a flood tide of excellent footage, the abbreviated length imposed cruel choices on newsreel editors. In April 1945 they had 30,000 feet available for one 700-foot release.[29]

While newsreels became shorter, like the documentaries they also became more grim. Reflecting military fears that civilians were weak and would falter if they saw "real" war, newsreels were initially mundane, with exultant and exhortatory narrations, little combat footage, few American casualties, and lots of high-ranking brass, logistical support, marching soldiers, naval guns firing, and planes flying overhead. By late 1943 the policy toward showing war's somber aspects and letting noncombatants know that "war is not all victory, with no losses" had changed. So dramatic was the transformation that administration officials complained that the newsreels "had softened war reports by self-censorship of scenes depicting American dead and wounded, action under fire, and other grim battlefront realities." Soon, according to one commentator, newsreels were "getting tougher. They are letting us have it right between the eyes.... They are showing the theatregoing public, after three years, that war is truly hell."[30]

II

While still pictures, documentaries, and newsreels provided information and sustained morale in general, the armed forces also produced still pictures and films specifically aimed at the work force. Stressing the direct link between home-front productivity and battlefield success, these industrial-incentive materials demonstrated the necessity for enormous quantities of weaponry and other war-related supplies. For example, the Army's Ordnance Department and the Navy's Bureau of Ordnance wanted scenes of artillery and naval guns in action for *Firepower*, a joint publication for distribution to employees in government owned ordnance industries.[31]

Generally, industrial-incentive films were much more important than still picture publications. The first such movie resulted from a meeting between Under Secretary of War Robert Patterson and his labor consultant, who suggested a film dramatizing industry's role in modern warfare. Completed in the spring of 1942, the ten-minute-long *The Arm Behind the Army* so impressed Patterson that he suggested a regular series of pictures that "would constitute an invaluable medium for continually bringing home to workers a realization of the necessity for ever-increasing effort."[32]

For most of the war the Army, through its Bureau of Public Relations, released two industrial-incentive films per month. A *Film Communique* of no more than twenty minutes in length was suitable for showing in any war plant; one appeared monthly until March 1945 when authorities concluded they had served their purpose. *Film Communique No. 1* consisted of three parts. The first showed a military-truck assembly plant in the North African theater, the second portrayed the Air Transport Command landing supplies and evacuating the wounded on New Guinea, and the third dealt with the men and equipment it cost to capture Rendova. The last communique, *No. 16*, centered on two sequences, one on the artifical ports and piers erected in support of the Normany invasion and the other on a typical carrier task force campaign. The Army's other monthly film targeted a specific industry. *Attack Signal* showed the importance of radios in a Pacific island invasion and emphasized the necessity for quality electronics. Medical suppliers received their due in *Lifeline*, which depicted the treatment of the wounded. *War on Wheels* (the automotive industry), *Men of Fire* (foundries), *Timber to Tokyo* (lumber), and *The Case of the Tremendous Trifle* (ball bearings), were other examples.[33]

The Army and AAF also produced emergency industrial "shorts" aimed at particular locales rather than specific industries. Labor trouble in Detroit compelled the Army to make six two-minute films to re-energize the area's work force. FMPU produced fifty-seven similarly brief films, ten each for Seattle, the Connecticut valley, and San Diego, eighteen for Los Angeles, and nine for Akron. In addition, Under Secretary Patterson requested FMPU to produce half a dozen labor shorts for nationwide distribution when Germany capitulated, "to remind civilian audiences that the war with Japan is by no means concluded."[34]

Navy representatives who saw *Combat Report*, the Army's second industrial film, were so impressed that they asked that the credits be changed to read "Produced by the Signal Corps for the Army and Navy." But the Navy was not content to follow in the Army's wake, and soon formed its own Industrial Incentive Division. Like the Army, the Navy orchestrated a two-tier film program, one dedicated to all industries making naval weapons and the other carrying a message for specific industries.[35] Illustrative of the first type was *This is Guadalcanal*, which paid tribute not only to the Marines who fought on the island but also to those who built the ships that took them there, produced their weapons, kept supplies coming, and made the planes that provided air cover. Marines, the narration explained, will always want "the all-important backing of you folks on the production line at home." *Full Speed Ahead* exemplified an industry-specific film, for it appealed to workers who built destroyers and their component parts by explaining the German submarine menace.

Combat footage dominated industrial-incentive films. The Army Bureau of Public Relations decreed that frontline scenes comprise at least 90 percent of each of its incentive films and the War Department insisted that no effort be made "to eliminate the tragic aspects of a battle or campaign," specifically requesting scenes of casualties. The head of the Navy's Industrial Incentive Division also specifically requested the Combat Photography Section to secure combat film for its use. The reason for this emphasis was that "production greatly improved if workers were given firsthand reports of the use of their products in actual combat."[36] *Business Screen Magazine*'s editor found that both labor and management preferred *"action films straight from the war fronts."* As one industrialist told him, "we need films showing some of the hardships and horror of the war in order to bring home to our employees the seriousness and importance of the work in which they are engaged."[37]

As with documentaries and newsreels, special promotions heralded a new industrial-incentive film. The Navy provided captioned still pictures, bulletin-board displays, employee-publication stories, and press and public-address-system announcements. With the cooperation of local Chambers of Commerce, it also sponored premiere showings attended by high-ranking officers and combat veterans.[38]

The incentive-film programs were not without problems. As each service vied for war-plant showings of its pictures, Army–Navy competition raised questions about duplication and market saturation to the point where the sheer number of films reduced their dramatic impact.[39] A second difficulty was that few factories contained adequate theater facilities; viewing them in poorly-darkened floor spaces, storage areas, or cafeterias was not conducive to rapt attention.[40] Much disagreement arose as to whether the films should be shown on workers' or employers' time. Employers argued "that work stoppage in large establishments results in serious production losses, which are not compensated by the mental stimulation afforded by motion pictures," but workers were reluctant to arrive early, stay late, or give up their lunch hour to see them.[41]

By the end of fiscal year 1944 approximately 6,000,000 workers saw Army films each month and during 1945 the number increased to 8,500,000; millions more saw Navy programs. Even though the programs grew enormously, questions remained about the films' effectiveness. As one APS officer confessed, no one knew exactly "how many man-hours industrial incentive films have added to the the work-power of the nation."[42] Yet the evidence indicates that the films had a powerful impact. For instance, in early January 1944 several thousand Lockheed Vega Corporation workers in Burbank, California, saw an incentive film featuring combat in Italy. One employee wrote that its effect "was terrific. Everyone to whom I spoke of it afterwards stated that it made them feel like slackers and that thereafter they would pay more attention to their work and cease taking time off."[43]

III

Money is the sinews of war and film was crucial in "selling" the war on the home front.

To help finance the war and control inflation the government not only raised taxes but also sold bonds. Although many officials initially favored a compulsory savings program, Secretary of the Treasury Henry Morgenthau, Jr. preferred voluntary bond purchases. Allowing individuals to buy bonds, he argued, gave them "a chance to have a financial stake in American democracy—an opportunity to contribute toward the defense of that democracy." Morgenthau favored Madison-Avenue-style advertising to *persuade* people to invest, thereby avoiding the bullying tactics used in World War I, when schoolchildren had been badgered and nonsubscribers had their homes doused in yellow paint. In the World War II loan drives the Treasury Department employed slogans, hoopla, Hollywood entertainers (especially voluptuous females), audacious stunts, and combat photography.[44]

"War Pictures *Sell War Bonds!*" proclaimed a Graflex photography ad extolling the selling power of the "GRAFLEX Sees the War" still-picture exhibit. During the Third War Loan Drive a Hollywood radio station displayed the original exhibit, and on CBS National Bond Sales Day the station booked orders for more than $14,000,000 in bonds. Before the drive ended over 10,000 people visited the studio, gazed at the photos, and bought more bonds. Encouraged by an impressed Treasury Department, Graflex made a new exhibit based on a "See Your War Bond Dollars in Action" theme, and provided copies to two hundred radio stations for the Fourth Drive. The appeal was again astonishing, necessitating two hundred additional exhibit sets for the Fifth Drive, and so on until war's end.[45]

By the Sixth Drive, conducted in the fall of 1944, the Treasury's War Finance Division was sponsoring a wide range of 16mm films to complement the still-picture advertising. "The potent force of sound motion pictures, packed with the dramatic action and sobering realism from America's war fronts," noted one essay, "has been harnessed to the Sixth War Loan Drive." Included were twelve special films.

Produced by the Navy expressly for the drive, five of them ran from nine to twenty minutes. Among them were *The 957th Day*, featuring the activities of the Fifth Fleet on July 20, 1944, *We Said We'd Come Back*, providing an account of the Navy's Pacific war, and *Freedom Comes High*, depicting a courageous but fatal destroyer-torpedo attack against a Japanese battleship. Six films produced by the War Department were three minutes long. *Just for Remembrance* opened with American bodies carpeting a battlefield, with GIs searching the dead soldiers' pockets for personal possessions to be returned to loved ones, and then cut to the Kansas City warehouse where clerks checked the personal effects packages—2,000 of them per month—before forwarding them to the next to kin. Another, simply titled *Silence*, contained scenes of wreckage strewn across a battlefield, with no movement and no sound. The narration then emphasized that a battle cannot be won without sound—the roar of artillery shells, trucks, tanks, and planes—and that bonds bought the machines that made the roar of victory possible.[46]

Depicting the European air war, the twelfth motion picture was *Combat America*. Originally intended as an aerial-gunnery training film, the movie was produced and narrated by Clark Gable, Hollywood idol and AAF officer, on General "Hap" Arnold's direct orders. Shot in 16mm color and with Captain Gable appearing in numerous scenes, the film had great potential appeal, and the AAF hoped to get it approved for 35mm theater distribution. But OWI rejected it because of the raw-stock film shortage and limited technicolor-processing facilities, and because of its thematic similarity to *The Memphis Belle*. The War Department authorized a black-and-white copy for the newsreels, which might use a few scenes, but it seemed as if Gable's complete production would get no public distribution. Then the Treasury Department adopted *Combat America* in 16mm color as a climax to the Sixth War Loan Drive, saving it from obscurity by arranging for simultaneous premieres in more than two hundred cities on New Year's Day, 1945.[47]

Although the Seventh War Loan Drive used Rosenthal's Iwo Jima flag-raising shot as its official symbol, it also showcased an array of short subjects, "impact" trailers, and feature-length pictures. The six shorts included *Remember These Faces*, a fifteen-minute color film on the care of wounded men; *Midnight*, an eighteen-minute account of the Navy's activities at midnight around the globe; and *Action at Angaur*, a twenty-two minute production on that island's capture. The two-and-a-half-minute trailers were *This Could be America, The Voice of Truth, Iwo Jima, Back Home, Time for Sale,* and *Mission Completed!*[48]   And the AAF contributed *The Fight for the Sky,* photographed by the 3rd CCU and consisting primarily of spectacular GSAP footage. It premiered in three hundred cities on May 21, 1945.[49]

Enormous numbers of Americans saw loan programs in factory aisles, grange halls, town squares, city parks, school auditoriums, private clubs, lodges, churches, union halls, and other niches where 16mm equipment could operate. The Seventh War Loan Drive had 141,615 showings of 16mm programs to 33,402,950 people.[50] Including the postwar Victory Loan Drive, the drives raised more than $150 billion, which meant that war bonds financed about half the government's expenditures on the war.

War consumed not only money but blood. To save wounded soldiers the armed forces needed enormous quantities of blood for transfusions. The best available blood source was the civilian population and the Red Cross cooperated with the government in obtaining civilian blood for military use. And combat photography aided the Red Cross in gaining widespread participation in its blood drives.[51]

The most famous photograph used in the blood-donor campaign was John Stephen Wever's shot of Private First Class Harvey White administering blood plasma to Private Roy W. Humphrey, who received a shrapnel wound on August 9, 1943.[52] Taken in an alley in Sant' Agata, Sicily, the shot showed Humphrey, from his blood-streaked face to his boots, lying on a stretcher in the foreground while White, wearing a Red Cross armband, administered the plasma. Five spectators were in the background. On the left were two girls and a woman in a doorway, in the center was an elderly woman standing against a wall, and on the extreme right, near the wounded G.I.'s boots, was a man sitting in a chair.

In composition and content the picture was compellingly eye-catching. It appeared on newspaper front pages from Baltimore to Los Angeles and received a 1944 Pulitzer Prize nomination. Noted photo critic Victor Keppler anointed it as "one of the greatest human-interest shots to come out of the war." Wever's picture sent record numbers of people, almost all of whom mentioned having seen the shot in their newspaper, streaming into local Red Cross Blood Banks. Wisely the Red Cross distributed prints to local chapters and featured it in

The caption on this Billy A. Newhouse photo was typical in its concern to identify individuals: "Four infantrymen, members of the two patrols that closed the escape gap east of Metz . . . shake hands after their mission has been accomplished. Left to right: S/Sgt Henry Tackett, Portsmouth, Ohio; S/Sgt Leonard Malicole, Cloverbottom, Ky; S/Sgt Frank B. Smith, Cleveland, Ohio; and Tec 5 Anoil T. Horbison, Rockville, Ind." *Photo provided by Newhouse.*

Of course the concern for identity applied only to the Allies. Fred Bonnard photographed a badly burned German body (left) while Morris Berman made a closeup of another dead German (right). Both men quickly moved on, making no effort to identify the dead enemy soldiers. *Photos provided by Bonnard and Berman.*

Considering the hard usage cameras received at the front, good camera repairmen were indispensable and the 163rd SPC had some of the best, including Chester E. Owens (on the phone) and Bernard Grubman (seated). *Photo provided by Owens.*

Because of film's importance for the war effort, photo outfits strove to get film processed quickly. Some even utilized courier planes. In this photo a pilot collects film just delivered from the 163rd SPC's far-flung cameramen and places it in a bag marked "URGENT U.S. Army Signal Corps PRESS FILM." Soon the pilot would be airborne, heading for a processing lab in London with his precious cargo. *Photo provided by Robert L. Lewis.*

Marine Corps cameraman William H. Genaust on Iwo Jima in this picture by another Marine photographer, Robert Campbell. Both Genaust and Campbell were atop Mount Suribachi when Joe Rosenthal made the famous still picture of the flag-raising there. Genaust shot the identical scene in motion pictures, which confirmed that Rosenthal did not pose it. Like three of the men who raised the flag, Genaust died in combat on Iwo Jima. *Photo provided by Tedd Thomey.*

Photographs of enemy positions allowed the Allies to understand the enemy's tactics and use of terrain. The top photo is of a Japanese coastal defense gun position on Okinawa, while the bottom photo shows the field of fire from this position. *Photos by Robert F. Albright. Photos provided by Albright.*

Shot by Marine cameraman Richard R. Dodds, this picture was part of a five-shot panorama taken from Japanese positions on Iwo Jima that let experts study the tactical situation from the enemy's perspective. *Photo provided by Dodds.*

Photos of enemy camouflage techniques, such as this one showing how the Germans camouflaged a powder plant by letting trees grow on the dirt-covered roof, alerted Allied forces so they would not be fooled. *Photo by Billy A. Newhouse. Photo provided by Newhouse.*

Billy A. Newhouse takes a terrain reconnaissance photo in Germany. Such photos were of tremendous tactical value since surprisingly few combatants could read military maps or interpret high altitude aerial photographs. *Photo by Harvey A. Weber. Photo provided by Weber.*

Many combat cameramen made low level reconnaissance photos from piper cubs, including the 166th SPC's Joseph M. Zinni shown here departing to photograph artillery fire during the Battle of the Bulge. The plane's name was rather descriptive: while flying close to the front line photographers often felt like clay pigeons with the entire enemy army shooting at them. *Photo provided by Zinni.*

Wherever high ranking officers went, photographers were nearby. In the top photo
General Walton H. Walker receives the Croix de Guerre. At least eleven photographers
were there—ten visible in the scene plus the man who took the shot, Harvey A. Weber.
Photo provided by Weber. At the bottom is the type of "brass" picture that never
became public. In the back seat are Secretary of War Stimson and General Omar
Bradley, and in the front is General George Patton, in an undignified pose. *Photo by
James LaFrano. Photo provided by LaFrano.*

Rewards for a dangerous job well done: Gordon T. Frye receives the Bronze Star for his superb front line photography (top); Frank J. Goetzheimer receives the Bronze Star for his role in a raid deep behind Japanese lines to release American prisoners (middle); and James M. Bray receives the Distinguished Flying Cross in a ceremony at FMPU (bottom). *Photos provided by Frye, Goetzheimer, and Bray.*

national advertising, crediting the photo to the "Associated Press from U.S. Army Signal Corps." "The gift of life is yours to give," read the ad. *"Will you give it?"*[53]

Wever's photo and others like it helped save the lives of servicemen who were hemorrhaging, burned, or in shock. During the war thirteen *million* pints of blood were collected and processed; this blood played a crucial role in reducing the mortality rate among casualties reaching frontline medical facilities from 8.1 percent in World War I to approximately 4 percent in World War II.

Wever undoubtedly spoke for all combat photographers when he learned that his photo was influencing the home front. "Glad to learn," he wrote to his mother after reading about the increase in Los Angeles blood donors following his shot's appearance in the *L.A. Times*, "that some of my pictures are at least doing a little bit of good."

13

"That Weapon Is Film"

Combat Film on the Fighting Fronts

In September 1943 AAF Major General Ira C. Eaker wrote a long letter to the Commanding General about an extremely important subject: the performance of the CCUs.

The general was distressed. "Hap" Arnold's hopes for the CCUs had not yet been realized and Eaker had "spent considerable time personally investigating the reasons." Part of the difficulty was that the CCUs were a new idea superimposed on an old organization, and finding their proper niche inevitably took time. But the primary problem was equipment. In the prewar era the AAF had developed planes and still-picture cameras for aerial photo recon, but had failed to appreciate the significance of motion pictures and had never designed planes to carry motion-picture cameras. The AAF was now paying a terrific price for its negligence, and Eaker was anxious to get the "new equipment required to make it possible for our combat camera units really to get battle pictures."[1]

Two years later Germany and Japan had been battered into submission. Like many Americans in and out of uniform, Eaker, now a lieutenant general and the Deputy Commander of the AAF, was reflecting on the causes of Allied success in World War II. He believed that one cause was the rapid progress that had been made in the CCUs' equipment and procedures, which allowed them to get indispensable battle pictures. "The important contribution of Army Air Forces motion pictures to final victory," he wrote, "cannot be overestimated." These films were instrumental in informing the public through documentaries and newsreels, but they were equally vital to the military for training films and tactical and technical studies. And they would be useful in the future, instructing "the youth of tomorrow on the important part played by the Army Air Forces in one of the greatest triumphs in American history."[2]

Eaker's intense interest in wartime photography had not been unique. Many leaders associated with the war effort at the highest levels knew that frontline film had helped make victory possible.[3]

I

As the armed forces mobilized for war, they confronted the urgent problem of suddenly having to teach a variety of skills to massive numbers of students but with only a handful of qualified instructors available. Most of the skills were novel, technical, and difficult. Making the situation worse was the necessity for frequent retraining as new weapons poured out of the factories and new techniques emerged from the battlefield. Two other complicating factors were uniformity and time. Whether from Portland, Maine, or Portland, Oregon, the recruits all had to perform a skill or technique in exactly the same way so that they could learn to work in unison in combat. Training also had to be done quickly, for training time was "a military asset that must be rationed as carefully as steel or copper or rubber. Time, unlike other military commodities, cannot be stretched out. There is no substitute for it."[4] The best way to save time was to make training more efficient.

The solution to these difficulties was the training film. When the war began, the services' training-film programs were ill conceived. The early movies were too long and excruciatingly dull, little more than filmed instruction manuals accompanied by a monotone voice delivering a factual "nuts-'n-bolts" narration. Most avoided using sound effects to dramatize their material, instead relying "upon the intrinsic interest of the subject and well-written commentary to hold the soldiers' attention."[5] Even a very great deal of intrinsic merit and excellent commentary did not command much attention from recruits, because trainers often used films as *alternatives* to training. During inclement weather, after lunch, or at the end of an active day—that is, at times when *real* training could not take place—trainees would be marched into darkened, cramped, poorly ventilated auditoriums to watch monotonous films. To soldiers, sailors, airmen, and Marines training films were the "big ether" because they seemed ideally designed to induce sleep.[6]

Although these problems never entirely disappeared,[7] training films and their use improved dramatically—but not without controversy. Many officers clung to the belief that these films should stress thoroughness and clarity since their purpose was to teach, not to entertain. They argued that education and entertainment were antithetical, and that the more entertaining a film was the less it would teach. As filmmakers with Hollywood experience donned uniforms they challenged this view, asserting that bored or snoozing soldiers learned nothing. Training films should avoid dullness by incorporating proven entertainment "values" such as plot, humor, dialogue, music, and animation. Production costs might rise and sometimes less information could be presented in a given amount of time, but the Hollywooders insisted that the results would compensate for these deficiencies.[8] Colonel Richard T. Schlossberg, the chief of APS early in the war, typified the reaction to such heresy: "You Hollywood big shots are all alike, all a pain in the ass.... You Hollywood guys just won't fit in with the Army way of producing films."[9]

Ultimately the Hollywood perspective prevailed, especially during the war's last two years, when a distinction emerged between training in the narrow sense of imparting procedural information and the broader sense of preparing men for combat.[10] One key to engaging the audience's emotional interest was incorporating combat footage "to so far project the soldier-in-training into the situation which he will face—its sounds, shadows, crowdings, surprises, and other troubles— that he will react immediately and correctly when the actuality is before him." As an APS report put it, "By placing stress on film actually shot at the front, the authenticity of Training Films is increased and the students' interest is intensified."[11]

Combat film proved especially suitable for technical and tactical films. As defined by the Army, the technical films illustrated "the use of weapons and equipment and the actions of an individual or of a group in performing an operation or a series of operations," while tactical films portrayed "the application of the basic principles of combat tactics of the different arms and services as set forth in the authorized training publications."[12] In these types of films, footage showing both correct and incorrect techniques was valuable. When trainees saw that proper training applied on the battlefield yielded success while mistakes often resulted in tragedy, they better understood why they were told to do certain things in certain ways.[13]

A filmmaker's ability to tinker with time and space was a tremendous asset in allowing recruits to conceptualize warfare. Events that took weeks and occurred over hundreds of square miles could be compressed by a filmmaker into a few minutes. For example, the cooperation of mechanized units, tactical airpower, artillery, and infantry was an essential component of modern war. Yet an individual soldier in any of these specialties could not readily grasp the entire operation since "his understanding is hemmed in by his personal horizon." But a well-crafted film could "bring him the whole story of the operation, showing him on the screen just how his immediate duty of running a tank, handling a machine gun or stringing a field-telephone line is integrated with each other part of the operation as a whole."[14]

"Hardly a picture now being made in [the Army's] Training Films Division is without film taken in the battle area," wrote Captain John G. Gilmour, the Division's Acting Director, in early 1945. The Army's Technical Films Branch had used 552,557 feet of frontline footage in 160 training films while the Army Ground Forces Projects Branch compiled a Let's Look at Ordnance film series from overseas footage.[15] Produced by the Corps of Engineers, Camouflage in Combat employed a split screen to show how camouflage as practiced in training was actually employed in the fighting zones.[16] AAF officials considered film so essential they held a conference to develop procedures for expeditiously transforming raw footage into training films. But the Marines, rather than hold lengthy conferences when time was of the essence, simply ignored established channels for procuring training films and made them directly from incoming footage.[17]

Supplementing and complementing combat footage were music and sound effects, a lively on-screen dialogue instead of an impersonal off-screen narration, and animation and humor, the latter two often closely linked.[18] Animation was useful in several ways. Photographing the interior of a field-artillery recoil mechanism was impossible, but through animated diagrams machines came alive, allowing trainees to visualize how their pistons and gears worked. Animation was also at the heart of *Camouflage Cartoon*. With Mr. Chameleon teaching novices about camouflage, the film won accolades "for successfully sugar-coating some darned valuable instruction." Other cartoon characters with a serious purpose included Thrust, Gravity, and Drag, teaching aircrews about the principles of flight, and Trigger Joe, an aerial gunner who learned everything through trial and error and more error.[19]

The most memorable cartoon character was Pvt. Snafu, whose moniker explained his soldierly ineptitude. Created by Theodore "Dr. Seuss" Geisel, Pvt. Snafu regularly appeared in *The Army-Navy Screen Magazine*, a biweekly release that epitomized the armed forces' increasingly clever filmmaking, especially through animation and combat film. The producer was Frank Capra, head of the 834th Signal Photographic Detachment and the director of the famous *Why We Fight*, *Know Your Allies*, and *Know Your Enemy* film series, which incorporated some combat footage. Designed "to stimulate morale, patriotism, and the will to win" and to broaden the combatants' perspective on the war, *Screen Magazine* was a twenty-minute potpourri of short subjects, a motion-picture equivalent of *Life*. It featured not only the incompetent Pvt. Snafu but also stories on an appreciative home front supporting the war, a "By Request" segment, a "Few Quick Facts" presenting military statistics in animated form, and combat scenes. The battlefield film updated the war's progress, stressed inter- and intraservice cooperation, and portrayed lessons gleaned from the global battleground.[20]

Along with producing films that kept trainees awake, the armed services also learned to integrate them into a broader training program. They showed movies at appropriate times and insisted that instructors preview a film in advance, introduce it to the trainees, and conduct follow-up activities emphasizing the film's major points. These might include discussing the film's contents, an examination, demonstrations, or letting the trainees practice the task shown in the film.[21]

Although studies found that the amount learned from a training film depended on the audience's educational and intellectual level, in all cases "some learning results from film showing." Research indicated that *good* films were superior to lectures and demonstrations in teaching facts, principles, and skills.[22] Well-crafted movies properly inserted into the training program ensured "that all students, regardless of location, have constant visual access to the latest approved methods as a standard in attaining their training objectives." Army studies also indicated that films reduced training time by as much as 30 percent.[23]

"A great percentage of our boys learned what to do under actual combat conditions the easy way," wrote Major Warren Wade, "through the training films that had been revised with combat footage."[24] As the Assistant to the Executive Producer at SCPC, Major Wade was not unbiased. Yet in this case his bias did not detract from the truth.

Medical training films were a special training-film category that relied heavily upon combat footage. In the 1840s, when photography was in its infancy, physicians used cameras to illustrate diseases and surgical results, and during the Civil War photos of wounds helped to train surgeons.[25] Since the 1860s the advent of motion pictures, slow motion, and color film (which made the differentiation of tissues and organs easier) added to film's virtues in medical training.

Army, AAF, and Navy cameramen all received frequent requests for medical-related photography. As the Navy's Chief of the Bureau of Medicine and Surgery told CINCPAC, his bureau had a "great need for motion pictures and still photographs of certain activities under your command in order to assist us in planning for equipment, supplies and research, and to be used in our training program." He requested film showing medical installations ashore and afloat, wounds of all types, different wound treatments and their results, methods used in evacuating the wounded, special medical problems in different environments, and caring for casualties under battle conditions.[26]

The demand for medical photography kept combat cameramen and special medical photographic units busy. In Italy the 3131st SSB's Donald J. Morrow filmed a story on the 33rd Field Hospital's 1st Platoon, an experimental surgical unit well within enemy artillery range. Consisting of a receiving-ward tent, an X-ray tent, three operating tables, and two recovery-ward tents, the platoon received patients who would die if they did not undergo major surgery promptly. But could a surgical unit survive so close to the enemy lines, and would surgeons be able to operate there effectively? The War Department hoped Morrow's film would supply the answer.[27]

On Morrow's first day on the job the receiving ward "was full of men—all delirious and very badly shot up." Surgeons worked day and night and so did Morrow, who used generator-powered interior lights to film gruesome operations. In one of these surgeons made a full-length belly incision to remove shrapnel, pulling out the man's intestines, liver, and stomach, just "like removing the innards of a chicken." For three days Morrow went virtually without sleep because of heavy cannonading. "The concussion," he scribbled in his diary, "raises the covers on your cot." On the fourth day Morrow moved forward to the 310th Clearing Station Hospital, tucked right against the Gothic Line. "It is here the patients are sorted out and serious and minor cases sent to hospitals handling those cases respectively," he wrote. "We photographed incoming patients and the details of distribution."

Working so close for so long to so many mangled men left Morrow depressed, but the situation got worse when he immediately began making another blood-filled film, this one on the veterinary treatment of wounded mules. By the time he completed the mule picture he was "fed up with seeing and photographing gory operations" and virtually fled from the hospital. "After weeks of seeing human beings and mules in this sort of condition this was too much."

Having used 16mm color film for several years before the war John Moyer fit perfectly into Naval Field Medical Photographic Unit #2, which consisted of five men and which specialized in color films. He joined the outfit in North Africa just before it transferred to Italy, where it photographed in several field hospitals as Allied forces ground their way northward. The unit then went to England, and on D-Day landed at Omaha Beach when the invasion there was still in doubt. During the Normandy campaign Unit #2 was so close to the front that Moyer lost much of his equipment when the Germans overran the field hospital he was filming. After a month of frontline service, the unit returned to England to film follow-up treatment of the wounded for several months before returning to the States with all the film.[28]

Studying medical photography yielded two benefits. First, it led to improved weaponry and equipment. For example, if the pictures revealed numerous leg wounds among AAF bomber crews this indicated the need for better armor in certain sections of the bombers.[29] Second, it allowed rear-area personnel to understand the best methods for preventing diseases and handling casualties. They incorporated their findings into training films such as the Bureau of Medicine and Surgery's ongoing series entitled *The Fundamentals of First Aid* and *Medicine in Action*.[30] Trained in the most modern procedures, medical personnel reduced the disease rate to a fraction of what it had been in

World War I, saved the lives of badly wounded men, and returned the less-severely injured to duty in the shortest possible time. In sum, medical films helped conserve the nation's manpower.

So important were training films that the armed forces operated Hollywood-type studios to produce them. The Army's SCPC was in the Paramount Studio at Astoria, New York; the AAF's FMPU was initially in the Vitagraph Studios but moved to the more spacious Hal Roach Studios in Culver City, California; and the Navy built its PSL to Hollywood standards. SCPC, FMPU, and PSL were, of course, multipurpose facilities. They also produced other types of films, such as documentaries and industrial shorts, and trained combat cameramen.

The service studios produced an increasingly large percentage of training films throughout the war, though industrial filmmakers and Hollywood also made them. At the military's request, armament manufacturers often supplied training films explaining the mechanical operation of their weapons. Industries supplied almost 4,000 reels (each about ten minutes long), more than 1,500 of them for the Navy, which relied more than the other services on industrial firms.[31] In addition, the Navy was Walt Disney Studios' largest customer, ordering from Disney a series of films on fog, wind currents, and ice formations, another series on naval aircraft identification, and a third on warship recognition.[32]

Initially the Army worked closely with the Hollywood studios, a relationship that went back to the early 1930s when the Research Council of the Academy of Motion Picture Arts and Sciences initiated a training program for Signal Corps officers. The large number of recruits who had to be trained after peacetime conscription began in 1940 overwhelmed the Signal Corps's filmmaking facilities, so the Research Council offered to help, agreeing to make films on a "negotiated-contract" nonprofit basis rather than on the basis of competitive bidding. Secretary of War Stimson accepted the offer in mid-December 1940. From the Army's perspective the beauty of the arrangement was that it did not have to deal separately with each producing company but only with the Research Council, which farmed out film contracts to various studios.[33]

The Signal Corps–Research Council partnership became so controversial that it sparked two investigations, one by the Army Inspector General and the other by a Senate committee chaired by Senator

Harry S. Truman. The interrelated issues were the question of education versus entertainment; the possible conflict of interest of Darryl F. Zanuck, who was simultaneously a Signal Corps colonel, chairperson of the Research Council, vice chairperson of the Council's Finance Committee, and a high-salaried executive and major stockholder with 20th Century-Fox, which produced a large number of training films; the near monopoly that a handful of big studios had on making training films; and whether the Army could acquire films more cheaply in its own facilities or through competitive bidding.

As a proponent of making films interesting, Zanuck had aroused the opposition of old-style Army officers, and his multiple positions hinted at conflicts of interest. The Research Council, chaired by Zanuck, allowed just four studios, including Zanuck's 20th-Century Fox, to produce two thirds of the training films, virtually excluding small companies from sharing in the government's largesse. Even worse, Zanuck's nonexistent accounting methods made it impossible to determine how much the government had paid for training films and how much profit the favored studios had made.

Neither the Inspector General nor the Truman Committee discovered any criminal behavior. Zanuck held his multiple positions with the Chief Signal Officer's blessing and received praise from Chief of Staff Marshall, whose integrity was almost superhuman. Small studios failed to receive contracts primarily because they lacked the facilities and personnel to produce high-quality films. While precise figures were hard to calculate, evidence indicated that the studios actually *lost* money producing the training films, which were usually excellent. What the investigations uncovered were some extraordinary arrangements made during an unprecedented emergency, arrangements that violated peacetime proprieties and procedures but were of tremendous benefit to the Army.[34]

Even as the investigations progressed, the emergency abated enough to allow the Signal Corps–Research Council relationship to be severed, eliminating even the appearance of wrongdoing. By early 1943 the war's great crisis period was over, new wartime procedures had been developed, and the Army had established the SCPC, a complete studio staffed with expert filmmakers. With the Research Council's assistance no longer vital, the Army shuffled Zanuck off to less prominent positions, negotiated directly with individual studios for the few Hollywood films it still needed, and began producing most of its own films at the SCPC.[35]

"To secure for the Air Corps the privilege of making its own films was a real battle with the Signal Corps in which the Air Corps emerged bloody but victorious," wrote an AAF officer who had been on the front lines during this brutal intra-Army conflict.[36] By making its own documentary, training, and historical films the AAF took an important step in its campaign toward independence from the Army. For the AAF leaders the most important postwar priority was service autonomy, and they worked assiduously for that goal during the war.[37]

When the war began the Signal Corps provided training films for all three Army commands (Ground Forces, Service Forces, and Air Forces), with the Wright Field Training Film Production Lab devoted to AAF films. But led by "Hap" Arnold, the AAF argued that aerial training films were so specialized that they required separate facilities under its direct control. The AAF Commanding General considered Signal Corps "interference" in this activity intolerable.[38] When the Signal Corps requested information regarding the AAF's training film requirements, the AAF—in a clever ploy— refused to respond, and when the Signal Corps needed airplanes for use in aerial film sequences the AAF deliberately failed to provide them. The AAF then argued that the Signal Corps's inability to provide timely training films and aerial footage proved that only the AAF could make them. The Signal Crops was not fooled. It understood that the main "point of dissension is the fact that the Army Air Forces do not desire to be dependent in any phase whatsoever upon the services of an outside organization," in this case the Signal Corps.[39]

In June 1942, Arnold confirmed the Signal Corps's suspicion that the training-films issue was a means to AAF independence when he wrote to Army Chief of Staff Marshall recommending that the Wright Field Lab be transferred to AAF control and that the AAF assume responsibility for all its own movies and still pictures. Even before receiving a reply the AAF established the FMPU, which the Army considered "an unjustifiable organization."[40] To resolve the issue, Signal Corps and AAF representatives held a conference in the office of Lieutenant General Brehon Somervell, the commander of the Army Service of Supply (the renamed Service Forces). The AAF emerged victorious, since the key decision was that the AAF could establish a photographic studio or studios under Arnold's "exclusive jurisdiction." As a result the Wright Field Lab now came under AAF supervision and was ultimately consolidated with FMPU, which prospered.[41]

II

Film was a vital combat military intelligence source regarding such factors as terrain, Allied and enemy deployments, enemy defenses, equipment, and tactics. As one officer wrote, "A picture is the positive detective—an extra thousand pairs of eyes through which the commander may see the enemy or may see his own troops in action."[42] Officers blessed with this extra vision could not only exploit enemy weaknesses but also mask or remedy their own.

For millennia maps and charts were inaccurate, few in number, and slow and expensive to reproduce. These defects often hindered both tactical and strategic operations. But by World War II maps and charts were far more accurate, and photography made them easy to reproduce quickly. Photographic units assigned cameramen to shoot still pictures of the daily situation maps at division, corps, Army, and Army Group headquarters (and the counterpart AAF and Navy headquarters). Map photos let commanders and intelligence personnel see frontline deployments at a glance and helped provide a uniform understanding of the daily situation to all concerned up and down the chain of command. In the pre-Xerox era, cameramen also photographed Allied and captured enemy documents for rapid duplication and dissemination.[43]

At the tactical-intelligence level photography often replaced or supplemented written or oral reports. A picture or movie scene substituted for many descriptive pages explaining how a piece of equipment performed in battle, and a film sequence invariably portrayed enemy tactics more clearly and briefly than a typical report. Photography was also less likely than a human observer to embody a bias. The camera was a mechanical device, impartially and impersonally recording scenes with greater accuracy and more detail than the human eye could see or the brain recall.[44]

The value of a photograph's accuracy cannot be overestimated. An AAF technical manual even defined photography as "an *accurate* [emphasis added] means of recording information of terrain, individuals, objects, and events." Commander Edward Steichen recounted an incident when enemy planes attacked the U.S.S. *Lexington*. The ship's officers varied considerably in describing what happened. "Later, when the photographs that were made on our ship and the other ships in the task group were assembled and studied," he wrote, "it was found that most of these eyewitness reports were inaccurate." And an AAF officer claimed that if seven men were debriefed, the debriefing officer would "get seven different stories, where just a little picture will tell the whole story."[45]

If possible a conscientious officer made a personal reconnaissance before an attack, but oftentimes this could not be done, in which case photography provided an excellent substitute. Before the invasions of North Africa and Tarawa, for instance, the Navy resorted to photographic reconnaissance, sending a sub to the invasion sites to take shots through the periscope depicting the terrain and beach defenses.[46] On land, cameramen equipped with telephoto lenses peered into enemy territory beyond the range of binoculars and peeped into areas too distant and dangerous to send a patrol. To perform these recon missions photographers took up positions on hills or in woods, buildings, or foxholes that were on the front lines or in advance of them. Marine Corps and Army cameramen also went aloft in Piper Cubs, flying slowly near or over enemy positions.

In Europe, the 163rd SPC's Ralph Thomas crept into an abandoned foxhole at night and then stayed there all the next day, popping up now and then to record a panoramic view of the enemy position. On Okinawa, Robert Albright and several other cameramen photographed Sugar Loaf Hill from as many angles as possible so that commanders could discover a way through the Japanese defenses. On one occasion they went "a little too far and found ourselves behind the Japanese lines." They discovered a way out—but it took them through an enemy minefield. The pictures Albright brought back were so vital that he received a Bronze Star.[47] As for low-level Piper Cub recon, Joe Zinni, Gordon Frye, and many others frequently took to the air. A flight was ordinarily bumpy, everything from rifles to artillery blazed away at such an obvious target, and if an enemy fighter plane appeared, "the one way these little planes get away is by just *diving* for the ground," usually without warning. "My head starts to whirl," Frye wrote to his wife, "my knees push up to my stomach, and my stomach does horrible things—what a thrill!!"[48]

Quickly processed in mobile labs, these tactical-level photos served many purposes. They pinpointed enemy strongpoints, supply depots, troop concentrations, and artillery positions so that they could be either attacked or avoided. Photos also often substituted for maps. The 16th CCU's Clifford Lefferts flew a mission to photograph Japanese artillery along the Salween River in Burma. His prints were soon in the hands of the attacking troops, who expeditiously demolished the enemy gun positions. British General Orde Wingate's February 1944

Burma offensive might not have taken place without the 10th CCU's Detachment #3. Commanded by Irving A. Greenspan, the Detachment was with the British 1st Air Commando Group, which was to support Wingate by landing in gliders behind Japanese lines and then constructing an airstrip. Visual reconnaissance a few days before the glider flight identified two obstacle-free rice paddies for the landings. Uneasy with mere human observation, Greenspan sent a cameramen to take low-level shots of the fields a few hours before the gliders departed. One hour and ten minutes after the photographer returned, Greenspan handed prints to the Air Commando Group revealing that one of the paddies had logs strewn across it, which "would have proven fatal to any attempt to land gliders." Within half an hour the Commandos arranged for all the gliders to land in the other paddy. Their commander wrote that Greenspan's *"QUICK WORK ON RECENT DAY SAVED OUR ENTIRE OPERATION FROM DISASTER WHICH WOULD HAVE COST US LIVES OF MANY OF OUR PEOPLE."*[49]

Low-level-oblique or ground-level panoramic photographs were often superior to military maps. During preparations for the Fifth Army's Italian offensive in the spring of 1944, "tactical commanders found increasing need for photographs of enemy-held terrain." So cameramen supplied 2,116 low-angle-air-oblique and ground shots, resulting in 54,688 prints, which were distributed from Army headquarters down to the platoon level. So many prints were necessary because many soldiers could not read military maps. Looking at a map grid superimposed on the prints, troops could visualize the terrain far more readily than they could from maps alone. Spread right before them were the enemy defenses and the hills, streams, woodlots, and fields they would have to traverse, making it possible for them to "see" the mission objective and to identify the best attack routes. Terrain photos also assisted the artillery in fire-direction control and were of extraordinary value in interrogating prisoners of war. The percentage of prisoners unable to read military maps or understand high-altitude vertical photographs was surprisingly high, noted a Signal Section report, but "when confronted with panoramic pictures of familiar terrain, they readily identified the location of installations, defensive positions, etc." Major General Geoffrey Keyes, the II Corps commander, attested that during the May offensive and in a subsequent drive against the Gothic Line photographs were a vital planning tool for the Corps' staff and all subordinate units.[50]

Once a position had been captured a cameraman's contribution to tactical success was far from over. Cameramen photographed the captured territory in detail, showing terrain contours, bridges, waterways, railroads, highways, ravines, lakes, buildings, and fortifications. Since the enemy sometimes recaptured a position, the Allied armed forces now had a visual record, an advance on-the-ground reconnaissance, upon which to base future assaults. Cameramen also went into enemy pillboxes and observation posts and photographed the American lines from the enemy viewpoint. Commanders studying these photos could then discern the strengths and vulnerabilities of their positions from the enemy's perspective.[51]

After cameramen had photographed the enemy's entrenchments, pillboxes, and camouflage techniques, prints circulated among the troops and intelligence agencies so that they could more easily recognize them at the next encounter. For example, on Iwo Jima Marine Corps cameraman Richard R. Dodds landed with the second wave. For the next three days he remained at the front line, photographing positions as soon as the Marines captured them. He then wrote the coordinates for each emplacement on a map and noted the weapons the Japanese deployed there. Such information was invaluable in calculating likely enemy positions and fields of fire.[52] Another example was the "XXIV Corps Photographic Study: Okinawa Campaign," which emphasized the relationship between terrain and enemy defenses. Since the armed forces expected to have future battles similar to those on Okinawa, the booklet had "been prepared to serve as a guide to photo interpreters and other intelligence agencies preparing for further operations against the Japanese." The enemy's "well-camouflaged underground positions in the dissected terrain" of Okinawa and other Pacific islands made it difficult to locate the Japanese main lines of resistance. "Only a systemized knowledge of enemy defensive methods, their use of terrain, and the limitations and deployment of their materiel will lead to the successful solution to such problems." To assist in acquiring the necessary knowledge, the book contained photos of Japanese pillboxes, machine-gun positions, antitank-gun emplacements, personnel pits, cave defenses, camouflaged supply areas, underground barracks, and captured weapons.[53]

Ground-level photos of enemy positions were also useful for AAF photo interpreters. High-altitude photos often failed to reveal subtle but important natural terrain features and camouflaged man-made positions. By making a comparative study of enemy installations, identified both in high-altitude aerial photos and from the ground, photo interpreters might become more proficient at spotting them. The Army War College's Intelligence Section, for instance, offered comparative photos from Munda (the southwest part of New Georgia island in the Solomon Islands). Although pre-attack interpretations for Munda had been about 90 percent correct, the expectation was that photo interpreters could do even better in the future.[54]

Because photos of hostile equipment could help ensure combat success, pictures were, in the words of a wartime technical intelligence study, "taken, developed, and printed of all new types of [enemy] equipment, fortifications, and operations insofar as possible."[55] Army Ground Forces wanted close-ups of captured armaments showing how they operated, so that American soldiers could use them if necessary.[56] Pictures of weapons could also reveal how to frustrate them. Photography was "highly instrumental" in defeating the V-1 "Buzz Bomb," and in nullifying the Germans' Lichtenstein SN-2 Airborne Interception radar.[57] Film revealed vulnerable features of enemy planes, alerting gunners to aim for those locations. When the 44th Division discovered new German mines on its front, it called on cameramen from the 163rd SPC, since the fastest and surest way to educate other units about the menace was to distribute photographs. Arriving at the Siegfried Line, the 166th SPC photographed various types of tank traps and sent the film to Army headquarters so that officers could devise methods to negate the traps.[58] And Army, AAF, and Navy intelligence agencies jointly dispatched an urgent request to CCUs for pictures of Japanese aircraft so they could "ascertain the new types of Japanese combat equipment so that necessary action may be taken to counteract enemy developments and tactics."[59]

Pictures (or rubbings or drawings) of nameplates from weapons yielded such important data that the War Department established a nameplate-analysis section. Cameramen were to photograph nameplates immediately so as "to win the race against the souvenir hunters and the destroyers of enemy equipment." The War Department also organized the 5250th Technical Intelligence Composite Company, Separate (Provisional) to collect this information. Before going into the field this company went through a training program that included films laced with combat photography on *Japanese Weapons*, *Japanese Small Arms*, and *Japanese Artillery*. Nameplate analysis was "one of the best sources of information regarding the locations, type, and amount of production of aircraft factories and other munitions plants, and of the number of weapons and major items of equipment the enemy has produced." Based on these data, analysts determined air-raid targets and learned much about the enemy's economic status.[60]

If photography taught Americans much about enemy war materiel, it also educated them about their own weapons. The Navy's Bureau of Ordnance requested combat pictures of ammunition being handled, fused, loaded, and fired, of depth charges and mines, and of star shells, rockets, and bombs, knowing that these scenes would be of "great value."[61] Pictures of malfunctioning weapons were often more useful than detailed reports in analyzing the causes of the failure. Cameramen were to photograph unsatisfactory equipment "in such a manner that the photographs will be of assistance in analyzing the reason for failure." Pictures of poorly-operating mortars, for example, provided "a virtual blueprint of changes needed," and photos of armaments damaged in battle revealed their weaknesses, which resulted in improvements.[62]

The anticipated and actual performance of American weapons and techniques could also be gauged from film. How effective would a smokescreen be in shielding an amphibious assault? Cameramen photographed a training rehearsal to find out. When was the most effective time to send supplies ashore after an amphibious assault began? The second wave? Third wave? Sixth wave? Film from previous assaults gave the Navy's Bureau of Supplies and Accounts the answer.[63] Was the A-36 a good dive-bomber? An Air Evaluation Board contingent visited the 12th CCU to view film of the planes in action. Were SHORAN-directed close air-support missions helping the ground troops? Cameramen from the 9th CCU provided GSAP footage so that an accurate assessment could be made.[64] When the AAF initiated the Aphrodite project employing remotely controlled B-17s laden with tons of explosives, the only way to *know* the results was to photograph the missions.[65]

Film made the study of enemy tactics more profitable than relying on eyewitness accounts alone. A prime example was the air war. The AAF high command emphasized photography's tactical value. One document called for a "Continuous, running account in motion pictures" of all bomber, strafing, and fighter missions because movies were "useful in evaluating tactical procedures such as formations before, during and after combat, flak and enemy fighter defenses, methods of approach, new tactics and techniques." The Chief of Air Staff ordered the CCUs to obtain film "for the purpose of analyzing enemy offensive and defensive tactics and the effectiveness of antiaircraft artillery fire." And a third document called for GSAP footage from fighter planes and aerial cinematography from the bombers. The former was vital in keeping "our own fighter techniques efficient" and in ascertaining the "offensive and defensive tactics of enemy fighter and bombardment aviation," while the latter provided material for analyzing enemy tactics and the effect of antiaircraft artillery, and for studying the "disposition of our own tactical formations to meet attacks by enemy fighter aviation."[66]

As film revealed changes in enemy tactics and deployments, the AAF modified its tactics to counter them. Soon, however, the adversary adjusted its methods to frustrate the Americans' new techniques. Photography revealed the enemy adjustments, compelling further tactical innovations. And so it went throughout the war.[67]

Two other invaluable applications of ongoing combat photography were for recognition training and for confirming "kills." Recognizing enemy and Allied weapons quickly under combat conditions permitted soldiers to fire at enemy forces before they got too close and to avoid inflicting "friendly-fire" casualties. The AAF's *Japanese Zero Fighter* used scenes of Zero fighter planes and freeze-frame techniques to teach pilots the features that differentiated the Zero from the American P-40. AAF filmmakers also produced an "Aircraft Recognition Proficiency Examination" featuring motion pictures of U.S., British, German, and Japanese planes in action.[68]

Like the AAF, the Army and Navy emphasized the importance of recognition training. Through their joint *U.S. Army-Navy Journal of Recognition*, published monthly beginning in September 1943, they "tried to present the latest information and best available pictures on various forms of operationally important materiel, both friendly and enemy." Typical stories included "British vs. Jap," which for comparative purposes contained four pictures of the British Hurricane and four of a new Japanese fighter called the Tony, and "Focke-Wulf Versus P-47," featuring five pictures of each plane. Because the P-47 and the Focke-Wulf 190 operated "at the same altitudes at the same time, it is essential that air gunners and pilots recognize them instantly in combat lest our own planes be shot down through carelessness, or enemy planes slip through our defenses." Since both the Allies and the Axis introduced new or modified weapons frequently, the urgent demand for new pictures never ceased. Designed in a *Life*-like format, the *Journal of Recognition* featured airplanes, warships, merchantmen, landing craft, tanks, self-propelled artillery, armored cars, and much more, all in an urgent effort to reduce tragic friendly-fire incidents and to "kill" the enemy.[69]

And how could authorities be sure that the enemy had in fact been "killed"? Whether on land, in the air, or on the sea, film often confirmed—or disproved—the claims of excited combatants that they had killed or damaged the enemy. For example, *The Fighting Lady's* narration noted that GSAPs recorded, "as no human eye and memory could record, just what our guns and bombs do to the enemy. These pictures enable our air combat intelligence officers to assess the damage as we swoop down upon Tinian." Knowing the extent of enemy losses not only prevented additional strikes against targets that had already been destroyed, but also helped intelligence agencies keep abreast of the enemy's order of battle.[70]

III

The military intelligence that battlefield film revealed was of greatest value if it could be disseminated throughout the armed forces, especially to rear-area staff officers who, paradoxically, rarely saw or participated in combat yet often made crucial decisions about the related factors of training, weapons, tactics, and strategy. Not surprisingly, the solution to disseminating vital information obtained from photography was to produce specialized types of combat films. A statement on combat film as it related to Chief of Staff Marshall observed that "In the final analysis, motion pictures must bring to his staff the war that is now spread all over the world."[71]

The Army produced *Staff Film Reports, Combat Bulletins, Film Bulletins, Technical Film Bulletins,* and *Project Technical Film Bulletins.* The secret *Staff Film Report* began in early 1944, appeared weekly thereafter, and consisted almost exclusively of combat photography. A *Report* usually ran about twenty minutes and dealt with at least half a dozen subjects. For example, *Report #1* showed a smokescreen; new combat clothing worn at Anzio; the repulse of an attack on Bougainville that showed flamethrowers in action and the interrogation of Japanese prisoners; protecting hospitals with sandbags and ditches; and amphibious assault training in England for the upcoming D-Day invasion. *Report #12* demonstrated the weather's influence by showing the effects of a Burmese monsoon; explained how the

Japanese use of naval mines on land created new mine-clearing problems; portrayed operations along the Gothic Line; discussed Karachi's importance as a supply base; and detailed the fighting in Normandy such as the capture of La-Haye-du-Puits, the British attack on Caen, and German equipment.[72]

All overseas theater staffs (including Allied staffs), the General Staff in Washington, and the staffs of Army Ground Forces, AAF, Army Service Forces, the Navy, and the Marines, saw the *Reports*, guaranteeing that staff officers in all services everywhere viewed "the most important happenings on all fronts and the latest developments in techniques and equipment." In essence, the *Staff Film Reports* were a liaison among the different theaters and between field commanders and military administrators, bridging the gap between the frontline warriors and the uniformed rear-area bureaucrats, who might otherwise misunderstand the battlefield's violent "language" and tribulations, and misperceive the terrain and climate in different regions. The APS considered the *Reports* its most valuable film contribution and the Chief Signal Officer agreed.[73]

In a sanitized form that omitted all sensitive intelligence material, the *Staff Film Reports* went to the troops at home and overseas as weekly *Combat Bulletins*, which were "the Army's own newsreel." Through frontline photography, the *Bulletins* emphasized "lessons learned in combat pertaining to teamwork, leadership, and adaptations to battle conditions, as well as to experience in the use of weapons, equipment, techniques, and local expedients. Both correct and incorrect practices will be pointed out." The Bulletins served "as a medium for exchanging experiences and training information between theaters of operations, as well as for training troops in the continental United States."[74] As with *Staff Film Reports, Combat Bulletins* employed sound effects and a narration.

Film Bulletins illustrated new equipment and weapons and recent developments in procedures and techniques, including some that worked but were not based on approved War Department doctrine. The first *Film Bulletin* appeared in 1942, and new issues appeared sporadically till war's end, approximately 200 of them in all, from six to forty-seven minutes in length. A few of the subjects were tank obstacles, smoke defense against air attack, camouflage dummies and decoys (in color), German infantry small arms, Japanese grenades and mines, medical services in the jungle, and the reduction of Japanese cave-type fortifications.[75]

To take advantage of the increasingly large amount of combat footage, in the fall of 1944 the War Department inaugurated two *Film Bulletin* variants. A *Project Technical Film Bulletin* was "a compilation of the best combat footage on any particular subject," often demonstrating tentative tactical conclusions or provisionally accepted equipment. If the subject proved particularly important and additional footage was available, a *Project Technical Film Bulletin* became a more comprehensive *Technical Film Bulletin*. To get these film reports to the troops quickly, most had brief captions and an accompanying written commentary but no sound track. By mid-1945 160 *Project Technical Film Bulletins* and ten *Technical Film Bulletins* had been produced on subjects ranging from "Frontline Chaplain" to "Flame Thrower Tactics."[76]

The Army was not alone in using motion pictures to disseminate intelligence. The AAF Combat Film Detachment in New York, which was the initial recipient of all CCU footage, produced *Combat Film Reports*, *Combat Weekly Digests*, and *Combat Film Subjects*. *Film Reports* depicted "the performance of men and materiel and the conditions under which the two work. They show procedures, modifications, and improvisations dictated by field conditions." If training films indicated how things *should* be done, the *Reports* showed how they *were* done. While collectively they covered a range of subjects, individual *Film Reports* presented "a unified treatment of material on a given strategic, tactical, or technical subject: and its purpose is to *inform*." The releases had a running time from as little as three minutes to as long as forty-five minutes.[77]

Weekly Digests were broader compilations than the *Reports*, while *Combat Film Subjects* were more narrow. *Weekly Digest #77*, for instance, had scenes of a P-80 (a new jet-aircraft prototype) taking off and landing, the search for a missing B-29, bombing attacks in the Philippines and Borneo, an improvised wheel dolly for changing tires on heavy bombers, aerial supply of partisans in France, Italy, and Yugoslavia, fighter kills, and bomb damage. Most *Weekly Digests* were about twenty minutes long, and often incorporated material that originally appeared in the *Film Reports*. The AAF produced relatively brief *Film Subjects* from December 1942 until September 1945, each containing footage on a specific topic, such as a supply mission or bomb damage to a particular locale.[78] The other services relied on analagous productions, including the Navy's *Combat Communiques* and the Marine Corps' *Combat Reports*.[79]

Intelligence dissemination occurred not only in motion pictures but also in still photos. The *U.S. Army-Navy Journal of Recognition* had a low-level security classification so that it could be widely disseminated. "This material," the *Journal* implored readers, "should be circulated among the fighters in the area just as rapidly as possible...."[80] In early 1945 the Army issued a 635-page classified *Handbook on German Military Forces* covering the enemy's organization, weapons, equipment, uniforms, tactics, fortifications, and defenses. When published in 1990 it featured an introduction by military historian Stephen E. Ambrose, who wrote that the "information it contains was exactly what men about to enter combat against the German Army needed." Ambrose praised the volume's clear writing and logical organization and noted that the "superb photographs speak for themselves." Dozens of them portrayed every aspect of the adversary—defenses ranging from tank obstacles to mobile steel pillboxes, weaponry from Lugers to tanks, equipment from gunner's quadrants to shortwave receivers, uniforms, and much more, all providing an accurate vision of what front line soldiers would encounter.[81]

As a final example, the Office of the Assistant Chief of Air Staff, Intelligence, published *Impact,* a classified monthly magazine, from April 1943 through September 1945. In the first issue Assistant Secretary of War for Air Lovett, AAF Commanding General Arnold, and *Impact*'s editor explained the project. Lovett had suggested to Arnold "that the value of classified aerial photography could be increased if disseminated in a regular manner" and recommended "a periodical devoted mainly to photographic portrayal of the methods and results of our operations, so that Air Force units and the Army as a whole might be kept informed of current developments." Arnold enthusiastically endorsed the secretary's concept as a means of giving the AAF information about itself and its enemies "in the form easiest to absorb—photography." As summed up by editor Edward K. Thompson, who subsequently edited *Life* and *Smithsonian,* the journal was "a medium for the dissemination, in graphic form, of air intelligence and correlated subjects."[82]

Impact fulfilled its mission, spreading 3,436 photographs over 1,730 pages in its thirty issues. The photo story headlines indicated the accompanying photographs. Typical headlines included "Air Photos Emphasize Campaign Lessons: New Guinea Air-Land Offensive Is Made More Realistic By Pictorial Study," "Study in Contrast Between Ground, Air Photographs," "P-47's Methods for Meeting (and

Evading) Rear Attack," and "Gun Cameras Enhance Value of the Kill: P-39 Tactics Against Japs Revealed by Films."[83]

———

When the Air Force Historical Foundation reprinted *Impact* in eight volumes in 1980 James Parton, who had been General Eaker's executive officer, wrote an introductory essay for the series explaining the magazine's origins and use. He praised the many "extraordinarily dramatic and instructive" photos that, he wrote, reflected "the remarkable talent" of the *editor*. Parton said nothing about the cameramen who had generated the photographs for the editor's selection.[84]

IV

Edwin P. Ramsey was one of the few Americans who did not surrender on Bataan. Instead he fled into Luzon's wilderness, helped organize Filipino resistance, and waged guerrilla warfare against the Japanese until American forces returned. By then Major Ramsey was suffering from malaria, amoebic dysentery, anemia, and acute malnutrition; he weighed only ninety-five pounds (down from 160), and was close to a nervous breakdown. Everyone at MacArthur's headquarters understood the role that Ramsey and his Filipino guerrillas had played in paving the way for the U.S. invasion by bleeding the occupation force. Now Ramsey was about to meet one of MacArthur's generals, Robert Beightler, whose jeep screeched to a halt in Meycauayan. As General Beightler alighted to shake hands with the bedraggled major he yelled to a reporter and a photographer, "Over here, snap it up!" Beightler struck a heroic pose while clasping Ramsey's hand as the cameraman took two shots. Then, brusquely brushing off Ramsey's pleas for rations for his ill, ravenous troops, Beightler hopped back in the jeep and sped off, no doubt searching for the next photo opportunity. Ramsay was furious. "My men were starving," he wrote, "but in his rush to make headlines the general would not spare us a mouthful of food."[85]

Ramsey had just confronted a phenomenon that most photographers witnessed repeatedly. For the high-ranking brass one of the most important purposes of combat photography was to generate pictures of them. To ensure that such photos were plentiful, combat camera units usually had to assign one of their men as the commander's personal photographer. Not only were the resulting pictures useful in promoting one's ego and career, but they also generated favorable publicity for the officer's service or branch or even his particular command. As the 162nd SPC's Jerry Kahn discovered, his initial assumption that SPC cameramen worked for the U.S. Army was wrong because "we were actually working as publicity men for a particular general and his troops."[86]

Although picking the top three publicity seekers necessitates excluding many worthy candidates, Generals Mark Clark, Douglas MacArthur, and George Patton win the contest. Their pursuit of photographic fame bordered on megalomania. "Photographed General Clark over at Fifth Army Headquarters this afternoon," Don Morrow wrote in his diary. "He is a big bastard & like most generals his head is big, too." He presented Medals of Honor to two GIs but insisted that the photographers "shoot so as to get a front view of his face—which gave us a rear view of the GIs. I can speak for all Signal Corps Photographers when I say that if we had our way General Clark would be one of the most unphotographed Generals in the Army." But they did not have their way. And woe to any cameraman who shot Clark so that his general's stars did not show! Few if any candid photos of MacArthur exist. Bill Avery encountered the general at a training exercise. Seeing the cameraman, MacArthur "immediately adjusted his hat to a jaunty angle, brought out his pipe, and started pointing." Avery took a dozen shots from different angles. "When I had completed the shots he asked me, 'Would you like to have some more, son?'" When Patton came ashore in Sicily from a command-ship conference, the 5th CPU was "ready for a 'grab shot,' or a picture taken on the fly. But not so with the General. Seeing the movie cameras grinding and the bulbs flashing, he stopped, adjusted his helmet, and gave us a smile. Then climbing aboard the command car, turned and grinned again."[87]

Paul Fussell has argued that World War II "was uniquely the Publicity War." Competition among the armed forces for favorable publicity was intense as each service organized a public-relations bureaucracy to further its organizational and budgetary interests.[88] Photography was always a significant factor in this endeavor. Most of the wartime documentaries reflected glowingly upon the service that made them, and each of the armed forces tried to get more newsreel coverage than the others. After seeing *The Battle of Midway* a reviewer wrote that if the film did not make a person "run to the nearest Navy recruiting office it isn't blood that runs in your veins." The importance of photographing AAF activities "cannot be stressed too strongly," wrote AAF Lieutenant General George E. Stratemeyer. "Such authentic presentations are of great assistance in establishing a powerful, influential and effective air force for the security of our country." The Navy created an office to produce special newsreel features as a means to get more naval footage on the big screen. But no service generated more publicity than the Marine Corps. In what may qualify as the understatement of the twentieth century, Marine public relations officer William P. McCahill acknowledged that "the Marine Corps came out of the war certainly in much better shape, PR-wise, than when it went in."[89]

Privates as well as generals loved pictorial publicity. Seeing pictures of themselves, their friends, their units, or at least their theater of operations was instrumental in maintaining their morale, convincing them that they were not anonymous and forgotten. "Nothing makes a fellow feel good," wrote McCahill, "whether he is a colonel or a private first class, than getting clippings from home with a picture and a story all about what he did, heroic or otherwise." Films, wrote General Ingles, "have a high morale value. The soldiers like to see operations that they themselves were engaged in." General Eaker agreed, asserting that the CCUs were "a prime factor in promoting the morale of our combat crews by depicting much of the remarkable work they are accomplishing."[90]

Troop reactions confirmed the officers' perceptions. After the release of Don Morrow's movies of a tank destroyer unit, its members showered him with candy, Cokes, and beer. "They fought their way through Africa, Sicily, and Italy," Morrow explained, "and yet this was their first publicity." Pictures of Darby's Rangers in Stars and Stripes and The New York Times gave the men who basked momentarily in the national spotlight "a new surge of pride and spirit at a crucial time when many were beginning to doubt the wisdom of joining the Rangers." Marauder Mission spotlighted the 323rd Bombardment Group, and when its members saw it they "cheered their own field and aircraft, howled with glee at recognizing self and friends on the screen, and laughed nervously as the flak popped closer than they like to see it." After the 81st Division's morale plummeted because the men felt that their role in conquering the Palau Islands had been slighted, APS produced Action at Angaur detailing the division's performance. The documentary had the intended tonic effect, especially since the Treasury Department used it in the Seventh War Loan Drive.[91]

Major Kenneth MacKenna stayed in the United States working with APS, a bit envious of those frontline photographers who would "spend an old age telling brave tales of heroic adventure." But he was also proud of the job he was doing. After all, those in the stateside military photographic community who transformed raw combat celluloid into its many usable formats were "wielding one of the most powerful and effective weapons that this Army employs against our enemies. That weapon is *film*."[92]

14

"Pix for a Price"

Casualties—and the War's Historical Image

Don Morrow and some of his photographic colleagues in Italy were tired of frontline troops derisively teasing them about being "rear-echelon men," so they did a little checking. Line infantry units normally had about 10 percent casualties, they learned, but photographers took 25 percent casualties.[1] The source of Morrow's information, which showed the infantrymen who the *real* combatants were, remains unknown. Perhaps he and his friends just sat around a stove one wintry night and, based on nothing more substantive than limited personal knowledge reinforced by an enormous amount of hearsay, concocted the percentages. If so they guessed reasonably well, though a bit low for photo outfits.

Perhaps the underestimation resulted from Morrow's misuse of the word "casualties." He referred only to cameramen killed and wounded in battle, but the term *casualties* includes both battle and nonbattle casualties. The former are those killed, wounded, or missing in action (KIA, WIA, or MIA) while the latter encompass individuals who suffer from disease or illness while in the battle zone or from injuries not directly attributable to enemy action. Although often overlooked, nonbattle casualties have a significant impact on military strength. Whether a person has died from an enemy bullet, pneumonia, or a jeep accident, troop strength had been depleted by one.

During World War II, for the first time in U.S. history, more men died from battle than from nonbattle causes. In the Civil War 200,000 soldiers were KIA but twice that number died from disease. By World War I the ratio was about even, with the Army suffering 50,000 battle and 56,000 nonbattle deaths (51,500 from disease, 4,500 from nonbattle injuries). In World War II 306,000 soldiers died—230,000 KIA and "only" 76,000 from nonbattle causes. The Army also had 16,745,000 hospital admissions for medical reasons, 16,145,000 of them for nonbattle causes.[2]

If the seventeen photographers featured here were representative, had Morrow included MIAs and nonbattle casualties his percentages would have been much higher. Six men (Caliendo, Joswick, Bray, Maslowski, Hatch, and Claveria) went through the war relatively unscathed, at least physically. One (Genaust) was KIA, seven (Frye, Herz, Chaney, Colgrove, Genaust, Watkins, and Friedman) were WIA, and one (Chaney) was MIA. Two (Frye and Colgrove) received injuries requiring medical attention and six (Avery, Ettinger, Goetzheimer, Chaney, Colgrove, and Jones) suffered seriously from disease or illness. In percentages, 35 percent of them were unharmed, 53 percent were battle casualties, and 47 percent were nonbattle casualties. The percentages total more than 100 percent because some men fit into multiple categories. Chaney was WIA and MIA during the same incident and later developed an intestinal tumor that sent him to a hospital, while Colgrove was ill and injured in China and then WIA in the Philippines.

Evidence indicates that this group was broadly representative. Norman Hatch believed his Marine Corps Photo Section had "pretty close to 50 percent casualties, wounded or dead" on Iwo Jima and the 6th Marine Division Photo Section had 37 percent (fourteen out of thirty-eight) killed or wounded during the first two months on Okinawa.[3] While serving in Sicily, Italy, and Southern France, the OIC of CPU #10, Dewey Wrigley, received two wounds, and two out of his three men also wore Purple Hearts.[4] Out in the Pacific all four members of CPU #3 had malaria in the fall of 1944, capping a succession of infections and illnesses that earned its OIC a stern lecture from a doctor "about the poor physical condition the men were in."[5] Between August 1943 and September 1944, fifteen of the 8th CCU's cameramen were battle casualties.[6] Six men who served in the 163rd SPC were KIA and one died in a jeep accident (one of 12,000 GIs killed in military-vehicle accidents during the war). Another 30, not all of them cameramen, received Purple Hearts, and some received more than one. Photographer Edward H. Peterson, for example, had a Purple Heart accompanied by three Oak Leaf Clusters.[7]

Casualties were so frequent that those who escaped unscathed marveled at the "fantastic and miraculous luck that got us out so often where others never got back."[8] Amid their collective anguish the survivors struggled to find solace as their friends went to their graves. Those who die, said an editorial in the 163rd SPC's weekly newsletter, "continue to live in the total life of their country. As long as America lives, they also live. In that sense, the Americans who die on the field of battle are immortal."[9]

Those immortals and their struggle to preserve America lived on in the wartime film, which reached staggering proportions. The question of how much film American military combat photographers shot between Pearl Harbor and the Japanese surrender cannot be answered precisely. Either the services did not systematically compile the necessary data, or if they did the records have not survived. Yet enough information exists to provide insight into the magnitude of the photographic effort.

The APS Still Picture Library in the Pentagon received 16,000 negatives between December 1941 and June 30, 1942; 28,000 in Fiscal Year (FY) 1943; 110,00 in FY 1944; 142,000 in FY 1945; and 56,000 between July and October 1945 (which fell in FY 1946).[10] These 352,000 negatives, however, represent less than the total number of still pictures taken. Not only did combat losses detract from the total, but editors often destroyed duplicate or technically imperfect negatives rather than forward them to APS.

Army motion-picture production also accelerated throughout the war. Between June 1942 and late February 1943 APS received 500,000 feet of film, but this escalated to 2,400,000 feet in FY 1944 and exploded to 9,100,000 feet in FY 1945.[11]

As with the Army, AAF photographic activities built to a crescendo in 1945. After shooting a negligible amount of film in 1942 the CCUs produced 597,000 feet of film in 1943, 1,962,000 in 1944, and approximately 2,500,000 feet in the first eight months of 1945.[12] These totals are low because editors disposed of some poor-quality film and combat claimed a considerable amount. The 6th CCU, for instance, reported

8,980 feet for December 1944, but that did not include the film lost when three cameramen were shot down returning from a mission.[13]

Although their primary concern was with movies, the CCUs also took stills. In December 1944 the 2nd CCU submitted 1,245 negatives, but such a large number was exceptional. The 1st CCU took as few as 100 and as many as 350 still pictures per month, the 5th CCU's figures ranged from "nil" to 660, and the 6th CCU reported a low of 77 and a high of 457. Combined, the CCUs produced thousands of negatives per month during 1944–45.[14]

The conversion of negatives and footage into usable products resulted in enormous numbers of prints. Each field army or army group, for instance, had an SOP guiding the number of prints made from each negative. The 12th Army Group required ten 4 × 5 prints and seven 8 × 10s, the 7th Army needed seven 4 × 5s and five 8 × 10s, and the 1st Allied Airborne Army wanted six 4 × 5s and five 8 × 10s.[15] These prints added up in a hurry. By the fall of 1944 the 163rd SPC lab was making at least 30,000 prints per month and the 166th's lab another 28,000.[16] Rear-area labs also made prints. Between January 1943 and July 1945 the APS Base Lab in London distributed more than 1,000,000 prints and the Paris Lab almost 500,000. In the States, the Signal Corps Photographic Lab made 895,000 prints in FY 1944 and 1,041,000 in FY 1945, while the Still Picture Library supplied 646,000 prints in FY 1945.[17] One authority estimated that toward war's end the armed forces as a whole made *twenty million prints per month!*[18]

Motion-picture film, like still-picture negatives, can be copied. Although APS received 2,400,000 feet of motion-picture film in FY 1944 it actually processed 20,800,000 feet, and in FY 1945 the number rose to 25,000,000 feet. Meanwhile the London APS lab and the United Kingdom commercial labs printed a combined total of 25,100,000 feet during the war.[19] And the Army utilized many other motion-picture labs that processed many more millions of feet.

Determining exactly how many cameramen served in the SPCs, SSBs, CCUs, CPUs, and Marine Corps Division Photo Sections is in many cases an impossibly complicated task. Not only are surviving records incomplete, but photo unit personnel, and the units themselves, were constantly shifting. Occasionally photo organizations were over strength, but ordinarily they were under strength, and the Marines never had a T/O&E for their Photo Sections, so an outfit's authorized strength is rarely an accurate guide to its actual strength. Sometimes units temporarily "borrowed" cameramen for a battle or campaign; these "loaners" may or may not appear in any official records. Tracing individual interunit transfers, such as Karl H. Maslowski transferring from the 9th to the 12th CCU, is often difficult because of incomplete records. Almost as puzzling can be the fate of entire units such as the 162nd SPC, which initially served as a cadre for other units, then deployed overseas, and was finally absorbed by the 3908th SSB.[20] Keeping track of replacements for photographers who were killed, discharged because of wounds, injuries, or illness, or transferred to other duties, can be equally challenging. Although the task was easy for CPU #1, which originally had four men but gained two new ones when reconstituted, identifying the replacements in such a small unit was significantly easier than it was for a 150-man Army SPC or even a 30-man AAF CCU for which only sporadic records exist.

Having said that, some calculated estimates are in order. Considering the T/O&Es and taking the above factors into account, the SPCs and SSBs contained about 1,330 photographers throughout the war. Probably not more than 350 cameramen served in the CCUs, approximately ninety officers and men were in the CPUs, and 430 Marines did photographic combat duty in the Pacific.

It warrants emphasis that these units were only parts, albeit extremely influential ones, of a larger photographic effort. The Army, for example, had more than 3,000 photographic personnel (including, of course, lab personnel and other technicians) overseas on June 30, 1945, and the Navy had more than 3,000 enlisted personnel alone assigned to photographic duties by March 1944, with one third working at PSL or doing photo interpretation and two thirds performing operational duties.[21]

I

Late in the war the 163rd SPC's *Foto-Facto* ran a story under the headline "Pix for a Price." The price paid was in blood. "Three 163rd photographers went down under German fire this week," the article reported, including one who had just recently been released from a hospital. Fortunately none of the wounds were serious.[22]

Aside from the bloodstains on the celluloid, did the World War II pictorial record have a different price tag attached? Has it helped mold the American vision not just of World War II, but of all war? Is that vision accurate? Answers to such questions must be speculative, since no methodology exists to measure photography's impact with precision. Still, such speculation may not be altogether idle.

Cameramen believed they were "the real historians of their time and place" and that they were making a living record of the war "for posterity's sake."[23] The armed forces as institutions were also history minded. They believed that history was their "laboratory," the one place where they could test theories and doctrines against experience. As an early twentieth-century Officer's Manual phrased it, "all study of war, strategy, tactics, military supplies and transport, and every other branch, brings us sooner or later to the study of Military History."[24] Unlike all previous eras, however, by World War II historical memory no longer depended on the written word alone. "After-action reports and other historical documents," wrote an officer, "when graphically illustrated by motion-picture film, acquire additional meaning."[25]

Consequently, the armed forces began systematically compiling historical film documents before the war ended. In late summer 1944, AAF Commanding General "Hap" Arnold ordered FMPU to reorder its priorities from training films to an AAF motion-picture history. Arnold was not interested in academic-style "objective" history. His film history, which would educate "future airmen and trainees, most of whom shall not have known this war," should "set forth factually and irrefutably" air power's vital significance and "hammer home the lesson that during the next peace there must be no check placed on a forward thinking, planning and acting Air Force—an Air Force that will be able to ward off the blow of any aggressor nation and simultaneously press home the attack."[26]

The Army, too, avidly pursued film history and began creating Theater Chronologies for future study and reference. Each chronology was a pictorial record of an individual campaign. Officers involved in producing them believed they would be a priceless record for "historians and for the military student in particular." Before the Axis nations surrendered, some chronologies had already been used as instructional tools at West Point and at Army service schools, such as the Command and General Staff School at Fort Leavenworth. APS was confident that the films would "continue to complement the textual material normally used for instruction," and that they would eventually be made "accessible to many government agencies and nongovernmental organizations for official and educational purposes."[27]

Impelled by the demands of the home front and the fighting fronts and by a sense of history, the cameramen preserved the war for posterity, and posterity has utilized their film repeatedly. Fifty years later, World War II footage appears almost nightly on television, and bookstores brim with heavily-illustrated histories. The Second World War lives in the collective American memory as if it had occurred only yesterday, the memory remaining so vivid that it has almost blotted out the history of American wars before and after 1941–1945, eradicating the past's complexity and variety. The exception to this nearly complete amnesia is the Civil War, which of all our other American wars most closely resembled World War II.

The Second World War's pictorial record has become analogous to a family photo album. In compiling a family album people make decisions about what images to preserve, about what they *want* to remember about their past and what they want others to remember about it[28]—birthdays (at least until age thirty or so), weddings, vacations, graduations, Thanksgiving dinner—good times, smiling faces, pleasant memories. People prefer to recall a happy past shorn of uncertainty, heartache, ugliness.

Despite occasional efforts by novelists and niggling historians to remind people that the war was not altogether wonderful, Americans recall World War II as The Good War with few "ifs, ands, or buts." Though the war's image has certainly acquired a sheen in the postwar decades, this perception is reasonably accurate. The crusade was against palpable evil—who can doubt the black hearts of the Nazi murderers or the Japanese militarists? The 163rd SPC's Joe Boyle perfectly expressed the collective attitude about the war's righteousness: "Holy God, thank the Lord that the Allies won the war because what would this world be like had the other side won?"[29] The war was wonderfully straightforward, in that the Allies fought for unconditional surrender, placed few restraints on the use of military force, and engaged in no morale-sapping, time-consuming negotiations with obstinate enemies. Comprehending the war's progress was easy as Allied forces steadily recaptured towns and territory, with joyous throngs greeting the liberators every step of the way. Since the Allies annihilated both German and Japanese power, the conflict left no ambiguity about who had won, about whether American aims had been fulfilled.

And the war's purported lessons were seductively simple. The commentary for *Victory at Sea*, the massive 1952 documentary that is still shown on television and available on VHS cassette, emphasized the fundamental "lessons" Americans learned about warfare from World War II. One was that "War is an act of force, and to the application of that force there is no limit, say the philosophers of war." A second was embodied in a series of equations: "Tarawa, Kwajalein, Eniwetok, *war*. Tarawa, Kwajalein, Eniwetok, *sacrifice*. Tarawa, Kwajalein, Eniwetok, *victory*." War equals sacrifice, which equals victory.[30]

The war's impact was so overpowering that citizens—ordinary lay people and high-ranking military officers, government leaders and leading scholars—not only embraced these lessons but also perceived World War II as typifying *the* American way of war. Reading the presumed lessons of World War II into the past, they argued that Americans had always preferred to wage unlimited total war, that they had always believed that "the complete overthrow of the enemy, the destruction of his military power, is the object of war," and that "most American strategists, through most of the time span of American history, [were] strategists of annihilation."[31]

In short, World War II was seen as the normal American way to wage war—to the hilt, with bipartisan support at home and without any politically-imposed limits on the exercise of violence in pursuit of the enemy's annihilation.

Considering this perception, more typical American-style wars such as Korea and Vietnam came as quite a shock.

The problem with featuring World War II and its presumed lessons in the American photo album is that its "lessons" were not universally applicable because that war was unique.

War is not simply an act of force waged without limit, as *Victory at Sea* suggested. The single most profound philosopher of war, the Prussian Karl von Clausewitz (1780–1831), postulated that war was "a continuation of political activity by other means." A nation wages war in pursuit of a policy objective; war is simply "the means of reaching it, and means can never be considered in isolation from their purpose." Nor could war—the means to an end—be divorced from its historical context, since the particular form a war took resulted "from ideas, emotions, and conditions prevailing at the time...." As the Prussian astutely recognized, "every age had its own kind of war, its own limiting conditions, and its own preconceptions," so "the events of every age must be judged in the light of their own peculiarities." Each war, in short, occurred within the context of its own singular circumstances.[32]

Clausewitz emphasized that wars varied "with the nature of their motives and of the situations which give rise to them," that "without any inconsistency wars can have all degrees of importance and intensity, ranging from a war of extermination down to simple armed observations." He understood that many roads could lead to success "and they do not all involve the opponent's outright defeat. They range from *the destruction of the enemy's forces, the conquest of his territory, to a temporary occupation or invasion, to projects with an immediate political purpose, and finally to passively awaiting the enemy's attacks.* Any one of these may be used to overcome the enemy's will: the choice depends on circumstances." Fundamentally, then, wars vary in magnitude and duration depending on the importance of the political objective and the general spirit or characteristics of the era in which they occur.[33] A large political objective such as national survival demands the utmost exertion. A lesser objective that did not directly involve the nation's fate, such as trying to preserve a non-Communist South Korea or a non-Communist South Vietnam, does not warrant an all-out effort.

The other supposed lesson, that of war and sacrifice followed by inevitable victory, was also faulty. Sometimes the equation is "war equals sacrifice, equals stalemate" as in the Quasi-War against France, the War of 1812, and the Korean conflict, or "war equals sacrifice, equals defeat" as in Vietnam. As the history of virtually every nation confirms, any of three equations, not just one, is applicable to warfare.

Two characteristics, never present in exactly the same mixture, have dominated all American wars except World War II. One was home front dissent by vociferous minorities. Since war is a *political* act the question of whether or not to go to war is a matter of political judgment, which may or may not be sound. In America's highly-educated and open society, vocal elements, often centered in the opposition political party, have usually questioned the judgment of the political leadership that committed the country to war: Tories during the Revolution; Jeffersonian Republicans during the Quasi-War; Federalists during the War of 1812; Whig politicans, abolitionists, and anti-expansionist Southern Democrats during the Mexican War; Copperhead Democrats in the North and Unionists in the South (approximately 100,000 Southerners fought *for* the Union) during the

Civil War; anti-imperialists during the Philippine–American War; socialists, pacifists, and anti-conscription elements during World War I; Republicans during the Korean War; a broad liberal coalition during the Vietnam War. Only two brief and quickly successful wars (the Spanish–American War and the recent United-Nations-sponsored action against Iraq) and World War II have been unaffected by significant home-front dissent. Therefore, when President Ronald Reagan, who served at FMPU throughout World War II, argued in 1984 that "We must restore America's honorable tradition of partisan politics stopping at the water's edge," he was projecting a romanticized past, since that condition existed *only* during the Second World War.[34]

The second prevalent characteristic of American wars has been that of limited aims pursued through limited war, aims that did not seek the enemy's annihilation as a precondition for peace. Beginning with the Quasi-War, which was the first international war waged under the Constitution, and continuing through the war with Iraq, most conflicts have been "mitigated" (to use Secretary of War James McHenry's word describing the conflict with France). They required neither the enemy's utter prostration nor the complete overthrow of the adversary's political system. As a result the wars ordinarily ended not with a bang, with the enemy's abject submission, but with a whimper in a negotiated armistice or peace: the Convention of 1800 with France; the Treaty of Ghent in 1814 with England; the Treaty of Guadalupe Hidalgo in 1848 with Mexico; the Treaty of Paris in 1898 with Spain; President Theodore Roosevelt's unilateral declaration on July 4, 1902, that the Philippine–American War was over; the armistice of November 11, 1918, with Germany, followed by the Treaty of Versailles the next year; the Korean armistice of July 27, 1953, after two years of angry negotiations; the peace accords signed with North Vietnam and the Viet Cong in January 1973 after prolonged, acrimonious negotiations.

World War II stands alone in the American experience. With national survival seemingly at stake, with the cause so unimpeachably just and necessary, home-front support between 1941 and 1945 was virtually unanimous in pursuit of the enemies' unconditional surrender. Only the Civil War rivaled World War II in the totality of its aims (like Germany and Japan, the Confederate States of America was annihilated) and no other war was so devoid of outspoken opposition.

The extensive World War II photographic record has permitted Americans to relive this unique war again and again, repeatedly reinforcing the collective historical memory. Television and VCR technologies have been especially influential in expanding the use of wartime motion pictures by making them readily available and familiar at all levels of society. And because motion pictures mate sight and sound, they can have a more intense impact than still photos. Sitting in their darkened dens and family rooms, people watch the same newsreels and documentaries that appeared on the home front during "the" war. For fifty years World War II has remained frozen in time, devoid of those fresh and searching historical perspectives that the passing decades ordinarily bring to events, even such momentous ones as "the Good War."

The depression Don Morrow experienced on his first day at the front soon turned to exhilaration, and even the subsequent knowledge of the high casualty rate among cameramen never stifled his enthusiasm. Like so many other photographers, he loved his wartime mission.

"There is something wonderful about the feeling one gets when he picks his scene, time, and place and presses that button," he noted in his diary on July 4, 1944, shortly after he had photographed the official raising of the American flag in liberated Rome. "When he knows, as in this case, that he has picked a moment out of time of which historians, great people, and just ordinary people, millions of people will see. The people of today, of my time, and the people of tomorrow, and the tomorrows thereafter will see this historic moment that I saw. They will see it through my eyes."[35]

ABBREVIATIONS USED IN THE NOTES AND BIBLIOGRAPHY

AAF   Army Air Force

AC   *American Cinematography*

AC/AS   Assistant Chief/Air Staff

AFHRA   Air Force Historical Research Agency (Maxwell Air Force Base, AL)

AP   *American Photography*

APS   Army Pictorial Service

BSM   *Business Screen Magazine*

BuAer   Bureau of Aeronautics (Navy)

CARL   Combined Arms Research Library (Fort Leavenworth, KS)

CAT   Combat Assignment Team

CCU   Combat Camera Unit (AAF)

CINPAC   Commander in Chief, Pacific Fleet

CPS   Combat Photography Section (Navy)

CPU   Combat Photography Unit (Navy)

FMPU	First Motion Picture Unit (AAF)
HS	Historical Section
IP	*International Photography*
JAH	*Journal of American History*
JCH	*Journal of Contemporary History*
JPSA	*Journal of the Photographic Society of America*
JSMPE	*Journal of the Society of Motion Picture Engineers*
MCHC	Marine Corps Historical Center (Washington, DC)
MOT	March of Time
MP	*Minicam Photography*
MPH	*Motion Picture Herald*
NA	National Archives (Washington, DC)
NCPD	Navy Combat Photography Division
NGM	*National Geographic Magazine*
OCSO	Office of the Chief Signal Officer
PP	*Popular Photography*
PSL	Photographic Science Laboratory (Navy)
RG	Record Group
SAB	Special Activities Branch
SCPC	Signal Corps Photographic Center (Army)
SPC	Signal Photographic Company (Army)
SSB	Signal Service Battalion (Army)
SWPA	Southwest Pacific Area
TCC	Troop Carrier Command
T/O&E	Table of Organization and Equipment
USC	*U.S. Camera*
USMC	United States Marine Corps

Notes

A Personal Note

1. Mayfield S. Bray and William T. Murphy, compilers, *Audiovisual Records in the National Archives of the United States Relating to World War II* (Washington: National Archives and Records Service, 1974), p. 30. Also see Nicholas Pronay, "The 'Moving Picture' and Historical Research," *Journal of Contemporary History (henceforth JCH)*, July 1983, p. 390.
2. The following quotes are from Gordon T. Frye to the author, Dec. 7, 1983 and Jan. 5, 1984; William H. Ettinger to the author, Dec. 11, 1980; Joseph D. Boyle to the author, Aug. 4, 1980 and undated [Fall 1980].

Prologue

1. This account of Donald J. Morrow relies on Donald J. Morrow's diary and Morrow's audio cassette responding to the author's inquiries, 1991.
2. Quoted in Geoffrey C. Ward, *The Civil War: An Illustrated History* (New York: Alfred A. Knopf, 1990), p. 161.
3. Alan Trachtenberg, *Reading American Photographs: Images as History, Mathew Brady to Walker Evans* ([New York]: Hill and Wang, 1989), p. 74.
4. Martha A. Sandweiss, Rick Stewart, and Ben W. Huseman, *Eyewitness to War: Prints and Daguerreotypes of the Mexican War, 1846–1848* (Washington, DC: Smithsonian Institution Press, 1989).
5. Michael Lesy, *Bearing Witness: A Photographic Chronicle of American Life, 1860–1945* (New York: Pantheon Books, 1982), pp. vii–viii; Jonathan Heller, ed., *War & Conflict: Selected Images from the National Archives, 1765–1970* (Washington, DC: National Archives and Records Administration, 1990), pp. 4–5; Trachtenberg, *Reading American Photo-*

graphs, pp. 72–74; Bureau of Naval Personnel, "Training Aids in World War II" (Washington, DC: U.S. Naval History Division, n.d.), p. 4.

6. Raymond Fielding, *The American Newsreel, 1911–1967* (Norman, OK: University of Oklahoma Press, 1972), pp. 5, 29–31.

7. Frank P. Liberman, "History of Army Photography," *Business Screen Magazine* (henceforth *BSM*), Dec. 30, 1945, pp. 16–17, 94; K. Jack Bauer, compiler, *List of World War I Signal Corps Films (Record Group 111)* (Washington, DC: National Archives and Records Service, 1957); Heller, *War & Conflict*, pp. 7–8; Robert L. Eichberg and Jacqueline Quadow, "Combat Photography" (Historical Section, Special Activities Branch, Office of the Chief Signal Officer [henceforth HS, SAB, OCSO], Nov. 1945), pp. 1–3, Combined Arms Research Laboratory (henceforth CARL), Fort Leavenworth, KS; Susan D. Moeller, *Shooting War: Photography and the American Experience of Combat* (New York: Basic Books, Inc., 1989), pp. 115–22.

8. PHCS Gerald T. DeForge, *Navy Photographer's Mate Training Series. Module 1. Naval Photography* (Pensacola, FL: Naval Education and Training Program Development Center, 1981) series 1–4, and Bureau of Aeronautics (henceforth BuAer), "Naval Aviation Photography and Motion Pictures" (Washington, DC: U.S. Naval History Division, 1957), pp. 1–3.

9. Jack O'Brine, "Studios on the Battlefields," *Popular Science*, Mar. 1943, pp. 108–109; Fielding, *American Newsreel*, pp. 92–96, 115–116, 124–125; Moeller, *Shooting War*, pp. 100, 114, 125, 136–137.

10. Army Pictorial Service (henceforth APS), "Army Pictorial Service Annual Report For The Fiscal Year 1 July 1944 to 30 June 1945" (OCSO, July 21, 1945), p. 45, National Archives (henceforth NA), Washington, DC; *Movies at War: Reports of War Activities Committee Motion Picture Industry, 1942–1945* (New York: War Activities Committee, Motion Picture Industry, 1942–1945), p. 3 (1942 Report); Jack Price, *A Guide for Military and News Photography* (New York: Falk Publishing Company, 1944), p. 12; F. Barrow Colton, "How We Fight with Photographs," *National Geographic Magazine* (henceforth *NGM*), Sept. 1944, p. 257.

11. Lt. Crolius to Carleton Mitchell, Apr. 22, 1944, Unit 11 (Lieut. Crolius) file, Records of the Navy Combat Photography Division (henceforth NCPD), NA, and LTC Sanford E. Greenwald, "Camera Command," *International Photography* (henceforth *IP*), Sept. 1945, pp. 20–24.

12. Tom Maloney, ed., *U.S. Camera 1946: Victory Volume* (n.p.: U.S. Camera Publishers, 1945), p. 370.

13. For Okinawa see "Tentative Operations Plan 1–45, Iceberg" (Feb. 15, 1945), CARL. For Kyushu, see "Chart No. 2. Organization of T/O 11-500 Photographic Co. and Plan of Assignment"; Chart No. 3. Organization of 167th Sig. Photographic Co. T/O&E 11–37 and Plan for Assignment of Missions"; and "Chart No. 4. Film Collecting and Processing Plan," all in CARL.

14. Alvin Wyckoff, "Cameramen Come Through," *American Cinematography* (*henceforth* AC), June 1944, p. 193, and "Newsletter," Apr. 1944, Records of the 7th CCU, Air Force Historical Research Agency (*henceforth* AFHRA), Maxwell Air Force Base.

15. Although the units named here are the primary focus of this book, they by no means exhaust the ranks of combat photographers. The APS also organized Production Units, Signal Service Photo Companies, Signal Service Photo Detachments of three different types, and Signal Service Photo Platoons. Every major naval-combat ship had a photographic unit, with aircraft carriers having a complement of anywhere from twelve to twenty-two men. Army Air Forces squadrons also had photographers assigned to them, such as John L. Nolan and Robert E. Hathorn of the 718th Squadron of the 449th Bombardment Group (Heavy). Nearly 200 photographers served in the Coast Guard, while dozens more worked for *Yank*, a magazine for and by enlisted men, and *Stars and Stripes*, the soldiers' daily newspaper. And "strays" showed up everywhere—among many others were Signal Corps cameramen Phil Stern with Darby's Rangers in the Mediterranean Theater and Warren A. Boecklen with Merrill's Marauders in Burma.

    Since accredited civilian photographers and aerial photo reconnaissance personnel have been studied previously, I have excluded them from this study. Moeller's *Shooting War* and Jorge Lewinski's *The Camera At War: A History of War Photography from 1848 to the Present Day* (New York: Simon & Schuster, 1978) deal almost exclusively with civilian photographers rather than military combat cameramen. Several excellent studies discuss photo reconnaissance. Among the best are Andrew J. Brookes, *Photo Reconnaissance* (London: Ian Allen Ltd., 1975) and Colonel Roy M. Stanley, II, *World War II Photo Intelligence* (New York: Charles Scribner's Sons, 1981).

16. See the entries in the *1986 Media Resource Catalog from the National Audiovisual Center* (Capitol Heights, MD: National Audiovisual Center, n.d.), and International Historic Films, Inc., *International Historic Films Videocassette Catalog 4-C* (Chicago: n.p., n.d.).

Chapter 1. "Those Guys Went Out Hunting Trouble"

1. Unless otherwise noted, this account of Gordon T. Frye relies on the Frye materials listed in the Bibliography and the "Movement of Company Headquarters Overseas," Records of the 163rd SPC, NA.

2. Tischler interview, Oct. 8, 1983.

3. Morehouse to the author, Nov. 5, 1989; Lewis to the author, Dec. 12, 1989; Culbertson interview, Oct. 7, 1983. Tischler also believed that the pilots mistook Caiazzo for Cassino; telephone interview, May 24, 1991.

4. Ned R. Morehouse's Papers contain a "casualty worksheet" that he kept of the 163rd's casualties; it lists those injured in the bombing.

5. This account of Harry A. Downard relies on Downard interview, June 16, 1980, and "'Photo by Signal Corps': The Story of the 166th," NA.

6. This account of Joseph M. Zinni relies on the Zinni materials listed in the Bibliography.

7. F. Bard Coatsworth to the author, Sept. 20, 1989.

8. Zinni to his wife, Sept. 13, 1944, Zinni Papers.

9. Frank H. Rentfrow, "Fighting Photographers," *Popular Photography* (*henceforth PP*), Oct. 1943, p. 94.

10. Donald J. Morrow Diary, Sept. 3, 1944 and Feb. 16, 18, and 27, 1945, Donald J. Morrow Papers; Morrow audio cassette responding to the author's inquiries, 1991.

11. *Foto-Facto*, Dec. 18, 1944, Records of the 163rd SPC.

12. Robert J. Goebel interview, Oct. 8, 1983.

13. Harold P. Leinbaugh and John D. Campbell, *The Men of Company K: The Autobiography of a World War II Rifle Company* (New York: William Morrow & Company, 1985), pp. 33–34; E. B. Sledge, *With the Old Breed at Peleliu and Okinawa* (Novato, CA: Presidio Press, 1981), pp. 302–03. For other examples of this attitude, see Lt. Arthur E. Arling, "Cameramen in Uniform," AC, Oct. 1943, p. 385, and Oral History Transcript: Major Norman T. Hatch, U.S. Marine Corps (Retired), Benis M. Frank, interviewer, pp. 82–83, Marine Corps Historical Center (*henceforth* MCHC).

14. William E. Teas interview, Nov. 6, 1981.

15. Charles R. Cooper to the author, Jan. 6, 1983; Edward C. Newell to the author, Mar. 7, 1981; Charles E. Sumners to the author, Aug. 1980. Many other cameramen made the same point.

16. Monthly report for Apr. 1945 in "History of the Fourth Combat Camera Unit: Second Phase—The ETO," Records of the 4th CCU, AFHRA; "Company History 1 January 1943 to 31 December 1944," Records of the 164th SPC, NA; commendation for Benedetto James Mancuso, Unit 3 (Lieut. Newcomb) file, NCPD, NA.

17. "Signal Corps U.S. Army ETOUSA: Signal Corps Responsibilities and Missions in the ETO. Section II" ([Washington, DC]: Department of the Army, 1944), p. 11; Robert L. Eichberg and Jacqueline Quadow, "Combat Photography" (HS, SAB, OCSO, Nov. 1945), Appendix N, CARL; War Department Pamphlet No. 11–2. *Standing Operating Procedure For Signal Photographic Units In Theaters of Operations* (War Department: Apr. 20, 1944); "Combat Photographic Operations" (undated), CARL.

18. As examples see Eichberg and Quadow, "Combat Photography," Appendices E, K, and M; "Company History 1 Jan. 1943 to 31 December 1944," Records of the 164th SPC, NA; "The Officers of the 168 Signal Photo Co.," Records of the 168th SPC, NA; APS, "Handbook for Motion Picture Photographers in the European Theater of Operations," (Signal Corps, United States Army, undated), pp. 18–20, Russell A. Meyer Papers.

19. Statement by the Commanding General, AAF, and AAF Memorandum No. 95–1, Oct. 21, 1943, both in Combat Camera file, AFHRA. Also see "Production Chart Guide For 16mm Motion Picture Unit," Combat Camera file, AFHRA; Regulation 95–9, Headquarters XXI Bomber Command, Feb. 2, 1945, in "Narrative History" covering Nov. 24, 1942 to Mar. 31, 1945, and memo on "Instructions, CCUs" from LTC Owen E. Crump to the Commanding Officer, 11th CCU, Aug. 1, 1943, both in Records of the 11th CCU, AFHRA.

20. Zinni to his wife, July 31, 1944, Zinni Papers; Karl H. Maslowski interview, Dec. 17, 1977; "'Photo by Signal Corps': The Story of the 166th."

21. "Cloak Removed From Activities of Photo Unit," undated newspaper clipping in "Unit History," Apr. 9, 1945, Records of the 10th CCU, AFHRA; Edward C. Newell to the author, Feb. 9, 1981; Zinni to his wife, Nov. 11, 1944, Zinni Papers; Mitchell to Lt. Samuel, Dec. 3, 1943, Combat Photography Unit 5 (Lt. Samuel) file, NCPD, NA.

22. Zinni to his wife, Aug. 29, 1944, Zinni Papers; group interview with seven former members of the 166th SPC, June 9, 1980; John D. Craig interview, Mar. 26–27, 1979.

23. Lt. Samuel to Carleton Mitchell, Friday [c. Jan. 1944], Combat Photography Unit 5 (Lt. Samuel) file, and Lt. Reiman to Mitchell, Dec. 16, 1943, Unit 7 (Lieut. Reiman) file, both in NCPD, NA.

24. Lt. Waterman to Carleton Mitchell, May 7, 1945, Unit 8 (Lt. Waterman) file, NCPD, NA; Phil Stern interview, June 11, 1980; William Cummings to the author, July 1980; Charles R. Cooper to the author, Jan. 22, 1983; James LaFrano to his mother and father, Jan. 17 [1945], James LaFrano Papers.

25. Robert Lewis to Warren [Kieft], Apr. 26, 1980, Joseph D. Boyle Papers.

26. Warren Kieft's comments on his diary, Aug. 1981, and Tischler interview, Oct. 8, 1983.

27. Jerome N. Kahn audio cassette responding to the author's inquiries, 1980.

28. Capt. Edwin T. Rhatigan, "The Tactical Employment of Photographic Troops" (n.d.), pp. 3–4, U.S. Army Signal Center and Fort Gordon, GA, and "Instructing U.S. Signal Corps Photographic Companies with Major Art Lloyd, A.S.C.," AC, July 1946, p. 258.

29. Capt. Frederick Reinstein, Project Officer, "Study of Signal Corps Officer Schooling, 1939–1944" (HS, SAB, OCSC, Dec. 1, 1944), pp. 162–63, 170, CARL; and John N. Harman, Jr. to the author, Dec. 1982.

30. "Through the Editor's Finder," AC, Dec. 1942, p. 517.

31. "Must mention this fact," wrote Samuel Tischler, "a total military minded Commanding Officer is good for discipline but not for photographing"; Tischler to the author, Sept. 17, 1981.

32. Reinstein, "Study of Signal Corps Officer Schooling," pp. 173–76, and "Unit History," June 1, 1944, Records of the 8th CCU, AFHRA.

33. Unless otherwise noted this account of Ned R. Morehouse relies on the Morehouse sources listed in the Bibliography.

34. Along with the sources in Note 9, see "History of the 163rd Signal Photographic Company," Feb. 10, 1943, Records of the 163rd SPC, NA; "WW2, 41–45, etc.," which is a 163rd SPC photo album that contains both pictures and documentary material, Robert L. Lewis Papers; Robert L. Lewis to the author, Dec. 12, 1989.

35. Kieft to the author, Aug. 8, 1981.

36. Warren Kieft Diary, Nov. 24, 1942, Warren Kieft Papers, and Kieft's comments on his diary, Aug. 1981.

37. *SIGPHO*, Feb. 17, 1943, John N. Harman, Jr. Papers, and Jack Price, *A Guide for Military and News Photography* (New York: Falk Publishing Company, 1944), pp. 73, 92. As Harman put it, combat cameramen were "often un-Army to the point of being impertinent"; Harman to the author, Aug. 17, 1981.

38. Kieft Diary, Jan. 6, 1943.

39. Tischler interview, Oct. 8, 1983; Zinni to his wife, Oct. 27, 1944, Zinni Papers; Teas interview, Nov. 6, 1981.

40. Donald J. Morrow Diary, Dec. 21, 1944, and a photograph of Morrow in a British uniform with a caption reading: "Ned wouldn't like this but the British uniform was much warmer than ours and I wore it a lot during the winter at the front"; both in the Donald J. Morrow Papers. Like the 163rd's, Morrow's attitude changed after the war. In 1991 he commented that Morehouse "really did a lot for me" and "I have come to think a lot of him"; Morrow audio cassette responding to the author's inquiries, 1991.

41. Audio cassette of an informal conversation among four members of the 166th SPC, 1980, Russell A. Meyer Papers; Russell A. Meyer interview, June 12, 1980; Harvey A. Weber to the author, Nov. 28, 1989; Teas interview, Nov. 6, 1981.

42. Teas interview, Nov. 6, 1981; Theodore W. Sizer interview, Aug. 31, 1983; Downard interview, June 16, 1980.

43. Kieft Diary, Jan. 6, 1943; and Goebel interview, Oct. 8, 1983.

44. Fred Bonnard audio cassette responding to the author's inquiries, 1980; and Jerry J. Joswick interview, Mar. 26, 1979.

45. Joseph D. Boyle audio cassette responding to the author's inquiries, 1980.

46. "Unit History," Apr. 9, 1945, Records of the 10th CCU, AFHRA.

47. *Time*, Nov. 6, 1944, pp. 70, 72.

48. "What About the Poor Photographers," *U.S. Camera* (henceforth *USC*), Dec. 1943, p. 38, and James LaFrano to his mother and father, Aug. 13, [1944], LaFrano Papers.

49. *Weekly Kodachrome*, Feb. 4, 1945, Russell A. Meyer Papers.

50. As examples see *Life*, Dec. 4, 1944, which featured color photos taken by the Navy's Orville L. Jenkins, and *Life*, Mar. 12, 1945, which gave credit to two Marines, George Dress and Robert Cooke, for photos taken on Iwo Jima.

51. *USC*, May 1946, p. 21; "50 Win Praise for Combat Film," *Close-Up*, Oct. 9, 1945, Frank J. Goetzheimer Papers; Capt. Raymond Henri, *Iwo Jima: Springboard to Final Victory* (New York: U.S. Camera Publishing Corporation, 1945).

52. Larry Sowinski, *Action in the Pacific As seen by US Navy photographers during World War 2* (Annapolis: Naval Institute Press, 1981); John Pimlott, *World War II in Photographs* (New York: The Military Press, 1984).

53. *The Combat Camera Chronicle*, Jan. 1991, p. 3, copy in the author's possession.

54. Glenn B. Infield, *Unarmed and Unafraid* (New York: Macmillan Publishing, 1970), pp. 4–14.

55. Infield, *Unarmed and Unafraid*, pp. 65–132, recounts several harrowing missions flown by recon pilots. Andrew J. Brookes, *Photo Reconnaissance* (London: Ian Allen Ltd., 1975), p. 117, argues that photo recon flights were like detective work.

56. Lee Blodget interview, June 17, 1980; Blodget to his wife, June 27, 1944 and Feb. 20, 1945, both in Lee Blodget Papers.

57. Eichberg and Quadow, "Combat Photography," Appendix N, and Rowland Carter, "Censored!," *PP*, Apr. 1942, p. 99.

58. Bruce Downes, "From Battlefront to Front Page," *PP*, Aug. 1943, p. 86, and Carter, "Censored!" pp. 99–100. As a Graflex advertisement proclaimed in regard to the Wartime Still Picture Pool, this arrangement gave "each service the benefits of the combined coverage of all four great picture-taking services"; see *Minicam Photography* (*henceforth MP*), Sept. 1945, p. 81.

59. The censoring procedures and organizations changed during the war, but for examples see Eichberg and Quadow, "Combat Photography," pp. 154–55, and memo on "Motion Picture film, handling of" from Leland P. Lovette, Director of Public Relations, to Capt. L. A. Pope, June 10, 1943, Aeronautics (Receipts, etc.) file, NCPD, NA.

60. For example, Air Force Historical Foundation, *Impact: The Army Air Forces' Confidential Picture History of World War II* (eight books, New York: James Parton and Company, 1980), Book 7 (May 1945) published three pictures by *Life's* Robert Capa; Book 7 (July 1945) published a number of pictures by *Life's* Margaret Bourke-White; and Book 8 (Sept.–Oct. 1945) used photos by *Life's* George Silk and W. Eugene Smith. The monthly *U.S. Army–Navy Journal of Recognition* also regularly gave credit to civilian photojournalists and news organizations; see *U.S. Army–Navy Journal of Recognition (September 1943–February 1944)* (Annapolis, MD: Naval Institute Press, 1990). Also see Capt. Halvor T. Darracott, "Produced by the United States Army Signal Corps," *Journal of the Society of Motion Picture Engineers* (henceforth JSMPE), Sept. 1943, pp. 206–09.

61. Memo on "Roto Pool Meetings, report on" from Carleton Mitchell to

the Director, Office of Public Relations, Oct. 17, 1942, Cooperation Still Agencies, MOT file, and memo on "Roto-pool photographs from Alaska Area" from Mitchell to Cdr. W. G. Beecher and Cdr. John E. Long, June 10, 1943, Combat Photography Unit 4 (Lt. Tacker) file, both in NCPD, NA; "Army Uses Censored Newsreel Footage," *Motion Picture Herald (henceforth MPH)*, Feb. 26, 1944, p. 28; "Newsreel Claim Denied by Army," MPH, Mar. 25, 1944, p. 60; "War and Newsreel," *MPH*, June 24, 1944, p. 7; memo on "Combat Correspondents" from Brig. Gen. Robert L. Denig to Maj. Gen. D. Peck, Jan. 24, 1944, Combat Correspondents (1) file, MCHC.

62. Memo on "Activity Report etc." from Lt. Drennan to Carleton Mitchell, Aug. 30, 1943, Unit 2 (Lieut. Drennan) file, NCPD, NA; group interview with five former members of the 163rd SPC, Sept. 26, 1987; Edward C. Newell to the author, Feb. 9, 1981; Harvey A. Weber to the author, Dec. 12, 1989.

63. Warren Kieft to the author, Aug. 8, 1981 and Feb. 9, 1984.

64. Oral History Transcript: Colonel William P. McCahill, USMC (Ret.), unknown interviewer, pp. 68–69, MCHC; Susan D. Moeller, *Shooting War: Photography and the American Experience of Combat* (New York: Basic Books, 1989), pp. 182–83; Editors of *Look*, *Movie Lot to Beachhead: The Motion Picture Goes to War and Prepares for the Future* (Garden City, NY: Doubleday, Doran and Co., 1945), p. 27.

65. Walton C. Ament, Chairman of the Newsreel Pool, to General Dwight D. Eisenhower, Mar. 21, 1945, in *Weekly Kodachrome*, Apr. 29, 1945, Russell A. Meyer Papers; Sherman Montrose, Still Pool Editor, to Lt. Col. Kenneth Clark, Public Relations Officer, Fifth Army, May 19, 1944, copy in Chester Owens Papers.

66. LaFrano to his mother and father, July 10, [1944], LaFrano Papers.

67. *Life*, Oct. 11, 1943, pp. 74–75, 77–78, 80, 82.

68. "Unit History," Apr. 9, 1945, Records of the 10th CCU; "Historical Record: Fifth Army Air Forces Combat Camera Unit," Records of the 5th CCU; "Unit History," Jan. and May 1945, Records of the 16th CCU. All in AFHRA.

69. Morehouse to the author, July 17, 1981; Boyle audio cassette, 1980; Zinni audio cassette, 1980; Bonnard audio cassette, 1980; Goebel interview, Oct. 8, 1983; group interview with 163rd SPC, Sept. 26, 1987; memo on "Combat Correspondents" from Denig to Peck, Jan. 24, 1944, Combat Correspondents (1) file, MCHC; Benis M. Frank, *Denig's Demons and How They Grew ... the Story of Marine Corps Combat Correspondents, Photographers and Artists* (Washington, DC: Moore & Moore, Inc., 1967), unpaged.

70. Hodges to Maj. Gen. Howard Davidson, Feb. 9, 1945, Records of the 10th CCU, AFHRA.

71. Memo on "Material for possible inclusion in Cominch memorandum"

from Carleton Mitchell to the Deputy Director, Oct. 10, 1944, Miscellaneous file; W. G. Beecher, Jr., Acting Director, to the Director of Photography, Bureau of Aeronautics, June 16, 1944, Photo Science Laboratory file; Mitchell to Lt. Drennan, July 28, 1943, Combat Photography Unit 2 (Lt. Drennan) file. All in NCPD, NA.

72. Peter P. Drowne, "An Investigation into the Evolution of Motion Picture Photography and Film Usage in the United States Marine Corps 1940–1945," (Unpublished Master's Thesis, University of California at Los Angeles, 1965), pp. 197–98; Henry L. Stimson Diaries, Feb. 4 and 25, 1943, microfilm edition of the Diaries from the Yale University Library; David Culbert, ed., *Film and Propaganda in America: A Documentary History*, 3 vols. (Westport, CT: Greenwood Press, 1990), Vol. II, Part 1, p. 381.

73. "Services Competing On Incentive Films," *MPH*, Feb. 19, 1944, p. 38.

74. Sanford E. Greenwald interview, June 11, 1980; LTC Sanford E. Greenwald, "Camera Command," *IP*, Aug. 1945, p. 26; monthly report for Mar. 1944 in "History of the Fourth Combat Camera Unit: Second Phase—The ETO"; memo on "Daily Activity Report" from Robert B. Miller, Chief, Motion Picture Services Division, to AC/AS, Intelligence, Executive, May 19, 1945, Motion Picture Services Division Activity Reports file, AFHRA.

75. Memo on "Army Air Forces Motion Pictures" from Col. H. W. Bowman, Chief, Office of Information Services, to All General Officers, Headquarters, Army Air Forces, Apr. 5, 1946, Henry H. Arnold Papers, AFHRA.

76. Keighley to All Officers of the Motion Picture Branch, June 30, 1943, in the 1944–Authority for Motion Picture Activities file; memos on "Daily Activity Report" from Robert B. Miller to Executive, AC/AS, Intelligence, Apr. 26 and 30 and June 6, 1945, Motion Picture Services Division Activity Reports file; Mason Sutherland to Captain Arnold N. Belgard, Apr. 10, 1945, Training Film Numbers file. All in AFHRA. "Statement for 'The Last Bomb'" by Curtis LeMay, Arnold Papers, AFHRA.

77. Zinni to his wife, Sept. 1, 1944, Zinni Papers.

78. W. G. Beecher, Jr. to Lt. Cdr. Charles G. Duffy, July 29, 1944, COM-NAVNAW file, NCPD, NA; and "Unit History," Dec. 1944, Records of the 7th CCU, AFHRA.

79. Newcomb to Carleton Mitchell, June 8, 1944, Unit 3 (Lieut. Newcomb) file, NCPD, NA.

80. [Carleton Mitchell] to Lt. Cdr. Peyton Anderson, June 2, 1945, Seventh Fleet file; Mitchell to Lt. Waterman, June 2, 1945, Unit 8 (Lt. Waterman) file; Mitchell to Lt. Wrigley, Unit 10 (Lieut. Wrigley) file; Mitchell to the Director of Public Relations, Aug. 24, 1944, Capt. Markey file. All in NCPD, NA.

81. Boyle to the author, [fall, 1980].

Chapter 2. "Survival of the Cleverest"

1. John D. Craig interview, Mar. 26–27, 1979; Craig's letter requesting consideration for a Regular Army commission, Jan. 14, 1946, John D. Craig Papers; "Valuable to Army Air Forces," *PP*, Aug. 1945, p. 123.
2. John S. Wever to his father, Dec. 1, 1943, John S. Wever Papers; L. Bennett Fenberg to the author, Feb. 17, 1981.
3. Joseph D. Boyle audio cassette responding to the author's inquiries, 1980; Joseph M. Zinni to his wife, Nov. 4, 1944 and Apr. 14, 1945, Joseph M. Zinni Papers; Christopher Phillips, *Steichen at War* (New York: Harry N. Abrams, Inc., 1981), p. 33; Billy A. Newhouse interview, Nov. 8, 1981; Warren Kieft to the author, Aug. 8, 1981; Edward C. Newell to the author, Apr. 25, 1981; George H. Meyer to the author, Oct. 12, 1980; Jerome N. Kahn audio cassette responding to the author's inquiries, 1980; PHCS Gerald T. DeForge, *Navy Photographer's Mate Training Series. Module 1. Naval Photography* (Pensacola: Naval Education and Training Program Development Center, 1981), Series 2–17.
4. Harry A. Downard interview, June 16, 1980; *Foto-Facto*, Mar. 13, 1945, Records of the 163rd SPC, NA; Harold Culbertson interview, Oct. 7, 1983; Robert J. Goebel interview, Oct. 8, 1983; James LaFrano to his mother, July 1, [1944], James LaFrano Papers; Zinni to his wife, Aug. 7 and Sept. 10, 1944, Zinni Papers.
5. Zinni to his wife, Nov. 22, 1944, Zinni Papers.
6. Zinni to his wife, July 5 and 29, 1944, Zinni Papers; "Unit History From Activation Through 31 March 1944" [This document actually begins with Apr. 1944 and includes monthly installments through Oct. 1945.], Aug. 1944, Records of the 6th CCU, AFHRA.
7. Peyton Anderson to Jack [?], Sept. 19, 1944, Seventh Fleet file, NCPD, NA.
8. Memo on "Authorization of Sleeve Insignia (Photographer)" from LTC C. F. Felstead to Commanding Officer, Headquarters Company and Headquarters Detachment, US Army SOS, Jan. 18, 1945, copy in William A. Avery Papers; Robert F. Albright audio cassette responding to the author's inquiries, 1991; photo of L. Bennett Fenberg showing him wearing an "Offical War Photographer" patch on his left shoulder, L. Bennett Fenberg Papers.
9. David Douglas Duncan, *Yankee Nomad: A Photographic Odyssey* (New York: Holt, Rinehart and Winston, 1966), pp. 9, 110–17, 152–53, 177.
10. James R. Palmer, "We Covered the B-29's," *IP*, Feb. 1946, p. 22; memo on "Employment of Official War Photographers" from Colonel W. G. Caldwell to Commanding Generals, All Corps and Divisions, Seventh Army, Nov. 1, 1944, copy in Edward C. Newell Papers; memo on

"Tacker, H. L., Lt. (jg) USNR" from the Vice Chief of Naval Operations to All District Commandants and Commanding Officers of All U.S. Naval Units, Jan. 20, 1943, CPU (Letters to all units) file, NCPD, NA.

11. Samuel Tischler to the author, Sept. 17, 1981, and Fenberg to the author, Feb. 17, 1981.

12. Lt. Samuel to Carleton Mitchell, June 28, 1943, Combat Photography Unit 5 (Lt. Samuel) file, and [Lt. Samuel] to Mitchell, May 21, 1944, Equipment Folder #2 file, both in NCPD, NA.

13. Group interview with five former members of the 163rd SPC, Sept. 26, 1987, and Robert J. Goebel to the author, May 28, 1981.

14. Emmett Bergholz interview, June 14, 1980, and Boyle audio cassette, 1980.

15. Karl H. Maslowski to the author, [late Aug. 1991]; Rick Rohde interview, June 14, 1980; "Historical Records and History of Organization," Oct. 9, 1944, Records of the 161st SPC, NA; Lt. Drennan to Carleton Mitchell, Oct. 1, 1943, Combat Photography Unit 2 (Lt. Drennan) file, NCPD, NA; Lt. Reiman to Mitchell, May 20, 1943, Combat Photography Unit 7 (Lt. Reiman) file, NCPD, NA; Theodore W. Sizer interview, Aug. 31, 1981.

16. "A Standing Operating Procedure for Combat Assignment Teams (SOPCAT)," (Headquarters 163rd SPC, Feb. 20, 1945), copy in Gordon T. Frye Papers, and Boyle audio cassette, 1980.

17. Sizer interview, Aug. 31, 1981; James A. Cuca and Ralph E. Thomas interview, Oct. 8, 1983; Kieft to the author, Aug. 8, 1981; "Unit History," Feb. 6, 1945, Records of the 10th CCU, AFHRA.

18. "Unit History," Mar. 10, 1945, Records of the 10th CCU, AFHRA, and Lt. Drennan to Carleton Mitchell, Aug. 31, 1943, Unit 2 (Lieut. Drennan) file, NCPD, NA.

19. APS, "Handbook for Motion Picture Photographers in the European Theater of Operations," (Signal Corps, United States Army, undated), p. 11, Russell A. Meyer Papers, and Ned R. Morehouse to the author, July 17, 1981.

20. Memo on "Photographic Coverage of the 14th Air Force" from Brig. Gen. Albert F. Hegenberger, Chief of Staff, Headquarters 14th Air Force, to Commanding Officers, All Tactical Units and Bases, 14th Air Force, June 23, 1945, copy in Allan L. Kain Papers. Also see memo on "Combat Correspondents" issued by Headquarters, 5th Marine Division, Camp Joseph H. Pendleton, Apr. 3, 1944, Combat Correspondents file, MCHC.

21. "Team History" from Team #2 for Feb. 28, 1945, Records of the 163rd SPC, NA.

22. Report of the Photo Officer covering teams with the 45th Infantry Division in "Company History" for Apr. 15–May 15, 1945, and "Weekly

Team Activity Report for March 14 to March 22, [1945]," both in Records of the 163rd SPC, NA; Robert L. Lewis to the author, Nov. 17, 1980.

23. Zinni to his wife, Sept. 1, 1944, Zinni Papers.

24. Zinni to his wife, July 26, Aug. 10, 12, 13, 17 and Sept. 14, 1944, Zinni Papers; Edward C. Newell to his mother, Oct. 1944; Kahn audio cassette, 1980.

25. Lt. Drennan to Carleton Mitchell, Aug. 19, 1945, Combat Photography Recent Letters file, and Lt. Wrigley to Mitchell, Aug. 15, 1943, CPU #10 (Lt. Wrigley[)] file, both in NCPD, NA.

26. The name of this individual is omitted to protect the guilty party.

27. United States Army Signal Corps, Southwest Pacific Area, "Exposure Under Fire: An Official History of Signal Corps Photography in the Luzon Operations" (Apr. 25, 1945), p. 11. Two versions of this document exist. The one in the Frank J. Goetzheimer Papers contains the photographers' names. The other, Document #R-11176, CARL, is an edited version that omits the photographers' names but contains a last page dated June 27, 1945, which the Goetzheimer version does not include. Unless otherwise noted I have used the Goetzheimer version.

28. "'Photo by Signal Corps': The Story of the 166th," NA.

29. Zinni to his wife, Mar. 25, 1945, Zinni Papers; and Frye to his wife, Mar. 27, [1945], Frye Papers.

30. Frye to his wife, Aug. 6, 1945, Frye Papers, and Newell to the author, Feb. 21, 1981.

31. For just a few examples of this diversity see Allan L. Kain interview, Dec. 26, 1978; Albright audio cassette, 1991; "WW2, 41–45, etc.," which is a 163rd SPC photo album that contains both pictures and documentary material, Robert L. Lewis Papers; "Combat Activities of Signal Corps Photographers in the Southwest Pacific Area," June 26, 1944, William A. Avery Papers; "Historical Records," Jan. and Feb. 1945, Records of the 9th CCU, AFHRA; Lt. Wrigley to Carleton Mitchell, Mar. 12, 1944, Unit 10 (Lieut. Wrigley) file, NCPD, NA; "Unit History," Nov. 1944 and May 1945, Records of the 1st CCU, AFHRA.

32. Sizer interview, Aug. 31, 1983, and Boyle to the author, [Fall 1980].

33. Warren Kieft's comments on his wartime diary, Aug. 1981, and Newell to the author, May 9, 1981.

34. Zinni to his wife, Oct. 25, 1944 and Jan 1, 1944 [sic: 1945], Zinni Papers.

35. LaFrano to his mother and father, July 10, Sept. 17, 18, 21, Oct. 2, 3, 8, [1944] and Jan. 6, 1945, LaFrano Papers. For similar sentiments see John S. Wever to his mother, Nov. 23, 1943, and Wever to his father, Feb. 10, 1944, both in Wever Papers.

36. Product Digest Section of *MPH*, Dec. 20, 1944, p. 2257.

37. S/Sgt. Dick Hannah, *Tarawa: The Toughest Battle in Marine Corps History* (n.p.: U.S. Camera Publishing Corp., 1944), p. 110.
38. "History of the 5th AAF Combat Camera Unit" in "Historical Record: Fifth Army Air Forces Combat Camera Unit," Nov. 24, 1942 to Dec. 31, 1943, Records of the 5th CCU, AFHRA; and Lt. Waterman to Carleton Mitchell, Mar. 7, 1945, Unit 8 (Lt. Waterman) file, NCPD, NA.
39. "Company History 1 January 1945 Thru 30 June 1945," Records of the 164th SPC, NA.
40. Zinni to his wife, Jan. 16, 1945, Zinni Papers; William H. Ettinger reminiscences on audio cassette; Samuel Tischler to the author, Sept. 17, 1981; William E. Teas interview, Nov. 6, 1981; Newell to the author, Mar. 1, 28, 1981; 1st Lt. Leonard Spinrad, "The Combat Photographer," *BSM*, Dec. 30, 1945, p. 84.
41. As examples see "Exposure Under Fire," p. 16, and Martin Friedman audio cassette responding to the author's inquiries, 1980.
42. "Exposure Under Fire," p. 24; Ettinger reminiscences on audio cassette; Maj. Kenneth MacKenna, "Photographic Work of the Army Pictorial Service," *The Journal of the Photographic Society of America (henceforth JPSA)*, Apr. 1945, p. 148; Kahn audio cassette, 1980; Frank J. Goetzheimer's handwritten caption sheet for Feb. 15–17, 1944, Goetzheimer Papers.
43. A. J. Erickson, "Press Flashes," *PP*, June 1942, p. 60.
44. "Company History 1 January 1943 to 31 December 1944," and "Company History 1 January 1945 Thru 30 June 1945," both in Records of the 164th SPC, NA.
45. W. Dean McWhirter to the author, June 12, 1981; and Lt. Wrigley to Carleton Mitchell, May 27, 1944, Unit 10 (Lieut. Wrigley) file, NCPD, NA.
46. Ralph Butterfield audio cassette responding to the author's inquiries, 1980, and Boyle to the author, Aug. 4, 1980. Fenberg spoke for most cameramen when he wrote that "luckily, I was never forced to drop my camera and fight. Even though I carried a gun at all times, I had no desire to shoot anything but my cameras"; Fenberg to the author, Feb. 17, 1981.
47. As Zinni wrote to his wife, Nov. 7, 1944, "the elements of late are our worst enemies & the Nazis seem to be only a harassing foe." Zinni Papers.
48. "Unit History," Mar. 1, 1943, Records of the 12th CCU, AFHRA; "Confessions of a Navy Combat Photographic Unit Officer," Combat Photography Unit 5 (Lt. Samuel) file, NCPD, NA; Jerry J. Joswick, with Lawrence A. Keating, *Combat Cameraman* (Philadelphia: Chilton Company, 1961), p. 43.
49. Clyde deVinna, "Field Hints for Military Cinematographers," AC, May, 1942, p. 228; APS, "Handbook for Motion Picture Photographers," pp.

39–40; Robert J. Goebel to the author, May 28, 1981; Zinni to his wife, Dec. 21 and 27, 1944 and Jan. 9, 1945, Zinni Papers.

50. Account by Sgt. John Blankenhorn in "'Photo by Signal Corps': The Story of the 166th"; Zinni to his wife, July 6, 7, 18 and Aug. 24, 1944, Zinni Papers; Morrow Diary, June 1, 1944, Morrow Papers.

51. "Company History," Records of the 167th SPC, NA, and "Weekly Team Activity Report" from Team #5 for Mar. 2–8, [1945], Records of the 163rd SPC, NA. Both the Records of the 163rd SPC and Zinni's letters to his wife, Zinni Papers, are replete with references to the miserable winter weather in northern Europe. Morrow's Diary, Morrow Papers, details the special agony of wintertime photography in northern Italy.

52. "Seabee Photographers," *MP*, Oct. 1943, p. 12; R. H. Bailey, "Tropical Problems in Aerial Camera Maintenance," *AC*, Aug. 1944, p. 263; 1st Lt. William R. McGee, "Cinematography Goes to War," *JSMPE*, Feb. 1944, p. 105; "U.S. Naval Photography, Some Comments Concerning" enclosed with Lt. Burlingame to Carleton Mitchell, Aug. 7, 1944, Movies—Unit 6—Burlingame file, NCPD, NA; Lt. Newcomb to Mitchell, Oct. 17, 1943, Combat Photography Unit 3 (Lt. Newcomb) file, NCPD, NA; "Narrative History" covering Nov. 24, 1942 to Mar. 31, 1945, Records of the 11th CCU, AFHRA; "Report Survey of the Proposed Move of the 16th Combat Camera Unit to Temporary Site at Peishiyi, China," June 2, 1945, Records of the 16th CCU, AFHRA.

53. "Company History 1 January 1943 to 31 December 1944," Records of the 164th SPC, NA.

54. DeVinna, "Field Hints," p. 226.

55. "Every Shot a Prize Winner," *United States Marine Corps Headquarters Bulletin*, June 1945, pp. 26–27, and Lt. Newcomb to Carleton Mitchell, June 8, 1944, Unit 3 (Lt. Newcomb) file, NCPD, NA.

56. Report to Carleton Mitchell [from Lt. Drennan], Information New CPU's file, NCPD, NA; Lt. Reiman to Mitchell, Oct. 14, 1943, Combat Photography Unit 7 (Lt. Reiman) file, NCPD, NA; Lieut. Arthur E. Arling, "Cameramen in Uniform," *AC*, Oct. 1943, p. 362.

57. "Narrative History," Nov. 24, 1942 to Mar. 31, 1945, Records of the 11th CCU, and a press release from the Public Relations Office, FMPU, May 17, 1944, Henry H. Arnold Papers, both in AFHRA.

58. "Unit History," June 11, 1944, Records of the 3rd CCU, AFHRA; "Unit History," July 1944, Records of the 8th CCU, AFHRA; John D. Craig to Col. William Keighley, Director of Photography, May 20, 1943, Craig Papers; memo on "Combat Camera Units" from William J. Keighley to General Arnold, Apr. 9, 1943, CCU Organization—General Arnold's folder, 9 Nov. 1942—9 Apr. 1943 file, AFHRA.

59. "Newsletter," Apr. 1944, Records of the 7th CCU, AFHRA.

60. "Photographic Activities of the 7th AAF Combat Camera Unit," June 6, 1944, Records of the 7th CCU, AFHRA; "The Story of the Fourth: An

Informal History of the 4th Combat Camera Unit, Army Air Forces," pp. 11–12, Records of the 4th CCU, AFHRA; memo on "Combat Photography Section, report on for year ending 30 June 1943" from Carleton Mitchell to [Navy] Director of Public Relations, July 9, 1943, Reports—Confidential file, NCPD; "Camera Equipment of CPUs," undated, Equipment file, NCPD, NA.

61. BuAer, "Naval Aviation Photography and Motion Pictures" (Washington, DC: U.S. Naval History Division, 1957), p. 59.

62. Memos on "CPUs, Equipment for," Jan. 1, 1943, "CPUs, Equipment for," Jan. 6, 1942 [*sic*: 1943], "CPUs, film requirements," Jan. 13, 1943, and "CPUs, still film requirements," Jan 14, 1943, all from Carleton Mitchell to Lt. Cdr. A. D. Fraser, Equipment file, NCPD, NA; Robert L. Eichberg and Jacqueline Quadow, "Combat Photography" (HS, SAB, OCSO), p. 27, CARL.

63. "Army Needs 35mm Movie Cameras," *MP*, Aug. 1942, p. 88; "Signal Corps Wants 35mm Movie Cameras," *MP*, Nov. 1942, p. 11; "The Signal Corps Needs," *IP*, Apr. 1943, p. 28; James V. Clarke, "Signal Corps Army Pictorial Service in World War II (1 September 1939—15 August 1945)" (HS, SAB, OCSO, Jan. 16, 1946), pp. 14–15, NA; Oral History Transcript: Major Norman T. Hatch, U.S. Marine Corps (Retired), Benis M. Frank, interviewer, p. 41, MCHC.

64. War Department, "History of Signal Corps Research and Development in World War II. Volume XV. Photographic Equipment" (Washington, DC: Army Service Forces, Dec. 1945), pp. 1–2, NA; and George R. Thompson and Dixie R. Harris, *The United States Army in World War II. The Signal Corps: The Outcome (Mid-1943 Through 1945)* (Washington, DC: Office of the Chief of Military History, 1966), pp. 565–66.

65. Eichberg and Quadow, "Combat Photography," p. 26.

66. Carleton Mitchell to Lt. Wrigley, July 28, 1944, Unit 10 (Lieut. Wrigley) file, NCPD, NA; Glenn Matthews, "Photoprogress in 1943," *JPSA*, May 1944, p. 259; George R. Thompson, et al., *The United States Army in World War II. The Signal Corps: The Test (December 1941 to July 1943)* (Washington, DC: Office of the Chief of Military History, 1957), pp. 408–11.

67. Carleton Mitchell to Lt. Crolius, May 16, 1944, Unit 11 (Lieut. Crolius) file, NCPD, NA; "Unit History," Jan. 1945, Records of the 7th CCU, AFHRA; "Unit History," July 1944, Records of the 12th CCU, AFHRA; "Historical Record: Fifth Army Air Forces Combat Camera Unit," Apr. 1945, Records of the 5th CCU, AFHRA.

68. "Notes and News," *American Photography* (*henceforth AP*), Dec. 1945, p. 58; Eichberg and Quadow, "Combat Photography," p. 39; C. Merwin Travis, "The Motion Picture Industry and the War Production Board," *JSMPE*, May 1943, pp. 273–76; "Through the Editor's Finder," AC, July 1945, p. 307; BuAer, "Naval Aviation Photography," p. 92. The figures

for square feet of film are in "Raw Stock Production Reaches New High in 1945," *BSM*, Nov. 28, 1945, p. 35.

69. Morrow Diary, Apr. 2, 1945, Morrow Papers. Also see memo from OIC [Carleton Mitchell], Combat Photography Section, to Officers in Charge, CPUs, Feb. 6, 1943, CPU Newsletter (Misc. Mtl. Sent) file, NCPD, NA; APS, "Report of Photographic Activities" (Signal Section, Headquarters, Fifth Army, Dec. 31, 1943), pp. 32–33, Records of the 163rd SPC, NA; Jacqueline M. Quadow, "Training Films in the Second World War, Supplement Jan 44 [*sic*] to August 1945" (HS, SAB, OCSO, May 13, 1946), pp. 10–12, NA.

70. Boyle audio cassette, 1980, and "U.S. Naval Photography, Some Comments Concerning," enclosed with Lt. Burlingame to Carleton Mitchell, Aug. 7, 1944, Movies—Unit 6—Burlingame file, NCPD, NA.

71. Bergholz interview, June 14, 1980.

72. Cuca and Thomas interview, Oct. 8, 1983.

73. "Report of Test of Combat Serviceability of Camera Equiptment [*sic*] P.H. 104" included in "History of the 163rd Signal Photographic Company," Feb. 10, 1943, and APS, "Report of Photographic Activities," p. 47, both in Records of the 163rd SPC, NA; William A. Avery to the author, Oct. 13, 1980.

74. Jack Lewis, "The Photo-Fighters: Part 1," *Creative Photography*, Oct. 1970, p. 35; and "A Digest of Combat Correspondents' Reports on Problems in the Field," Combat Correspondents (1) file, MCHC.

75. War Department, "History of Signal Corps Research," Introduction, pp. 1–2.

76. Lewis, "Photo-Fighters," p. 35; Lt. Reiman to Carleton Mitchell, Feb. 22, 1944, Unit 7 (Lieut. Reiman[)] file, NCPD, NA; MacArthur to LTG Brehon Somervell, July 26, 1943, RG 4, Box 10, War Department Correspondence 13 May 1943–1 Sept. 1943, MacArthur Memorial Archives. I am indebted to Professor Allison Gilmore of The Ohio State University at Lima for bringing the MacArthur document to my attention.

77. Lt. Spafford to Carleton Mitchell, Dec. 1, [1944], Unit 13 (Lieut. Spafford) file, NCPD, NA.

78. APS, "Handbook for Motion Picture Photographers," p. 32; [Drennan] to Carleton Mitchell, undated, Information New CPUs file, NCPD, NA; Lt. Tacker to Mitchell, Oct. 25, 1943, Combat Photography Unit 4 (Lt. Tacker) file, NCPD, NA; APS, "Report of Photographic Activities," p. 43.

79. Lt. Waterman to Carleton Mitchell, Mar. 30, 1945, Unit 8 (Lt. Waterman) file, NCPD, NA; Albright audio cassette, 1991; "Unit History From Activation Through 31 March 1944" [This document actually contains monthly installments through Oct. 1945.], Dec. 1944, Records of the 6th CCU, AFHRA.

80. For the "combat camera" see Eichberg and Quadow, "Combat Photography," pp. 32–33; and "New Designs in Combat Cameras," *PP*, Sept. 1945, p. 72.

81. "U.S. Naval Photography, Some Comments Concerning," enclosed with Lt. Burlingame to Carleton Mitchell, Aug. 7, 1944, Movies—Unit 6— Burlingame file, NCPD, NA; APS, "Report of Photographic Activities," p. 45; *Weekly Kodachrome*, Apr. 22, 1945, Russell A. Meyer Papers.

82. Glenn E. Matthews, "Photoprogress in 1941," *JPSA*, Apr. 1942, p. 164; Boyle audio cassette, 1980; "WW2, 41-45, etc.," Lewis Papers; Jonathan Heller, *War & Conflict: Selected Images from the National Archives, 1765–1970* (Washington, DC: National Archives and Records Administration, 1990), p. 15.

83. APS, "Report of Photographic Activities," p. 45; Ignatius Gallo to the author, Aug. 15, 1982; Kieft to the author, Aug. 8, 1981; Morehouse to the author, Sept. 5, 1981.

84. "New Designs in Combat Cameras," p. 72; Glenn E. Matthews, "Photoprogress in 1942," *JPSA*, Apr. 1943, p. 152; William Stull, "The First Real Combat Camera," *AC*, Nov. 1942, pp. 474, 490; "Technical Progress in 1942," *AC*, Jan. 1943, p. 6.

85. Lt. Spafford to Carleton Mitchell, Dec. 1, [1944], Unit 13 (Lieut. Spafford) file, and memo on "Cunningham Combat Cameras, request for," from Mitchell to Director of Photography, Bureau of Aeronautics, Dec. 12, 1944, Equipment Folder #2 file, both in NCPD, NA.

86. Matthews, "Photoprogress in 1941," *JPSA*, Apr. 1942, p. 165; F. Barrows Colton, "How We Fight with Photographs," *NGM*, Sept. 1944, p. 270; Maj. Gen. H. H. Arnold, "Aerial Color Photography Becomes a War Weapon," *NGM*, June 1940, pp. 757–58.

87. Memo to "All Combat Photo Unit Officers" from Carleton Mitchell, Dec. 1, 1943, Information New CPUs file; Mitchell to Lt. Drennan, Apr. 25, 1944, Unit 2 (Lieut. Drennan) file; Mitchell to the Director of Public Relations, Aug. 24, 1944, Capt. Markey file; all in NCPD, NA. APS, "Army Pictorial Service Annual Report For The Fiscal Year 1 July 1944 to 30 June 1945" (OCSO, July 21, 1945), pp. 50–51, NA.

88. William A. Palmer, "Direct-16mm vs. 35mm for Training Film Production," *AC*, Mar. 1943, p. 112; *Life*, Aug. 7, 1944, pp. 55–57; R. S. Quackenbush, Jr., "The Gun Camera," *JSMPE*, May 1945, pp. 368–69.

89. Lt. Walter Evans, "The Contribution of Color to Navy Training Films," *BSM*, June 10, 1945, pp. 60–61; Joseph A. Bors, "Navy Photo Science Laboratory," *PP*, May 1944, p. 89; W. Keener to Carleton Mitchell, June 10, 1941 [sic: 1944], Unit 3 (Lieut. Newcomb) file, NCPD, NA.

90. George Stevens, Jr., and Max Hastings, *Victory in Europe: D-Day to VE Day In Full Color* (Boston: Little Brown and Company, 1985), p. 8.

91. Peter P. Drowne, "An Investigation into the Evolution of Motion-Picture Photography and Film Usage in the United States Marine Corps

1940–45" (Unpublished Master's Thesis, University of California at Los Angeles, 1965), pp. 41–42.

92. "In combat," wrote one 35mm-motion-picture cameraman, "we would run out of film because we could not carry enough"; William H. Ettinger to the author, Dec. 11, 1980.

93. John N. Harman, Jr., to the author, Feb. 26, 1992; Evans, "Contribution of Color," p. 60; Carroll H. Dunning, "16mm Color to 35mm Black-and-White," AC, Dec. 1944, p. 407; "Hints on Outdoor Camerawork for Army Combat And Training Films," AC, June 1943, p. 207.

94. APS, "Handbook for Motion Picture Photographers" p. 37; Eichberg and Quadow, "Combat Photography," Appendix F; memo to "All Combat Photo Unit Officers" from Carleton Mitchell, Dec. 1, 1943, Information New CPUs file, NCPD, NA; "Photographic Activities of the 7th AAF, Combat Camera Unit," June 6, 1944, Records of the 7th CCU, AFHRA.

95. Eichberg and Quadow, "Combat Photography," pp. 154, 168–69; Ansco ad in *Life*, May 14, 1944, p. 61; Palmer, "Direct-16mm vs. 35mm," pp. 112–13.

96. Darryl F. Zanuck, *Tunis Expedition* (New York: Random House, 1943), p. 78; and APS, "Report of Photographic Activities," p. 45.

97. Eichberg and Quadow, "Combat Photography," pp. 140–41, and "Photographic Activities of the 7th AAF, Combat Camera Unit."

98. The two men sent to Italy were Morris Berman and Frank S. Errigo; for their activities see Berman reminiscences, Nov. 11, 1987, Berman Papers; Berman to the author, mid-Oct. 1987; Tech. Sgt. Frank S. Errigo, "Shooting Army Color: A Factual Report of Army Experiences in Illustration," BSM, Dec. 30, 1945, pp. 50–51.

99. Eichberg and Quadow, "Combat Photography," pp. 66–67.

100. Craig interview, Mar. 26–27, 1979.

101. The SFPs can be followed in the "Daily Activity Reports" from the Chief, Motion Picture Services Division, to Executive, AC/AS, Intelligence, Jan.–Aug. 1945, in Motion Picture Services Division Activity Reports file, AFHRA. Also see "History of First Motion Picture Unit Army Air Forces, Culver City, California," Sept. 1–30, 1945, AFHRA.

102. Orders issued by Robert B. Miller, Acting Chief, Motion Picture Services Division, Feb. 1, 1945, John D. Craig Papers.

103. "History of the Fourth Combat Camera Unit: Second Phase—The ETO," Feb.–June 1945, Records of the 4th CCU; "Unit History," Feb.–Aug. 1945, Records of the 3rd CCU; "Historical Record: Fifth Army Air Forces Combat Camera Unit," monthly reports for 1945, Records of the 5th CCU; "Unit History From Activation Through 31 March 1944" [This document actually contains reports through Oct.

1945.], monthly reports for 1945, Records of the 6th CCU; "Unit History," reports for 1945, Records of the 8th CCU; "Narrative History," Apr. 1–May 31, June 1–30, and July 1–31, 1945, Records of the 11th CCU. All in AFHRA.

104. "Statement for 'The Last Bomb'" by Curtis LeMay, Henry H. Arnold Papers, AFHRA; "AAF's 'Last Bomb' Sensational," AC, Feb. 1946, p. 44.

105. Stevens and Hastings, *Victory in Europe*, pp. 7–11.

106. "Unit History From Activation Through 31 March 1944," pp. 13–17, Records of the 6th CCU, AFHRA.

107. "History of First Motion Picture Unit Army Air Forces, Culver City, California," May 1–31, 1944, Appendix D, p. 2, AFHRA; and interview of Commanding Officer Mollwitz by 1st Lt. Vincent P. Hughes, Sept. 14, 1945, enclosed in "Narrative," Records of the 11th CCU, AFHRA.

108. "Combat Photographic Operations," (undated), CARL; Thompson, et al., *The Test*, pp. 403–406; Thompson and Harris, *The Outcome*, p. 570; Eichberg and Quadow, "Combat Photography," Appendix N; Lt. Reiman to Carleton Mitchell, Apr. 25, 1943, Combat Photography Unit 7 (Lt. Reiman) file, NCPD, NA; memo on "Material for possible inclusion in Cominch memorandum," from Mitchell to the Deputy Director, Oct. 10, 1944, Miscellaneous file, NCPD, NA.

109. "U.S. Naval Photography, Some Comments Concerning," enclosed with Lt. Burlingame to Mitchell, Aug. 7, 1944, Movies—Unit 6—Burlingame file, NCPD, NA.

110. William C. Barry to Carleton Mitchell, Apr. 26, 1945, Combat Photography Recent Letters file, NCPD, NA.

111. Eichberg and Quadow, "Combat Photography," pp. 74–75 and Appendix N; APS, "Report of Photographic Activities," pp. 9, 33, 39–40, 50; MacArthur to Somervell, July 26, 1943.

112. "Interview of Captain Roy E. Steele, Commanding Officer of 2nd Combat Camera Unit, made and prepared by 1st Lt. James P. McFarland," Sept. 6, 1945, and "Unit History," Aug. 1945, Appendix A, both in Records of the 2nd CCU, AFHRA; "Unit History," July 1944, Records of the 8th CCU, AFHRA; "Confessions of a Navy Combat Photographic Unit Officer," Combat Photography Unit 5 (Lt. Samuel) file, NCPD, NA.

Chapter 3. "Jeez, This Is Just Like in the Movies"

1. Manny Farber, "One for the Ages: *Desert Victory*," in Lewis Jacobs, ed., *The Documentary Tradition: From Nanook to Woodstock* (New York: Hopkinson and Blake, 1971), p. 212, and *Life*, Apr. 5, 1943, p. 54.

2. Henry L. Stimson Diaries, May 8, 1943, microfilm edition of the Diaries from the Yale University Library.

3. *Life*, Apr. 5, 1943, p. 54.
4. Darryl F. Zanuck, *Tunis Expedition* (New York: Random House, 1943), p. 159.
5. Quoted in Myra MacPherson, *Long Time Passing: Vietnam & the Haunted Generation* (New York: Doubleday and Company, 1984), p. 43.
6. *Time*, July 31, 1944, p. 50, and Theodore W. Sizer interview, Aug. 31, 1983.
7. Harold P. Leinbaugh and John D. Campbell, *The Men of Company K: The Autobiography of a World War II Rifle Company* (New York: William Morrow & Company, 1985), p. 46.
8. Chief Signal Officer quoted in George R. Thompson and Dixie R. Harris, *The United States Army in World War II. The Signal Corps: The Outcome (Mid-1943 Through 1945)* (Washington, DC: Office of the Chief of Military History, 1966), p. 570.
9. Ned R. Morehouse to the author, July 17, 1981.
10. "History of First Motion Picture Unit Army Air Forces, Culver City, California," May 1–31, 1944, p. 12, AFHRA, and "Real War Differs From War Films, Says Gable," *MPH*, Nov. 6, 1943, p. 64.
11. Byron Haskins, "'Special Effects' and Wartime Production," AC, Mar. 1943, p. 89.
12. Lt. Gerretson to Carleton Mitchell, June 17, 1944, and Mitchell to Gerretson, June 24, 1944, both in Unit 8 (Lieut. Gerretson[)] file, NCPD, NA; Ignatius Gallo to the author, May 1982; Fred Mandl interview, June 13, 1980.
13. Donald J. Morrow Diary, July 12, 1944, Morrow Papers, and Captain J. Winston Lemen, "Combat Photography in the U.S. Marine Corps," *JPSA*, May 1945, p. 198.
14. "Confessions of a Navy Combat Photo Unit Officer," Combat Photography Unit 5 (Lt. Samuel) file, NCPD, NA; Larry Sowinski, *Action in the Pacific as Seen by US Navy Photographers during World War 2* (Annapolis: Naval Institute Press, 1981), p. 44; "Every Shot a Prize Winner," *United States Marine Corps Headquarters Bulletin*, June 1945, pp. 26–27.
15. As one expert phrased it, "The difficulties of working under actual fire prevent him [a cameraman] from indulging his artistic inclinations," Jack Price, A *Guide for Military and News Photography* (New York: Falk Publishing Co., 1944), p. 21.
16. Capt. M. S. Blankfort, "The Camera Is A Weapon," AC, Jan. 1944, p. 14; Jerome N. Kahn audio cassette responding to the author's inquiries, 1980; Robert F. Albright audio cassette responding to the author's inquiries, 1991.
17. Report from CPU #2 by Myrl A. Yeaman, undated, Data CPU file, NCPD, NA.

18. Major General Harry C. Ingles, Chief Signal Officer from 1943–1947, made some of these points in an April 1944 press conference; see the extract from a Signal Corps "Technical Information Letter," William A. Avery Papers.

19. Robert L. Eichberg and Jacqueline Quadow, "Combat Photography," (HS, SAB, OCSO, Nov. 1945) pp. 105–06, CARL.

20. Hatch's footage appeared in both *With the Marines at Tarawa* and *I Was There: Tarawa.* Peters' footage appeared in *Fury in the Pacific.* Also see "Jap Vs. Camera: Blast Buries Film in Mud," *USC,* Feb. 1945, p. 48.

21. For example, *7th Infantry Division* contained a scene of four Japanese soldiers running along a ridgeline, and former Marine Corps cameraman Martin Friedman has a VHS cassette, entitled *The Battle of Okinawa* and released by the United States Marine Corps (*henceforth* USMC) Combat Correspondents Association, of footage from Okinawa showing more than fifty Japanese soldiers running along a hillside to escape an American mortar barrage.

22. Eichberg and Quadow, "Combat Photography," pp. 92–105.

23. Memo on "Combat Correspondents" from the Divison of Public Relations, Headquarters USMC, Apr. 7, 1943, Combat Correspondents (2) file, MCHC; memo on "Comments on Mr. Selznick's plan" from Leland P. Lovette to the Vice Chief of Naval Operations, Oct. 9, 1942, Photostats file, NCPD, NA; Lt. Wrigley to Carleton Mitchell, Apr. 13, 1944, and Mitchell to Wrigley, Apr. 29 and May 16, 1944, all in Unit 10 (Lieut. Wrigley) file, NCPD, NA.

24. "Production Chart Guide For 16mm Motion-Picture Unit," AFHRA.

25. Photo Memo No. 5 for "All Photographic Personnel" from Maj. Linden G. Rigby, May 17, 1944, Donald J. Morrow Papers. Some cameramen even followed this policy into the postwar era. For example, Gordon T. Frye's personal album contains six photos showing a wounded machine gunner, a medic giving him aid, and then the man being carried off on a stretcher; Frye's notation reads: "One of series of 'Give Blood for your Buddy'—also part of Red Cross job (Reenacted—Not Actual Combat)."

26. Morrow Diary, July 17, 1944, Morrow Papers.

27. Fred Owens to the author, July, 1980; William E. Teas interview, Nov. 6, 1981; Harvey A. Weber to the author, Dec. 12, 1989.

28. Barney Wolf, "Explosions—Made to Order," *AC,* Dec. 1942, p. 510, and Tom Maloney, ed., *U.S. Camera 1946: Victory Volume* (n.p.: U.S. Camera Publishers, 1945), pp. 58–59.

29. *Time,* May 28, 1984, p. 29.

30. "Special Memo to All Cameramen, Notably *Still* Men" from Lewis, Mar. 18, 1945, Frye Papers.

31. Morrow repeatedly noted the battlefield stench; see his Diary entries for May 31, June 4, 5, and July 14, 15, 1944, Morrow Papers.

32. Joseph M. Zinni to his wife, Feb. 1, 1945, Zinni Papers.

33. The film's title is *San Pietro*, although commentators (including Huston and some of his biographers!) often refer to it as *The Battle of San Pietro*.

34. *New York Post*, undated clipping, Gordon T. Frye Papers; Product Digest Section of *MPH*, Mar. 10, 1945, p. 2351; *Time*, May 21, 1945, pp. 94, 96.

35. William J. Blakefield, *Documentary Film Classics*, 2nd ed., (Washington, DC: National AudioVisual Center, n.d.), p. 37; Clyde Jeavons, A *Pictorial History of War Films* (Secaucus, NJ: The Citadel Press, 1974) p. 150; Douglas W. Gallez, "Patterns in Wartime Documentaries," *The Quarterly of Film, Radio and Television*, Winter 1955, p. 132; Jeanine Basinger, *The World War II Combat Film: Anatomy of a Genre* (New York: Columbia University Press, 1984), p. 127.

36. Richard Griffith, "The Use of Film by the U.S. Armed Services," Appendix I, p. 357, in Paul Rotha, *Documentary Film*, 3rd ed. rev., (New York: Hastings House, 1952); and Roger Manvell, *Films and the Second World War* (New York: Dell Publishing Company, 1974), p. 181.

37. Quoted in Robert Hughes, ed., *Film: Book 2. Films of Peace and War* (New York: Grove Press, 1962), p. 20; David H. Hackworth and Julie Sherman, *About Face* (New York: Simon and Schuster, 1989), pp. 361–62.

38. "'San Pietro' Tells Graphically How Town Was Taken," *MPH*, July 14, 1945, p. 29; Gerald Pratley, *The Cinema of John Huston* (New York: A. S. Barnes and Company, 1977), pp. 54–56; Hughes, *Film: Book 2*, p. 26.

39. John Huston, *An Open Book* (New York: Alfred A. Knopf, 1980).

40. Martin Blumenson, *United States Army in World War II: The Mediterranean Theater of Operations. Salerno to Cassino* (Washington, DC: Office of the Chief of Military History, 1969), Chapter XVI. The following account also relies on Robert L. Wagner, *The Texas Army: A History of the 36th Division in the Italian Campaign* (Austin: n. p., 1972), and Robert Wallace and the Editors of Time-Life Books, *The Italian Campaign* (Alexandria, VA: Time-Life Books, 1981).

41. Richard W. Steele, "American Popular Opinion and the War Against Germany: The Issue of Negotiated Peace, 1942," *Journal of American History*, (henceforth *JAH*), Dec. 1978, pp. 704–23, and Mark H. Leff, "The Politics of Sacrifice on the American Home Front in World War II," *JAH*, Mar. 1991, pp. 1296–1318.

42. John Morton Blum, *V Was for Victory: Politics and American Culture During World War II* (New York: Harcourt Brace Jovanovich, 1976), pp. 21–30; Clayton R. Koppes and Gregory D. Black, *Hollywood Goes to War: How Politics, Profits, and Propaganda Shaped World War II Movies* (New York: The Free Press, 1987), pp. 52–60; Susan D. Moeller, *Shooting War: Photography and the American Experience of Combat* (New York: Basic Books, 1989), p. 8.

43. Samuel I. Rosenman, ed., *The Public Papers and Addresses of Franklin D. Roosevelt*, 13 vols., (New York: Harper & Brothers, 1938–1950). Vol. XII covers 1943; the quotations are from pp. 6, 113, 389, 399.

44. Ibid. The quotations are from pp. 182, 324, 399.

45. Germany confronted the same dilemma during World War II, as did the Union during the Civil War and the United States during the recent conflict with Iraq. See George L. Mosse, *Fallen Soldiers: Reshaping the Memory of the World Wars* (New York: Oxford University Press, 1990), p. 202; Alan Trachtenberg, *Reading American Photographs: Images as History, Mathew Brady to Walker Evans* ([New York:] Hill and Wang, 1989), p. 93; "Networks plan all-out war coverage but limits could stem flow of hard news," *Lincoln* [Nebraska] *Journal*, Jan. 15, 1991, p. 9; "Will We See the Real War?" *Newsweek*, Jan. 14, 1991, p. 19.

46. William L. Chenery, *So It Seemed* (New York: Harcourt, Brace and Company, 1952), pp. 278–79.

47. Memo on "Release of Pictures" from [AAF] Lt. Col. Curtis Mitchell, Chief, Pictorial Branch, Bureau of Public Relations, enclosed with memo on "Report on Motion-Picture Footage Forwarded by CCUs" from William J. Keighley to the Commanding Officer, 9th CCU, May 13, 1943, Records of the 9th CCU, AFHRA; and "Hoyt Asks More Realism in War News Coverage," *MPH*, Oct. 2, 1943, p. 14.

48. "Morale Photography," *Newsweek*, May 24, 1943, p. 15, and "Photo With a Message," ibid., p. 27.

49. "War Photo Confusion," *Newsweek*, Oct. 11, 1943, p. 12; "Realism for Breakfast," *Newsweek*, Sept. 20, 1943, p. 98; *Life*, Aug. 2, 1943, p. 23. Although the new realism first manifested itself in still pictures, the newsreels were not far behind; see "War Newsreels," *MPH*, Sept. 11, 1943, p. 7.

50. "Realism for Breakfast;" Letters to the Editor in *Life*, Oct. 11, 1943, pp. 4, 6; "Asks Newsreels Drop Gruesome Shots," *MPH*, Oct. 23, 1943, p. 48; "Report on War," *MPH*, Jan. 1, 1944, p. 7; "War Photo Rush," *Newsweek*, Nov. 1, 1943, p. 16.

51. For an inkling of the types of wounds and death *not* shown during the war consult Maj. James C. Beyer, ed., *Wound Ballistics* (Washington, DC: Office of the Surgeon General, 1962).

52. "Realism to Feature War Loan Film," *MPH*, Dec. 25, 1943, p. 33, and "Special Memo to All Cameramen, Notably *Still* Men," from Lewis, Mar. 18, 1945, Gordon T. Frye Papers.

53. James J. Gibson, ed., *Motion Picture Testing and Research (Report No. VII of Army Air Forces Aviation Psychology Program Research Reports)*, (Washington, DC: U.S. Government Printing Office, 1947), pp. 16–17.

54. For example, see Paul Fussell, *Wartime: Understanding and Behavior in the Second World War* (New York: Oxford University Press, 1989), pp. 269–72.

55. *With the Marines at Tarawa.* In *To the Shores of Iwo Jima* the narrator said, "It was tough going. Many didn't make it," and in *US Marines Capture Tarawa!*, produced by Castle Films, the narrator talked about the 1,026 dead and 2,557 wounded Marines and said, "The price of victory was high."

56. The impact of constant repetition can be overpowering; see Nicholas Pronay, "The 'Moving Picture' and Historical Research," *JCH*, July 1983, p. 370.

57. APS, "Report of Photographic Activities" (Signal Section, Headquarters Fifth Army, Dec. 31, 1943), Records of the 163rd SPC, NA. Except where noted the next ten paragraphs rely primarily on this document, but also include material from APS, "Report on Motion Picture Progress" (Signal Section, Headquarters Fifth Army, Dec. 25, 1943), Records of the 163rd SPC, NA.

58. Warren Kieft Diary, Sept. 28, 1943, Kieft Papers.

59. For the members of the 163rd who worked with Huston, see Gordon T. Frye, "Rhode Island to the Rhine"; Frye to the author, Jan. 1984; *New York Post*, undated clipping that names the cameramen and has Frye's handwritten notations, Frye Papers.

60. Robert L. Lewis to the author, Nov. 17, 1980 and Jan. 10, 1981; Lewis to Joseph D. Boyle, Sept. 9, 1980; Robert J. Goebel interview, Oct. 8, 1983. Eric Ambler, *Here Lies Eric Ambler: An Autobiography* (London: Weidenfeld and Nicolson, 1985), pp. 201–204, describes an incident when the camera crew "deserted" Huston.

61. The filmmaker was John Grierson, quoted in R. C. Raack, "Historiography as Cinematography: A Prolegomenon to Film Work for Historians," *JCH*, July 1983, p. 424; Holmes quoted in James West Davidson and Mark Hamilton Lytle, *After the Fact: The Art of Historical Detection*, 2 vols., 2nd ed., (New York: Alfred A. Knopf, 1986), Vol. II, p. 237.

62. Susan Sontag, *On Photography* (New York: Farrar, Straus and Giroux, 1977), pp. 68–70, and John Tagg, *The Burden of Representation: Essays on Photographies and Histories* (Amherst: University of Massachusetts Press, 1988), pp. 2–3, 164–65.

63. Gibson, *Motion Picture Testing and Research*, pp. 174–76.

64. Wagner, *Texas Army*, p. 90.

65. Lawrence Grobel, *The Hustons* (New York: Charles Scribner's Sons, 1989), p. 239; Huston, *An Open Book*, pp. 102–104; Tony Aldgate, "Mr. Capra Goes to War: Frank Capra, the British Army Film Unit, and Anglo-American Travails in the Production of 'Tunisian Victory'," *Historical Journal of Film, Radio and Television*, No. 1, 1991, pp. 21–39. The end message of *Tunisian Victory* states that "When necessary, for purposes of clarity, certain stock shots were used and a few authentic reenactments were photographed under War Department or War Office supervision."

66. Ambler, *Here Lies Eric Ambler*, pp. 205, 210–11.
67. Ibid., p. 192, and Grobel, *The Hustons*, p. 249. Ambler left Italy on Dec. 22, 1943.
68. Frye, "Rhode Island to the Rhine"; Frye to the author, Jan. 1984; Frye's audio cassette responding to the author's inquiries, 1983; telephone interviews with Frye, Dec. 19, 1989 and Sept. 29, 1990; Tischler to the author, Sept. 17, 1981; Tischler interview, Oct. 8, 1983; telephone interviews with Tischler, Oct. 18, 1990 and Dec. 4, 1990.
69. "Record-of-Film-Shot-During-War," Tischler Papers.
70. Morehouse to the author, Sept. 5, 1981. Also see Lewis to the author, Feb. 18, 1981, and Goebel interview, Oct. 8, 1983.
71. Lance Bertelsen, "San Pietro and the 'Art' of War," *Southwest Review*, Spring 1989, pp. 253–54.
72. "Record-of-Film-Shot-During-War"; Tischler interview, Oct. 8, 1983; Tischler to the author, Sept. 17, 1981; Frye to his parents, July 8, 1944, Frye Papers.
73. David Culbert, ed., *Film and Propaganda in America: A Documentary History*, 3 vols. (Westport, CT: Greenwood Press, 1990), Vol. II, Part 2, pp. 229–52, reproduces all but one of the index cards for the outtakes; the card Culbert inexplicably omits is ADC 703–2.
74. APS, "Report on Motion Picture Progress"; the following three paragraphs are also based on this document.
75. Culbert, *Film and Propaganda in America*, Vol. II, Part 2, p. 277.
76. The film's revisions can be followed in Culbert, pp. 253–99; also see Grobel, *The Hustons*, p. 250.
77. Blakefield, *Documentary Film Classics*, p. 33; William T. Murphy, "John Ford and the Wartime Documentary," *Film & History*, Feb. 1976, p. 6; James M. Skinner, "*December 7*: Filmic Myth Masquerading as Historical Fact," *Journal of Military History*, Oct. 1991, pp. 508–509.
78. Boyle audio cassette, 1980.
79. Frye to his wife, Dec. 31, 1943, Frye Papers.

Chapter 4. "We Shoot 'em with a Camera—Only"

1. Unless otherwise noted, the material on Gordon T. Frye in this chapter relies on the sources listed in Note 1, Chapter One.
2. Frye was one of the original four soldier-cameramen on the *Yank* staff; see Victor Keppler, "The *Yank* is Coming," *USC*, Sept. 1942, p. 26.
3. "WW2, 41–45, etc.," a 163rd SPC photo album that contains both pictures and documentary material, Robert L. Lewis Papers, and *Foto-Facto*, Dec. 18, 1944, Records of the 163rd SPC, NA.
4. Fred Bonnard audio cassette responding to the author's inquiries, 1980. The 165th SPC's Robert C. Reinhart made *nine* first-wave landings; Reinhart to the author, Nov. 12, 1991.
5. Robert L. Eichberg and Jacqueline Quadow, "Combat Photography"

(HS, SAB, OCSO, Nov. 1945), pp. 162–63, CARL. Apparently the 195th SPC was never deployed.

6. "Historical Records and History of Organization," July 10, 1943, Records of the 161st SPC, NA; Eichberg and Quadow, "Combat Photography," pp. 15–20; War Department, "Summary Report on Photographic Activities of the Signal Corps Since August 4, 1941 in the Fields of Motion Pictures & Visual Aids" (OCSO, Feb. 26, 1943), pp. 129–30, 350–51, NA; John N. Harman, Jr., "In Retrospect: A 'Gon Editor Recalls Typical Events of Last Thirty-five Years," clipping dated 1964, John N. Harman, Jr. Papers.

7. "Historical Records and History of Organization," July 10, 1943, Records of the 161st SPC, NA; Special Orders No. 87, Apr. 9, 1942; "History of the 163rd Signal Photographic Company," Feb. 10, 1943; and "The Story of the 163rd Signal Photo Co." All in the Records of the 163rd SPC, NA.

8. War Department Table of Organization and Equipment No. 11-37. *Signal Photographic Company* (War Department: Feb. 12, 1944); Eichberg and Quadow, "Combat Photography," Appendix M; "The Officers of the 168 Signal Photo Co.," Records of the 168th SPC, NA; "Combat Photographic Operations" (undated), CARL.

9. "Historical Records and History of Organization," Oct. 9, 1944, Records of the 161st SPC, NA; "Company History 1 January 1943 to 31 December 1944," Appendix A, Records of the 164th SPC, NA; "Company History," Records of the 167th SPC, NA; "Company History," July 15 to Aug. 15, 1944, Records of the 163rd SPC, NA.

10. Eichberg and Quadow, "Combat Photography," Appendix N.

11. Ibid., pp. 24, 82, 117, and Appendix N.

12. The 163rd SPC considered the T/O&E a "handicap"; see "The Story of the 163rd Signal Photo Co.," Records of the 163rd SPC, NA. Various other companies developed methods other than the use of Corps Photo Liaison Officers to gain better coordination and utilization of the assignments units. As commander of the 161st, John N. Harman, Jr. performed essentially the same function as the Corps Photo Liaison Officers by traveling "to the various field locations where our combat assignment units were stationed on attached duty with Corps and Divisions in the field." He made sure that the frontline units understood the photographers' mission "and that our combat cameramen would have authority and freedom to do their job"; Harman to the author, Feb. 26, 1992.

13. "A Standing Operating Procedure for Combat Assignment Teams (SOPCAT)" (Headquarters 163rd SPC, Feb. 20, 1945), Gordon T. Frye Papers.

14. *Foto-Facto*, Jan. 22, 1945. The 163rd's monthly "Company History" for

Jan.–May, 1945, showed CATs numbered 1 through 24; Records of the 163rd SPC, NA.

15. "Company History 1 January 1943 to 31 December 1944," second Appendix C, Records of the 164th SPC, NA.

16. War Department Pamphlet No. 11-2. *Standing Operating Procedure For Signal Photographic Units in Theaters of Operations* (War Department, Apr. 20, 1944).

17. "Standard Operating Procedure For Signal Photographic Units," HQ Seventh Army, Mar. 27, 1945, in "WW2, 41-45, etc.," Lewis Papers, and APS, "Handbook for Motion-Picture Photographers in the European Theater of Operations" (Signal Corps, United States Army, undated), pp. 1, 16, Russell A. Meyer Papers.

18. Joseph D. Boyle audio cassette responding to the author's inquiries, 1980; John S. Wever to Kyme Meade, Apr. 22, 1980, and Marvin R. Pike to Meade, Aug. 12, 1980, both in Joseph D. Boyle Papers.

19. "Company History," Mar. 15 to Apr. 15, 1945; "Story of the 163rd"; "History of the 163rd," Feb. 10, 1943; "Company History: Extract for Calendar Year 1943," Appendix B; "Report of Activities To 20 November 1943." All in the Records of the 163rd SPC, NA.

20. Boyle audio cassette, 1980, and Boyle to the author [Fall, 1980].

21. In addition to the sources cited in Note 19 above, see Warren Kieft Diary, Aug. 24, 29, 1943, Kieft Papers, and Kieft's comments on his diary, Aug., 1981.

22. Kieft Diary, Sept. 2, 14, and 28, 1943, and "Story of the 163rd."

23. "Record of Laboratory Movement"; "Movement of Company Headquarters Overseas"; "Story of the 163rd"; "Company History" beginning with the monthly entry for Aug. 15 to Sept. 15, 1944. All in Records of the 163rd SPC, NA.

24. APS, "Report of Photographic Activities," (Signal Section, Headquarters Fifth Army, Dec. 31, 1943), p. 15, Records of the 163rd SPC, NA.

25. *Foto-Facto*, Nov. 13, 1944.

26. "Company History" monthly entries from July 15 to Oct. 15, 1944, and "Army Assignments of the 163rd Signal Photo Company," Records of the 163rd SPC, NA; Kieft Diary, July 1 and 21, 1944; Samuel T. Tischler to Joseph D. Boyle, Aug. 15, 1980, Boyle Papers; Bronze Star Medal citation, Tischler Papers. Also see memo on "Amphibious Assault Information" from Col. G. F. Wooley to Chief Signal Officer, Mediterranean Theater of Operations, Jan. 28, 1945, in "Information on Signal Personnel and Equipment in Amphibious Assault Landings" (undated), CARL.

27. Newell to his mother, Aug. 16, 1944, Edward C. Newell Papers.

28. Kieft Diary, Aug. 15, 1944.

29. Ibid., Sept. 20, 1944.

30. "Team History" for CAT #18, May 10–17, 1945, Records of the 163rd SPC, NA.

Chapter 5. "Sticking Their Necks Out Doing Their Weird Things"

1. Unless otherwise noted, this account of Arthur H. Herz relies on the Herz materials listed in the Bibliography.

2. On Skorzeny and his unit see Charles B. MacDonald, A *Time for Trumpets: The Untold Story of the Battle of the Bulge* (New York: William Morrow and Company, 1985), pp. 87–89, 224–27, and on General Bradley see William K. Goolrick, Ogden Tanner, and the Editors of Time-Life Books, *The Battle of the Bulge* (Alexandria, VA: Time-Life Books, 1979), p. 59.

3. The basic source is Ruth F. Sadler, "History of the Signal Corps Affiliated Plan, August 1944" (Personnel Branch, Personnel and Training Service, OCSO, Jan. 5, 1946), CARL. Also see Jacqueline M. Quadow, "Training Films in the Second World War" (HS, SAB, OCSO, Apr. 26, 1946), p. 5, NA, and War Department, "Summary Report on Photographic Activities of the Signal Corps Since August 4, 1941, in the Fields of Motion Pictures & Visual Aids" (OCSO, Feb. 26, 1943), pp. 137–39, NA.

4. Sadler, "History of the Signal Corps Affiliated Plan," p. 100 and Exhibits F and G.

5. Billy A. Newhouse interview, Nov. 8, 1981, and Ralph Butterfield audio cassette responding to the author's inquiries, 1980.

6. War Department, "Summary Report on Photographic Activities," pp. 218–19.

7. Sadler, "History of the Signal Corps Affiliated Plan," p. 101; "A.S.C. and Academy to Train Cameramen for Army Service," AC, June 1942, pp. 255, 278; "Uncle Sam's Cameramen Are Coming!" AC, Sept. 1942, pp. 395, 418; Sgt. Herb A. Lightman, "The Men Behind The Combat Cameramen," AC, Oct. 1945, pp. 332, 355. Other services, such as the Marines, also sent cameramen to Hollywood for training; see Harrold A. Weinberger, unpublished autobiography, Weinberger Papers.

8. Butterfield audio cassette, 1980; Russell A. Meyer interview, June 12, 1980; Billy A. Newhouse to the author, Oct. 31, 1991.

9. Sadler, "History of the Signal Corps Affiliated Plan," Exhibit F; William E. Teas interview, Nov. 6, 1981; Paul N. Fox to the author, July 21, 1980; audio cassette of an informal conversation among four members of the 166th SPC, 1980, Russell A. Meyer Papers; "Instructing U.S. Signal Corps Photographic Companies with Major Art Lloyd, A.S.C.," AC, July 1946, p. 258. Other APS cameramen trained other units. For example, T/Sgt. Herold E. Baldwin and Capt. Andrew L. Gold worked with the 164th SPC; see "Company History 1 January 1943 to 31 December 1944," Records of the 164th SPC, NA.

10. Memo to "All Combat Photography Unit Officers" from Carleton Mitchell, Dec. 1, 1943, Information New CPUs file, NCPD, NA.

11. "Company History from date of Activation thru December 31, 1942," and "Company History 1 January 1943 to 31 December 1944," both in Records of the 164th SPC, NA.

12. "Company History," Records of the 167th SPC, NA.

13. "'Photo By Signal Corps': The Story of the 166th," NA; Harvey A. Weber audio cassette responding to the author's inquiries, 1981; Weber to the author, undated; Weber, "Photographer at War," *American Heritage*, April/May 1985, p. 49. (*American Heritage* garbled some of the information in Weber's story, so this essay contains numerous errors.)

14. "'Photo By Signal Corps': The Story of the 166th."

15. Ibid.; Weber audio cassette, 1981; Weber to the author, undated; Weber to the author, Nov. 28, 1989; George H. Meyer to the author, Oct. 12, 1980; William E. Teas interview, Nov. 6, 1981; Joseph M. Zinni to his wife, Feb. 23, 1945, Zinni Papers.

16. Robert L. Eichberg and Jacqueline Quadow, "Combat Photography" (HS, SAB, OCSO, Nov. 1945), Appendix N, CARL; *Foto-Facto*, Dec. 4 and 11, 1944, and "Company History," Nov. 15—Dec. 15, 1944, both in Records of the 163rd SPC, NA.

17. "Unit History From Activation Through 31 March 1944 [actually through Oct. 1945]," June, Aug., and Sept. 1945, Records of the 6th CCU, AFHRA.

18. "Unit History," Aug. 8, 1945, Records of the 10th CCU, AFHRA; "Unit History," May and June 1944, and "Unit War Diary," May and June 1944, Records of the 12th CCU, AFHRA.

19. "War Diary," Feb. 8, 1945, in "Historical Records," Feb. 1945, Records of the 9th CCU, AFHRA.

20. Major General Davenport Johnson to Major General James P. Hodges, AC/AS Intelligence, Nov. 28, 1944, Henry H. Arnold Papers, AFHRA.

21. Unless otherwise noted, this account of Bernard J. Caliendo relies on the Caliendo materials listed in the Bibliography.

22. Newhouse interview, Nov. 8, 1981.

23. Adrien Salvas to the author, Mar. 1990.

24. Aside from the sources in Notes 1 and 21, above, see also the account of this episode in "'Photo By Signal Corps': The Story of the 166th."

25. Weber to the author, Dec. 12, 1989; in a VHS cassette that he narrated entitled *The Battle of Okinawa*, Martin Friedman explained that he did not have the heart to shoot pictures of dead Marines; *The History of Photography Series*, Robert Delpire, producer, *Edward Steichen* (Millerton, NY: Aperture, Inc., 1978), p. 10.

26. Donald Ornitz wrote that upon entering a village near Bastogne, "I found my friends—their clothes blown [to] shreds hanging, caught on trees (I've photographs), their bodies dead, loss of blood; you could see

the quantity—measurable on the snow.... My pictures were used, but not the ones I wanted seen—my friends dead"; "'Photo by Signal Corps': The Story of the 166th."

27. *Time*, May 28, 1984, pp. 12–13.

28. "Special Memo to All Cameramen, Notably *Still* Men" from Robert L. Lewis, Mar. 18, 1945, Gordon T. Frye Papers.

29. Martin W. Sandler, *American Image: Photographing One Hundred Years in the Life of a Nation* (Chicago: Contemporary Books, Inc., 1989), pp. 203 and 206; and Sandler to the author, Feb. 2, 1990. Another egregious error is in *Time*, Jan. 11, 1993, p. 30, where a photo taken on a tropical isle is labeled "Taking the beach at Iwo Jima, 1945."

30. For an example of a D-Day daylight paratroop drop see the segment in the *Victory at Sea* series titled *D-Day: Normandy*. This episode also intermingles rehearsal scenes and real combat footage. The former can usually be identified by the lack of defensive beach obstacles, the absence of battlefield debris, and the small amount of smoke and dust. CPU #2 shot rehearsals so that the footage "can be worked into the final story on 'the real thing.'" See Lt. Drennan to Carleton Mitchell, May 24, June 1, and June 7, 1944, Unit 2 (Lieut. Drennan) file, NCPD, NA.

31. Martha A. Sandweiss, Rick Stewart, and Ben W. Huseman, *Eyewitness to War: Prints and Daguerreotypes of the Mexican War, 1846–1848* (Washington, DC: Smithsonian Institution Press, 1989), pp. 213–14, proves that a Mexican War daguerreotype usually identified as a "View in Parras, Mexico" is actually a view of Saltillo, Mexico.

32. Sylvia E. Danovitch, "The Past Recaptured? The Photographic Record of the Internment of Japanese-Americans," *Prologue: The Journal of the National Archives*, Summer 1980, p. 103.

33. When the Nebraska educational television station produced a documentary on the 35th Division, which included the Nebraska National Guard, producer Joel R. Geyer screened footage in the NA showing the 35th Division's attack on St. Lô in the summer of 1944. As Geyer viewed the work of the two photographers who shot much of the film, Caliendo's superior camerawork was obvious to him; interview with Joel R. Geyer, May 21, 1991.

34. Harry A. Downard interview, June 16, 1980.

35. Carleton Mitchell's memo to "All Combat Photography Unit Officers." Also see "Photographic Accomplishments of the 7th AAF CCU," Aug. 22, 1944, Records of the 7th CCU, AFHRA.

36. Memo to "All Combat Photography Unit Officers"; and Mitchell to Lt. Drennan, June 8, 1944, Unit 2 (Lieut. Drennan) file, NCPD, NA.

37. "Every Shot a Prize Winner," *United States Marine Corps Headquarters Bulletin*, June 1945, pp. 26–27.

38. Detachment report dated Apr. 15, 1944 in "History of the Fourth Combat Camera Unit: Second Phase—The ETO," Records of the 4th

CCU, AFHRA; "Newsletter," Apr. 1944, Records of the 7th CCU, AFHRA; Ken Chaney interview, June 16, 1980; Allan L. Kain interview, Dec. 26, 1978.

39. Lt. Burlingame to Carleton Mitchell, Oct. 14, 1944, Unit 6 (Lieut. Burlingame) file, NCPD, NA.

40. APS, "Report of Photographic Activities" (Signal Section, Headquarters Fifth Army, Dec. 31, 1943), pp. 34–35, 41–43, Records of the 163rd SPC, NA.

41. "Unit History," May 1944, Records of the 12th CCU, AFHRA, and "Company History 1 January 1945 Thru 30 June 1945," Records of the 164th SPC, NA.

42. "Unit History," July 9, 1945, Records of the 10th CCU, AFHRA.

Chapter 6. "It Seemed Like a Lifetime"

1. *Time*, Dec. 28, 1942, p. 20. For historical accounts of the Papuan campaign see Samuel Milner, *Victory in Papua* (Washington, DC: Office of the Chief of Military History, 1957), and Lida Mayo, *Bloody Buna* (Garden City, NY: Doubleday & Company, 1974).

2. Narration for *Attack! The Battle for New Britain. The Sunset Division*, the Army's historical film on the 41st Division, also graphically portrayed the deplorable conditions in SWPA.

3. William H. Ettinger Diary, Feb. 12, 1943, Ettinger Papers. In his Diary for Aug. 8, 1943, Ettinger noted, "Christ, what a war; clothes rot off in a month." In a letter to the author, July 28, 1990, Ettinger wrote that "I just got back from a dermatologist with three kinds of medicine for New Guinea fungus."

4. Ettinger Diary, Apr. 30, 1943, Ettinger Papers.

5. "Reunion in New York For Alumni of 832nd" *Close-Up*, Oct. 9, 1945, Frank J. Goetzheimer Papers; William H. Ettinger to Les Feeny, Jan. 17, 1990, John N. Harman, Jr. Papers; War Department Table of Organization and Equipment No. 11-500. *Signal Service Organization* (War Department, Sept. 22, 1944); "Combat Photographic Operations" (undated), CARL.

6. Robert L. Eichberg and Jacqueline Quadow, "Combat Photography" (HS, SAB, OCSO, Nov. 1945), Appendix C, CARL.

7. Unless otherwise noted, this account of William A. Avery relies on the Avery materials listed in the Bibliography.

8. Milner, *Victory in Papua*, pp. 369, 374.

9. Undated newspaper clipping, John N. Harman, Jr. Papers.

10. Unless otherwise noted, this account of William H. Ettinger relies on the Ettinger materials listed in the Bibliography.

11. Mark Twain, *Life on the Mississippi* (New York: Harper & Brothers Publishers, n.d.) pp. 358–59.

12. John Tagg, *The Burden of Representation: Essays on Photographies and*

Histories (Amherst: University of Massachusetts Press, 1988), p. 188. Also see Susan Sontag, *On Photography* (New York: Farrar, Straus and Giroux, 1977), pp. 23, 108–09.

13. "A Standing Operating Procedure for Combat Assignment Teams (SOPCAT)" (Headquarters 163rd SPC, Feb. 20, 1945), Annex C, Exhibit 1, Gordon T. Frye Papers; and APS, "Handbook for Motion Picture Photographers in the European Theater of Operations" (Signal Corps, United States Army, undated), p. 33, Russell A. Meyer Papers.

14. APS, "Army Pictorial Service Annual Report For The Fiscal Year 1 July 1944 to 30 June 1945" (OCSO, July 21, 1945), p. 50, NA, and "Newsletter," June 1944, Records of the 7th CCU, AFHRA.

15. War Department Pamphlet No. 11-2. *Standing Operating Procedure For Signal Photographic Units in Theaters of Operations* (War Department: Apr. 20, 1944), pp. 8–9. Also see Eichberg and Quadow, "Combat Photography," Appendices E and M.

16. War Department Pamphlet No. 11-2, pp. 4-5, and APS, "Handbook for Motion Picture Photographers," p. 36.

17. Fred Owens to the author, July 30, 1980; Samuel T. Tischler to the author, Nov. 3, 1983; *Foto-Facto*, Nov. 20, 1944, Records of the 163rd SPC, NA.

18. "Unit History," July 31, 1944, Records of the 10th CCU, AFHRA, and War Department Pamphlet No. 11-5, *Combat Photography* (Mar. 22, 1945), p. 4, copy enclosed with Eichberg and Quadow, "Combat Photography."

19. Larry Sowinski, *Action in the Pacific As seen by US Navy photographers during World War 2* (Annapolis: Naval Institute Press, 1981), p. 5.

20. Bernard J. Caliendo audio cassette responding to the author's inquiries, 1980.

21. Arthur H. Herz to the author, Feb. 12, 1990.

22. Paul Fussell, "Images of Anonymity," *Harper's*, Sept. 1979, pp. 76–77; also see Jonathan Marwil, "How We Remember the Good War," *LSAmagazine*, Fall 1991, p. 9.

23. Susan D. Moeller makes this argument in *Shooting War: Photography and the American Experience of Combat* (New York: Basic Books, 1989).

24. William A. Avery to the author, Oct. 1, 1980; APS, "Report of Photographic Activities" (Signal Section, Headquarters Fifth Army, Dec. 31, 1943), p. 33, Records of the 163rd SPC, NA.

25. Memo on "Report on Motion-Picture Footage Forwarded to CCUs" by William J. Keighley to the Commanding Officer, 9th CCU, May 13, 1943, Records of the 9th CCU, AFHRA; and Christopher Phillips, *Steichen at War* (New York: Harry N. Abrams, Inc., 1981), p. 33.

26. Memo for Combat Correspondents from Division of Public Relations, Headquarters USMC, Mar. 10, 1943, Combat Correspondents (2) file, and "Official Style Book for Marine Corps Public Relations Officers and

Combat Correspondents," Combat Correspondents' Memo file, both in MCHC.

27. Karal Ann Marling and John Wetenhall, *Iwo Jima: Monuments, Memories, and the American Hero* (Cambridge, MA: Harvard University Press, 1991); for the ongoing controversy see "New inquiry sought into famous photo," *Lawrence* [Kansas] *Journal-World*, Nov. 11, 1990, p. 14.

28. Wever's caption on a print of the photograph, John S. Wever Papers, and Wever to the author, Oct. 31, 1981 and May 10, 1989.

29. Unless otherwise noted, this account of Frank J. Goetzheimer relies on the Goetzheimer materials listed in the Bibliography.

30. For the events recounted in this paragraph and the next one, see United States Army Signal Corps, Southwest Pacific Area, "Exposure Under Fire: An Official History of Signal Corps Photography in the Luzon Operations" (Apr. 25, 1945), pp. 1–4, 7–15, Goetzheimer Papers.

31. Donald J. Morrow Diary, Apr. 1, 1945, Morrow Papers.

32. In addition to the sources in Note 29, this account of the raid relies on Forest Bryant Johnson, *Raid on Cabanatuan* (Las Vegas: A Thousand Autumns Press, 1978), and "Exposure Under Fire," pp. 4–5.

33. In addition to the Goetzheimer materials listed in the Bibliography, this account of the recapture of Corregidor relies on Lt. Gen. E. M. Flanagan, Jr., *Corregidor: The Rock Force Assault, 1945* (Novato, CA: Presidio Press, 1988); "Exposure Under Fire," pp. 25–27; Pfc. George Willard Woodruff, "Into Action on Corregidor," *AP*, July 1945, pp. 12–13.

Chapter 7. "Some Incident of Danger to Maintain Their Good Humor"

1. Unless otherwise noted, this account of Jerry J. Joswick relies on the Joswick materials listed in the Bibliography. Particularly important is Jerry J. Joswick with Lawrence A. Keating, *Combat Cameraman* (Philadelphia: Chilton Company, 1961), which must be used with care since some of it cannot be confirmed by wartime documents or by those who served with him, and parts are exaggerated.

2. Memo on "Pictorial Coverage of Air Force Activities" from Gen. H. H. Arnold to the Commanding General, 9th Air Force, Nov. 9, 1943, Records of the 9th CCU, AFHRA; memos on "Pictorial Coverage of Air Force Activities" from General Arnold to the Commanding Generals of the 7th Air Force and the 8th Air Force and to the Director of Photography, all dated Nov. 9, 1942, CCU Organization—General Arnold's Folder, 9 Nov. 1942–9 Apr. 1943 file, AFHRA; Sanford E. Greenwald, "Camera Command," *IP*, Apr. 1945, p. 8; Greenwald interview, June 11, 1980; Burr McGregor, "Cameramen at War," *AC*, May 1944, pp. 150–51.

3. "Brief Historical Record," May 24, 1943, and memo on "Motion Picture Coverage of AAF Activities in Combat Theaters" from William J.

Keighley, Chief, Motion Picture Section, to the Commanding General of the 9th Air Force, Dec. 12, 1942, both in Records of the 9th CCU, AFHRA; John D. Craig interview, Mar. 26–27, 1979; Craig to Keighley, May 20, 1943, Craig Papers.

4. Kenneth M. Chaney interview, June 16, 1980.

5. On combat fatigue, see Wesley Frank Craven and James Lea Cate, *The Army Air Forces in World War II*. VII, *Services Around the World* (Chicago: The University of Chicago Press, 1958), pp. 365–476; Max Hastings, *Bomber Command* (New York: A Touchstone Book reprint, 1989), pp. 213–22; Stephen L. McFarland and Wesley Phillips Newton, *To Command the Sky: The Battle for Air Superiority Over Germany, 1942–1944* (Washington, DC: Smithsonian Institution Press, 1991), pp. 110–11.

6. Quoted in Ronald Schaffer, *Wings of Judgment: American Bombing in World War II* (New York: Oxford University Press, 1985), p. 66.

7. Unless otherwise noted, this account of James M. Bray relies on the Bray materials listed in the Bibliography.

8. Quoted in Stanley Rubin, "They Put the Air War on Film," *Western Flying*, Sept. 1944, p. 48.

9. The account of this mission also relies on a telephone interview with George Groff, May 4, 1992.

10. McGregor, "Cameramen at War."

11. Craig to Keighley, May 20, 1943, Craig Papers.

12. Lt. Col. Jack L. Warner, "Creation of an Army Air Forces Motion Picture Unit," Apr. 30, 1942, in Suggested Plan of Operation for the Motion Picture Activities Division file, AFHRA.

13. Memo on "Motion Picture Coverage of AAF Activities in Combat Theaters" from Gen. H. H. Arnold to the Director of Photography, Nov. 10, 1942, CCU Organization—General Arnold's Folder, 9 Nov. 1942–9 Apr. 1943 file, and Gen. Arnold to Lt. Gen. George C. Kenney, Apr. 15, 1944, Combat Camera file, both in AFHRA.

14. See the annotated list of CCUs in Combat Camera Units—Information and Notes file, AFHRA.

15. "Production Chart Guide for 16mm Motion Picture Unit," AFHRA; brief histories of four of the units in an unlabeled folder in Microfilm Reel A0492, AFHRA; rosters of the 16mm units, Photo Units: Motion Picture Units—Rosters file, AFHRA; "Photographic Operations Report—16mm Units" in "History of the First Motion Picture Unit Army Air Forces, Culver City, California," Feb. 1–29, 1944 and Dec. 1–31, 1944, Appendix A, AFHRA.

16. Almost all the CCU histories contain information on the Manning Table; a copy of T/O&E 1-708 is in the Emmett Bergholz Papers. For the possibility of larger CCUs, see "Unit History," Dec. 1944, Records of

the 7th CCU, AFHRA, and "Unit War Diary," Nov. 7, 1943, Records of the 12th CCU, AFHRA.

17. Almost all the CCU histories contain information on unit strength.
18. Memo on "AAF Motion Picture Activities" from Maj. Gen. H. A. Craig to Gen. White, Aug. 11, 1944, and memo on "AAF Motion Picture Activities" from Maj. Frank W. G. Lloyd to Maj. Gen. Craig, Aug. 18, 1944, both in 1944—Authority for Motion Picture Activities file, AFHRA.
19. See the monthly reports for Jan. 1944, Oct. 1944, and Mar. 1945 in "History of the Fourth Combat Camera Unit: Second Phase—The ETO," Records of the 4th CCU, AFHRA.
20. "Unit History From Activation Through 31 March 1944 [This document actually begins with Apr. 1944 and includes monthly installments through Oct. 1945.]," July and Aug. 1944, Records of the 6th CCU, AFHRA.
21. "Historical Records," Feb. 1945 (War Diary entry for Feb. 8), Records of the 9th CCU, AFHRA.
22. Unless otherwise noted, this account of Kenneth M. Chaney relies on the Chaney materials listed in the Bibliography. Raymond Fernstrom was the cameraman who commended Chaney's bravery; quoted in McGregor, "Cameramen at War."
23. Craig interview.
24. "History of the First Motion Picture Unit," Mar. 1–31, 1944.
25. Ibid., Feb. 1–29, 1944, and "The Story of the Fourth: An informal history of the 4th Combat Camera Unit, Army Air Forces," Apr. 1944, Records of the 4th CCU, AFHRA.
26. For some of the film stories Joswick filed, see "Public Relations Stories Covered" for June and July, 1944 in "The Story of the Fourth," and "History of the Fourth Combat Camera Unit: Second Phase—The ETO," Oct. 1944. All in Records of the 4th CCU, AFHRA.
27. "History of the Fourth Combat Camera Unit: Second Phase—The ETO," July 1944.
28. Memo on "Daily Activity Report" from James W. Chapman to The Executive, AC/AS, Intelligence, Dec. 30, 1944, Motion Picture Services Division Activity Reports file, AFHRA.
29. Unless otherwise noted, the following account of the IX TCC CCU comes from the unit's monthly reports for Dec. 1944 and Jan., Feb., Mar., and Apr. 1945, which are in the Records of the 9th CCU, AFHRA. The Army also covered Operation Varsity; see "Signal Report on Operation 'Varsity,'" CARL.
30. The 3rd and 8th CCUs also covered Operation Varsity; see "Unit History," Mar. 1945, Records of the 3rd CCU, AFHRA.
31. Along with the sources listed in Note 7 above, this account of Henry and Bray relies on Malcolm E. Henry to the author, Feb. 19, 1981.

Chapter 8. "The New Battlefront, the Air Front"

1. Unless otherwise noted, this account of Karl H. Maslowski relies on the Maslowski materials listed in the Bibliography.
2. "Unit History," July 1944, Records of the 12th CCU, AFHRA.
3. Quoted in Stanley Rubin, "They Put the War on Film," *Western Flying*, Sept. 1944, p. 98.
4. Unless otherwise noted, this account of *The Memphis Belle* relies on the following sources: William Wyler interview, June 14, 1980; William Clothier interview, June 11, 1980; John Sturges interview, Mar. 24, 1979; S/Sgt. James F. Scanlan, "Filming 'Memphis Belle,'" *IP*, May 1944; and the film's narration.
5. "History of the First Motion Picture Unit Army Air Forces, Culver City, California," Oct. 1–31, 1944, AFHRA.
6. Ibid., Jan. 1–31, 1944.
7. "Pictures to the Editor," *Life*, Aug. 2, 1943, p. 92; "The last B-17F," *Aerospace Historian*, Winter/Dec. 1984, pp. 283–84; "B-17 has a new home," *The Kansas City Star*, May 18, 1987, p. 6B.
8. Unless otherwise noted, this account of *Thunderbolt* relies on the following sources: Wyler interview, June 14, 1980; Sturges interview, Mar. 24, 1979; the Maslowski Papers; Maslowski interviews, Dec. 17, 1977 and Aug. 25, 1978; and the film's narration.
9. "War Diary," June 4 and 12, 1944, and "Unit History," June 1944, both in Records of the 12th CCU, AFHRA.
10. "Unit History," July 1944, and "Account of Special Events," both in Records of the 12th CCU, AFHRA.
11. "War Diary," July 13 and Aug. 11, 1944, and "Account of Special Events," all in Records of the 12th CCU, AFHRA.
12. "Unit History," Aug. 1944, and "Account of Special Events," both in Records of the 12th CCU, AFHRA.
13. "Account of Special Events," Records of the 12th CCU, AFHRA.
14. "War Diary," Sept. 20–30, 1944, Records of the 12th CCU, AFHRA.
15. In this case they saw it after the war, since the editing was not completed until after both Germany and Japan had surrendered.
16. R. H. Bailey, "Movies of Bullets," *AC*, Apr. 1944; F. Barrows Colton, "How We Fight with Photographs," *NGM*, Sept. 1944; "The 'Guzap' That Went to War," *AC*, Oct. 1945; Reed N. Haythorne, "Sixteen Millimeter Teaches Airmen To Shoot," *AC*, June 1941, and "The Air Corps' Newest Camera-Gun," *AC*, Jan. 1942; "Gun Camera Trains Pilots," *PP*, Sept. 1942; R. S. Quackenbush, Jr., "The Gun Camera," *JSMPE*, May 1945; and "Aircraft Camera Equipment and Techniques in AAF," Jan. 1944, in "AAFSAT ANSCOL Course. Class E-1944. Course Number 200...." CARL.
17. "Interview of Capt. Roy E. Steele, Commanding Officer of 2nd Combat Camera Unit, made and prepared by 1st Lt. James P. McFarland," Sept. 6, 1945, and "Unit History," Aug. 1945, Appendix A, both in Records of the

2nd CCU, AFHRA; "History of the Fourth Combat Camera Unit: Second Phase—The ETO," Feb. 1945, Records of the 4th CCU, AFHRA; "Historical Record: Fifth Army Air Forces Combat Camera Unit," Feb. 1945, Records of the 5th CCU, AFHRA; "History of Motorized Conversion of 35mm A-4 Motion Picture Camera (Bomb Spotter)," enclosed with "Unit History," Dec. 12, 1944, Records of the 10th CCU, AFHRA; "Unit History," Apr. 1944, Records of the 12th CCU, AFHRA.

18. "Unit History," Aug. 1944, Records of the 12th CCU, AFHRA.
19. Colton, p. 277.
20. Memo on "AN Type N4 and N4A 24 Volt Gun Cameras" from The Chief of the Bureau of Ordnance to The Chief of Naval Operations, Oct. 14, 1943, Equipment Folder #2 file, NCPD, NA, and "Gunsight Camera Repaired," *PP*, Aug. 1945, p. 76.
21. "War Diary," Feb. 23, 1945, Records of the 9th CCU, AFHRA.
22. The three cameramen killed in this accident were Harold A. Bollerman (the 9th CCU's commanding officer), Richard Fowkes, and Casimir Karas, who had previously won a Silver Star and was, in Maslowski's words, "a Polish immigrant who was 110 percent American." Almost fifty years later, tears still welled up in Maslowski's eyes when he recounted this incident.
23. The "War Diary," May 2 and 3, 1944, Records of the 9th CCU, AFHRA, confirms Maslowski's observation.
24. "War Diary," June 15, 1945, Records of the 9th CCU, AFHRA.

Chapter 9. "Frankly, I Wouldn't Have Picked This as an Assignment"

1. Unless otherwise noted, this account of Earl F. Colgrove and Douglas B. Jones relies on the Colgrove and Jones materials listed in the Bibliography; the CPU #1—Lieut. Colgrove file; the Combat Photography Unit 1 (Lt. Colgrove) file, and the Unit 1 (Lieut. Colgrove) file, all in NCPD, NA; Colgrove, "Camping on a Sampan," *IP*, Sept. 1944, and "On the Move with SACO," *IP*, Jan. 1946. For place names in China I have used the World War II spelling, not the modern spelling.
2. David O. Selznick, "Tentative Plan for Establishment of Bureau of Photography," Sept. 17, 1942, Photostats file, NCPD, NA.
3. Memo on "Comments on Mr. Selznick's plan" from Leland P. Lovette to the Vice Chief of Naval Operations, Oct. 9, 1942, Photostats file, NCPD, NA.
4. For the relevant documents see the Photographic Board file, NCPD, NA. For a complete discussion of the board see BuAer, "Naval Aviation Photography and Motion Pictures" (Washington, DC: U.S. Naval History Division, 1957).
5. Memo on "Photography, Use of, in the Navy for Historical and Publicity Purposes" from the Secretary of the Navy to All Ships and Stations, Jan. 2, 1942, Ready Information CPU's file, and W. G. Beecher, Jr., Acting

Director, [Navy] Office of Public Relations to Capt. P. V. Mercer, June 15, 1944, Miscellaneous file, both in NCPD, NA.

6. Memo on "Combat Photography Section, information on" from Carleton Mitchell to the Director of Photography, BuAer, and Assistant Director of Photography, BuAer, Nov. 13, 1943, Aeronautics, (Bur. of) Letters file; Mitchell to James J. Butler, Apr. 8, 1943, Miscellaneous Correspondence file; Mitchell to Lt. Drennan, Oct. 20, 1943, Combat Photography Unit 2 (Lt. Drennan) file. All in NCPD, NA.

7. A brief biography is enclosed with a press release titled "Navy Sets Up Combat Photographic Unit," Dec. 12, 1942, Miscellaneous file, NCPD, NA.

8. [Carleton Mitchell,] "Notes For Talk To Public Relations Officers," undated, Naval Districts Bulletin file; [Carleton Mitchell,] "Preliminary Outline: Combat Photography Section," Oct. 15, 1942 and "Operational Outline: Combat Photography Section," Oct. 30, 1942, both in Operational Outline file. All in NCPD, NA.

9. [Mitchell,] undated essay enclosed with a memo on "CPUs, report on" from Carleton Mitchell to Captain H. W. Taylor, May 11, 1943, Miscellaneous file; and memo on "Lt. John H. Levick, USNR, duties of as OIC, CPU" from Leland P. Lovette to Commanding Officers Concerned, Jan. 14, 1943, Aeronautics, (Bur. of) Letters file, both in NCPD, NA.

10. Carleton Mitchell to Lt. Gerretson, Dec. 14, 1943, Combat Photography Unit 8 (Lt. Gerretson) file, and Mitchell's essay enclosed with memo on "Naval Districts Bulletin, February issue, contribution for" from Mitchell to W. L. Huggins, Jr., Jan. 27, 1943, Naval Districts Bulletin file, both in NCPD, NA.

11. Carleton Mitchell to Capt. H. B. Miller, Nov. 15, 1944, Miscellaneous file; memo on "CPU 10, orders for" from Mitchell to the Director of Photography, Dec. 14, 1944, Unit 10 (Lieut. Wrigley) file; Mitchell to Lt. Wrigley, Feb. 17, 1944, Unit 10 (Lieut. Wrigley) file. All in NCPD, NA.

12. Carleton Mitchell to James J. Butler, Apr. 8, 1943, Miscellaneous Correspondence file; Mitchell to Capt. Gene Markey, July 29, 1944, Capt. Markey file; memo on "Combat Photography Section, Organization of" from Mitchell to the Director, Oct. 15, 1942, Miscellaneous file. All in NCPD, NA.

13. "Combat Photography Section (Personnel and Assignment of Combat Units as of February 1, 1943)," Addresses—CPU Units file; memo on "Combat Photography Section, report on for the year ending 30 June 1943" from Carleton Mitchell to the Director of Public Relations, July 9, 1943, Reports—Confidential file; memos from Mitchell to the Director of Photography requesting the transfer of CPUs #12 and #13 to CINC-PAC's Staff, Sept. 15, 1944, Orders file. All in NCPD, NA.

14. Lt. Samuel to Carleton Mitchell, June 29, 1943, Combat Photography Unit 5 (Lt. Samuel) file, NCPD, NA.

15. Carleton Mitchell to Captain Stuart Palmer, Feb. 28, 1944, Miscellaneous (1944) file, and memo on "Combat Photography Section, report on for the year ending 30 June 1943" from Mitchell to the Director of Public Relations, July 9, 1943, Reports—Confidential file, both in NCPD, NA.

16. For Miles and SACO see Vice Admiral Milton E. Miles, USN (as prepared by Hawthorne Daniel from the original manuscript), *A Different Kind of War: The Unknown Story of the U.S. Navy's Guerrilla Forces in World War II* (Garden City, NY: Doubleday & Company, 1967), and Roy Olin Stratton, *SACO—The Rice Paddy Navy* (Pleasantville, NY: C. S. Palmer Publishing Co., 1950).

17. Secretary of the Navy (Director of Public Relations) to CINCPAC, Sept. 20, 1944, Combat Photo Units file, NCPD, NA.

18. Edward Steichen, ed., *U.S. Navy War Photographs: Pearl Harbor to Tokyo Bay* (New York: Bonanza Books, 1984 ed.), p. 79. For examples, see Rafael Steinberg, *Return to the Philippines* (Alexandria, VA: Time-Life Books, 1979), p. 103, and The Editors of Time-Life Books, *WW II: Time-Life Books History of the Second World War* (New York: Prentice-Hall, 1989), p. 390. Steichen credits Colgrove with the photo; the other two books credit "U.S. Navy, National Archives."

19. Carleton Mitchell to Lt. Drennan, Feb. 15, 1944, Unit 2 (Lieut. Drennan) file; memo on "CPUs" from Mitchell to Capt. H. B. Miller, Sept. 6, 1944, Reports-Confidential file; Mitchell to the Director, Nov. 6, 1944, Personnel file; memo on "CPUs, information on" from Mitchell to the Director, Dec. 29, 1944, Miscellaneous file. All in NCPD, NA.

20. Carleton Mitchell to Lt. Colgrove, Nov. 17, 1943, Combat Photography Unit 1 (Lt. Colgrove) file; memo on "Procurement and distribution of still and motion pictures" from Mitchell to the Director of Public Relations, Aug. 24, 1944, Capt. Markey file; Mitchell to the Director, Nov. 6, 1944, Personnel file. All in NCPD, NA.

21. Memo on "CPUs, relief and reassignment of" from Officer in Charge, Combat Photography Section [Carleton Mitchell] to Director of Public Relations and Director of Photography, BuAer, May 15, 1944, Policy file; and memo on "Material for possible inclusion in Cominch memorandum" from Mitchell to the Deputy Director, Oct. 10, 1944, Miscellaneous file, both in NCPD, NA.

22. Memo on "Material for possible inclusion in Cominch memorandum" from Carleton Mitchell to the Deputy Director to the Deputy Director, Oct. 10, 1944, Miscellaneous file; Mitchell to the Director of Public Relations, Aug. 24, 1944, Capt. Markey file; memo on "Improvement of Photographic Coverage Emanating from the Pacific Area" enclosed with memo on "CPUs in the Pacific Area" from Mitchell to the Director,

July 7, 1944, Miscellaneous file; Mitchell to Lt. Sorenson, Mar. 22, 1944, Unit 9 (Lieut. Sorenson) file. All in NCPD, NA.

23. Carleton Mitchell to Capt. H. B. Miller, Nov. 15, 1944, Miscellaneous file; Mitchell to the Director of Public Relations, Aug. 24, 1944, Capt. Markey file; Mitchell to Lt. Burlingame, June 9 and Oct 27, 1944, Unit 6 (Lieut. Burlingame) file; Mitchell to Director of Photography, BuAer, Sept. 15, 1944, Reports—Confidential file; Mitchell to Lt. Sorenson, Mar. 22, 1944, Unit 9 (Lieut. Sorenson) file. All in NCPD, NA.

24. Abstract of letter from Capt. H. B. Miller to Rear Adm. A. S. Merrill, Oct. 31, 1944, CPU General file; and Capt. H. B. Miller to Mitchell, Nov. 7, 1944, Miscellaneous file; both in NCPD, NA.

25. Mitchell to Lt. Cdr. Peyton Anderson, Mar. 30, 1945, Seventh Fleet file; Mitchell to Richard M. Blanco, May 9, 1945, Combat Photography Recent Letters file; Mitchell to Lt. Waterman, Sept. 7, 1945, Unit 8 (Lt. Waterman) file. All in NCPD, NA.

26. Unless otherwise noted, this account of Edward Steichen relies on the following sources: Edward Steichen, *A Life in Photography* (Garden City, NY: Doubleday & Company, 1963); Edward Steichen, *The Blue Ghost: A Photographic Log and Personal Narrative of the Aircraft Carrier U.S.S. Lexington in Combat Operations* (New York: Harcourt, Brace and Company, 1947); Edward Steichen, compiler, *Power in the Pacific* (New York: U.S. Camera Publishing, 1945); Edward Steichen, ed., *U.S. Navy War Photographs: Pearl Harbor to Tokyo Bay* (New York: Bonanza Books, 1984 ed.); Matthew Josephson, "Commander with a Camera," *The New Yorker*, June 3 and 10, 1944; The Museum of Modern Art, *Steichen the Photographer* (New York: Doubleday & Company, 1961); Christopher Phillips, *Steichen at War* (New York: Harry N. Abrams, Inc., 1981).

27. *Time*, Apr. 23, 1945, p. 50.

28. *Time*, Jan. 22, 1945, p. 91. Also see *Life*, Mar. 5, 1945 pp. 76-78, and Product Digest Section of *MPH*, Dec. 23, 1944, p. 2237.

29. *MPH*, Feb. 15, 1945, p. 8.

30. MG James P. Hodges to MG Howard C. Davison, Feb. 9, 1945, Records of the 10th CCU, AFHRA.

31. Lee Blodget to his wife, Mar. 2, 1945, Blodget Papers.

32. *USC*, Aug. 6, 1945, p. 38.

33. Both Colgrove and Jones received citations for "exceptionally meritorious photography" at the first awards ceremony on October 27, 1945.

34. The following information on the CINCPAC photo pool comes from the Rohde materials listed in the Bibliography. Shortly after the war Rohde sent out questionnaires to the pool members because he intended to write a book about the pool. He received dozens of responses but never wrote the book, and generously gave all the material that he collected to the author.

Chapter 10. "Old Glory Was Raised and, Boy, Tears Ran Down My Cheeks"

1. Quoted in S/Sgt. Dick Hannah, *Tarawa: The Toughest Battle in Marine Corps History* (n.p.: U.S. Camera Publishing, 1944), p. 110.
2. Unless otherwise noted, this account of Norman T. Hatch relies on Oral History Transcript, Major Norman T. Hatch, U.S. Marine Corps (Retired), Benis M. Frank, interviewer, MCHC.
3. Peter P. Drowne, "An Investigation into the Evolution of Motion Picture Photography and Film Usage in the United States Marine Corps 1940–45" (Unpublished Master's Thesis, University of California at Los Angeles, 1965), pp. 60–61, and "Letter of Instruction No. 1077," July 12, 1945, from Commandant A. A. Vandegrift to All Commanding Officers, MCHC.
4. See David Douglas Duncan, *Yankee Nomad: A Photographic Odyssey* (New York: Holt, Rinehart and Winston, 1966).
5. Benis M. Frank, *Denig's Demons and How They Grew ... The Story of Marine Corps Combat Correspondents, Photographers and Artists* (Washington, DC: Moore & Moore, Inc., 1967); Garry M. Cameron, *Last to Know, First to Go: The United States Marine Corps' Combat Correspondents* (Capistrano Beach, CA: Charger Books, 1988); Oral History Transcript: Brigadier General Robert L. Denig, U.S. Marine Corps (Retired) Oral Interview, Benis M. Frank, Alvin M. Josephy, Jr., and Brigadier General Robert L. Denig, Jr., USMC (Ret.), interviewers, MCHC; Robert L. Denig, "U.S. Marines Develop Fighting Cameramen," *PP*, Mar. 1943; Frank H. Rentfrow, "Fighting Photographers," *PP*, Oct. 1943; Jack Lewis, "The Photo-Fighters: Part I," *Creative Photography*, Oct. 1970.
6. "No. 22, Marine Corps Script Series, Division of Public Relations, Headquarters, United States Marine Corps. *Marine Combat Correspondents*," Combat Correspondents' Memo file; and memo on "Combat Correspondents" from the Director, Division of Public Relations to the Director, Division of Plans and Policies, Jan. 8, 1943, Combat Correspondents (1) file, both in MCHC.
7. Cameron, *Last to Know, First to Go*, p. 55.
8. "Opportunity," *MP*, Mar. 1944, p. 4, and "Combat Photographers," *MP*, June 1944, p. 11.
9. Oral History Transcript. Lieutenant Colonel Karl T. Soule, Jr., U.S. Marine Corps (Retired), Benis M. Frank, interviewer, pp. 9–14, MCHC.
10. As Carleton Mitchell wrote to the OIC of CPU #7, the Marines "did an exceptionally good job. Some of their footage of the early phases of the attack constitute some of the finest material that has come out of the war"; Mitchell to Lt. Reiman, Dec. 9, 1943, Combat Photography Unit 7 (Lt. Reiman) file, NCPD, NA.

11. On Hayward's asthma see Oral History Transcript: Hatch, p. 70.

12. Hatch's film, for example, appeared in *Attack in the Central Pacific: Makin and Tarawa* and in Castle Film's *U.S. Marines Capture Tarawa!*

13. Memo on "Combat Correspondents" from Brig. Gen. Robert Denig to Maj. Gen. D. Peck, Jan. 24, 1944, Combat Correspondents (1) file, MCHC, and Cameron, *Last to Know, First to Go*, p. 237.

14. Unless otherwise noted, this account of William H. Genaust relies on the Genaust materials listed in the Bibliography and on the Harrold A. Weinberger Papers, which contain an unpublished autobiography that describes what fighting and photographing were like in the Marianas.

15. Unless otherwise noted, this account of Harold L. Watkins relies on the Watkins materials listed in the Bibliography.

16. Realizing how flammable film was, some cameramen carried their spare rolls in a hand held pouch so they could throw it far away in an emergency; see Theodore W. Sizer interview, Aug. 31, 1983.

17. On the Honolulu conference see Oral History Transcript: Hatch, pp. 150–52, 169–73; Weinberger autobiography, pp. 327-29; "Newsreels Bring Bloody Iwo Home," *MPH*, Mar. 10, 1945, p. 36. Although the AAF did not participate in the conference it committed the 7th CCU to Iwo Jima, both in the air and on land; see "Unit History," Jan. 1945, and "Description of Scenes Submitted by Cameraman Grayner Regarding His Photography on Iwo Jima," Mar. 6, 1945, both in Records of the 7th CCU, AFHRA.

18. Hannah, pp. 110–11.

19. Oral History Transcript: Hatch, pp. 157–58, 160–61, and Oral History Transcript: Soule, pp. 7, 24–26.

20. Frank, *Denig's Demons*, unpaged, and Oral History Transcript: Hatch, p. 190.

21. Bill D. Ross, *Iwo Jima: Legacy of Valor* (New York: Vanguard Press, 1985), pp. 96–98. Ross' book has the facts straight regarding the photographers who climbed Mount Suribachi on February 23.

22. Joe Rosenthal with W. C. Heinz, "The Picture That Will Live Forever," *Collier's*, Feb. 18, 1955, pp. 62–67; Ross, pp. 100–102; Susan D. Moeller, *Shooting War: Photography and the American Experience of Combat* (New York: Basic Books, 1989), pp. 244–46; copy of a letter from Weinberger to the Editor, *Los Angeles Times*, Oct. 14, 1982, Genaust Papers; and Weinberger autobiography, p. 341. Since civilian correspondents received favored treatment, Rosenthal's photos arrived at the lab on Guam many days before Lowery's. Rosenthal's famous shot had already been displayed in the U.S. as *the* flag raising, so some officials suggested that Lowery's negatives be destroyed, which, of course, was not done; see Oral History Transcript: Colonel William P. McCahill, USMC (Ret.), unknown interviewer, pp. 53–55, MCHC.

23. For an explanation of how the truth of what happened atop Mount

Suribachi became distorted, see Karal Ann Marling and John Wetenhall, *Iwo Jima: Monuments, Memories, and the American Hero* (Cambridge, MA: Harvard University Press, 1991). Unfortunately, this book is not accurate in regard to Genaust's fate.

24. *Victory at Sea* titled its episode on Iwo Jima *Target Suribachi*, implying that Suribachi was *the* target, and used Genaust's scene as the climax.

25. In addition to the Genaust Papers, see Ross, pp. 284–85, and two newspaper articles about Genaust by Tedd Tomey, who served in the 5th Division at Iwo Jima: "A Neglected Hero of Iwo Jima," Long Beach, CA, *Press-Telegram*, Mar. 14, 1983, and "Marines finally honor Iwo Jima cameraman," *Orange County Register*, Feb. 22, 1984. Along with Leo Harry McGrath and Genaust, Marine cameraman Donovan R. Raddatz also died on Iwo Jima.

26. *Life*, May 28, 1945, p. 87.

27. Unless otherwise noted, this account of Martin Friedman relies on the Friedman materials listed in the Bibliography.

28. Unless otherwise noted, this account of Federico Claveria relies on the following sources: Claveria interview, June 13, 1980; "Proud To Be ...," *Leatherneck*, Jan. 1986; "Numismatic Profile," *Numismatic Digest*, Feb. 1969; a copy of Claveria's advertisement for the La Tolteca Tortilla Factory; and Claveria to Mrs. Genaust, June 23, 1945, Genaust Papers.

Chapter 11. "The Fringe Necessities"

1. Robert W. McFarren to the author, Jan. 6, 1981.

2. James V. Clarke, "Signal Corps Army Pictorial Service in World War II (1 September 1939–15 August 1945)" (HS, SAB, OCSO, Jan. 16, 1946), p. 37, NA.

3. Robert L. Eichberg and Jacqueline Quadow, "Combat Photography" (HS, SAB, OCSO, Nov. 1945), pp. 12, 22, CARL; "Instructing U.S. Signal Corps Photographic Companies with Major Art Lloyd, A.S.C.," AC, July 1946, p. 258; "A.S.C. and Academy to Train Cameramen for Army Service," AC, June 1942, p. 255. The armed forces missed some skilled photographers in their mobilization efforts. Ernie Pyle met a soldier in Italy with eighteen years' experience as a cameraman, but the Army had made him a cook and then an artilleryman; see David Nichols, ed., *Ernie's War: The Best of Ernie Pyle's World War II Dispatches* (New York: Random House, 1986), p. 181.

4. Joseph D. Boyle audio cassette responding to the author's inquiries, 1980, and Charles E. Sumners to the author, Aug. 1980.

5. War Department, "Summary Report on Photographic Activities of the Signal Corps Since August 4 1941 in the Fields of Motion Pictures & Visual Aids" (OCSO, Feb. 26, 1943), pp. 16–65, 118–19, 141–76, 284–92, NA; Clarke, "Signal Corps Army Pictorial Service," pp. 12,

44–46, 78, 85, numerous blind-folio charts showing reorganizations; Eichberg and Quadow, "Combat Photography," pp. 8–10; Jacqueline M. Quadow, "Training Films in the Second World War, Supplement Jan 44 [sic] to August 1945" (HS, SAB, OCSO, May 13, 1946), pp. 34–42, NA.

6. Clarke, "Signal Corps Army Pictorial Service," p. 122.

7. Except where noted, this paragraph and the next one rely on the following sources: Capt. Frederick Reinstein, "Study of Signal Corps Officer Schooling, 1939–1944" (HS, SAB, OCSO, Dec. 1, 1944), pp. 176–79, CARL; Eichberg and Quadow, "Combat Photography," p. 164; War Department Pamphlet No. 11-5, *Combat Photography* (War Department, Mar. 22, 1945) pp. 6–7; "Signal Corps Photo School," USC, Apr. 1944; "Training Combat Cameramen," USC, Aug. 1944; "Signal Corps Movie School," USC, Nov. 1944; "Training Combat Photographers," MP, Jan. 1944; Maj. Arthur L. Gaskill, "Training the Army Cameraman," BSM, Dec. 30, 1945.

8. APS, "Army Pictorial Service Annual Report For The Fiscal Year 1 July 1944 to 30 June 1945" (OCSO, July 21, 1945), p. 82, NA. Some of these graduates were, of course, lab personnel rather than photographers.

9. "The Story of the Fourth: An informal history of the 4th Combat Camera Unit, Army Air Forces," Records of the 4th CCU, and "Unit History," June 11, 1944, in Records of the 3rd CCU; both in AFHRA.

10. The records of virtually all the CCUs contain material on these matters, as does the "History of First Motion Picture Unit Army Air Forces, Culver City, California," AFHRA. Also see 1st Lt. William R. McGee, "Cinematography Goes to War," JSMPE, Feb. 1944; Maj. Ralph Jester, "Operations of Army Air Forces Combat Camera Units in the Theaters of War," JSMPE, Aug. 1943; reports for weeks ending Nov. 14 and 26, 1943, in "Combat Film Service Weekly Reports, 4 October 1943 [sic: 18 September 1943]–2 Jan [sic] 1944," AFHRA.

11. "History of First Motion Picture Unit," monthly reports for Jan.–June 1945.

12. PHCS Gerald T. DeForge, *Navy Photographer's Mate Training Series. Module 1. Naval Photography* (Pensacola: Naval Education and Training Program Development Center, 1981), Series 2-22, 2-23, 2-24; Herbert C. McKay, "The Navy Builds Cameramen," PP, Jan. 1943; "The Miniature Camera," AP, Nov. 1942; Carleton Mitchell to Cdr. T. A. Nicholson, Aug. 28, 1943, Miscellaneous Correspondence file, and Mitchell to Lt. Elliott D. Pemberton, Sept. 20, 1944, Aeronautics, (Bur. of) Letters file, both in NCPD, NA.

13. Frank H. Rentfrow, "Fighting Photographers," PP, Oct. 1943; Capt. J. Winston Lemen, "Combat Photography in the U.S. Marine Corps," JPSA, May 1945; Peter P. Drowne, "An Investigation into the Evolution of Motion Picture Photography and Film Usage in the United States

Marine Corps 1940–45" (Unpublished Master's Thesis, University of California at Los Angeles, 1965), pp. 13–16.

14. Eichberg and Quadow, "Combat Photography," pp. 10, 14; Sgt. Alfred W. Rohde, Jr., "Marines Man the Movie Cameras," AC, July 1941; DeForge, *Navy Photographer's Mate*, Series 2-10; Robert W. Marks, "Life's School For Fighting Photographers," MP, June 1942.

15. Advertisements for these schools regularly appeared in PP and other photography magazines.

16. Carleton Mitchell to Lt. Cdr. W. G. Beecher, Jr., Oct. 5, 1942, Miscellaneous file; memo on "Combat Photography Section, organization of" from Mitchell to the Director, Oct. 15, 1942, Organization Combat Photography file; *"Operational Outline: Combat Photography Section,"* Nov. 2 1942, Operational Outline File; Mitchell to Duty Officer, Third Naval District, Nov. 4, 1942, Miscellaneous file; Mitchell to Lt. Cdr. George Dunbaugh, [c. Dec. 1942], Applications file; memo on "Combat Photography Section, report on for year ending 30 June 1943" from Mitchell to the Director of Public Relations, June 30, 1943, Reports—Confidential file; "Training Schedule for Combat Camera Officers" [c. Nov. 1942], Training file; "Training Schedule for Combat Photographic Officers (Tentative Final Four Weeks at March of Time)" [c. Nov. 1942], Miscellaneous file. All in NCPD, NA.

17. Eichberg and Quadow, "Combat Photography," p. 124; Joseph M. Zinni to his wife, Dec. 1, 4, 5, 7, 8, 15, 1944, Zinni Papers; "Company History," Records of the 167th SPC, NA; "Every Shot a Prize Winner," *United States Marine Corps Headquarters Bulletin*, June 1945, pp. 26–27.

18. Alfred Toombs, "Wanted: Photo Inventions," PP, July 1942, and memo on "Report on Motion Picture Footage Forwarded by CCUs" from William J. Keighley to the Commanding Officer, 9th CCU, May 13, 1944, Records of the 9th CCU, AFHRA.

19. Lt. Drennan to Carleton Mitchell, Oct 28, 1943, Combat Photography Unit 2 (Lt. Drennan) file; Lt. Tacker to Mitchell, Sept. 30, 1943, Combat Photography Unit 4 (Lt. Tacker) file; Lt. Gerretson to Mitchell, Feb. 14, 1944 and Mitchell to Gerretson, Mar. 20, 1944, both in Unit 8 (Lieut. Gerretson[)] file; "U.S. Naval Photography, Some Comments Concerning" enclosed with Lt. Burlingame to Mitchell Aug. 7, 1944, Movies—Unit 6—Burlingame file. All in NCPD, NA.

20. "Field Reports from the 4th AAF CCU," undated, in "History of the Fourth Combat Camera Unit: Second Phase—The ETO," Records of the 4th CCU, AFHRA; memo on "Daily Activity Report" from William J. Keighley to the Executive, AC/AS, Intelligence, Nov. 14, 1944, Motion Picture Services Division Activity Reports file, AFHRA.

21. See the discussion of GSAPs in Chapter 8.

22. "History of the Sixteenth AAF Combat Camera Unit, 1 May 1943 to 31

December 1944," entry for Mar. 1944, Records of the 16th CCU, AFHRA.

23. This account relies on War Department, "History of Signal Corps Research and Development in World War II. Volume XV. Photographic Equipment" (Washington, DC: Army Service Forces, December 1945), NA; Clarke, "Signal Corps Army Pictorial Service," pp. 91–93, 127–71; APS, "Army Pictorial Service Annual Report," pp. 60–76; War Department Pamphlet No. 11-5, *Combat Photography*, p. 11; *Annual Report of the Army Service Forces for the Fiscal Year 1944*, p. 196, CARL.

24. "Company History 1 January 1943 to 31 December 1944," Records of the 164th SPC, NA.

25. War Department Technical Manual No. 1-219, *Basic Photography* (War Department, July 1, 1941), pp. 280, 314–19.

26. *Army Signal Forces Catalog SIG 3. Signal Supply Catalog. List of Items for Troops Use* (Headquarters, Army Service Forces, Sept., 1945). I am indebted to Mr. Ted Wise of the Signal Corps Museum for alerting me to this document.

27. BuAer, "Standard Photographic Stock List and Quarterly Report" (April 1944) in Inventory-CPU Equipment file, NCPD, NA, and "U.S. Naval Photography, Some Comments Concerning."

28. Col. Robert B. Miller to The Director, AAF Technical Services Command, Dec. 23, 1944, in the 18th AAF Base Unit—General file, AFHRA.

29. BuAer, "Naval Aviation Photography and Motion Pictures" (Washington, DC: U.S. Naval History Division, 1957), p. 59.

30. "Company History 1 January 1943 to 31 December 1944," Records of the 164th SPC, NA.

31. "Report of The General Board, United States Forces, European Theater. Signal Supply, Repair, and Maintenance. Study No. 110," pp. 23–27, CARL; "Unit History," July 1944, Records of the 3rd CCU, AFHRA; "A Standing Operating Procedure for Combat Assignment Team (SOP-CAT)" (Headquarters 163rd SPC, Feb. 20, 1945), Annex D, Gordon T. Frye Papers; Carleton Mitchell to Captain H. B. Miller, Nov. 15, 1944, Miscellaneous file, NCPD, NA.

32. Robert L. Lewis to the author, Feb. 13, 1985; "A Standing Operating Procedure for Combat Assignment Team," Annex D; Chester Owens to the author, Nov. 20, 1987.

33. Letter of Commendation to Chester Owens from Ned R. Morehouse, Mar. 2, 1944, Owens Papers.

34. "Historical Records and History of Organization," Oct. 5, 1943 and Jan. 4, 1944, Records of the 161st SPC, NA; "'Photo by Signal Corps': The Story of the 166th," NA; "Company History," Records of the 167th SPC, NA.

35. Brief biographies of Joe M. Ritchie and William Markus in "The Enlisted Men of the 168 Signal Photo Co.," Records of the 168th SPC, NA.
36. "Report of Activities From 24 November to 24 December 1943," Records of the 163rd SPC, NA.
37. Zinni to his wife, Mar. 5, 1945, Zinni Papers.
38. Zinni to his wife, June 29 and Oct. 24, 1944, Zinni Papers, and "Company History," Jan. 15–Feb. 15, 1945, Records of the 163rd SPC, NA.
39. Robert J. Goebel interview, Oct. 8, 1943.
40. "E. K. Co.'s Portable Darkroom," *MP*, Nov. 1943, pp. 78–79; Eichberg and Quadow, "Combat Photography," p. 43 and Figure 12a; Joseph D. Boyle audio cassette responding to the author's inquiries, 1980.
41. United States Army Signal Corps, Southwest Pacific Area, "Exposure Under Fire: An Official History of Signal Corps Photography in the Luzon Operations" (Apr. 25, 1945), pp. 30–31; M/Sgt. Rex D. McDowell, "Darkroom Task Force," *JSMPE*, Nov. 1945; Lt. Morton Sontheimer, "Photographic Operations in the Pacific," *BSM*, Dec. 30, 1945.
42. William Stull, "A Portable Developing Machine For Field Service With The Army," *AC*, Nov. 1942.
43. "History of the Fourth Combat Camera Unit: Second Phase—The ETO," Mar. 1944 and June 1945, Records of the 4th CCU; "Historical Data of 13th AAF CCU," Feb. 29, 1944, Records of the 13th CCU; "16th Combat Camera Unit History, January 1st to Nov. 2 1945," Mar. 1945, Records of the 16th CCU. All in AFHRA.
44. DeForge, *Navy Photographer's Mate*, Series 2-17; "Notes on the Preparation of Data Sheets and the Shipment of Film," undated, Information New CPU's file, NCPD, NA; "V-J Day Arrival Halts Films for Army-Navy," *MPH*, Aug. 25, 1945, p. 26.
45. Eichberg and Quadow, "Combat Photography," pp. 55, 63–66, 122–23, 142–55, Appendix C, Appendix E; "Signal Corps U.S. Army ETOUSA," p. 12; Clarke, "Signal Corps Army Pictorial Service," pp. 206–207; Quadow, "Training Films," pp. 80–81; War Department Pamphlet No. 11–2, *Standing Operating Procedure For Signal Photographic Units In Theaters of Operations* (War Department, Apr. 20, 1944), pp. 4–5.
46. Eichberg and Quadow, "Combat Photography," pp. 119–122, Appendix C.
47. "Naval Aviation Photography and Motion Pictures," pp. 56, 75.
48. Joseph D. Boyle to the author, Feb. 6, 1981.
49. "Company History 1 January 1943 to 31 December 1944," July 15, 1944, Records of the 164th SPC, NA.
50. Memo on "Instructions to Combat Cameramen" from 2nd Lt. Howard W. Pennebaker to All Personnel, Nov. 23, 1943, Allan L. Kain Papers,

and Maj. Gen. James P. Hodge to Commanding General, CBI Sector, Oct. 16, 1944, in Records of the 10th CCU, AFHRA.

51. Carleton Mitchell to Lt. Gerretson, Sept. 20, 1943, Combat Photography Unit 8 (Lt. Gerretson) file, and Mitchell to Lt. Reiman, Oct. 27, 1943, Combat Photography Unit 7 (Lt. Reiman) file, both in NCPD, NA.
52. "163 Stretches Air Arm," *Foto-Facto*, Mar. 20, 1945. Also see APS, "Army Pictorial Service Annual Report," p. 45, and War Department Pamphlet No. 11-2, *Standing Operating Procedure*, p. 8.
53. Warren Kieft Diary, June 5, 1944, Kieft Papers.
54. Kieft Diary, Aug. 15, 1944, and Kieft's comments on his diary, Aug. 1981.
55. "Company History," Dec. 15, 1944 to Jan. 15, 1945, and Mar. 15, 1945 to Apr. 15, 1945, Records of the 163rd SPC, NA; "163rd Gets Speedier Courier Service," *Foto-Facto*, Feb. 17, 1945; "About the Area," *Foto-Facto*, Mar. 6, 1945. The 166th SPC also established an air courier service; see "'Photo by Signal Corps.'"
56. A. J. Ezickson, "Press," *PP*, May 1945, p. 65, and "Coverage," *MPH*, Feb. 24, 1945, p. 9.
57. Quoted in Tom Maloney, ed., *U. S. Camera 1946: Victory Volume* (n.p.: U. S. Camera Publishers, 1945), p. 370.

Chapter 12. "My Pictures Are at Least Doing a Little Bit of Good"

1. H. G. Nicholas, ed., *Washington Despatches, 1941–1945: Weekly Political Reports from the British Embassy* (Chicago: University of Chicago Press, 1981), p. 15.
2. Ibid., pp. 2, 4, 5, 9, 18–22, 24, 37, 44, 45, 98, 99, 102, 120. By mid-March 1942 Secretary of War Stimson was receiving warnings about "the hostile public opinion to our war effort which seems to be growing up throughout the country," and agreed "that drastic efforts must be taken to create public unity." See Henry L. Stimson Diaries, March 16, 1942, microfilm edition of the Diaries from the Yale University Library.
3. Arthur Brackman, "Calling All Cameras!" *MP*, Dec. 1942, p. 19, and Robert W. Marks, "Life's School For Fighting Photographers," *MP*, Jan. 1942, p. 42.
4. Defining "propaganda" in a unanimously acceptable way is impossible; see David Culbert, ed., *Film and Propaganda in America: A Documentary History*, 3 vols. (Westport, CT: Greenwood Press, 1990), Vol. I, pp. ix–x. For a detailed discussion of propaganda see Terence H. Qualter, *Opinion Control in Democracies* (London: The Macmillan Press Ltd., 1985).
5. In early 1944 *Life* changed this statement to read "All material, which in the opinion of the editors involves military security, has been submitted to competent military or naval authority for review as to security."

6. "To Our Readers: A Statement of Policy For *U.S. Camera* During These War Times," *USC*, Apr. 1942, p. 57.

7. Hermine Rich Isaacs, "War Fronts and Film Fronts," *Theater Arts*, June 1944, p. 344, and John G. Morris, "Photographers Ran the War," *PP*, Feb. 1946, p. 142.

8. *Life*, Dec. 11, 1944, p. 27 and *Life*, Apr. 2, 1945, pp. 26–27.

9. Joris Ivens, "Making Documentary Films to Meet Today's Needs," AC, July 1942, pp. 298, 333. For similar sentiments see John Grierson, "Documentary Films in Wartime," AC, Mar. 1942, p. 101.

10. An excellent brief discussion of these matters is K. R. M. Short, ed., *World War II Through the American Newsreels, 1942–1945: An Introduction and Guide to the Microfiches* (229 microfiches, Oxford and New York: Oxford Microfilm Publications, 1985), pp. 1–5. Also see *Movies at War: Reports of War Activities Committee Motion Picture Industry, 1942–1945* (New York: War Activities Committee Motion Picture Industry, 1942–1945), pp. 4–5 (1942 report).

11. *Movies at War*, p. 6 (1942 report).

12. This account is based on the following sources: William Stull, "Hollywood's Own Film Unit Volunteers to Film the Navy," AC, Oct. 1941, pp. 466–67, 494; "Ford Films Midway," *IP*, July 1942, p. 25; Jack Mackenzie, Jr., "With Ford at Midway," *IP*, Jan. 1943, pp. 3–4; Hermine Rich Isaacs, "Shadows of War on the Silver Screen," *Theater Arts*, Nov. 1942, p. 691; "The Battle of Midway," AC, Oct. 1942, p. 456; Andrew Sinclair, *John Ford* (n.p.: The Dial Press/James Wade, 1979), pp. 101–13.

13. Richard Dyer MacCann, "World War II: Armed Forces Documentary," in Richard Meran Barsan, ed., *Nonfiction Film Theory and Criticism* (New York: E. P. Dutton & Co., 1976), p. 136; Peter Rollins, "Document & Drama in *Desert Victory*," *Film & History*, May 1974, p. 11; Frank J. Wetta and Stephen J. Curley, *Celluloid Wars: A Guide to Film and the American Experience of War* (Westport, CT: Greenwood Press, 1992), p. 9.

14. Isaacs, "War Fronts," p. 344.

15. Maj. Bertram Teitelbaum, "A *Survey*: Operations and Functions of the First Army Air Forces Combat Film Detachment" (Jan. 7, 1944), p. 15, AFHRA.

16. Target Tokyo—A Production of the First Motion Picture Unit AAF file, AFHRA, and "'Target Tokyo' Vivid Telling Of First Attack by B-29s," *MPH*, May 19, 1945, p. 26.

17. "Timely Newspaper Breaks Publicize 'Fighting Lady,'" *MPH*, Mar. 17, 1945, p. 58.

18. *Time*, Mar. 26, 1945, p. 96.

19. Maj. Gen. Harry C. Ingles, Chief Signal Officer from 1943 to 1947, quoted in "Signal Corps Technical Information Letter," Apr. 1944, in William A. Avery Papers.

20. *Time*, Apr. 9, 1945, p. 96, and "War Reports," *MPH*, Mar. 24, 1945, p. 7.

21. *Time*, Aug. 13, 1945, p. 94.

22. See Raymond Fielding, *The American Newsreel, 1911–1967* (Norman, OK: University of Oklahoma Press, 1972), and Short, *World War II Through the American Newsreel*. Newsreels were equally important in Britain; see Clive Coultass, *Images for Battle: British Film and the Second World War, 1939–1945* (Newark, DE: University of Delaware Press, 1989).

23. "D-Day Newsreels Given Special Exploitation," *MPH*, June 24, 1944, p. 78, and Short, *World War II Through the American Newsreel*, which contains issue sheets in almost every microfiche.

24. Many of the CPU files in the NCPD, NA, contain examples of these descriptions and caption sheets.

25. The draft script is in Short, *World War II Through the American Newsreel*, microfiche No. 209 (2 Mar. 1945–13 Mar. 1945) and the final narration is in *V for Victory*, a 9-videocassette compilation of WW II newsreels, Vol. IX.

26. *Movies at War*, p. 16 (1942 report), p. 45 (1943 report), p. 19 (1944 report); "Newsreels Give 80% of Footage to War News," *MPH*, Feb. 3, 1945, p. 14; Editors of *Look*, *Movie Lot to Beachhead: The Motion Picture Goes to War and Prepares for the Future* (Garden City: Doubleday, Doran and Company, 1945), p. 26.

27. Fielding, *American Newsreel*, p. 289.

28. Short, *World War II Through the American Newsreel*, p. 9; "War and Newsreel," *MPH*, June 24, 1944, p. 7; "Expect Quicker Screening of War Pictures," *MPH*, Feb. 26, 1944, p. 28; "First Newsreels of the Invasion Take Audiences to the Beachheads," *MPH*, June 17, 1944, p. 9.

29. Fielding, *American Newsreel*, p. 295, and "Shortends," *Close-Up*, Apr. 24, 1945, Frank Goetzheimer Papers.

30. "Newsreels Show The War As It Is, Editors Insist," *MPH*, Jan. 1, 1944, p. 13, and Bosley Crowther, quoted in Fielding, *American Newsreel*, p. 293.

31. Memo on "Request for Photographic Material" from The Chief of the Bureau of Ordnance to The Executive Office of the Secretary, Navy Director of Public Relations, May 7, 1943, Data CPU Men file, NCPD, NA.

32. War Department, "Summary Report on Photographic Activities of the Signal Corps Since August 14, 1941 in the Fields of Motion Pictures & Visual Aids (OCSO, Feb. 26, 1943), pp. 306–307, and James V. Clarke, "Signal Corps Army Pictorial Service in World War II (1 September 1939–15 August 1945)" (HS, SAB, OCSO, Jan. 16, 1946), pp. 187–89.

33. For descriptions of the industrial-incentive films, see War Department Field Manual FM 21-7, *List of War Department Films, Film Strips, and Recognition Film Slides* (War Department, Jan. 1946), pp. 75–81.

34. George R. Thompson and Dixie R. Harris, *The United States Army in World War II. The Signal Corps: The Outcome (Mid-1943 Through 1945)* (Washington, DC: Office of the Chief of Military History, 1966),

pp. 553–54; "History of First Motion Picture Unit Army Air Forces, Culver City, California," entries for Jan., Apr., May, Sept., and Oct. 1944, AFHRA; Project Synopses file, AFHRA.

35. Clarke, "Signal Corps Army Pictorial Service," pp. 189-90; Rear Admiral C. H. Woodward, "The Motion Picture Program of the Industrial Incentive Division, U.S. Navy," *JSMPE*, Feb. 1944; "Navy Films for War Plant Use," *BSM*, July 1, 1943, p. 8.

36. Clarke, "Signal Corps Army Pictorial Service," p. 190; "Historical Data of 13th AAF CCU," Mar. 31, 1944, Records of the 13th CCU, AFHRA; memo on "Combat Photographic Service" from C. H. Woodward to the Director, Office of Public Relations, Dec. 16, 1942, Request for Combat Pictures file, NCPD, NA.

37. O. H. Coelln, Jr., "Blood, Tears and the Production Line," *BSM*, Feb. 15, 1943, p. 13.

38. "On the Navy's Smokestack Circuit," *BSM*, Dec. 30, 1944, p. 21.

39. "Services Competing On Incentive Films," *MPH*, Feb. 19, 1944, p. 38.

40. "The Worker Learns About War," *BSM*, Apr. 25, 1943, p. 15, and Charles F. Hoban, Jr., *Movies That Teach* (New York: Dryden Press, 1946), p. 36.

41. Culbert, *Film and Propaganda in America*, Vol. III, part 2, p. 428.

42. *Annual Report of the Army Service Forces for the Fiscal Year 1944*, pp. 197–98, CARL; War Department Pamphlet No. 11-5, *Combat Photography* (War Department, Mar. 22, 1945), pp. 1–2; Major Kenneth MacKenna, "Photographic Work of the Army Pictorial Service," *JPSA*, Apr. 1945, p. 153.

43. Quoted in M. E. Gillette, Colonel, Signal Corps, to All Motion Picture Cameramen, Feb. 28, 1944, Samuel Tischler Papers.

44. For brief discussions of these matters, see John Morton Blum, *V Was For Victory: Politics and American Culture During World War II* (New York: Harcourt Brace Jovanovich, 1976), pp. 16–17, and Richard Polenberg, *War and Society: The United States, 1941-1945* (Philadelphia: J. B. Lippincott Company. 1972), pp. 29–30.

45. Graflex ads in *MP*, Mar. 1944, p. 69, Aug. 1944, p. 69, and Nov. 1944, p. 43, and in *AP*, Apr. 1944, p. 45 and Feb. 1945, p. 43.

46. "16mm Films Join the 6th War Loan Drive," *BSM*, Oct. 28, 1944, pp. 21, 24.

47. "History of First Motion Picture Unit," 1–31 Aug. and 1–30 Sept., 1944; "'Combat America' to Bond Shows," *BSM*, Dec. 30, 1944, p. 15; "Already Made," *MPH*, Nov. 25, 1944, p. 8; memo on "Daily Activity Report" from James Chapman to The Executive, AC/AS, Intelligence, Sept. 26, 1944, and memo on "Daily Activity Report" from William J. Keighley to The Executive, AC/AS, Intelligence, Nov. 24, 1944, both in Motion Picture Services Division Activity Reports file, AFHRA.

48. "Mobilize All Facilities of Visual Industry for Seventh War Loan Film Program," *BSM*, Apr. 5, 1945, p. 17.
49. "'Fight For The Sky,'" *IP*, July 1945, p. 22, and memo on "Daily Activity Report" from Robert B. Miller to The Executive, AC/AS, Intelligence, May 2, 1945, Motion Picture Services Division Activity Reports file, AFHRA.
50. "Showings to Millions," *BSM*, Sept. 15, 1945, p. 22.
51. For a discussion of the wartime blood supply see James Phinney Baxter, 3rd, *Scientists Against Time* (Cambridge, MA: The M.I.T. Press, 1946), Chapter XXI, "Blood and Blood Substitutes."
52. Unless otherwise noted, this account of Wever's photograph relies on the Wever materials listed in the Bibliography.
53. See the identical ads in *MP*, Nov. 1943, p. 71 and *IP*, Nov. 1943, p. 19. For a different battlefield plasma-giving shot used by the Red Cross see *AP*, Apr. 1945, p. 43.

Chapter 13. "That Weapon Is Film!"

1. Ira C. Eaker to Barney M. Giles, Sept. 29, 1943, Ira C. Eaker Papers, Box 17, Barney M. Giles file, Library of Congress. I am indebted to noted air-power historian Maj. Mark Clodfelter for calling this letter to my attention.
2. Quoted in T/Sgt. James Scanlan, "History of 18th AAF Base Unit (Motion Picture Unit) (Formerly Designated 1st Motion Picture Unit): A Report for War Activities Committee of the Motion Picture Industry," frontispiece, AFHRA.
3. Secretary of War Stimson, for example, had a projector installed in his home so he could watch combat film there, and the Pentagon devoted an auditorium and four special "preview rooms" to motion pictures. See memo on "Daily Activity Report" from William J. Keighley to The Executive, AC/AS, Intelligence, Nov. 20, 1944, Motion Pictures Services Division Activity Reports file, AFHRA, and "4 Film Rooms in Pentagon Help Army Map Strategy," *IP*, Sept. 1944, p. 23.
4. "Signal Corps Photographic Center," *IP*, Dec. 1942, p. 9.
5. Capt. Vernon G. Fleury, "The Signal Corps Photographic Center" (Nov. 1949), p. 3, U.S. Army Signal Center and Fort Gordon, Fort Gordon, GA; Jacqueline M. Quadow, "Training Films In the Second World War" (HS, SAB, OSCO, Apr. 26, 1946), p. 61, NA; Kenneth Macgowan, "Film Making for the Army," *IP*, Jan. 1942, p. 27.
6. Quadow, "Training Films," pp. 108–109; James J. Gibson, ed., *Motion Picture Testing and Research (Report No. VII of Army Air Forces Aviation Psychology Program Research Reports)* (Washington, DC: U.S. Government Printing Office, 1947), p. 46; Charles F. Hoban, Jr., *Movies That Teach* (New York: Dryden Press, 1946), p. 39.

7. William A. Palmer, "Direct-16mm. vs 35mm. for Training Film Production," AC, Mar. 1943, p. 91; Lt. Herbert R. Jensen, "Camera vs. the Microphone in Training Film Production," AC, Jan. 1945, p. 16; Lt. Richard B. Lewis, "Blunders in Training Films—Their Causes and Cures," *JSMPE*, May 1945, pp. 343–48.

8. Hoban, *Movies That Teach*, pp. 87–91; Gibson, *Motion Picture Testing and Research*, p. 242; David Culbert, ed., *Film and Propaganda in America: A Documentary History*, 3 vols., (Westport, CT: Greenwood Press, 1990), Vol. II, Part 1, pp. xx, 375–76; Lt. William Exton, Jr., "Training Films in the U.S. Navy," AC, June 1942, p. 253; Ross H. Vincent, Jr., "A Historical Study of the Army Air Forces First Motion Picture Unit (18th AAFBU) in World War II" (Unpublished Master's Thesis, University of Southern California, 1959), p. 59–60; Alex Greenberg and Malvin Wald, "Report to the Stockholders," *Hollywood Quarterly*, July 1946, p. 415.

9. Frank Capra, *The Name Above the Title: An Autobiography* (New York: Macmillan Publishing Company, 1971), p. 318.

10. Jacqueline M. Quadow, "Training Films in the Second World War, Supplement Jan 44 [sic] to August 1945" (HS, SAB, OCSO, May 13, 1946), p. 12, NA.

11. Quadow, "Training Films," p. 70, and APS, "Army Pictorial Service Annual Report For the Fiscal Year 1 July 1944 to 30 June 1945" (OCSO, July 21, 1945), p. 4, NA.

12. War Department Army Regulations No. 105–260. *Signal Corps Training Films* (War Department, Mar. 22, 1940).

13. Robert L. Eichberg and Jacqueline Quadow, "Combat Photography," (HS, SAB, OCSO, Nov. 1945), p. 157, Appendix A, Appendix E, CARL; memo from Hqs. U.S. Army Service of Supply, OCSO, Signal Corps Pictorial Service, June 27, 1944, in William A. Avery Papers.

14. "Movies For National Defense," AC, Mar. 1941, p. 132.

15. Capt. John G. Gilmour, "Training Films," *Close-Up*, Apr. 24, 1945, Frank J. Goetzheimer Papers.

16. APS, "Army Pictorial Service Annual Report," p. 5.

17. Memos on "Daily Activity Report" from William J. Keighley to The Executive, AC/AS, Intelligence, Oct. 25 and 31, 1944, Motion Picture Services Division Activity Reports file, AFHRA; Peter P. Drowne, "An Investigation into the Evolution of Motion Picture Photography and Film Usage in the United States Marine Corps 1940–1945" (Unpublished Master's Thesis, University of California at Los Angeles, 1965), p. 62.

18. R. C. Raack, "Historiography as Cinematography: A Prolegomenon to Film Work for Historians," *JCH*, July 1983, pp. 418–19; Drowne, "An Investigation," p. 128; Newton E. Meltzer, "The War and the Training Film," AC, July 1945, p. 230.

19. Capt. Rodell C. Johnson, "Animation for Army Films," *BSM*, Dec. 30, 1945, p. 44; Allen Warren Elliott, "Uncle Sam Presents," *PP*, May 1942, p. 105; Capt. Richard P. Creyke to Capt. Richard Baer, May 20, 1945, in Training Film Numbers file, AFHRA; Lt. William R. McGee, "Cinematography Goes to War," *JSMPE*, Feb. 1944, p. 111; Greenberg and Wald, "Report," pp. 413–15.

20. "Private SNAFU," *BSM*, Dec. 30, 1945, p. 89; William J. Blakefield, *Documentary Film Classics* (Washington, DC: National AudioVisual Center, n.d., 2nd ed.) pp. 22–23; APS, "Army Pictorial Service Annual Report," pp. 14–16; War Department, "Summary Report on Photographic Activities of the Signal Corps Since August 4, 1941 in the Fields of Motion Pictures & Visual Aids" (OCSO, Feb. 26, 1943), pp. 429–33, NA; James V. Clarke, "Signal Corps Army Pictorial Service in World War II (1 September 1939–15 August 1945)" (HS, SAB, OCSO, Jan. 16, 1946), pp. 180–81, NA.

21. War Department Field Manual FM 21-7. *List of War Department Films, Film Strips, and Recognition Film Slides* (War Department, Jan. 1946), pp. 3–6.

22. Hoban, *Movies That Teach*, pp. 6–7, 10–16, 38.

23. "Movies for Army Air Forces," *IP* July 1942, p. 12; *List of War Department Films*, pp. 3–4; Exton, "Training Films," pp. 252–53; Richard Griffith, "The Use of Films by the U.S. Armed Services," in Paul Rotha, *Documentary Film*, 3rd ed., rev., (New York: Hastings House Publishers, 1952), pp. 348–49; Colonel Emanuel Cohen, "Film Is A Weapon," *BSM*, Dec. 30, 1945, p. 43.

24. Maj. Warren Wade, "How Is Combat Footage Used?" *BSM*, Dec. 30, 1945, p. 70.

25. Stanley B. Burns, *Early Medical Photography in America (1839–1883)* (New York: The Burns Archive, 1983), p. iv, and Alan Trachtenberg, *Reading American Photographs: Images as History, Matthew Brady to Walker Evans* ([New York]: Hill and Wang, 1989), p. 116.

26. Memo on "Procurement of Medical Films" from The Chief of the Bureau of Medicine and Surgery to CINCPAC, Feb. 18, 1943, Requests for Combat Pictures file, NCPD, NA.

27. This account of Donald J. Morrow relies on the Morrow sources listed in the Bibliography.

28. John Moyer audio cassette responding to the author's inquiries, 1987, and Moyer's correspondence with the author.

29. Hal Hall, "Fighting With Film," *AC*, Sept. 1943, pp. 324–25.

30. Lt. Walter Evans, "The Contribution of Color to Navy Training Films," *BSM*, June 10, 1945, p. 61.

31. "Producers of War Training Films Get WPB Recognition," *BSM*, Apr. 5, 1945, p. 18; "On the Production Line," *BSM*, Dec. 30, 1945, p. 24; "Set Army Lab Output Records," *BSM*, Dec. 30, 1945, p. 24.

32. Thorton Delehanty, "The Disney Studio at War," *Theater Arts*, Jan. 1943, pp. 31–32.

33. War Department, "Pertinent Facts Regarding The Army Training Films Program" (War Department, Aug. 21, 1941), unpaged, in War Department, "Summary Report on Photographic Activities"; Quadow, "Training Films," pp. 12–23, Appendix A; Major General Dawson Olmstead, "The Signal Corps," *JPSA*, Apr. 1942.

34. For the Inspector General's investigation see Culbert, *Film and Propaganda*, Vol. II, Part 1, pp. 81–371; for the Senate investigation see U.S. Congress (78th Cong., 1st Sess.). Senate. *Hearings Before a Special Committee Investigating the National Defense Program. Part 17. Army Commissions and Military Activities of Motion Picture Personnel* (Washington, DC: Government Printing Office, 1943).

35. Quadow, "Training Films," p. 40.

36. Memo from [William J. Keighley] to General Craid [*sic*: Craig], July 21, 1944, in 1944—Authority for Motion Picture Activities file, AFHRA.

37. Perry McCoy Smith, *The Air Force Plans for Peace, 1943–1945* (Baltimore: The Johns Hopkins Press, 1970), pp. 14–21.

38. "Brief Outline of the Photographic Activities of the Army Air Forces," undated, in 1944—Authority for Motion Picture Activities file, AFHRA.

39. War Department, "Summary Report on Photographic Activities," pp. 440–52.

40. Memo on "Transfer to AAF of Responsibility for Procurement (by Production or Otherwise), Storage, and Issue of All Motion Picture and Still Picture Films Required by the AAF" from Gen. Arnold to Chief of Staff [George C. Marshall], undated, in 1944—Authority for Motion Picture Activities file, AFHRA; George R. Thompson, et al., *The United States Army in World War II. The Signal Corps: The Test (December 1941 to July 1943)* (Washington, DC: Office of the Chief of Military History, 1957), p. 392.

41. Memo on "Photographic Activities" from Lt. Gen. Brehon Somervell to the Chief Signal Officer, July 19, 1942, in 1944—Authority for Motion Picture Activities file, AFHRA; Clarke, "Signal Corps Army Pictorial Service," p. 25.

42. Maj. H. L. Patterson, "The Photographic Branch of the Signal Division in a Combined Theater of Operations" (Mar. 1950), p. 3, U.S. Army Signal Center and Fort Gordon, Fort Gordon, GA.

43. Martin van Creveld, *Technology and War From 2000 B.C. to the Present* (New York: The Free Press, 1989), pp. 43–45, 116–18. As examples of map and document copying, see the weekly "Team History" reports for CAT #4, Records of the 163rd SPC, NA; the excerpted reports by Norris Ewing, OIC of G Detachment, in "Company History 1 January 1943 to 31 December 1944," and the reports from the Chungking Detachment

in "Company History 1 January Thru 30 June 1945," both in Records of the 164th SPC, NA; Maj. Andrew H. Berding, Special Counter-Intelligence Detachment, to 167th Signal Photo Intelligence Company, Nov. 18, 1944, and Brig. Gen. A. Franklin Kibler to the Commanding Officer of the 167th SPC, May 11, 1945, both in "Company History," Records of the 167th SPC, NA.

44. Eichberg and Quadow, "Combat Photography," p. ix.
45. War Department Technical Manual No. 1-219. *Basic Photography* (War Department, July 1, 1941), p. 3; Edward Steichen, *The Blue Ghost: A Photographic Log and Personal Narrative of the Aircraft Carrier U.S.S. Lexington in Combat Operations* (New York: Harcourt, Brace and Company, 1947), p. v; speech by Lt. Col. Hal Roach, May 5, 1944, in "History of First Motion Picture Unit Army Air Forces, Culver City, California," May 1-31, 1944, Appendix D, AFHRA.
46. PHCS Gerald T. DeForge, *Navy Photographer's Mate Training Series. Module 1. Naval Photography* (Pensacola: Naval Education and Training Program Development Center, 1981), Series 2–20, and F. Barrows Colton, "How We Fight with Photographs," NGM, Sept. 1944, p. 258.
47. Ralph E. Thomas interview, Oct. 8, 1983, and Robert F. Albright audio cassette responding to the author's inquiries, 1992.
48. Gordon T. Frye to his wife, Mar. 27 [1945], Frye Papers.
49. "History of the Sixteenth AAF Combat Camera Unit, 1 May 1943 to 31 December 1944," June 1944, Records of the 16th CCU, AFHRA; "Historical Report," Mar. and Apr. 1944, Records of the 10th CCU, AFHRA.
50. Eichberg and Quadow, "Combat Photography," Appendix N.
51. Ibid.; Jack Price, *A Guide for Military and News Photography* (New York: Falk Publishing Company, 1944), pp. 59–62; Colton, "How We Fight," pp. 266–67.
52. Richard R. Dodds interview, July 1, 1987; citation from the Commanding General, 5th Marine Division, in Dodds Papers.
53. P.I., G-2 Section, XXIV Corps, "XXIV Corps Photographic Study: Okinawa Campaign, 1 April 1945 to 21 June 1945," CARL.
54. Price, *A Guide*, p. 62, and Air Force Historical Foundation, *Impact: The Army Air Forces' Confidential Picture History of World War II*, 8 books (New York: James Parton and Company, 1980), Book 3, Jan. 1944, pp. 34–35.
55. U.S. Army Technical Intelligence Center, "History of Technical Intelligence: Southwest and Western Pacific Areas, 1942–1945," 2 vols. (Dec. 7, 1945), Vol. I, p. 23, CARL.
56. Eichberg and Quadow, "Combat Photography," Appendix A.
57. Robert L. Eichberg, "Photography Beat the Buzz Bomb," AP, June 1945, and R. V. Jones, *The Wizard War*, p. 393.
58. Hall, "Fighting With Film," p. 325; "Speaking of Pictures ... Gun

Camera Films Nazi Planes Hit by American P-47s," *Life*, Nov. 1, 1943, pp. 20–21; "Company History: 15 Nov. to 15 Dec. 1944," Records of the 163rd SPC, NA.

59. Memo on "Daily Activity Report" from Capt. Miller to The Executive, AC/AS, Intelligence, Jan. 9, 1945, and memo on "Daily Activity Report" from Lt. Col. Owen E. Crump to The Executive, AC/AS, Intelligence, Jan. 25, 1945, both in Motion Picture Services Division Activity Reports file, AFHRA; "Unit History," Mar. 10, 1945, Records of the 10th CCU, AFHRA.

60. Technical Intelligence Center, "History of Technical Intelligence," Vol. I, p. 18, and the relevant documents in Vol. II.

61. Memo on "Motion picture films, Request for" from the Chief, BuAer, to CINCPAC, undated, CPU General file, NCPD, NA.

62. William H. Eichberg and Quadow, "Combat Photography," p. 160, Appendix A.

63. William H. Ettinger Diary, entry for Nov. 6, 1943, Ettinger Papers; Ettinger reminiscences on audio cassette; Lt. Charles M. Warren, "From the Islands to the Lab: The Story of the U.S. Naval Photographic Science Laboratory," *BSM*, June 10, 1945.

64. "Unit History," Sept. 1944, and "Unit War Diary," Sept. 1944, Records of the 12 CCU, AFHRA; "Historical Records," Feb. 1945, Records of the 9th CCU, AFHRA.

65. Larry Barbier to the author, Aug. 11, 1980; Emmett E. Bergholz interview, June 14, 1980; Ralph Thierry interview, June 14, 1980; "Unit History," Aug. 1944 and Jan. 1945, Records of the 8th CCU, AFHRA; "Unit History," July and Aug. 1944, Records of the 3rd CCU, AFHRA.

66. "Production Chart Guide For 16mm Motion Picture Unit," AFHRA; AAF Memorandum No. 95-1, Oct. 21, 1943, in Combat Camera file, AFHRA; "Brief Outline of the Photographic Activities of the Army Air Forces," see Note 38 above.

67. John D. Craig interview, Mar. 26–27, 1979.

68. Captain Walter S. Bell, "The Marines Get Action With Visual Training," *BSM*, June 10, 1945, p. 50; "Japanese Zero Fighter" in Project Synopses file, AFHRA; Gibson, *Motion Picture Testing and Research*, pp. 99–105.

69. See the U.S. *Army-Navy Journal of Recognition* (*September 1943–February 1944*) (Annapolis, MD: Naval Institute Press, 1990); the quotation is from the Feb. 1944 issue, p. 3, and the stories are in the Dec. 1943 and Jan. 1944 issues.

70. Much other evidence emphasizes the importance of verifying the destruction of enemy forces and equipment; as just one example, see "History of the Sixteeenth AAF Combat Camera Unit, 1 May 1943 to 31 December 1944," Dec. 1943, Records of the 16th CCU, AFHRA.

71. Quoted in Eichberg and Quadow, "Combat Photography," p. xi.

72. The Motion Picture Branch, NA, has a number of *Staff Film Reports* on VHS cassettes available for public viewing; it also contains entry cards for all the *Reports* in Record Group 111.

73. APS, "Army Pictorial Service Annual Report," pp. 20, 35; Quadow, "Training Films, Supplement," p. 3; Cohen "Film Is A Weapon," p. 74.

74. APS, "Army Pictorial Service Annual Report," p. 21; Quadow, "Training Films, Supplement," p. 8. Also see *Annual Report of the Army Service Forces for the Fiscal Year 1944*, p. 198, CARL. The Motion Picture Branch, NA, has a number of *Combat Bulletins* available on VHS cassettes for public viewing. For a description of each *Bulletin*, see Department of the Army Pamphlet 108-1. *Index of Army Motion Pictures, Film Strips, Slides, and Phono Recordings* (Department of the Army, 1957), pp. 178–82.

75. *Annual Report of the Army Service Forces for the Fiscal Year 1945*, p. 146, CARL; APS, "Army Pictorial Service Annual Report," pp. 4, 7–10; War Department Pamphlet No. 11-5, *Combat Photography* (War Department, Mar. 22, 1945), p. 3; *List of War Department Films*, pp. 1, 51–56.

76. APS, "Army Pictorial Service Annual Report," pp. 4, 7–10; Quadow, "Training Films, Supplement," pp. 9–10; *Annual Report of the Army Service Forces for the Fiscal Year 1945*, p. 133, CARL; Eichberg and Quadow, "Combat Photography," Appendix H; George R. Thompson and Dixie R. Harris, *The United States Army in World War II. The Signal Corps: The Outcome (Mid-1943 Through 1945)* (Washington, DC: Office of the Chief of Military History, 1966), p. 551.

77. "Newsletter," June 1944, Records of the 7th CCU, and Maj. Bertram Teitelbaum, "A *Survey*: Operation and Functions of the First Army Air Forces Combat Film Detachment" (Jan. 7, 1944), both in AFHRA.

78. Mayfield S. Bray and William T. Murphy, compilers, *Audiovisual Records in the National Archives of the United States Relating to World War II* (Washington, DC: National Archives and Records Service, 1974), pp. 12–13. For a list of the *Film Reports* and *Weekly Digests*, see "Catalogue—AAF Combat Film Reports and Weekly Digests," July 1, 1945, in "History of 1st Army Air Forces Combat Film Detachment, One Park Avenue, New York," AFHRA.

79. Memo on "CPUs in the Pacific Area" from the Director to Carleton Mitchell, July 7, 1944, Reports—Confidential file, NCPD, NA; and Drowne, "An Investigation," pp. 157–60, 196–97.

80. *Journal of Recognition*, Dec. 1943, p. 3.

81. U.S. War Department, *Handbook on German Military Forces* (Baton Rouge: Louisiana State University Press, 1990). The Army produced an analogous volume on the Japanese; see U.S. War Department, *Handbook on Japanese Military Forces* (Novato, CA: Presidio Press, 1991).

82. *Impact*, Book 1, Apr. 1943, inside front cover, and Book 1, May 1943, inside front cover.
83. *Impact*, Book 1, June 1943, p. 26; Book 1, July 1943, pp. 26–27; Book 2, Oct. 1943, p. 12; Book 2, Dec. 1943, p. 21.
84. James Parton, "How *Impact* Began, Was Edited and Used During World War II," Book 1, p. vi.
85. Edwin Price Ramsey and Stephen J. Rivele, *Lieutenant Ramsey's War* (Los Angeles: Knightsbridge Publishing Co., 1990) pp. 311–12.
86. Jerome N. Kahn audio cassette responding to the author's inquiries, 1980.
87. Donald J. Morrow Diary, June 10, 1944, Morrow Papers; James A. Cuca interview, Oct. 8, 1983; William A. Avery to the author, Oct. 1, 1980; "Confessions of a Navy Combat Photographic Unit Officer," Combat Photography Unit 5 (Lt. Samuel) file, NCPD, NA.
88. Paul Fussell, *Wartime: Understanding and Behavior in the Second World War* (New York: Oxford University Press, 1989), Chapter 11, "Accentuate the Positive."
89. "Movies Photographers Should See," MP, Nov. 1942, p. 67; Lt. Gen. George E. Stratemeyer to Capt. Edward R. Evans, June 8, 1945, in "Unit History," July 1945, Records of the 10th CCU, AFHRA; "Navy Newsreel," MPH, Mar. 3, 1945, p. 9; Oral History Transcript: Colonel William P. McCahill, USMC (Ret.), unknown interviewer, p. 57, MCHC.
90. Oral History Transcript: McCahill, pp. 70–71; Gen. Ingles quoted in Memo from Hqs. U.S. Army Service of Supply, OCSO, Signal Corps Pictorial Service, June 27, 1944, William A. Avery Papers; Lt. Gen. Ira C. Eaker to Capt. Charles A. [sic: S.] Geckler of the 9th CCU, Feb. 13, 1945, copy in the Karl H. Maslowski Papers.
91. Morrow Diary, Mar. 9, 1945, Morrow Papers; James Altieri, *The Spearheaders* (New York: Bobbs-Merrill Company, 1960), pp. 154–55; "History of the Fourth Combat Camera Unit: Second Phase—The ETO," field report for Mar. 11–18, 1944, Records of the 4th CCU, AFHRA; Cohen, "Film Is A Weapon," p. 72.
92. Maj. Kenneth MacKenna, "Photographic Work of the Army Pictorial Service," JPSA, Apr. 1945, p. 147.

Chapter 14. "Pix for a Price"

1. Donald J. Morrow Diary, Jan. 9, 1945, Morrow Papers.
2. Frank A. Reister, *Medical Statistics in World War II* (Washington, DC: Office of the Surgeon General, Department of the Army, 1975), graphs on pp. 11 and 13.
3. Oral History Transcript: Major Norman T. Hatch, U.S. Marine Corps (Retired), Benis M. Frank, interviewer, p. 197, MCHC, and Letter of

Appreciation from The Commanding General to The Photographic Section, Sixth Marine Division, June 5, 1945, copy in Martin Friedman Papers.

4. PHCS Gerald T. DeForge, *Navy Photographer's Mate Training Series. Module 1. Naval Photography* (Pensacola: Naval Education and Training Program Development Center, 1981) Series 2–18 and 2–19.

5. See the correspondence between Carleton Mitchell and Lt. Newcomb from June through Nov. 1944, in Unit 3 (Lieut. Newcomb) file, NCPD, NA.

6. Document entitled "8th AAF Combat Camera Unit," Dec. 20, 1944, in Emmett E. Bergholtz Papers.

7. "Roll of Honor: 163rd Signal Photo Company," Arthur K. Elliott Papers, and Warren Kieft Diary, May 1, 1945, Kieft Papers.

8. Edward C. Newell to his mother, Aug. 16, 1945, Newell Papers.

9. "Those Who Die (An Editorial)," *Foto-Facto*, Jan. 22, 1945, Records of the 163rd SPC, NA.

10. George R. Thompson, et al., *The United States Army in World War II. The Signal Corps: The Test (December 1941 to July 1943)* (Washington, DC: Office of the Chief of Military History, 1957), p. 411; James V. Clarke, "Signal Corps Army Pictorial Service in World War II (1 September 1939—15 August 1945)" (HS, SAB, OCSO, Jan. 16, 1946), p. 206, NA; Donald O. Wagner, "Army Pictorial Service During Demobilization, 15 August—31 December 1945" (HS, SAB, OCSO, n.d.), p. 27, NA.

11. War Department, "Summary Report on Photographic Activities of the Signal Corps Since August 4, 1941 in the Fields of Motion Pictures & Visual Aids" (OCSO, Feb. 26, 1943), p. 356, NA; Clarke, "Signal Corps Army Pictorial Service," pp. 127–28.

12. "Newsletter," Apr. 1944, Records of the 7th CCU, AFHRA; memo on "Monthly Report on Receipts of 35mm Film from Combat Camera Units" from Lt. Col. Ralph K. Jester to the Commanding General, AAF, Jan 8, 1945, in Combat Camera Units—Information and Notes file, AFHRA; "AAF Motion Picture Service," *IP*, Feb. 1946, p. 30. The "History of 1st Army Air Forces Combat Film Detachment, One Park Avenue, New York," AFHRA, contains detailed monthly totals of the 35mm film that each CCU submitted.

13. "Unit History," Dec. 1944, Records of the 6th CCU, AFHRA.

14. "Unit History," Dec. 1944, Records of the 2nd CCU; the figures for the 1st, 5th, and 6th CCUs come from their monthly unit histories. All in AFHRA.

15. Robert L. Eichberg and Jacqueline Quadow, "Combat Photography" (HS, SAB, OCSO, Nov. 1945), p. 127, CARL.

16. "Company History," 15 Aug. to 15 Sept. 1944, Records of the 163rd SPC, and "'Photo by Signal Corps': The Story of the 166th," both in NA.

17. Eichberg and Quadow, "Combat Photography," p. 132; Clarke, "Signal Corps Army Pictorial Service," pp. 68–69; APS, "Army Pictorial Service Annual Report For the Fiscal Year 1 July 1944 to 30 June 1945" (OCSO, July 21, 1945), p. 48, NA.
18. Dr. Walter Clark, "The Photographic Year: A Review of Progress in 1945," *PP*, Jan. 1946, p. 20.
19. Clarke, "Signal Corps Army Pictorial Service," pp. 68–69, and Eichberg and Quadow, "Combat Photography," chart following p. 145.
20. Eichberg and Quadow, "Combat Photography," p. 122.
21. APS, "Army Pictorial Service Annual Report," p. 88, and BuAer, "Naval Aviation Photography and Motion Pictures" (Washington, DC: U.S. Naval History Division, 1957), p. 75.
22. "Pix for a Price," *Foto-Facto*, Apr. 24, 1945.
23. *Close-Up* (Oct. 9, 1945), p. 2, Frank J. Goetzheimer Papers, and "History of the Sixteenth AAF Combat Camera Unit, 1 May 1943 to 31 December 1944," Jan. 1944, Records of the 16th CCU, AFHRA.
24. Quoted in Carol Reardon, *Soldiers and Scholars: The U.S. Army and the Uses of Military History, 1865–1920* (Lawrence: University Press of Kansas, 1990), p. 203. Also see Larry D. Roberts, *CSI Report No. 12. Evaluating Historical Materials* (Fort Leavenworth, KS: Combat Studies Institute, n.d.), p. 13.
25. Capt. Edwin T. Rhatigan, "The Tactical Employment of Photographic Troops" (n.d.) pp. 8–9, U.S. Army Signal Center and Fort Gordon, Fort Gordon, GA.
26. Memo on "Motion Picture Records" from LTC Clayton W. Williams, Chief, Historical Division, AC/AS, to Management Control, Organization Planning Division, Sept. 11, 1944; Maj. Gen. James P. Hodges, Assistant Chief of Air Staff, Intelligence, to Maj. Gen. Willis H. Hale, Nov. 16, 1944; and Hodges to Maj. Gen. William E. Kepner, Jan. 23, 1945. All in the Henry H. Arnold Papers, AFHRA. Also see memo on "Motion Picture History of the Army Air Forces" from Col. H. H. Bassett to the Commanding Officer, AAF Weather Wing, Asheville, NC, Nov. 21, 1944, and memo on "Report on Historical Program" from Capt. Arthur E. Orloff to Col. Miller, Apr. 6, 1945, both in Arnold Papers.
27. War Department Pamphlet No. 11-5. *Combat Photography* (War Department, Mar. 22, 1945), p. 2; Maj. Kenneth MacKenna, "Photographic Work of the Army Pictorial Service," *JPSA*, Apr. 1945, p. 154; Col. Emanuel Cohen, "Film Is a Weapon," *BSM*, Dec. 30, 1945, p. 74; APS, "Army Pictorial Service Annual Report," pp. 55–59. The Army completed only fourteen of its projected fifty-nine chronologies.
28. David Thelan, "Memory and American History," *JAH*, Mar. 1989, p. 1122.
29. Joseph D. Boyle audio cassette responding to the author's inquiries, 1980.

30. The first quotation is from the episode entitled "Two If By Sea: Peleliu and Angaur" and the second from "The Conquest of Micronesia: Carrier Warfare in the Gilberts and Marshalls."

31. The quotations come from one of the seminal studies in American military history, Russell F. Weigley's *The American Way of War: A History of United States Military Strategy and Policy* (New York: Macmillan Publishing Company 1973), pp. xx–xxii.

32. Karl von Clausewitz, *On War*, ed. and trans. by Michael Howard and Peter Paret (Princeton: Princeton University Press, 1976), pp. 87, 580, 593–94.

33. Ibid., pp. 81, 88, 92, 94.

34. "America's Foreign Policy Challenges for the 1980s," in United States Department of State, *Realism, Strength, Negotiation: Key Foreign Policy Statements of the Reagan Administration* (Washington, DC: Bureau of Public Affairs, May, 1984).

35. Morrow Diary, July 4, 1944, Morrow Papers.

Bibliography

This bibliography includes only primary sources, which were of four major types: information from former World War II combat cameramen; unpublished manuscripts and documents, plus a few additional primary sources; World War II-era magazines and journals; and wartime motion-picture film.

Several problems arose with these sources. One was wartime censorship, which detracted from the value of letters and diaries. "I'd love to tell you about my daily experiences more in detail," wrote Joe Zinni, "but for security's sake, I'm not permitted to do so." "I know it's seemed to you that I was being nasty and holding out information on you," Gordon Frye half-apologized, half-explained to his wife, "but I just couldn't write one-tenth of what I'd like to tell you," because of censorship guidelines. "Had a lecture from the censor today," noted Bernard Abramson. "You know, there's really not very much that I'm allowed to write." As for diaries, military regulations forbade keeping them overseas, so they are relatively scarce. Moreover, realizing that they were doing something illegal, diarists sometimes mitigated their crime by keeping the entries sporadic, brief, and innocuous. Fortunately some photographers so disdained regulations that they ignored the prohibition against diaries and made regular, lengthy entries.

Another difficulty was the question of reliability raised by oral interviews, correspondence, and audio cassette communications with former combat cameramen. Research has demonstrated that the memory is not a vast reservoir automatically storing all the "facts," which a person can then retrieve at will. Instead individuals actively construct and recon-struct their memories, which can (and do) change dramatically according to the audience for whom an individual is "recalling" an event. The cam-eramen whom I contacted realized that their memories were imperfect: "The memory even in the best of us is not that accurate," wrote Edward C. Newell. "I realize I have dates wrong and some stories not exactly right, but it's been forty-five years or so since these things happened to me," said William H. Ettinger. "As you remember it you remember the good parts, the fun parts, and you forget all the misery," commented William E. Teas. Actually, in cross-checking the memories of various indi-viduals with each other and with official documents and wartime letters and diaries, most were far more accurate than anticipated.

Finally, surviving official records are often uneven and incomplete. For example, the records for the 163rd SPC comprise hundreds of pages, those for the 167th just one brief document, and no official doc-uments survive for the 166th SPC. Even the 163rd's extensive docu-mentation has weaknesses. The company had three commanders, but while the records include dozens of documents from two of them they contain only one document from the third commander.

I have done a modest amount of editorial work to avoid the con-stant use of [sic], bracketed material, and ellipses. Examples include writing "thru" as "through," "praise worthy" as "praiseworthy," "cloths" as "clothes," and "PWs" as "prisoners of war." In interviews and their audio cassettes cameramen sometimes made an important point in a slightly awkward way and on a few occasions I have slightly modified their quotes so as to make them read more smoothly. For example, on an audio cassette that Joe Boyle sent he said "Holy God, thank the Lord that the Allies won the war because what would this world be had the other side won the war?" I rendered this as "Holy God, thank the Lord that the Allies won the war because what would this world be like had the other side won?" That is, I added the work "like," which was implied in Boyle's words, and omitted the words "the war" at the end of the quote since they were repetitious. I have also corrected most misspelled words and grammatical errors. These minor editorial changes have probably made the cameramen seem better versed in the English language and less harried than they were.

I. Former World War II Combat Cameramen

The following list gives the name, primary unit(s), and contribution of the cameramen who assisted my research. In some cases a cameraman served in several different units, so I have listed only the one or two units most relevant to the material in this book. Almost all those cameramen with surviving wartime papers graciously allowed me unrestricted access to them, either giving me the originals or permitting me to make photocopies of them for my files. In a few instances my correspondence with a cameraman consisted of only a letter or two, but in other cases it involved many letters over a number of years. The audio cassettes varied considerably as well; a handful were no more than twenty or thirty minutes long while others contained hours of information. Since practically every cameraman had a photograph collection I have not denoted them individually.

Abrams, Eugene M. (161st SPC, 166th SPC)—Papers (small collection of articles, clippings, documents); correspondence.

Abramson, Bernard (Navy aerial reconnaissance photographer)—Papers (large number of personal letters); interview (June 9, 1980).

Albright, Robert F. (3231st Signal Photo Detachment)—Papers (very small collection of official documents, articles); audio cassettes responding to the author's inquiries (1991). My thanks to Mr. Douglas Clanin of the Indiana Historical Society, who interviewed Albright as part of the Society's oral history collection, for putting me into contact with him.

Avery, William A. (161st SPC/832nd SSB)—Papers (official documents, complete personnel file); correspondence.

Barbier, Lawrence L. (3rd CCU, 8th CCU)—Correspondence.

Barr, William T. (Navy photographer aboard the carrier *Enterprise*)—Correspondence.

Bergholtz, Emmett E. (13th CCU, 8th CCU)—Papers (clippings, official documents, complete personnel file); interview (June 14, 1980).

Berman, Morris (163rd SPC, special mission to shoot color film)—Papers (includes brief memoirs); interview (Sept. 27, 1987); correspondence.

Blodget, Lee (Navy aerial reconnaissance photographer)—Papers (small collection of personal letters, clippings); interview (June 17, 1980).

Boecklen, Warren A. (Signal Corps photographer with Merrill's Marauders)—Papers (small collection of personal letters). These are located at the U.S. Army Military History Institute, Carlisle Barracks, PA. My thanks to Lieutenant Colonel Frederick A. "Rick" Eiserman (Ret.) for calling these papers to my attention.

Bonnard, Fred (163rd SPC)—Papers (articles, clippings); correspondence; audio cassettes responding to the author's inquiries (1980).

Boyle, Joseph D. (163rd SPC)—Papers (official documents, postwar correspondence among members of the 163rd, a copy of "The First Hitch: The 163 Signal Photo Company," copies of *Foto-Facto*); correspondence; audio cassettes responding to the author's inquiries (1980). Boyle served as a conduit between many members of the 163rd and the author, funneling many of their photos and documentary sources to me. His assistance on this project has been invaluable.

Bray, James M. (9th CCU, IX TCC CCU [Provisional])—Papers (substantial collection including personal letters, clippings, articles); telephone interview (Apr. 24, 1982); correspondence; recordings of three wartime radio programs done in Oct. 1943 that featured Bray (Ralph Edwards' "Report to the Nation," an interview with Sam Hayes, and a dramatic re-enactment of his exploits for "I Was There"); James M. Bray as told to Keith Ayling, "Seeing the Bombs Home," *Liberty Magazine* (Dec. 11, 1943). Many of Bray's Papers and the three radio recordings are in the possession of Bray's sister, Ms. Mary Bird, who kindly gave me access to them.

Butterfield, Ralph (166th SPC)—Audio cassette responding to the author's inquiries (1980).

Caliendo, Bernard J. (166th SPC)—Papers (small collection of personal letters); correspondence; audio cassette responding to the author's inquiries (1980).

Chaney, Kenneth M. (9th CCU)—Interview (June 16, 1980); correspondence; Ken Chaney, "The Milk Run," *Argosy*, Apr. 1959.

Claveria, Federico (USMC)—Papers (small collection of articles); interview (June 13, 1980).

Clothier, William H. (worked with William Wyler, 4th CCU)—Interview (June 11, 1980).

Colgrove, Earl F. (CPU #1)—Papers (large collection of personal letters, diary, official documents); interview (June 10, 1980); correspondence.

Cooper, Charles R. (161st SPC)—Correspondence.

Craig, John D. (9th CCU)—Papers (complete personnel file); interview (Mar. 26-27, 1979).

Cuca, James A. (163rd SPC)—Papers (small collection of clippings); interview (Oct. 8, 1983).

Culbertson, Harold (163rd SPC)—Interview (Oct. 7, 1983).

Cummings, William (166th SPC)—Correspondence.

Dodds, Richard R. (USMC)—Papers (small collection of official documents); interview (July 1, 1987).

Downard, Harry A. (166th SPC)—Papers (small collection of clippings, official documents); interview (June 16, 1980).

Elliott, Arthur K. (163rd SPC)—Papers (contain a set of the Records of the 163rd SPC from the NA, as well as other important documents, such as the "Roll of Honor: 163rd Signal Photo Company" listing all the unit members killed in action and all those in the unit who earned medals and Presidential Citations). Elliott was instrumental in inviting me to attend 163rd SPC reunions in Kansas City in 1983 and 1987, and to attend a reunion of all the SPCs in Las Vegas in 1991.

Ettinger, William H. (161st SPC/832nd SSB)—Papers (substantial collection containing diary, official documents); correspondence; reminiscences on audio cassettes (four hours).

Feather, James W. (163rd SPC)—Interview (Oct. 7, 1983).

Faillace, Gaetano (161st/832nd SSB)—Papers (publicity sheet for his postwar lecture film *Australia to Tokyo*).

Fenberg, L. Bennett (163rd SPC)—Interview (Sept. 27, 1987); correspondence.

Fox, Paul N. (166th SPC)—Correspondence.

Friedman, Martin (USMC)—Papers (substantial collection including diary, complete personnel file, official documents); telephone interviews (Nov. 8, 1990, Dec. 1, 1990); correspondence; audio cassettes responding to the author's inquiries (1980); VHS cassette entitled *The Battle of Okinawa*, which is narrated by Friedman and contains color film shot by USMC cameramen and a story by NBC-TV's News 4 New York in New York City on Friedman receiving his Bronze Star almost forty-five years after the war; VHS cassette also entitled *The Battle of Okinawa* released by the USMC Combat Correspondents Association in 1986.

Frye, Gordon T. (163rd SPC)—Papers (substantial collection of personal letters, clippings, official documents, drawings, copy of "A Standing Operating Procedure for Combat Assignment Team [SOPCAT]" [Headquarters 163rd SPC, 20 Feb. 1945]); telephone interviews (Dec. 19, 1989, Sept. 29, 1990); correspondence; audio cassette responding to the author's inquiries (1983); Frye's reminiscences entitled "Rhode Island to the Rhine" recorded on audio cassettes (six hours).

Gallo, Ignatius (166th SPC)—Correspondence.

Genaust, William H. (USMC)—Papers (personal letters, clippings). These are in the possession of Mrs. Rowland E. Dobbins, the former Mrs. Genaust, who generously shared them with me and also kindly wrote me about Genaust's service. My thanks, also, to Mr. Tedd Thomey, a member of the 5th Marine Division in World War II and a postwar journalist, whose help in reconstructing Genaust's activities was invaluable.

Goebel, Robert J. (163rd SPC)—Interviews (Oct. 8, 1983, Sept. 26, 1987); correspondence.

Goetzheimer, Frank J. (161st SPC/832nd SSB)—Papers (substantial collection of officials documents, clippings, several issues of SCPC's *Close-Up*, copy of United States Army Signal Corps, Southwest Pacific Area, "Exposure Under Fire: An Official History of Signal Corps Photography in the Luzon Operations" [Apr. 25, 1945]); telephone interview (Dec. 18, 1991); correspondence.

Greenwald, Sanford E. (9th CCU)—Papers (small collection of offical documents); interview (June 11, 1980).

Groff, George (bomber pilot who flew cameraman James M. Bray)—Telephone interview (May 4, 1992).

Harman, John N., Jr. (161st SPC)—Papers (substantial collection of personal letters, clippings, complete personnel file); correspondence.

Hathorn, Robert E. (photographer in 449th Bombardment Group [Heavy])—Correspondence.

Henry, Malcolm E. (fighter pilot who flew cameraman James M. Bray)—Correspondence.

Herz, Arthur H. (166th SPC)—Papers (small collection of official documents, brief memoir entitled "Amerika, America!"); correspondence.

Jones, Douglas B. (CPU #1)—Papers (small collection of official documents); interview (June 10, 1980).

Joswick, Jerry J. (9th CCU, IX TCC CCU [Provisional])—Interview (Mar. 26, 1979); with Lawrence A. Keating, *Combat Cameraman* (Philadelphia: Chilton Company, 1961).

Kahn, Jerome N. (162nd SPC)—Papers (small collections of official documents); audio cassette responding to the author's inquiries (1980).

Kain, Allan L. (16th CCU)—Papers (small collection of official documents); interview (Dec. 26, 1978); audio cassettes responding to the author's inquiries (1985).

Kieft, Warren (163rd SPC)—Papers (diary, plus an almost daily log of abbreviated notes that began Dec. 7, 1941 and ended May 12, 1945); correspondence; audio cassette responding to the author's inquiries (1981).

Kiely, Arthur J. (USMC)—Papers (official documents, script to accompany a slide presentation about his World War II experiences, entitled "Island by Island with U.S. Marine Corps Combat Photographers"); correspondence.

LaFrano, James (162nd SPC)—Papers (personal letters); correspondence.

Leuders, William R. (163rd SPC)—Interview (Sept. 27, 1987).

Lewis, Robert L. (163rd SPC)—Papers ("WW2, 41–45, etc." album filled with photos and official documents); correspondence.

McCroby, Budd J. (163rd SPC)—Interview (Sept. 27, 1987).

McFarren, Robert W. (161st SPC/832nd SSB)—Correspondence.

McWhirter, W. Dean (163rd SPC, 196th SPC)—Papers (small collection of official documents); correspondence.

Mandl, Fred (165th SPC, 166th SPC)—Interview (June 13, 1980).

Maslowski, Karl H. (9th CCU, 12th CCU)—Papers (official documents, substantial collection of personal letters [the bulk of these are in the author's possession but the Cincinnati Museum of Natural History has a number of letters written from Maslowski to his friend Christian J. Goetz]); interviews (Dec. 17, 1977, Aug. 25, 1978); correspondence.

Meyer, George H. (166th SPC)—Correspondence.

Meyer, Russell A. (166th SPC)—Papers (substantial collection including official documents, clippings, copies of *Weekly Kodachrome*, copy of APS "Handbook for Motion Picture Photographers in the European Theater of Operations" [Signal Corps, United States Army, undated]); interviews (June 12, 1980; Apr. 17, 1983; Oct. 9, 1991). Meyer's assistance was indispensable in getting me into contact with many other members of the 166th. He set up a group interview with six members of the 166th SPC (Fred Mandl, Ralph Butterfield, Paul N. Fox, Robert Curry, James Ryan, Billy A. Newhouse) in his home on June 9, 1980. He sent me audio cassettes of an informal conversation he and three other 166th SPC members (Harry H. Johnson, Homer L. Foreman, Charles E. Sumners) had in Horton, Alabama in 1980. And he invited me to attend a 166th SPC reunion at Camp Crowder, Missouri, as his guest.

Morehouse, Ned R. (163rd SPC)—Papers (official documents, photos with extensive captions); correspondence.

Morrow, Donald J. (3225 Signal Photo Production Unit, 3131st SSB)—Papers (substantial collection including diary, official documents); audio cassette responding to the author's inquiries (1991).

Moyer, John (Naval Field Medical Photographic Unit #2)—Correspondence; audio cassette responding to the author's inquiries (1987).

Newell, Edward C. (163rd SPC)—Papers (substantial collection of personal letters, official documents, clippings, articles); correspondence.

Newhouse, Billy A. (166th SPC)—Interview (Nov. 8, 1981); correspondence.

Nichols, Gene (166th SPC)—Interview (Nov. 6, 1981); correspondence.

Nolan, John L. (Photographer in 449th Bombardment Group [Heavy])—Correspondence.

Owens, Chester E. (163rd SPC)—Papers (small collection of official documents); correspondence.

Owens, Fred R. (166th SPC)—Correspondence.

Pitts, Robert L. (163rd SPC)—Correspondence.

Reinhart, Robert C. (165th SPC)—Correspondence.

Rohde, Rick (CINCPAC photo pool)—Papers (substantial collection, including postwar questionnaires from dozens of cameramen in the CINCPAC photo pool); interview (June 14, 1980).

Salvas, Adrien (166th SPC)—Correspondence.

Sizer, Theodore W. (166th SPC)—Papers (small collection of official documents); interview (Aug. 31, 1983); correspondence.

Stern, Phil (Signal Corps photographer with Darby's Rangers)—Papers (official documents, clippings, articles); interview (June 11, 1980).

Sturges, John (12th CCU)—Interview (Mar. 24, 1979).

Sumners, Charles E. (166th SPC)—Correspondence.

Teas, William E. (166th SPC)—Interview (Nov. 6, 1981).

Thierry, Ralph (3rd CCU, 8th CCU)—Interview (June 14, 1980).

Thomas, James J. (166th SPC)—Correspondence.

Thomas, Ralph E. (163rd SPC)—Interview (Oct. 8, 1983).

Tischler, Samuel T. (163rd SPC, 3131st SSB)—Papers (small but important collection, including official documents with annotations, his "Record-Of-Film-Shot-During-War"); interview (Oct. 8, 1983); telephone interviews (Oct. 8, 1990, Dec. 4, 1990, May 24, 1991); correspondence.

Wagoner, William H. (Army photographer who remained in the U.S.)—Correspondence.

Watkins, Harold L. (USMC)—Papers (scrapbook with official documents, clippings, articles); interview (June 13, 1980).

Weber, Harvey A. (166th SPC)—Papers (substantial collection, including a daily photo assignment sheet for the detachment he commanded, list of the detachment's command post locations indicating to which unit the detachment was attached, official documents); correspondence; audio cassette responding to the author's inquiries (1981).

Weinberger, Harrold A. (USMC)—Papers (unpublished autobiography); correspondence.

Wever, John Stephen (196th SPC)—Papers (personal letters, official documents, clippings, articles); correspondence.

Wyler, William (AAF photographer/director on special assignments)—Interview (June 14, 1980).

Zinni, Joseph M. (166th SPC)—Papers (substantial collection of personal letters); a photo album with an introduction by Colonel Elton F. Hammond, Signal Officer, Headquarters Third U.S. Army, *Third U.S. Army, ETO:*

Ireland, England, France, Belgium, Luxembourg, Germany, Austria, Czechoslovakia, 1944–45); telephone interview (Aug. 4, 1992); audio cassette responding to the author's inquiries (1980); an 802-page unpublished novel closely based on his wartime experiences and entitled *Combat Photographer.*

II. UNPUBLISHED MANUSCRIPTS AND DOCUMENTS

The following materials are in the NA, Washington, DC:

APS, "Army Pictorial Service Annual Report For the Fiscal Year 1 July 1944 to 30 June 1945" (OCSO, July 21, 1945), RG 111.

Clarke, James V., "Signal Corps Army Pictorial Service in World War II (1 September 1939–15 August 1945)" (HS, SAB, OCSO, Jan. 16, 1946), RG 319.

"'Photo By Signal Corps': The Story of the 166th [SPC]," RG 407. A copy of this document is also in the Russell A. Meyer Papers.

Quadow, Jacqueline M., "Training Films in the Second World War" (HS, SAB, OCSO, Apr. 26, 1946), RG 319.

Quadow, Jacqueline M., "Training Films in the Second World War, Supplement Jan 44 [sic] to August 1945" (HS, SAB, OCSO, May 13, 1946), RG 319.

Records of the NCPD, RG 38. These contain several different files for each CPU and dozens of other files pertaining to related matters. Some of the files have similar labels. For example, one is CPU #7 Lieut. Reiman, another is Unit 7 (Lieut. Reiman[)], and a third is Combat Photography Unit 7 (Lt. Reiman). In another instance one is Personnel, another Personnel—Combat Units, a third Personnel—Miscellaneous, and a fourth Personnel Records.

Records of the 161st SPC, RG 407.
Records of the 162nd SPC, RG 407.
Records of the 163rd SPC, RG 407.
Records of the 164th SPC, RG 407.
Records of the 165th SPC, RG 407.
Records of the 167th SPC, RG 407.
Records of the 168th SPC, RG 407.

Wagner, Donald O., "Army Pictorial Service During Demobilization, 15 August–31 December 1945" (HS, SAB, OCSO, n.d.), RG 319.

War Department, "History of Signal Corps Research and Development in World War II. Volume XV. Photographic Equipment" (Washington, DC: Army Service Forces, Dec. 1945), RG 319.

War Department, "Summary Report on Photographic Activities of the Signal Corps Since August 4, 1941 in the Fields of Motion Pictures & Visual Aids" (OCSO, Feb. 26, 1943), RG 319.

The following are in the AFHRA, Maxwell Air Force Base:

Arnold, Henry H. Papers.

CCU Organization—General Arnold's Folder 9 Nov. 1942–9 Apr. 1943 file, Microfilm Reel A2987.

Combat Camera file, Microfilm Reel A2987.

Combat Camera Units—Information and Notes file, Microfilm Reel A2987.

"Combat Film Service Weekly Reports, 4 October 1943 [sic: 18 September 1943]–1 Jan [sic] 1944," Microfilm Reel A2987.

18th AAF Base Unit—General file, Microfilm Reel A2987.

General file, Microfilm Reel A2987.

"History of 1st Army Air Forces Combat Film Detachment, One Park Avenue, New York," Microfilm Reels A2987 and A2988.

"History of First Motion Picture Unit Army Air Forces, Culver City, California," Microfilm Reel A2987.

Motion Picture Services Division Activity Reports file, Microfilm Reel A1033.

1944—Authority for Motion Picture Activities file, Microfilm Reel A2987.

Photo Units: Motion Picture Units—Rosters file, Microfilm Reel A2987.

"Production Chart Guide For 16mm Motion Picture Unit," Microfilm Reel A0492.

Project Synopses file, Microfilm Reel A2986.

Records of the 1st CCU.
Records of the 2nd CCU.
Records of the 3rd CCU.
Records of the 4th CCU.
Records of the 5th CCU.
Records of the 6th CCU.
Records of the 7th CCU.
Records of the 8th CCU.
Records of the 9th CCU.
Records of the 10th CCU.
Records of the 11th CCU.
Records of the 12th CCU.
Records of the 13th CCU.
Records of the 16th CCU.
Records of the IX TCC CCU (Provisional).

[Note: The Records of the CCUs are available on Microfilm Reels A0483, A0484, A0485, A0486, A0487, A0488, and A0489.]

Scanlan, T/Sgt James, "History of 18th AAF Base Unit (Motion Picture Unit

(Formerly Designated 1st Motion Picture Unit): A Report for War Activities Committee of the Motion Picture Industry," Microfilm Reel A2986.

Suggested Plan of Operation for the Motion Picture Activities Division file, Microfilm Reel A2987.

Target Tokyo—A Production of the First Motion Picture Unit AAF file, Microfilm Reel A0492.

Teitelbaum, Major Bertram, "A *Survey*: Operations and Functions of the First Army Air Forces Combat Film Detachment" (Jan. 7, 1944) Microfilm Reel A2987.

Training Film Numbers file, Microfilm Reel A2986.

The following materials are in the MCHC, Washington, DC:

Combat Correspondents' Memo file

Combat Correspondents file

Combat Correspondents (1) file

Combat Correspondents (2) file

Combat Correspondent file

"Letter of Instruction No. 1077," July 12, 1945 from Commandant A. A. Vandegrift to All Commanding Officers.

Oral History Transcript: Brigadier General Robert L. Denig, U.S. Marine Corps (Retired), Benis M. Frank, Alvin M. Josephy, Jr., and Brigadier General Robert L. Denig, Jr., USMC (Ret.), interviewers.

Oral History Transcript: Colonel William P. McCahill, USMC (Ret.), unknown interviewer.

Oral History Transcript: Lieutenant Colonel Karl T. Soule, Jr., U.S. Marine Corps (Retired), Benis M. Frank, interviewer.

Oral History Transcript: Major Norman T. Hatch, U.S. Marine Corps (Retired), Benis M. Frank interviewer.

The following materials are in the U.S. Army Signal Center and Fort Gordon, Fort Gordon, GA:

Fleury, Captain Vernon G., "The Signal Corps Photographic Center" (Nov. 1949).

Patterson, Major H. L., "The Photographic Branch of the Signal Division in a Combined Theater of Operations" (Mar. 1950).

Rhatigan, Captain Edwin T., "The Tactical Employment of Photographic Troops" (n.d.).

The following materials are in the CARL, Fort Leavenworth, KS:

"AAFSAT ANSCOL Course. Class E-1944. Course Number 200. 13 Nov—2 Dec 1944. Taught at the AAF School of Applied Tactics, Staff and Special Training Department, Orlando, Fla.," Document N-5269.

"Annex #12: Communications Zone Signal Plan to Communications Zone Plan For Operation Overlord (Final Draft)" (May 12, 1944), in Document N-6607.

Annual Report of the Army Service Forces for the Fiscal Year 1943, Document N-5345.

Annual Report of the Army Service Forces for the Fiscal Year 1944, Document N-5345.

Annual Report of the Army Service Forces for the Fiscal Year 1945, Document N-5345.

"Chart No. 2. Organization of T/O 11-500 Photographic Co. and Plan of Assignment."

"Chart No. 3. Organization of 167th Sig. Photographic Co. T/O&E 11-37 and Plan for Assignment of Missions."

"Chart No. 4. Film Collecting and Processing Plan."

"Combat Photographic Operations" (undated), Document N-12765.

Eichberg, Robert L. and Quadow, Jacqueline, "Combat Photography" (HS, SAB, OCSO, Nov. 1945), Document N-14853-68.

"Fifth Air Force Second Phase Photo Intelligence Report," in Document N-3063.

Hall, Dr. Courtney R., "Administrative Demobilization of the Office of the Chief Signal Officer, 15 August—31 December 1945" (HS, SAB, OCSO, Feb. 1946), Document R-15366.

"Information on Signal Personnel and Equipment in Amphibious Assault Landings" (undated), Document N-8247.

"Memorandum from Captain Elmer D. Roscoe, Commanding, to General Godfrey. Subject: Airborne Mission of Company 'A', 879th AB Engr. Avn. Bn." (June 5, 1944), in Document N-2955.

"Memorandum from Garland C. Black, Colonel, Signal Corps, to Signals Division, Supreme Headquarters, AEF, APO 757, US Army, Attn: Brigadier General F. H. Lanahan, Jr. Subject: Recommendations on Personnel and Training Activities in the US" (Jan. 11, 1945), in Document 5857.

P.I., G-2 Section, XXIV Corps, "XXIV Corps Photographic Study: Okinawa Campaign, 1 April 1945 to 21 June 1945," Document 12229.

Reinstein, Captain Frederick, "Study of Signal Corps Officer Schooling, 1939-1944" (HS, SAB, OCSO, Dec. 1, 1944), Document R-15371.1.

"Report of The General Board, United States Forces, European Theater. Signal Supply, Repair, and Maintenance. Study Number 110," Document R-12937.110-2.

Sadler, Ruth F., "History of the Signal Corps Affiliated Plan, August 1944" (Personnel Branch, Personnel and Training Service, OCSO, Jan. 5, 1946)," Microfilm Reel M-N1033.

"Signal Report on Operation 'Varsity'," Document N-11312.

"Tentative Operations Plan No. 1-45, Iceberg" (Feb. 15, 1945), in Document N-8633.

"The Development of the Office of the Chief Signal Officer. Part II. 1 July 1943 throught 15 August 1945" (HS, SAB, OCSO, Nov. 1945), Document R-15367.

United States Army Signal Corps, Southwest Pacific Area, "Exposure Under Fire: An Official History of Signal Corps Photography in the Luzon Operations" (Apr. 25, 1945), Document R-11176.

U.S. Army Technical Intelligence Center, "History of Technical Intelligence: Southwest and Western Pacific Areas, 1942–1945," 2 vols. (Dec. 7, 1945), Documents N-14450A and N-14450B.

Some additional important primary sources are:

Air Force Historical Foundation, *Impact: The Army Air Forces' Confidential Picture History of World War II*, 8 books (New York: James Parton and Company, 1980).

Army Signal Forces Catalog SIG 3, Signal Supply Catalog. List of Items for Troops Use (Headquarters, Army Service Forces, Sept. 1945). I am indebted to Mr. Ted Wise, Director/Curator of Science and Technology, Signal Corps Museum, Fort Gordon, GA, for calling my attention to this document.

BuAer, "Naval Aviation Photography and Motion Pictures" (Washington, DC: U.S. Naval History Division, 1957).

Bureau of Naval Personnel, "Training Aids in World War II" (Washington, DC: U.S. Naval History Division, n.d.).

Culbert, David, ed., *Film and Propaganda in America: A Documentary, History*, 3 vols. (Westport, CT: Greenwood Press, 1990).

"History of the Office of Censorship," 3 reels (A Microfilm Project of University Publications of America, Inc.).

Short, K. R. M., ed., *World War II Through the American Newsreels, 1942–1945: An Introduction and Guide to the Microfiches* (229 microfiches, Oxford and New York: Oxford Microfilm Publications, 1985).

Steichen, Edward, ed., *U.S. Navy War Photographs: Pearl Harbor to Tokyo Bay* (New York: Bonanza Books, 1984 ed. [originally published in 1946]).

Stimson, Henry L. Diaries (microfilm edition of the Diaries from the Yale University Library).

U.S. Army–Navy Journal of Recognition (September 1943–February 1944) (Annapolis, MD: Naval Institute Press, 1990).

U.S. Congress (78th Cong., 1st Sess.). Senate. *Hearings Before a Special Committee Investigating the National Defense Program. Part 17. Army Commissions and Military Activities of Motion Picture Personnel* (Washington, DC: Government Printing Office, 1943).

War Department Army Regulations No. 105–260. *Signal Corps Training Films* (War Department, Mar. 22, 1940).

War Department Pamphlet No. 11-2. *Standing Operating Procedure For Signal Photographic Units in Theaters of Operations* (War Department, Apr. 20, 1944).

War Department Pamphlet No. 11-5. *Combat Photography* (War Department, Mar. 22, 1945).

War Department Table of Organization and Equipment No. 11-37. *Signal Photographic Company* (War Department, Feb. 12, 1944).

War Department Table of Organization and Equipment No. 11-500. *Signal Service Organization* (War Department, Sept. 22, 1944).

War Department Technical Manual No. 1-219. *Basic Photography* (War Department, July 1, 1941).

III. Wartime Magazines and Journals

I read all available issues of the following from 1940–1946:

American Cinematography (AC)

American Photography (AP)

Business Screen Magazine (BSM)

International Photography (IP)

Journal of the Photographic Society of America (JPSA)

Journal of the Society of Motion Picture Engineers (JSMPE)

Life

Minicam Photography (MP)

Motion Picture Herald (MPH)

Newsweek

National Geographic Magazine (NGM)

Popular Photography (PP)

Theater Arts

Time

U.S. Camera (USC)

IV. Films

I have studied many World War II documentaries, newsreels, and other types of motion pictures that are available either on video cassette from commercial firms or in the NA. Three commercial houses with large selections of material on video cassette are:

Boomerang Publishers, 6164 W. 83rd Way, Arvada, CO 80003 (303-423-5706).

Cumberland Marketing International, Inc., Box 40461, Nashville, TN 37204 (615-298-1401).

International Historic Films, Inc., Box 29035, Chicago, IL 60629 (312-927-2900).

For a general description of the NA's World War II film records, such as *Staff Film Reports, Combat Bulletins,* and training films, see Mayfield S. Bray and William T. Murphy, compilers, *Audiovisual Records in the National Archives of the United States Relating to World War II* (Washington, DC: National Archives and Records Service, 1974).

For lists and brief individual descriptions of many of the NA's film records, consult War Department Field Manual FM 21-7. *List of War Department Films, Film Strips, and Recognition Film Slides* (War Department, Jan. 1946), and Department of the Army Pamphlet 108-1, *Index of Army Motion Pictures, Film Strips, Slides, and Phono Recordings* (Department of the Army, 1957).

Anyone interested in war and film should consult Major Frederick A. Eiserman, compiler, *Historical Bibliography No. 6. War on Film: Military History Education Video Tapes, Motion Pictures, and Related Audiovisual Aids* (Fort Leavenworth: Combat Studies Institute, U.S. Army Command and General Staff College, n.d.), and Frank J. Wetta and Stephen J. Curley, *Celluloid Wars: A Guide to Film and the American Experience of War* (Westport, CT: Greenwood Press, 1992).

ACKNOWLEDGMENTS

I began doing research on this book in October 1977. In the intervening years I have received help and encouragement from a large number of people and institutions.

Foremost would be my family—wife Pern (aka Linda Ann Pernack Maslowski), son Jed, and daughter Laurel—for all the incredible joy and excitement they have provided. Life with them is never dull, that's for sure. My parents, Edna and Karl H. Maslowski, deserve special thanks, too, at the very least for the wartime letters that Dad sent home and that Mom had the good sense to save. But I am indebted to them for much more than that, as they and I both know.

Without the gracious cooperation and generosity of these men who served in World War II photographic units I could never have completed this project:

Eugene M. Abrams	Emmett E. Bergholtz
Bernard Abramson	Morris Berman
Robert F. Albright	Lee Blodget
William A. Avery	Warren A. Boecklen
Lawrence L. Barbier	Fred Bonnard
William T. Barr	Joseph D. Boyle

James M. Bray
(and two pilots who
flew him during the war,
George Groff and
Malcolm E. Henry)

Ralph Butterfield

Bernard J. Caliendo

Kenneth M. Chaney

Federico Claveria

William H. Clothier

Earl F. Colgrove

Charles R. Cooper

John D. Craig

James A. Cuca

Harold Culbertson

William Cummings

Richard R. Dodds

Harry A. Downard

Arthur K. Elliott

William H. Ettinger

James W. Feather

Gaetano Faillace

L. Bennett Fenberg

Paul N. Fox

Martin Friedman

Gordon T. Frye

Ignatius Gallo

William H. Genaust

Robert J. Goebel

Frank J. Goetzheimer

Sanford E. Greenwald

John N. Harman, Jr.

Robert E. Hathorn

Arthur H. Herz

Douglas B. Jones

Jerry J. Joswick

Jerome N. Kahn

Allan L. Kain

Warren Kieft

Arthur J. Kiely

James LaFrano

William R. Leuders

Robert L. Lewis

Fred Mandl

Karl H. Maslowski

Budd J. McCroby

Robert W. McFarren

W. Dean McWhirter

George H. Meyer

Russell A. Meyer

Ned R. Morehouse

Donald J. Morrow

John Moyer

Edward C. Newell

Billy A. Newhouse

Gene Nichols

John L. Nolan

Chester E. Owens

Fred R. Owens

Robert L. Pitts

Robert C. Reinhart

Rick Rohde

Adrien Salvas

Theodore W. Sizer

Phil Stern

John Sturges

Charles E. Sumners

William E. Teas

Ralph Thierry

James J. Thomas

Ralph E. Thomas

Samuel T. Tischler

William H. Wagoner

Harold L. Watkins

Harvey A. Weber

Harrold A. Weinberger

John Stephen Wever

William Wyler

Joseph M. Zinni

I especially need to thank four of these men. Joe Boyle was not only my initial contact with the members of the 163rd SPC, but was also one of my most prolific sources. The late Gordon Frye was my "anchor" for more than a decade because I always *knew* that the first sentence of the first chapter would be "Gordon Frye was finally getting a well-deserved rest," and as many authors will attest, composing the first sentence is often the hardest part of writing a book. Russ Meyer copied much of his tremendous collection of 166th SPC materials for me and introduced me to dozens of that unit's members, including Arthur Herz and Bernard Caliendo. No matter how often I badgered him, Earl Colgrove always responded enthusiastically, even when I asked him to retell a substantial portion of his wartime story after my cassette player chewed up part of our original interview.

Several individuals critiqued the manuscript, including Pern, who may not understand much about history but who knows when something does not make sense. Amidst their busy schedules Major (soon to be Lieutenant Colonel) Mark Clodfelter, Professor Calvin L. Christman, and Professor Jerry M. Cooper, three of the best historians I know, read the manuscript with special care, for which I am profoundly in their debt. Don Winslow not only gave me the benefit of his exceptional intellect, but also provided entertainment, both from his novels (A *Cool Breeze on the Underground* and *The Trail to Buddha's Mirror*) and the trout fishing near his Riverton, Connecticut, home. How I would love to blame any errors of fact or interpretation on these scholar-friends! But, of course, the full responsibility for any such errors is exclusively mine.

Various grants from the University of Nebraska–Lincoln Research Council, which has been extraordinarily generous to me during the nearly two decades I have worked at the university, were indispensable.

Although I supposedly went to the Combat Studies Institute of the U.S. Army Command and General Staff College at Fort Leavenworth as a teacher, I still feel guilty about how *much* the staff members there taught me and how *little* I taught them. To Denny Frasché, Roger Spiller, Bob Ramsey, Bob Berlin, Glenn Robertson, Chris Gabel, Rick Eiserman, Gary Griffin, Jim Gebhardt, and all the rest, thank you: 1986–87 *was* the best year of my life.

Over the years the staffs at the Combined Arms Research Library at Fort Leavenworth, the Air Force Historical Research Agency at Maxwell AFB, the Marine Corps Historical Center, and the National Archives have been unfailingly helpful. Like World War II military cameramen, the people who work in these repositories are anonymous, talented, and dedicated, and have an incredibly important mission. My thanks to all of them.

Since 1975 I have been fortunate to live next door to John F. Sanders, who is not only a good friend but also a professional photographer with his own lab. When cameramen sent me their personal photographs to study I often asked John to make negatives from the prints and then make new prints for my files. So deft was he in doing this that his prints were often superior to the original pictures. Virtually every photo in this book has benefited from his extraordinary skill.

Sandra Pershing and Joan Curtis, respectively the University of Nebraska–Lincoln History Department's talented staff assistant and head secretary, have been of great assistance. Without their help in ways both large and small, I sometimes wonder if I could have ever completed this book.

Donald E. Robinson, a cartographic technician whom I first met when he was an undergraduate, made the excellent map showing CPU #1's route.

I have had the wonderfully good fortune to work with Joyce Seltzer, Vice President and Senior Editor at The Free Press, and with Robert Harrington, Editorial Production Supervisor at The Free Press, on two projects, of which this book is the second. In both cases their guidance has greatly improved the book. Thanks, Joyce and Bob.

Peter Maslowski
North Lake (in spirit anyhow),
Nebraska
February, 1993

INDEX

399